"After a diet of turgid perorations by Xi Jinping, a reader needs relief. Zimmerman's tale of the 1923 hijacking of the Peking Express is just such an antidote. Not only has he done his research, but he spins a helluva good yarn!"

—Orville Schell, author of *My Old Home*

"*The Peking Express* takes readers on a journey across China's countryside where a train robbery opens windows onto the tumultuous politics of twentieth-century China. Painting lively portraits of heroes, villains, saviors, and victims—but which was which?—Zimmerman tells a story that sets the stage for war and revolution, with echoes that persist to this day."

—Jay Carter, author of *Champions Day*

PRAISE FOR *THE PEKING EXPRESS*

"*The Peking Express* is a fascinating story, and the author has done an amazing amount of research. It's really an intriguing, impressive work."

—Ian Johnson, Pulitzer Prize–winning journalist
and author of *The Souls of China*

"*The Peking Express* is a vivid, exhilarating account of China's greatest train robbery of the early twentieth century. A true story about bandits, kidnapping, forced marches across the countryside, a pursuing Chinese army, diplomatic intrigue, and a cast of rather unique characters in 1923 China—what's not to love???"

—Paul French, author of *Midnight in Peking* and *City of Devils*

"*The Peking Express* is a dramatic story of survival, heroism, and political intrigue. It takes the reader from the bustling cosmopolitan city of Shanghai to the impoverished, rural landscape of the mysterious and breathtakingly beautiful mountains of southern Shandong. Zimmerman delivers a gripping account that captivates the reader from beginning to end—an ending that is both climactic and riveting in its description of the horrors and excesses of China's warlord era. This is a book that readers will never forget!"

—Lingling Wei, award-winning journalist; chief China correspondent
the *Wall Street Journal*; and coauthor of *Superpower Showdow*

THE
PEKING
EXPRESS

JAMES M. ZIMMERMAN

THE PEKING EXPRESS

THE BANDITS WHO STOLE A TRAIN, STUNNED THE WEST, AND BROKE THE REPUBLIC OF CHINA

PUBLICAFFAIRS

New York

PublicAffairs
Hachette Book Group
1290 Avenue of the Americas, New York, NY 10104
www.publicaffairsbooks.com
@Public_Affairs

Printed in the United States of America

First Edition: April 2023

Published by PublicAffairs, an imprint of Perseus Books, LLC, a subsidiary of Hachette Book Group, Inc. The PublicAffairs name and logo is a trademark of the Hachette Book Group.

The Hachette Speakers Bureau provides a wide range of authors for speaking events. To find out more, go to www.hachettespeakersbureau.com or email HachetteSpeakers @hbgusa.com.

PublicAffairs books may be purchased in bulk for business, educational, or promotional use. For more information, please contact your local bookseller or the Hachette Book Group Special Markets Department at special.markets@hbgusa.com.

The publisher is not responsible for websites (or their content) that are not owned by the publisher.

Various photos courtesy of the State Historical Society of Missouri Manuscript Collection, SHSMO Research Center, Columbia, Missouri, John Powell's papers (C3662); the Colonel Roland W. Pinger Family; the General Wallace C. Philoon Family; Library of Congress; Rhode Island Historical Society; and Ulrico Hoepli, publisher of D. Musso, *La Cina Ed I Cinesi: Loro Leggi E Costumi* (China and the Chinese: Their Laws and Customs, 1926). Every effort was made by the author to communicate with copyright holders, and the author welcomes hearing from anyone in this regard.

Print book interior design by Amy Quinn.

Library of Congress Cataloging-in-Publication Data

Names: Zimmerman, James M., 1958– author.
Title: The Peking Express : the bandits who stole a train, stunned the
    West, and broke the Republic of China / James M. Zimmerman.
Other titles: Bandits who stole a train, stunned the West, and broke the
    Republic of China
Description: First edition. | New York, NY : PublicAffairs, 2023. |
    Includes bibliographical references and index.
Identifiers: LCCN 2022035230 | ISBN 9781541701700 (hardcover) | ISBN
    9781541701724 (ebook)
Subjects: LCSH: Lincheng Outrage, Lincheng Xian, China, 1923. | Lincheng
    Xian (China)—History—20th century. | Hijacking of
    trains—China—History—20th century. | Peking Express (Express
    train)—History. | Train robberies—China—Lincheng Xian—History—20th
    century.
Classification: LCC DS793.L5233 Z56 2023 | DDC 951/.152—dc23/eng/20221025
LC record available at https://lccn.loc.gov/2022035230

ISBNs: 9781541701700 (hardcover), 9781541701724 (ebook)

LSC-C

Printing 1, 2023

To the bandits, hostages, interlocutors, rescuers, and other participants in the Lincheng Incident, as well as family and friends in my life who encouraged and supported this writing project: this book is dedicated to you.

CONTENTS

A NOTE ON ARCHIVAL SOURCES AND LANGUAGE USAGE

I HAVE USED AUTHENTIC QUOTATIONS AND DIALOGUE FROM EXISTING historical sources, including Chinese and English-language governmental and academic archives on the events and political affairs at the time; the extensive personal memoirs, correspondence, diaries, statements, and family records of the participants; and foreign and Chinese-language media reports. As a result, many of the comments and statements reflect the views of the times, and I have tried to provide contemporary context. In addition, and to be consistent with historical sources from 1923, all geographic references and names use the Wade-Giles Romanized transliteration system in effect at the time. The following is a comparison of the Wade-Giles system, current Pinyin spelling, and simplified Chinese characters.

Wade-Giles	Pinyin	简体字
Anhwei	Anhui	安徽
Chekiang	Zhejiang	浙江
Chihli	Zhílì	直隶
Ch'ing	Qing	大清
Chungking	Chongqing	重庆
Hangchow	Hangzhou	杭州
Hankow	Wuhan	汉口
Honan	Henan	河南
Kiangsu	Jiangsu	江苏
Peking	Beijing	北京
Shantung	Shandong	山东
Soochow	Suzhou	苏州
Süchow	Xuzhou	徐州
Tientsin	Tianjin	天津
Tsaochuang	Zaozhuang	枣庄
Tsinan	Jinan	济南
Tsingtao	Qingdao	青岛
Whangpoo	Huangpu	黄浦江
Woosung	Wusong	吴淞区

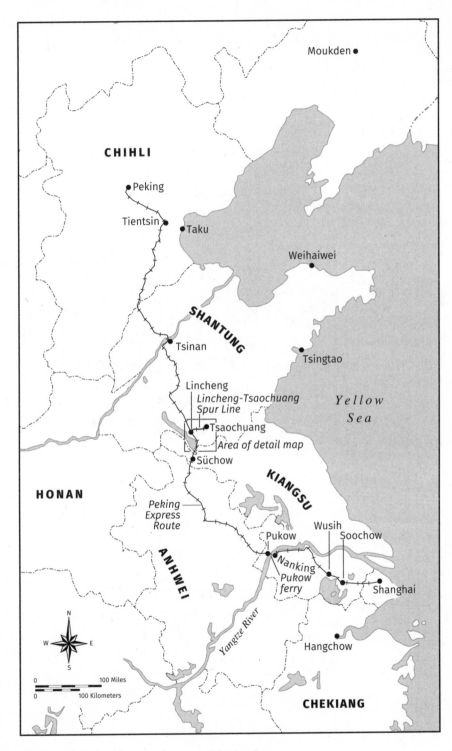

Route of the Peking Express. See page xii for detail map.

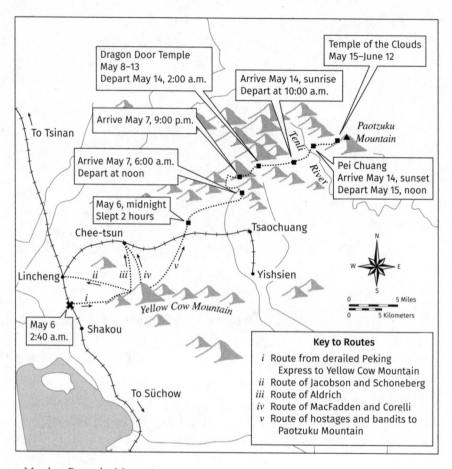

March to Paotzuku Mountain

PROLOGUE

About the only difference between a bandit and a soldier is the matter of army pay, a uniform and a gun.

—John B. Powell, American publisher and hostage[1]

MAY 1923

After the revolution of 1911 ended more than two thousand years of imperial rule in China, the country ruptured into regional political factions, each jockeying for power in a constant state of internecine warfare. The armies of the provincial military warlords, the *tuchuns*, dominated the countryside as the hapless leaders of the Republic of China in Peking struggled to maintain a semblance of control over a fractured nation. The warlord armies obeyed no higher authority than the warlord himself—they were in effect personal armies made into military satrapies, independent of national-level authorities.[2]

In June 1922, Li Yuan-hung was installed as president of the nation. A highly respected former rebel army leader in the 1911 revolution who had then served as president in 1916-1917, President Li was now regarded as an antimilitarist who would unify the country with a national constitution as well as disband the tuchuns and their armies. After ten years of warlord intrigue, corruption, and destruction, Li's ambitious plan was a welcome relief to both the Chinese people and the international community. But he needed to move quickly: there was much trouble brewing in the heartland.

For more than a decade, rival warlords had settled scores by resorting to arms, and after each battle their defeated soldiers scattered for survival. Poor and starving, most of these soldiers sought to be reinstated into an army, anyone's army. But others became outlaws. By 1923, bandits, or *tufei*, had become an existential threat to the Chinese government. Every day, swarms of men armed with rifles and sabers swept through the country-side, looting factories, hijacking trade routes, and kidnapping children.[3]

To neutralize the bandits, the warlords initiated ruthless suppression campaigns, laying siege over entire regions and engaging in bloody wars of attrition that destroyed village after village. Outside train stations and vil-lage gates, the rotting heads of executed bandits were tethered from poles and baskets, dangling in the wind as gruesome trophies to dissuade former soldiers—and any peasants caught in the cross fire—from becoming tufei.

Few Westerners ever set foot in the lawless interior of the country, where the bandits and warlords did battle. Yet in 1923, China's newly launched express trains—a showcase of its modernity—passed right through the heart of bandit country, their seats filled with prominent and wealthy pas-sengers traveling back and forth between the raucously cosmopolitan city of Shanghai and the nation's more austere but still thriving capital, Peking.

An attack on an express train by marauding brigands could threaten Chi-na's national sovereignty and bring the unstable Republican government to its knees. It would not only strike a blow to China's economically critical rail system but also put the country in the crosshairs of the foreign powers that increasingly took the view that China couldn't govern itself. Much as during the opium wars of the nineteenth century and the Boxer Rebellion just a few decades earlier, various foreign governments were itching for a reason to intervene militarily to protect their treaty rights and expand their territorial ambitions. Much was indeed at stake. So when, in early May 1923, the inevitable happened—an attack on the Peking Express, a hostage situation, and a diplomatic crisis that captured the attention of the globe— it not only changed the lives of those caught up in the affair; it also changed China and its relationship with the rest of the world. This is that story.

PART 1

THE JOURNEY

CHAPTER 1

ALL ABOARD!

All in all, travel on the regular routes is as safe in China as in any other part of the world. Robbers and pirates exist, of course, and there is usually a revolution or rebellion going on in some part of the country, but these things add zest rather than danger to the journey.

—*The Travelers' Handbook for China* (1921)[1]

MAY 5, 1923, 8 A.M., SHANGHAI

John Benjamin Powell had a train to catch. The publisher of Shanghai's *Weekly Review* and the *Chicago Tribune*'s man in China handed his baggage and portable typewriter to his driver and kissed his wife, Martha, and two small children good-bye. At the age of thirty-four, he looked lean and smart in his three-piece wool suit, wingtip shoes, and dark-gray Stetson fedora. He had remembered to shave, and his hair was slicked back with brilliantine. He got dolled up like this only for the important assignments. On most days, he wore rugged olive-green khakis and rolled-up shirtsleeves. His round black wire-rimmed glasses gave him a studious look, and he never left home without pencils, a notebook, and his beloved corn-cob pipe to remind himself of his midwestern roots.

He had certainly come a long way from his native Missouri. Powell lived in a two-story Tudor-style house in "French Town"—the French Concession area of Shanghai—where the leafy lanes and vibrant commerce made him feel as if he were walking the streets of Paris. The area had become the neighborhood of choice for the growing American colony, as well as the rich Taipans, or foreign-born business tycoons, who had built Shanghai into a modern metropolis.

Powell's taxi passed by the gated mansions, heading east and then north, in the direction of the Whangpoo River toward the Shanghai-Nanking Railway Station. On Avenue Edward VII, the taxi breezed past Powell's newsroom in the Great Northern Telegraph Company, a stately office building from which messages were sent around the clock over lines connecting China to Russia, Europe, and Imperial Japan. During the past six years, Powell had wired firsthand accounts of famine, earthquakes, rebellions, bloody regional wars, and the seemingly vain efforts of the Republican government to unite the country and improve the lot of the Chinese people.

Most of his stories were ugly and dark, but today's assignment was good news for a change. Powell was headed six hundred miles north to Shantung Province to cover the completion ceremony of a major river-reclamation project funded by the American Red Cross and built with the help of

Journalist and publisher John B. Powell on a reporting trip in China, ca. 1920. (SHSMO)

American contractors and twenty-three thousand Chinese laborers.[2] This initiative—which involved the construction of a diversion dam, levees, and a massive rail trestle built out of Oregon pine timber—was an example of the emergent friendship between the United States and China. And it would save lives. Two years earlier in this same spot, the restless Yellow River had broken through its north bank, laying waste to five hundred villages.

Although this was an important story, it also gave Powell the excuse he was waiting for to book a first-class ticket on the Peking Express, a luxurious overnight train service that had launched just four months earlier. In addition to the creature comforts such a journey would provide, Powell knew he would meet interesting, important people—catnip for new story ideas.

Powell's taxi was now crawling in traffic along the city's principal waterfront. On his right was the nine-mile river frontage, full of a motley assortment of sampans, crimson-colored masted junks, fishing and trading boats, and passenger ferries traversing the smooth, steel-gray-colored river and clogging the docks and ramps extending from the shoreline promenade. Farther on, across to the shore of the east bank of the river, Powell could see the wharves, the gray warehouses (godowns), and the smokestacks of factories standing tall in the skyline. From this vantage point, Shanghai looked like any other industrial city in Europe or America.

The noise on the crowded streets was ear piercing, the fumes choking. The taxi dodged a strange mixture of vehicles: tramcars, carriages, motorcars, lorries, and rickshaws. In the bustle, Powell saw the whole pecking order of Shanghai's social fabric, from British aristocrats and foreign and Chinese businessmen in bespoke suits to stern-looking Sikh traffic policemen in khakis and turbans, barking orders to pedestrians and drivers alike. Also here were many Chinese who made their living on the street: pigtailed peddlers hawking curios; slender courtesans (or "sing-song girls") in their form-fitting and sleeveless silk *cheongsam*, or mandarin gowns; and skeletal rickshaw pullers restless for passengers so they could earn enough for their daily meal.

In 1923 Shanghai had a population of thirty-five thousand foreigners and two million Chinese. You could live a modern, urbane life in Shanghai the same way you could in any major city of the West, never encountering the rural, impoverished China that lay just beyond the city limits. Powell was one of the few Westerners who knew, and loved, both sides of the country: the international concessions and the "real" China that many of his expat friends wouldn't dare explore.

Powell and his family spent their weekends touring the city, beguiled by that interesting mixture of East and West. The shops were always dark and mysterious and had the inescapable but welcoming aroma of smoky sandalwood incense, pots brewing jasmine tea, and lantern candles burning cold vegetable tallow. Understanding the shopkeepers was a challenge, but they knew some pidgin English—a combination of English and Chinese words that was predominant in the foreign concessions—and Powell spoke enough Chinese to get by.

He loved how so many different cultures met and mingled in Shanghai: not only every kind of European and Chinese but also Malays, Parsees, Annamese, Brahmins, Hindus, Persians, Turks, and Javanese. And although he enjoyed the city's rich diversity, Powell also lamented the discrimination toward the native population. In the public parks along the Bund, for instance, no Chinese, except for those working as servants to foreigners, were even allowed to enter.[3] Shanghai also had its dark side, which he knew well enough to avoid: several streets were notorious for gambling, prostitution, grogshops, and opium joints catering to all kinds.

The Shanghai Bund in 1923, a mile-long stretch of stately buildings lining the western bank of the Whangpoo River. (Ulrico Hoepli)

Powell was amazed by how much he loved China, by how Shanghai had really become home, despite the fact that six years earlier he couldn't find it on a map. Back in 1916, he was teaching journalism at the University of Missouri when Thomas Millard, a well-known international political correspondent in Asia for the *New York Herald*, sent a telegram to the dean of the school searching for young journalists interested in working in the Orient. Millard summarized his editorial policy as printing "anything we damn well please." That sounded good to Powell. So did the glamour of becoming a foreign correspondent.

Shanghai would be quite the adjustment for him and his young family. To prepare himself, Powell read the only two books on China in the university library, both of which were written by missionary Arthur H. Smith, whose description of the Chinese people was meant to be humorous but was in fact condescending—if not racist. The few Chinese students at the university bitterly complained about Smith's supercilious point of view. Even with no experience in China, Powell was turned off by the chapter headings in Smith's popular and widely read 1894 tome that characterized the Chinese people as having a "Talent for Misunderstanding" and "Intellectual Turbidity."[4] America needed a more objective view of China and the Chinese people, and Powell believed that he was the right man for the job.

When he arrived in Shanghai in February 1917, Powell quickly realized that he would be starting the magazine from scratch. Over time, he added staff, and the *Review* grew exponentially in both subscribers and advertising revenues.[5] As a weekly newsmagazine, the *Review* provided coverage with greater depth than the daily newspapers, and had a more US-centric analysis of current events than the other British- and European-oriented publications in Shanghai. In 1920 Powell bought out Millard and changed the name of the publication to the *Weekly Review of the Far East*.[6] By the early 1920s, his magazine had become the journal of choice, not only for the Anglo-American colony but for anyone in China with an international outlook. Whereas many foreign publications were dismissive of Chinese subscribers, Powell discovered that the largest English-reading group was actually a younger generation of Chinese— the intellectuals and the students of mission and municipal schools— who took a keen interest in world affairs.

As his magazine's stature grew, so did Powell's influence. He developed close ties to both the business community and the government. And unlike many foreigners, who had exploitive, colonial mind-sets, Powell advocated for a strong and independent China. He often ruffled feathers in the foreign business community by calling for the abandonment of the special extraterritorial privileges that exempted foreigners from the jurisdiction of local courts and gave them freedom from arrest by local officials. Powell, like many of his young liberal Chinese readers, also supported China's current president, Li Yuan-hung. Li was a scholar and a modernizer, Powell believed, who wanted to turn the page on the warlord era and unify China.[7] Although he was never shy to criticize the president, Powell was optimistic that good times were ahead, if only the country could just stay on the rocky course toward democracy and the rule of law.

As the taxi pulled into the jammed driveway of the railway station, it was met by a swarm of hawkers elbowing one another for the prize of acting as Powell's unofficial porter. Everywhere there were men and women peddling tobacco, newspapers, and refreshments for the train ride. Within seconds, the station's official porters—red-capped and uniformed—freed Powell from the scrum.

"J. B.!," someone shouted out to him over the gaggle of voices. "Glad you could make it, pal!"

Powell smiled, sensing a trace of sarcasm in the wise-guy voice, which belonged to Lloyd Lehrbas, a young reporter and cameraman with the *China Press* whom everyone called Larry. Young and handsome, Lehrbas was a newcomer to the newspaper game in China, and Powell admired that he was aggressively ambitious when it came to getting a good story. But he found his personal style—the endless skirt chasing and male bravado—a bit much. As the two newsmen exchanged greetings, they were distracted by the arrival of a spanking-new blue sedan that forced its way to the front portico of the station, blasting its horn incessantly.

Out of the motorcar came thirty-nine-year-old Leon Friedman, a wealthy Shanghai automobile dealer who would be traveling on the Peking Express to visit his branch operation in the capital city. A master salesman, gregarious and gracious, Friedman always loved to show off his inventory. Leon and his brother Max were typical of the self-made foreign business-man who thrived in Shanghai. Although they now owned the China Motors Federal Company, which sold cutting-edge brands of the day—such as Hupmobile, Dodge, and Chandler—from showrooms across China, they had begun their adult lives with practically nothing, having escaped the anti-Semitic pogroms of their native Romania around the turn of the century.[8] They arrived in Shanghai in 1919 after a colorful career in the United States as promoters for stunt pilots and barnstorming, including the Wright brothers. The ease of encountering such personalities with truly fascinating backstories was one of the things Powell liked best about life in Shanghai.

As he made his way past the ticket booths and into the station's cavernous waiting hall, Powell observed a mix of businessmen and holiday makers. There were reporters from Chinese-language newspapers heading north to cover the reclamation project, as well as a large group of well-dressed young men whom Powell recognized as major players in the city's Jewish merchant community.[9] Lee Solomon, the leading exporter of mahjong sets to the West, was there. So was the heavy-set Shanghai-based Italian lawyer Giuseppe D. Musso, who represented the Shanghai Opium Combine, which drove the opium trade before and after it became outlawed. Musso was also a well-known confidant of Italy's new fascist leader, Benito Mussolini.[10] Accompanying Musso was his very young and dainty secretary, Alba Corelli. Powell also clocked a mysterious face in the crowd that belonged to a tall, well-dressed gentleman who suspiciously eyed the other passengers and shooed away the porters from his very heavy baggage.

Whatever's in that guy's bag, Powell thought, *he doesn't want anyone to touch it.*

The most conspicuous personality, however, was an older American lady, who seemed at ease in her surroundings yet was dressed more for an Easter-bonnet parade than an overnight train ride. Lucy Aldrich was the sister-in-law of American financier John D. Rockefeller Jr., heir to the fortune of the Standard Oil Company of New York. She was wealthy and politically connected in her own right. Aldrich had come to Shanghai on her second circumnavigation of the globe and had been traveling for months in the company of her very proper secretary and a French maid.

The call to board the train was announced over a tinny public-address system. A stampede of mostly Chinese passengers ran down the raised platform to the second- and third-class coaches at the front of the train. The first-class passengers were in the rear cars, away from the smoke and cinders that the coal-burning steam locomotive spewed into the air. Aldrich, her companions, and the other foreign passengers were ushered by the first-class compartment porters to their assigned carriage. The engineer then sounded the large, swinging brass bell cradled atop the locomotive again and again—a signal to both the station crew and passengers that it was time to get on board or get out of the way. As the hissing steam was blown out from the cylinder cocks on the sides of the engine and the exhaust from the smokestack started to belch, the train moved forward. The journey had begun.

BEFORE THE RAILROAD CAME TO CHINA, PEOPLE TRAVERSED THE MASsive country by watercraft, horse, sedan chair, cart, wheelbarrow, mule, camel, and rickshaw. Or they could walk. Beasts of burden bore the cargo— packhorses, donkeys, oxen, and very often human beings who used hanging baskets at the ends of a carrying yoke. China's often impassible roads lived up to their notorious reputation.

The railroad would end up revolutionizing travel within China, yet its arrival was anything but auspicious. The first Chinese train track was constructed in 1876, a nine-mile narrow-gauge passenger line between Shanghai and the port town of Woosung. The Ch'ing government's approval for the project was granted, withdrawn, and then reinstated several times. One year after the train began operating, the government had the railroad dismantled on the grounds that the service unfairly disrupted the occupations of the locals (who operated canal boats and ferries) and that the track damaged neighboring farmland.[11] By the turn of the century, only ten miles of railroad track existed in all of China. The United States, by contrast, had 193,000 miles of railroads, crisscrossing the continent to reach practically every frontier town in North America. China wasn't so much behind the times, industrially speaking, as it was another planet altogether.

Yet the Chinese government slowly began to warm up to the economic and strategic value of railroads.[12] By 1909, China had about 5,000 miles of railroads and another 4,700 miles planned or under construction. After the 1911 revolution, which was directed at the inability of the Ch'ing court to put the country on a path of technological and commercial advancement, the unstable Republican government made the building of railroads a national priority to both unify the fractured country and drive its economic development. But the government had neither the money nor the technological expertise to lay the thousands of miles of track it needed. Sensing opportunity, foreign governments and bankers jockeyed for a stake in China's rapidly expanding railroad system. Several agreements were reached with European financial groups for construction funds, but each deal had strings attached, including usurious interest rates and provisions making sure that the respective country's own industries would control and profit from every aspect of the project, from construction and equipment to export fees.

Back in 1898, a deal had been reached to build the Tientsin-Pukow line, the longest portion of the railroad artery that would eventually connect Peking and Shanghai. The project was split between German and British contractors. German capital and engineers built the northern half; the British built the southern half. The Tientsin-Pukow line was politically significant because it marked the first railway project in China where the construction and the control were vested wholly with the Chinese government. Before the Tientsin-Pukow line was completed, a voyage between Shanghai and Peking was made primarily by oceangoing vessel and took three to five days to complete, weather permitting. The Tientsin-Pukow line would cut down the travel time significantly.

The rail service was immediately popular among merchants, missionaries, bankers, and diplomats, but it was also of interest to an increasing number of Western visitors. By the early 1920s, foreign tourism was booming in China, and advertisements enticed travelers with images of the mysterious dynastic walled city of Peking, the teeming commercial metropolis of Shanghai, the beautiful lakefront of Hangchow, the ancient capital of the Manchus in the northern city of Moukden, and more. One advertisement claimed that China "remains as interesting and strange as it was to

Europeans who more than five hundred years ago read Marco Polo's amazing account of the land of the Great Khan."[13]

For the first ten years of service, travel on the Tientsin-Pukow line took place mainly during the daylight hours, with a dozen stops along the way. Then, in autumn 1922, the Tientsin-Pukow Railway took delivery of a new set of carriages designed for fast, overnight, luxury travel. Built in America, the carriages were technological marvels. A huge investment for the railway, this new express train was more spacious, faster, and safer than any previous mode of transportation in China. The overnight service would cut down travel time to a predictable thirty-eight hours, door to door, from Shanghai to Peking: a distance of 892 miles.[14]

Compared to wood-framed passenger cars, the block-steel carriages reduced the risk of fire and prevented the telescoping of carriages in the event of a collision.[15] But the steel carriages also had another benefit: they were practically bulletproof. In fact, the Peking Express was designed specifically to withstand attacks from the bandits who terrorized the Chinese countryside. The train would be a kind of leviathan on wheels, with two sandbagged machine-gun emplacements atop the carriages and a small army of private security guards. There seemed to be nothing to fear from the overnight journey. The advertisement for the all-steel construction underscored that it was even well suited for passage through remote, bandit-ridden territory—the solid state of the cars provided the Peking Express with an impregnable level of security from robbers and highwaymen. Or so everyone thought.

CHAPTER 2

THE BANDIT CHIEF

Our cause is righteous, and our army marches fearlessly over the length and breadth of Shantung. Our object is to protect the poor, to bring about equality among men, and to kill all unscrupulous officials and wicked gentry; to reform the Government's rotten policy which has done so much harm to the people, and to establish a stable government.

—Sun Mei-yao, commander in chief, Self-Governed
Army for the Establishment of the Country[1]

MAY 5, 1923, TOWN OF LINCHENG, SHANTUNG PROVINCE

Sun Mei-yao saw himself as a soldier, not a thief, yet he was about to pull off the biggest train heist in the history of China. Twenty-five years old and born to a prestigious family clan in southern Shantung Province, Sun had begun his career as an officer in a local militia. He stood out for his intelligence, charisma, and ambition. He had tried to fight with honor, but the tuchuns who vied for power and plunder in rural China did not care about honor. To them, Sun and his men were little more than cannon fodder. And when peace was made, his unit was disbanded, and his men were left to starve. Sun decided he would no longer be a soldier of fortune, a slave to the spurious for-profit campaigns of the warlords. He told his troops not to lay down their arms. He said their next battle would be different. It would be an economic insurgency, a chance to fight back against the warlords and business interests that extracted local resources from Shantung and gave nothing in return.

Sun was an opportunist, but his aims were revolutionary. He hoped to wrest control of southern Shantung from the tuchuns, to have his troops be recognized by the Republican government in Peking, and to change the balance of power in his native province. He started small by smuggling salt, a controlled commodity used by the Chinese government to pay off foreign loan obligations, and extorting local coal-mining companies that operated under concessions from the warlords.[2] As his raids got more audacious, he relied more on the villagers for refuge and supplies. He could sometimes buy their allegiance cheaply—a sack of rice, a bag of salt, or a bolt of cloth was all that was needed to make a friend.

Shantung was a resource-rich province, a crossroad for trade routes, and a hub for agricultural products from the fertile soil of the wide plain across its northern borders. Moving south, the flat land became craggy and mountainous. This landscape was steeped in mysticism. Shantung was the birthplace of Confucius and a dominant center for folk religions, Taoism, and Chinese Buddhism.

Yet in 1923, Shantung was also beset by political intrigue. Japan had relinquished control over eastern Shantung Province and its railroads just months before, in 1922. The Japanese had taken control of Tsingtao only a few years earlier, when the Germans were forced to give it up after losing the Great War. But the Japanese Empire's political interest in the region continued. Indeed, diplomats along with journalists like Powell assumed that from the moment the empire gave up Shantung, it had been busy plotting ways to destabilize the region in the hopes of eventually recapturing it. In the year since Japan's departure, various warlord cliques—from inside and outside the province—now fought over the spoils left behind.

Sun thought that he could exploit this political vacuum. But standing in his way was General Tien Chung-yu, the Chinese military governor of Shantung Province, who ran Shantung as a kind of mafia state and staunchly objected to bandits claiming a share of the protection fees from local businesses that he thought should go only to him. In July 1922, Tien decided to send Sun a brutal message. He had Sun's older brother, Sun Mei-tsu, a scholar and well-known intellectual in the region, murdered, and his severed head was hung from the train station in Lincheng.[3] To avenge his family's honor, Sun and his allies took up arms against Tien's troops, leading to conditions in southern Shantung Province that by the spring of 1923 were akin to civil war.

Tien made no distinction between Sun's troops and the local villagers who got in the way. In pursuit of Sun, he razed homes, burned down farms, and killed women and children. Such tactics only increased the loyalty that the locals felt toward Sun, who had established a base of operations at Paotzuku Mountain, a remote fortress-like pinnacle thirty-odd miles east of Lincheng.[4] Sun was also charismatic in his own way. Boyish looking and clean shaven, he had a wide, pleasing smile and a calm and self-assured manner about him. He walked with a cane, not because of any injury or disability but to convey a dignified image of social stature. Though thoroughly at ease with his fellow bandits, he always carried a pistol hidden under his cloak, given the constant threats to his life.

Caught in the cross fire, the villagers preferred Sun and the bandits (whom they feared) to the soldiers (whom they despised). The longer the government troops besieged the region, the greater the suffering would be for the people of southern Shantung. Sun and his allies believed that something needed to be done, something big.

Sun's target was the Peking Express. His idea was to brazenly attack the country's main railway artery, derailing the train and kidnapping its passengers. Only by taking people hostage—not only scores of rich Chinese but also prominent foreigners—would Sun get the world's attention and thus the leverage he needed to strong-arm Peking and make his revolutionary plans a reality.

THE ENORMOUS OX SIZZLED OVER A MASSIVE BED OF COALS. ALL DAY long the bandits had been drinking *samshu*, a cheap, potent, liqueur-like wine made from glutinous rice. Sensing it was almost mealtime, the hungry bandits crowded around the spectacle as the carvers sliced the tender

meat from the seared crust. They went still and solemn as Sun, dressed
in a wide-brimmed hat, smoke-tinted oval glasses, and a long, dark brown
changshan—a Chinese-styled gown—received the honor of taking the first
bite. With much ceremony, the bandit chief nodded in approval as he slowly
relished the delicious meat. Then he proceeded to hand out portions to his
overjoyed compatriots.

The night before the feast, a team of men had dug a pit in an open field
and started a massive fire. By early morning, they had amassed a deep glowing bed of coals. They slaughtered an ox and suspended its gutted carcass
on a pole over a makeshift trestle. They began cooking at dawn, basting and
roasting all day. The ox weighed more than three hundred pounds, and it
was cooked whole (including its head), providing enough meat to feed the
entire bandit crew of a thousand men.

This banquet was a welcome luxury. Bandits, like most Chinese peasants, had very little meat in their diet. Sun's reed-thin troops were weak
from malnutrition, yet if this raid on the Peking Express were to be a success, he needed them to be at their best—bold and energetic and fearless.
So to raise morale, he decided that he would hold an elaborate feast in the
early evening, right before the attack. He spared no expense, aiming to impress upon his fellow bandits the importance of the coming task.

SUN GAVE HIS GANG THE GRANDIOSE TITLE OF THE "SELF-GOVERNED
Army for the Establishment of the Country." They had an unusually ide-
alistic agenda, calling for an end to the warlord system and for national
peace. But to the government in Peking and the warlords, these men were
nothing more than a confederation of rabble, the same breed of bandits
(tufei) who wreaked havoc across the Chinese countryside. The word *tufei*
means "local badness coming out of the ground," and it hinted at how the
bandits seemed to be everywhere at once, how impossible they were for
the authorities to snuff out.[5] Most, like Sun, were ex-military men, hastily
armed and trained, then discarded by the Chinese government or some
tuchun as soon as the latest war or insurrection was over.

Some bandits had served in the China Labor Corps in the Great
War, during which they served the Allied armies on the Western Front.

Shantung Province, and particularly the port cities of Weihaiwei and Tsingtao, were key recruiting grounds for the roughly 150,000 laborers who supported both the war and the reconstruction efforts. Contracted for a pittance to do menial jobs such as building trenches and digging graves, they had returned to China knowing their way around modern weapons and speaking a few words of English or French. This made them comparatively sophisticated compared to the homegrown bandits.[6] The second group of men were drawn from various sources. Some hailed from famine districts and were literally starved into a life of crime. Some were drug addicts, infected by the epidemic of opium that had ravaged the Chinese countryside. And some were out for revenge, in search of a way of fighting back against a local warlord who had murdered a member of their family or seized their property.[7] For them, banditry was the only kind of justice available in China, which at the time lacked an effective system of legal redress even for rich urbanites, much less powerless peasants.

Sun may have had noble ambitions for his "self-governed army," but in order to consolidate his power he had to often make deals with the devil. Standing beside him at the feast was Liu Shou-t'ing, also known as Po-Po Liu, a bandit who was much more interested in money and opium than politics. His nickname, Po-Po, came from his childhood, when he was a street peddler of dumplings.[8] Yet there was nothing soft or doughy about Po-Po Liu. He had terrorized both the Germans and the Japanese during their respective governance of eastern Shantung Province. By the early 1920s, he had a price on his head in the city of Tsingtao, so he moved southwest to the Lincheng area to continue his vocation.

Whereas Sun was poised and self-controlled, Liu was blunt and ruthless—he and his comrades in arms represented the dark underbelly of Chinese banditry. Unlike Sun, Liu lacked both charisma and oratorical skills, although he carried himself calmly—until provoked. Liu was in his early forties but looked much older. He had chronically bloodshot eyes and a dry voice from his opium and alcohol addictions. He was balding on top, with thin hair on the sides of his head, and he wore a full, ungroomed mustache.

Sun had approximately seven hundred men in his gang, and Po-Po Liu had three hundred. Theirs was an uneasy alliance—a blood brotherhood—yet Sun needed Po-Po Liu to boost his numbers. Plus, Liu's battle-hardened troops, though difficult to control, fought with savage intensity. The bandits in Sun's inner circle, by contrast, had a veneer of discipline about them. They wore old, ill-fitting army uniforms and had unkempt military-style haircuts. Most ordinary bandits—like Po-Po Liu's men—were lucky if they had shoes. They dressed in rags and wore their coal-black braided hair into tight knots, tied in place with a red ribbon. They carried an assortment of weapons— some modern, some medieval—but all stolen or captured in battle.

The bandit gang had two subchiefs who were, compared to their peers, worldly and sophisticated. One would earn the nickname "Russky" and the other the "Frenchman." Prior to the Great War, Russky had drifted northward to Siberia and eventually worked as an assistant to a Russian army officer. He followed him to the Eastern Front to fight the army of the Kaiser, and then during the Russian Civil War traveled to Moscow, Petrograd, and Omsk to fight the Bolsheviks. When his master was killed in battle, Russky deserted his post and returned to his hometown in Shantung Province, where he joined Sun's bandit army. He proudly carried a well-cared-for Russian rifle, as well as a small automatic pistol and a brass-and-bone-handled knife that he had acquired during his sojourns. Stolid and scar-faced, Russky was fluent in Russian and had a penchant for vodka, caviar, and singing Russian ballads.

The Frenchman had spent three years in Europe during the Great War as a member of the China Labor Corps. Jaded by the callousness of war and violence, the Frenchman had little interest in going back to a subsistence lifestyle of farming when he returned to his native Shantung. So he threw his lot in with the bandits. He was an attractive man, spoke French with confidence, and always wore what looked like a wide-brim Panama hat over his closely shaven head.

In essence, the bandit army was a mixed bag, a compound of combustible elements: drug addicts, starving peasants, ex-soldiers of fortune, and gravediggers from the killing fields of Europe—men who had seen the backside of Hell and who knew life was cheap, men who had nothing left to lose. They may not have made for ideal soldiers, but Sun believed that with the right leadership and the right luck, they might just change history.

CHAPTER 3

A PICTURESQUE VIEW

Now there were miles after miles of rice paddies, with little brown villages with straw-thatched roofs scattered here and there—no roads except paths on the narrow dikes for little donkeys and tiny oxen. Not many folks were about, but we wondered what manner of people lived in these earthy little habitations.

—Major Roland Pinger, American tourist and hostage[1]

MAY 5, 1923, AFTERNOON, TIENTSIN-PUKOW LINE, NANKING

Before they settled into their luxurious sleeping cars, passengers leaving Shanghai on the Peking Express had to travel two hundred miles northwest to the Nanking terminus on the south bank of the Yangtze River.[2] They then boarded a two-story passenger ferry to cross the wide, slow-moving Yangtze River to the Pukow terminus on the north bank, where they would find their compartments for the overnight ride north to Peking.[3] A shallow-draft flat-bottomed boat with a coal-burning steam engine, the ferry was privately owned by the railroad. The ride took about twenty minutes or so.

"That's a reassuring sight," said US Army major Roland Pinger, pointing to the stars and stripes on the river vessel. All eyes on the ferry had turned toward the USS *Monocacy* of the Yangtze River Patrol Force (YangPat), a US naval operation of shallow-draft gunboats built specifically for service in China and designed to protect American-flagged passenger and cargo ships operating along all nine hundred miles of the river.[4]

"These navy boys have been busy fighting river pirates and warlords," Pinger remarked to fellow passenger Robert Allen, another US Army major, as both men waved to the gunboat's crew in the distance. Pinger was stationed at Fort Santiago in the Philippines, a US military facility acquired after the Spanish-American War. Allen was also based in the Philippines—he was a physician with the Army Medical Corps at Fort McKinley in Manila. The two officers had met through social events at the Army & Navy Club of Manila, and both men decided to take a side trip with their families through China on their way home to the United States after the completion of their tours of duty.

They had the same rank and got along well enough, but the majors had very different personalities. Pinger, thirty-four, had an infectious smile and a professorial bearing. He was an army ordnance officer who was responsible for ensuring that weapons systems, motor vehicles, and military equipment of all kinds were in perfect working condition for deployment. An engineer by training, he had a highly technical and encyclopedic mind and carefully observed everything from the perspective of logic and science. Pinger got excited about ships, trains, and anything mechanical, and he loved his work in the army, which was more of a passion than a job to him.

By contrast, Allen was pessimistic and cynical. He was forty-six years old, but his nearly all-white hair made him look much older. He always seemed to be inconvenienced by some little thing and had strong opinions about race and religion. Unlike Pinger, Allen had been underwhelmed by his time in the army. He wanted to gain valuable medical experience dealing with battlefield injuries, but in peacetime he was limited to treating soldiers for gonorrhea and syphilis. What he did get in Southeast Asia was a crash course in tropical diseases—the effects of which he hoped he would never see again. He looked forward to leaving the military once stateside and planned to return to private practice in Tacoma, Washington. Pinger's wife, Miriam, and

Allen's wife, Martha, were devoted military housewives, enjoying the adventure of an overseas assignment as well as the prestige that came from being an officer's wife.

As the ferry neared the landing dock on the Pukow side of the river, Miriam Pinger gathered her two children—nine-year-old Roland Jr. and three-year-old Edward—and stepped ashore behind her husband. Major Allen and Martha followed suit, along with their twelve-year-old son, Bobby.

The mile-long Pukow waterfront was composed of gritty godowns, port cranes, wharves, and floating pontoons large enough to support freighters from abroad. Smaller masted watercraft were tied together like cordwood along the river's edge. There were piles of steel rails, treated-wood railroad ties, lumber for buildings, and other construction materials stacked here and there. As far as the eye could see, tents and roughly built shanties topped with woven-reed matting crowded the river embankment and adjoining fields, home to the more than thirty thousand railway and riverboat workers and their families. Once an uninhabited river beach covered in rushes, Pukow had become a drab, treeless port—yet it was of strategic and economic importance as a transfer point for both passengers and goods, including much of the country's coal output from the northern provinces.

As the passengers disembarked from the ferry and walked the short distance to the train platform, they couldn't help noticing the dozens of bedraggled, barefoot children darting about on the idle train tracks, picking up bits of coal that fell from the uncovered and overloaded transport cars. Their faces, bare hands and feet, and clothing were blackened by coal. This coal could either be sold or used for cooking and heating. Seeing these young scavengers gave the foreign passengers pause—a Dickensian moment that indicated how some in China were going through the worst of times.

The attention of the passengers quickly changed as they saw the royal-blue express train waiting just ahead at the Pukow station. Buzzing around the platform were scores of smartly dressed sleeping-car porters, eager to help with luggage and to locate assigned compartments. As the passengers stepped on board, there was a sense of awe at the elegance and grandeur of this technological marvel—their new home for the overnight ride northward.

The Peking Express consisted of two first-class cars, two second-class cars, two third-class cars, a dining car, a "drawing-room" car, and one car each for baggage and mail. All the passenger cars were sleepers, equipped with beds for overnight travel. A corridor ran down the left side of sleeping compartments. The first-class cars consisted of two berths, the bottom-sleeping berth being a "lower," which could be used as a seat during the daytime. The second-class cars were four-berth compartments; the third-class cars had six berths per compartment. Up in third class close to the locomotive, the ordinary Chinese passengers and a few impoverished foreigners were packed together on hard beds in dormitory-like sleeping arrangements.

By contrast, the first-class cabins came with every luxury—from hot water to silk sheets—and the pleasure of privacy. The first-class passengers had access to the common drawing-room car, which was equipped with wide windows on both sides for observation. On one end was a Victorian-style parlor with velvet upholstered couches and chairs lining the walls, and at the other end a full bar with tables and chairs for card games. The dim lights of the corridors burnished the smart craftsmanship of paneled woodworking decorated with inlaid designs. Passengers also enjoyed the modern comforts of shared washrooms and toilet facilities, with sanitation under the personal supervision of a qualified medical officer. The heating system included a thermostat, allowing each compartment to regulate the temperature as desired. The lighting was electric, with individual reading lamps for each berth. Temperature was controlled by electric fans and ventilation. The sole dining car—which serviced the first-class passengers only—featured a modern kitchen complete with refrigeration, steam tables, sinks, sanitation equipment, and utensils. In the dining room, tables were laid with silver and linen. All in all, the Peking Express resembled a luxury hotel on wheels, and many of the foreign passengers believed that they were on the trip of a lifetime, getting a glimpse of the countryside that few Westerners had ever seen.

As the Peking Express lumbered northward, the scenery changed, and the passengers saw mile after mile of rice paddies and straw-thatched-roof villages, with no roads except for narrow paths for oxen and donkeys. As the sun set across the vast horizon of China's central plains, the passengers went to the dining car for an elaborate five-course banquet featuring enormous prawns, fresh-steamed garden vegetables and salad, French cheeses and breads, Swiss chocolates and pastries, and an assortment of fine wines. As if in an elegant restaurant, all the passengers dressed in their swanky best for the onboard dining experience. Over dinner and drinks, they talked about the sights and shopping they had enjoyed in Shanghai and the things they planned to see in Peking.

After dinner, the American heiress Lucy Aldrich and her two companions moved to the drawing-room car to listen to music from the Victrola. Aldrich was drinking tea and enjoying the music, but she could see that her secretary and traveling companion, Minnie MacFadden, was less enthusiastic about the atmosphere. She sat glaring at a table of American and British men who were drinking whiskey and playing poker at the other end of the drawing-room car. "It's very bad taste to play in public, and before the Chinese!" the prim MacFadden remarked loudly.[5]

"Hush! Let them enjoy themselves," Aldrich countered. "It helps pass the time."

This was 1923, the height of Prohibition in America. The Rockefeller clan of which Aldrich was a part vigorously supported the dry cause and was also one of the largest contributors to the militant Anti-Saloon League, an organization instrumental in securing the passage of dry laws and, eventually, the Eighteenth Amendment. In China, however, temperance propaganda held sway only over the Protestant missionaries. It had no apparent effect on the Chinese or other foreigners. In fact, many people in Shanghai thought that Prohibition was American puritanism at its worst.

Aldrich and MacFadden watched as the men finished their game. The winner, a tall, Eastern-European-looking gentleman, jammed a big wad of bills into his pocket and strolled out of the car, jingling silver in both hands. MacFadden shook her head in disapproval.

Aldrich just smiled and cupped her hand over her ear to better hear the music playing on the gramophone. Aldrich was nearly deaf, but as with so many challenges she faced, she never let this disability keep her from living life to its fullest. Though a product of a stodgy New England upbringing, Aldrich was much more liberated than her sententious companion. She was highly educated, politically astute, and well traveled, having taken her first trip abroad four decades earlier. In her own way she was a free spirit and even a provocateur, and at times she wanted others to see her as a bit rebellious—lively, witty, *fun*. Her love for Asian fabrics, garments, and fancy headwear showed that she was not constrained by convention and popular ideas of "good taste." MacFadden was often aghast at her playfulness and caprice, yet Aldrich took pleasure in shocking her uptight companion, who was nevertheless devoted to her and had been in her service now for six years.

The two American army brats, Roland Pinger Jr. and Bobby Allen, had taken control of the Victrola and started singing along and snapping their fingers to Ted Weems and his orchestra's rendition of "Somebody Stole My Gal," a hit that was just then topping the charts:

> Gee, but I'm lonesome, lonesome and blue.
> I've found out something I never knew.
> I know now what it means to be sad,
> For I've lost the best gal I ever had,
> She only left yesterday,
> Somebody stole her away.

Bobby was taller than most twelve-year-olds and strong enough to wind up the tight spring that powered the music box. Roland was nine, much smaller but very clever. He took it upon himself to sort through the records of popular American musicians and knew just how to pick the right tune to please the crowd. With precision, he set the needle on the black hard-vinyl disk, which rocked slightly with the subtle, rhythmic movement of the carriage. Roland and Bobby looked like Boy Scouts. They were well-mannered, handsome, and tanned from life in the tropical weather of Manila. Dreamers, they both had a taste for adventure, and they loved reading the stories of Mark Twain and Robert Louis Stevenson.

Roland somehow knew just what the boisterous table of card players wanted to hear. At a certain point, these men began to sing along so loudly that they drowned out the Victrola. Aldrich took this as her cue to leave. Around ten o'clock she, MacFadden, and their French maid, Mathilde Schoneberg, stood up just as a song ended. Bobby and Roland took a bow, then shook hands with the gamblers, who gave the boys a round of applause for their exceptional command of the phonograph.

Roland Pinger found his parents in their connecting cabins and got ready for bed. He had to be careful as he climbed into the upper berth, above the compartment window, not to wake his younger brother, Edward, who was asleep on the lower berth.

As Roland drifted off to sleep, his parents talked about the events of the day, reflecting on how this trip was a nice way of ending their family adventure in Asia—an experience that they and the boys would never forget. As she lay in her lower berth, glancing at the boys soundly asleep, Miriam took off her rings and unconsciously put them in a little silk envelope with her hairpins. She closed her eyes and was lulled to sleep by the soothing carriage movement and rhythmic *chuff, chuff, chuff* of the steam locomotive engine driving the train northward.

AFTER THE WOMEN AND CHILDREN LEFT THE DRAWING-ROOM CAR, THE atmosphere changed. Now smoke and drunken laughter filled the whole length of the carriage. Powell made his way down to the bar and ordered another whiskey. He could hear the soft and slow melodic plucking of a banjo from one of the tables, creating a pensive, almost mournful ambience. He then settled into an armchair next to his cabinmate, Marcel A. Berubé, a French veteran of the Great War who worked as a senior official with the Chinese Salt Administration. The government agency administered the *gabelle* (tax) on salt, which had provided the Peking government with a key source of revenue for two thousand years.[6] It was Berubé's job to control revenue collection on salt sales so that China's foreign debts could be repaid, including its railroad infrastructure loans, which financed projects like the Peking Express.

Berubé was on his way to Tientsin, a coastal commercial and trading hub in northern China, where he lived with his American-born wife, Elizabeth. Powell and Berubé had never met before, but they quickly were enamored by each other's personal stories, travels, and views on China. As Powell sipped his drink, he introduced Berubé to Friedman and Lehrbas, and the men all began comparing notes. Powell couldn't help but think about how this train encapsulated life in China. On one passenger carriage you had international travelers, the multicultural expatriate set, and the wealthy and privileged Chinese, all being waited on by porters representing China's huge working class. Then there were those in the tightly packed third-class cars to the front of the train, impatiently waiting to get to the next stop.

Larry Lehrbas was going on about how cheap booze was in Shanghai, how there was even a bar in the offices of his newspaper. Chomping his cigar, Friedman replied that drinking brandy and selling automobiles went hand in hand, and he couldn't imagine how anyone could close a deal under Prohibition.

Powell listened to the lighthearted conversation, but he was distracted by the table of card players nearby. He knew these men by reputation—the Shanghai cousins. All in their twenties, related to one another by marriage, they belonged to powerful Jewish mercantile families. They, like Berubé, were headed to Tientsin. One of them, Victor Haimovitch, was a jockey on his way to compete in the spring horse races there, and his cousins had come along to root for him.

The Shanghai cousins represented a blend of nationalities. Haimovitch held US citizenship. Theo Saphiere and the brothers Eddie and Freddie Elias were technically British "protégés," a political designation held by many Mediterranean, Middle Eastern, and Baghdadi Jews who lived in regions under British protective status and were thus neither colonial subjects nor naturalized citizens. Emile Gensburger was a French protégé, with family roots in Alsace-Lorraine. But their common Jewish background was their real identity. In the late nineteenth and early twentieth centuries, Shanghai was considered an attractive business destination and safe haven because it was an open port city without strict immigration requirements. More than forty thousand Jews emigrated to Shanghai and other cities in China, including merchants from India and Iraq looking for economic opportunities, as well as refugees escaping the pogroms of Eastern Europe and Russia.

Eddie Elias was a book-smart stockbroker working for the Hong Kong & Shanghai Banking Corporation. He was just twenty-three but already serious and businesslike, and he was described by his family as a "God-loving, gentle bore." In contrast, his big brother, twenty-eight-year-old Freddie, didn't like to read, yet he was fluent and garrulous in spoken Chinese. He also worked as a stockbroker, enjoyed gambling on the horses with his clients, and loved socializing with the film stars who visited Shanghai. He was a handsome, fashionable playboy and was attracted to young Chinese men—which was not necessarily taboo in Shanghai.[7]

Like Freddie, Emile Gensburger was a natural entertainer, with the wit and traits of a vaudeville actor, and he was always the life of the party. He had just returned to China from Paris and Monte Carlo, showing off his pricey European clothing. Haimovitch was an up-and-coming jockey who, when not racing, helped with the family jewelry business. While attending college in California, he had worked for a time as an actor in San Francisco. Traveling with the cousins was their friend, musician Alfred Zimmerman, whose parents were Russian Jews who had emigrated to the United States from the city of Vladivostok in 1888 before eventually moving to Shanghai to build a life in China.

Sitting next to Eddie Elias was Hung Shi-chi, a Shanghai personality who was well-known to the cousins as well as to Powell. Given his taste for expensive automobiles, he had been one of Friedman's best customers. Hung had graduated from Brown University in 1909 and had lived in New York City for many years before returning to his native China, where he infamously squandered a vast fortune inherited from his businessman father on a lavish and dissolute lifestyle. He also gave up a lucrative sinecure that his father paid a vast sum of money for—he simply did not want to carry on the family business. Now in his late thirties, Hung had settled into the duller life as an English-language professor, yet he did not shy away from enjoying a night of drinking with his foreign friends. Hung was dressed fashionably in a well-fitted Western suit and carried himself more like a banker than a professor.

As the night wore on and the liquor flowed, China's political pendulum was the talk of the drawing-room. Powell's hopes had soared, he said, when just the week before, President Li Yuan-hung announced his plans to abolish the warlord system.[8] President Li had come out of retirement six months earlier to lead the country once again. His ambitious plans were a welcome relief to both the Chinese people and the international community after ten years of warlord thievery and destruction. Yet

Li Yuan-hung, president, Republic of China (1916–1917, 1922–1923). Li was regarded as an antimilitarist and scholar, and he sought to unify the country with a national constitution, as well as to disband the warlords (tuchuns) and their armies, a step that was met with much resistance. (Ulrico Hoepli)

disbanding the warlord armies would take much more money than the government in Peking had.

In 1923 the central government was effectively bankrupt, and new forms of taxation payable to the central government were resisted by the tuchuns, although they kept nine-tenths of China's national taxation.[9] To make matters worse, state revenues from trade and customs, the salt monopoly, and other taxes were allocated to pay foreign debts, including the railroad loans and reparations forced upon China by foreign governments to compensate for past outrages against foreign interests. China's national debt had soared to $950 million, including $100 million in unpaid civil and military expenses. The foreign indebtedness of China wasn't new; it had started in the late 1800s with the financing of its war efforts against the Japanese in 1894-1895. After China lost the war, the Japanese exacted a large indemnity. Following the Boxer Rebellion, during which a military force of the Eight-Nation Alliance invaded China to lift the siege of the Peking legations,

China incurred additional debt to pay for property losses and the cost of the foreign expeditionary forces that entered China to protect their nationals.

Without a financial incentive, the warlords had no motivation to give up the money they squeezed out of the territories under their command or to disband the provincial troops they needed to remain in power.[10] And if they did disband their armies, what would become of the thousands of troops who now had no way of earning their keep? "The end result is that there are gangs of disbanded soldiers that roam the countryside just looking for something to eat, or looking for trouble," Powell said, as he pointed out the window toward the dark countryside beyond the tracks. Lehrbas shook his head and clicked his tongue, while Friedman raised his eyebrows as he took a long drag on his cigar.

"Oh, jeesh! Is it safe to run the trains through the countryside at night?" Lehrbas asked the obvious as Berubé nodded and looked to Powell for the answer.

"Let's just hope so," he said, finishing his drink.

The train then started to slow down for a scheduled water and coal stop at the central Chinese town of Süchow, and most of the people in the drawing-room car realized it was well past midnight and time to turn in. Powell asked Berubé if he wanted to step outside to smoke one last cigarette before retiring for the night.

UNDER THE MOTHY STATION LIGHTS, POWELL ADMIRED THE EXTERIOR of the passenger cars with their uniform, royal-blue paint and gold lettering in both English and Chinese. He and Berubé watched from a distance as the railway staff quickly swung a long standpipe from an enormous water tank adjacent to the track to replenish the engine's supply. The water was used not only to generate steam to move the locomotive but also to operate other devices such as the air compressor for the brakes, the passenger-car heating system, and the train whistle. A small, steam-driven generator also powered the headlight, with illumination sufficient to see at least 800 feet ahead on the tracks.

Together with the loading of water, the coal chute was positioned to feed the fuel supply into the tender. Even while in the station, the engine crew worked continuously, stoking and tending the firebox. The relentless shoveling of coal was hellishly hot, backbreaking, and dirty work, and Powell and Berubé felt a twinge of guilt seeing the toil required for them to travel in such speed and comfort. The shirtless workers at the coal bin were coated from head to toe with glistening black soot.

Then, just as Powell and Berubé were about to climb back aboard, they noticed something strange. Several Asian men—well-dressed in stylish dark suits, leather gloves, and black fedora hats—stridently boarded the train and, with the help of the railway staff, roused several passengers in the sleeping compartments. A few minutes later, Powell watched as a half-dozen disheveled, barely awake male passengers hastily disembarked with their satchels and were hustled away. All of them appeared to speak Japanese.

Powell checked his watch: it was nearly one o'clock in the morning. He and Berubé assumed that this late hour meant that these passengers had overslept and missed their stop. An attendant motioned for the pair to get back onboard. Puzzled, Powell hesitated for a moment before he and Berubé tossed their cigarette stubs aside and returned to their shared compartment.

Fueled by coal, the engine's side rods slowly began to move the main driving wheels of the locomotive. The two men then heard the cadenced chuffing sound of steam and smoke being released with each engine stroke, and the train lurched forward into the darkness of the night.

CHAPTER 4

THE OUTRAGE

I peered through the window, and in the darkness could just discern a crowd of ghostly-looking men with pigtails wound around their heads, in ragged garb and with rifles and bayonets, bounding towards the stationary carriages.

—William Smith, British tourist and hostage[1]

MAY 6, 1923, 2:40 A.M., EIGHT LI SOUTH OF LINCHENG

As darkness descended, Sun Mei-yao led his men—emboldened by their feast of meat and *shamsu*—to a specific section of the rail line just south of the town of Lincheng, a southern Shantung boomtown along the Tientsin-Pukow line that served as a junction for the spur lines servicing the vast coal mines twenty miles to the east. His spies had informed him that on this weekend, all the senior officers of the railway police, who were responsible for the protection of both the track and the trains, were in Tientsin, 377 miles to the north, attending the birthday party of their commander. The junior officers left behind either chose not to go to work, given the absence of their bosses, or were bribed to stay home. In any case, only a few rank-and-file guards were there to protect the entire train system.

Once in position, Sun's troops seized the few railway police on duty in the vicinity and forced some railroad workers to remove the steel nails and fishplates connecting sixteen rails—without actually removing the rails from the sleepers, or railroad ties. Each fishplate, joining two rails together on the track for alignment, had six large bolts that could be removed only with a special wrench. Without fishplates and nails holding the rails to the sleepers, the track could not support the weight of an oncoming train.

The spot chosen was eight *li*—about two and a half miles—south of Lincheng, where the track was on a slight uphill grade and curve. This uphill curve not only forced approaching locomotives to slow down, but it also made it difficult for any train crew to see far ahead. Sun knew that his plan was audacious. He would be taking the typical kidnapping and thievery practiced by bandits in the Chinese countryside to a whole new level. But he did not realize, as his men lay their trap for the Peking Express, that he was also about to become an international media sensation and a subject of major concern in halls of power around the world.

POWELL HAD DRUNK TOO MUCH WHISKEY, AND INSTEAD OF MAKING HIM happy, it only made him anxious. Something bothered him about the sight of those Japanese businessmen sneaking off the train in their pajamas. They were, like all the other passengers, clearly headed much farther north, to the cities of Tsinan, Tientsin, or Peking. Why would they suddenly disembark here, in the middle of nowhere, in the middle of the night? He couldn't figure it out, and it offended his sense of himself as a journalist that there should be things that others knew and he did not.[2]

He lay awake in his bunk, swaddled in silk sheets, talking to Berubé. Powell had taken the upper berth, which was above the compartment's window; Berubé was on the lower bunk, which ran perpendicular to Powell's and served as a couch during the daytime. The spring night was cool and fresh, and the green landscape appeared soft and welcoming as it rolled by in the moonlight. Powell listened to the pleasant rattle of the wheels and hiss of the steam engine until finally drifting off to sleep.

He dozed for about forty minutes while the train snaked its way through the flat, central plains and then crossed a rail bridge above China's Grand

Canal. Carved out in the fifth century BCE, this 1,100-mile waterway is the world's longest artificial river. It meanders south from Peking, just grazing Shantung Province.[3]

Without warning, the train lurched sharply side to side, and the brakes squealed like a pig being slaughtered. Then came a loud crashing sound. Powell nearly toppled out of his bunk onto the compartment floor before he caught himself on the bed frame and climbed down from the berth. He looked outside but couldn't see a station in the darkness, only the faint moonlit silhouette of the Shantung mountain peaks toward the east. For a moment there was an uncanny silence. Powell looked at his pocket watch and noticed the time was two-forty in the morning.

Then came the first gunshots. They seemed to be coming from all sides at once. The reports looked like distant firecrackers lighting up the hillsides. Powell could see raiders lying in the fields and firing, and others dashing across the embankment toward the now-still carriages. "Good lord, we are *under attack!*" Powell shouted.

Berubé instinctively dropped to the floor. Powell drew his head from the window and placed his back against the wall of the carriage. The bullets continued to ring up and down the train cars. *Christ—how many are there?* A rifle appeared in the window of the carriage. The shot went off inches from Powell's head, and the deafening blast reverberated in the steel-encased carriage, instantly shattering his eardrums. Everything went silent; then slowly the silence was filled by a high-pitched ringing.

"Get your gun!" Powell screamed to Berubé as he pulled his own .25 caliber automatic revolver from his travel bag.[4] Both men readied their weapons. The electric lights had gone out. But Powell noticed in the darkness the glow of hand torches and lanterns, balls of light careening through the brushed-wood and steel carriages. And he could hear cries in Chinese:

"*Tsou, tsou!*"—go, go!

"*Sha, sha*"—kill, kill![5]

The voices were accompanied by shattering glass. It was a sound the passengers of the Peking Express would never forget. One survivor described it as the music "under which our hopes vanished"—the simultaneous smashing of a hundred windows, the slithering of two thousand thick-soled sandals, and the screams of women and children.[6]

Powell ducked outside the carriage door into the hallway. He could see the bandits working their way toward his compartment, armed with rifles and pistols and in some cases *miaodaos*—sabers used by Chinese soldiers and bandits alike. Ransacking compartments as they went along, they faced no resistance. Something was not right. Where were the guards, the rooftop machine-gun emplacements that were supposed to have protected them, the veritable army that made "the most luxurious train in the orient" also reputedly the safest?[7]

As it turned out, the two dozen armed guards—either because of cowardice or because they were paid off in advance—ran from the train as soon as the bandits opened fire. The commanding officer, Chao Te-ch'ao, was for some reason not in uniform at the time of the attack and took no apparent action to defend the passengers. He was sleeping peacefully in one of the compartments when confronted by the bandits, and he quickly surrendered.[8]

SUN MEI-YAO AND PO-PO LIU WANTED TO STOP THE TRAIN WITHOUT causing serious damage. They had planned it all perfectly—or almost perfectly. When the train approached the site, the engine's powerful headlight did not reveal that the tracks had been loosened, creating an ideal trap. But the engineer saw movement in the fields and men lurking around the side of the track. So as a precaution he slowed the train to 10 miles per hour.[9]

When the locomotive reached the booby-trapped section, the engine jolted sideways and came to a grinding halt as it slipped from the loosened rails and sunk into the gravel ballast. The engine stayed upright, but the loosened rails could not bear the load of the weight of the cars, and a few of them toppled over. One rail came up under the engine and bent in an arch. That bent rail actually jammed into the engine's undercarriage and helped prop up the engine, keeping it from tipping over.

As the train sank into the gravel embankment, the engineer slammed on the brakes, but the steam that drove the mechanism had no time to circulate to the rear of the train, so the brakes were not uniformly engaged. As a result, the coal tender, baggage car, and other carriages behind the engine went sideways and slipped down the embankment as the track started to snap off the railroad ties in what Major Pinger described as "a series of deafening and bone-shaking concussions."[10]

Everything seemed to happen in slow motion as one of the third-class coaches veered off into the fields until it finally came to a stop, leaning sideways at a forty-five-degree angle. Miraculously, no one was killed in the derailment itself. The deaths and injuries came once the bandits stormed aboard.

THEY SET UPON THE PEKING EXPRESS IN WAVES. THE FIRST GROUP RANsacked compartments and grabbed any cash, coins, jewelry, watches, and other small objects of value that could be traded for ammunition, supplies, and opium. The second wave was the gleaners—removing the less precious items left behind (clothing, hats, bedding, and fixtures from the train), which the bandits could put to their own use or barter for food and shelter with the villagers. The final group of bandits was the kidnappers. It was their job to sweep through the train cars and take passengers hostage.[11]

Powell was about to encounter the first wave of attackers, those looking for valuables. He and Berubé went back inside their compartment, loaded their pistols, and got ready to make a stand. Though in his pajamas, Berubé looked like he was once again peering over a trench on the Western Front. He raised his arms to take aim. They could hear the bandits in the neighboring compartments; then suddenly they were right outside their room. A rifle barrel crashed through the glass door. As Powell readied his pistol to open fire, he quickly realized that resistance might be a deadly mistake. Glass was breaking all around them. The bandits poured into the compartment through the windows and from both of the neighboring carriages. "There are at least a half-dozen of these bastards!" Powell then motioned to Berubé to hand over his gun. "And mine too," he said, holding out his pistol to the bandits.[12]

Both men raised their hands in surrender. Now Powell had a chance to size up his captors. They looked not all that different from the beggars he would see in Shanghai. Most of the bandits were short and wore a braided ponytail wrapped around their head. Some carried the same kind of carbines as Chinese soldiers, meaning they were probably ex-army. As the outlaws fumbled with and admired their new weapons, Powell and Berubé used the time to get dressed. This was a smart move—many of the other travelers were being pushed off the train in only their nightgowns and pajamas.

Powell, never fussy about his appearance, even put on his necktie as if going to a dinner party. He wanted to delay the bandits some more and give Berubé the opportunity to scrounge whatever he could from their compartment. When they were finally dressed, the two passengers stood nervously with hands slightly raised. One of the bandits, seeing a ring on Powell's left hand, forcefully attempted to remove it. Rather than risking injury, Powell surrendered his cherished University of Missouri class ring.

Suddenly, four more bandits, now the third wave, appeared and pushed the pair of men down the narrow corridor that ran the length of the left side of the carriage and off the train onto the embankment. Almost every window in the train was broken. Great piles of glass lay everywhere. Passengers, including women and children, were being dragged off in their nightclothes without shoes. Once everyone was outside, the bandits swept through the entire train once again, breaking open travel bags and ripping up the fixtures in the sleeping compartments.

Slowly it dawned on the passengers that they were not just waiting for the bandits to finish robbing the train—they were being taken hostage. They begged to be let back into their compartments to collect shoes and warmer clothes. Over the shouting, Powell could distinctly make out the sound of a mature female voice. "Socony!" she screamed. "Socony! Socony!" Powell chuckled, amused that Miss Aldrich believed that a Chinese bandit would be impressed by her connection to the venerable Standard Oil Company of New York or to the Rockefeller family. *Socony*, he thought, *is certainly not going to be much help out here!*

JOSEPH ROTHMAN WOKE TO THE SOUNDS OF GUNFIRE AND THE SCREAM-ing of passengers. Either someone was coming after him or he was in the wrong place at the wrong time. With no time to lose, he quickly got dressed, putting on his suit coat and shoes, and then readied his two revolvers. At the fore of his mind were the stacks of cash and silver coins in his baggage, including his poker winnings from earlier that evening. While securing the cash, he pulled out the first of several large boxes of ammunition. He had a small arsenal with him, including almost two hundred rounds. Looking at his pile of money, he thought it had been too hard-earned to be filched by a bunch of savages. He was ready for a firefight.

A naturalized British citizen originally from Romania, Rothman was a fifty-eight-year-old army veteran of the Second Anglo-Boer War in the Cape Colony in southern Africa. Because he had fought for the Crown, he was granted British citizenship in 1902. Once discharged from the military, he traveled to Singapore, Hong Kong, Manila, and finally Shanghai. By the early 1920s, Rothman was well-known to the British authorities in China as a shady character, notorious for his work as a crewing agent in the Straits Settlement of Singapore—conscripting crew members for ships, sometimes by coercion or even by kidnapping them.[13] He hunted for his prey in the waterfront saloons and boardinghouses, searching for unsuspecting men to supply live bodies for sailing crews. Crewing agents often drugged and beat their hapless victims, shanghaiing them into back-breaking service on ships that plied the waters of the Orient. He was apparently on his way to Tientsin to continue his trade, although he had previously been deported from China for his criminal activities. Rothman had every reason to be worried that someone might be coming after him.

After banging and banging on the compartment door, a group of bandits charged into Rothman's room, likely assuming that behind the door was another unarmed, frightened foreign tourist. Instead, Rothman wildly opened fire with both of his pistols, but one of his guns must have jammed and the other missed its mark. The bandits fired back. Staggering, the tall foreigner realized that he had taken a bullet in his lower chest.

The bandits momentarily ceased fire but yelled at the man to drop his pistols. Rothman dropped one of his guns as he balanced himself on the berth, but then he pulled up his second pistol and took aim at the gang in his doorway. Instantly, one of the bandits rushed forward, raised his rifle, and shot the injured man point-blank in the face. Mortally wounded, Rothman's last desperate act of defiance was to grab a tea kettle and throw it at the intruders from across the room.[14] He then stumbled sideways and collapsed on the compartment floor, dying almost immediately.

Not wanting to climb over the sprawling body or the blood-covered floor, the bandits didn't take Rothman's baggage and never discovered his cache of money and ammunition. In addition to Rothman, two Chinese passengers who put up resistance also sustained fatal gunshot wounds during the initial raid.

ALTHOUGH SHE WAS PARTIALLY DEAF, LUCY ALDRICH HAD HEARD THE attack break out—the gunfire and the shouting—but to her ears it all sounded like a "queer crackling noise." She thought perhaps the train had collided with something. Moments later Minnie MacFadden mouthed to her what was happening: *The Peking Express was under attack!* In an instant, five bandits had occupied the neighboring compartment belonging to Mathilde Schoneberg. MacFadden could hear Schoneberg's sobs coming through the walls.[15] The heiress was not frightened as much as outraged. *Don't these fools know who I am?*

Aldrich peeked out through the curtain and in the dim light saw swarms of gaunt figures surrounding the train. As the guns kept popping outside,

Lucy Truman Aldrich, daughter of Rhode Island senator Nelson Aldrich and the sister-in-law of American financier John D. Rockefeller Jr., 1923. (RIHS)

she quickly grabbed her passports and letters of credit. Then Aldrich yelled to the faithful Mathilde, imploring her not to fight back and to give the bandits everything they demanded. (She did not know that her crafty maid had already secreted away her diamonds and emeralds in a sachet, which she then hid in her undergarments.)[16]

MacFadden heard the bandits next door, "ransacking, pulling, turning everything out" of their luggage. Then she noticed someone violently yanking the doorknob to their locked compartment. "Should I just let them in?" MacFadden whispered, thinking that the inevitable was about to happen anyway.[17]

A cauldron of emotions was boiling inside Aldrich: fear, anger, but also curiosity. She wanted to face these outlaws who had upset her carefully planned trip. She had always pictured railway bandits as "bold, romantic looking chaps with neatly turned up hat brims and red handkerchiefs knotted about their necks."[18] But the half-dozen men who entered the compartment were ragged and barefoot. Pointing their revolvers at the women, the outlaws ripped through the handbags with dagger-like knives and rifled through the pockets of their nightgowns and overcoats. One of the bandits had cut his hand on a piece of glass and was dripping blood around the room. He went on thrashing and pawing through their belongings as blood streamed all around.

Aldrich was losing her temper. "Here, take this!" she said, handing him a handkerchief. The young bandit smiled and said something in Chinese, which the two women took to be an expression of thanks.

MacFadden then picked up a box of candy that the bandits had overlooked and thrust it into the hands of the bleeding bandit. "Here is something to eat," said MacFadden. "Take it and *get out!*"

The two self-assured women then nudged the bandits into the corridor and thought that the whole affair was over.[19] Moments later, in came another group of bandits who milled around the compartment to see if there was anything else of value. When the bandits ripped through MacFadden's handbag, they found a red case containing their documents and some Japanese currency. Aldrich snatched it out of a bandit's hand, but seconds later another bandit wrestled it back. Then one of the thieves grabbed a string of jade beads belonging to MacFadden, but Aldrich pushed him away. "No, you don't!"

The bandit grabbed Aldrich's fingers and pulled the jade beads toward him but ended up breaking the string and scattering the beads across the floor. "You pick those up!" Aldrich fumed.[20]

This was something that the bandits did not expect, that their fiercest resistance would come from two dowdy, aging American spinsters. The bandit flinched, surprised by Aldrich's overly confident order. He glared at the woman, who got down on all fours and started to pick up the beads; the bandit kneeled down to help her. Finally, the bandit seemed to realize that this troublesome woman had no business ordering him around. He straightened up and held his revolver to her head for a half-minute, rattling off a string of pungent Chinese phrases that the two cowering women interpreted as expletives.

Then he suddenly laughed, shoving Aldrich aside and continuing to rummage through her belongings. She seemed to realize at once how close she had come to death. The bandits were now everywhere: "They seemed literally to boil up out of the floor." Aldrich turned to MacFadden and took a deep breath. "Right here and now, we need to obey orders without quibbling."[21]

With pistols in their backs, Aldrich, MacFadden, and Schoneberg were led down the corridor and out of the train.

CHAPTER 5

TAKING PRISONERS

They said "Sha, Sha" which means "Kill, Kill." We heard screaming and howling. They were dragging people off the train. They took everything they could find.

—Alfred Zimmerman, American passenger and escapee[1]

MAY 6, 1923, 4:00 A.M., EIGHT LI SOUTH OF LINCHENG

Sun Mei-yao and Po-Po Liu watched as the first wave of bandits brought from the train the cash, jewelry, and other valuable objects looted from the passengers and handed the cache over to a trusted subchief, who took inventory and placed the treasure into a pilfered portmanteau. One by one, the young bandits ran toward Sun and Liu to show off their finds. The chiefs were pleased, Liu especially, and nodded with approval. As the second wave passed through the train, Sun started to get impatient. He told his subchiefs to better control their men, some of whom were spending too much time carrying unwieldy items, such as bedding and kitchen fixtures, off the train. Sun didn't want anything to slow them down. They had more important things to accomplish than removing every bit of loot from the train.

Sun was most interested in the passengers, especially the foreigners. He watched as the third wave of men swept through the train cars looking for passengers, room by room. Sun smiled when he saw the foreigners being carried off the train and onto the embankment where he was standing. This was exactly what he wanted for his grand political agenda: hostages. They were a motley group of frail and frightened old men and women, young boys, and sturdy-looking men such as Powell and Friedman—would-be heroes who needed to be carefully watched, he thought. He had already been told that at least one foreigner was shot to death after fighting back.

"Separate them all!" Sun called out. He didn't want the foreigners talking with one another, possibly plotting their escapes. "I want every foreigner guarded by at least three of our men, if not more."

Sun could hear the frightened passengers pleading to go back to the train for their shoes and clothing, but he rejected their entreaties. Instead, he ordered his men to gather up the shoes and some clothing, which would be handed out later when they got away from the derailed train.

MAJOR ROBERT ALLEN WAS JOLTED AWAKE BY THE CRASH, WHICH sounded to him like something out of a war zone. Then, there was a "death-like silence" followed by the crackling of rifle shots in the distance. "Outlaws!" Allen shouted.

Bobby and Martha rose to their feet in the dark compartment. Falling back on his basic training, the major steeled himself for battle and instinctively dressed as he heard the attackers running toward the train. In a few moments, Chinese voices could be heard outside the corridor, along with the frightened outcries of the foreign passengers.

Allen took from his pocket two rolls of Chinese paper currency. The first he divided between Martha and Bobby, giving a larger share to his wife, who concealed the wad of cash in her nightgown. The major held the other roll of money in his hand, hoping the bandits would accept it and move on. Allen saw no use in resistance; there were too many of them to fight.

The door to the compartment was locked, but the bandits broke through the window, thrust aside the curtain with a lantern, and reached in to open the door. As they entered, one of the bandits yelled at Allen while making nervous gestures with his firearm. Allen immediately offered the bandits the roll of currency in his hand, which they quickly snatched. They searched his pockets, taking the few silver coins he had on him. One bandit grabbed Martha's hands and forcefully removed her wedding ring. She screamed as the bandit tore it off her finger. The bandits then left the Allens sitting alone in the darkness of their compartment, vainly hoping that their ordeal was now over.

Oh Lord! thought Allen, hearing the terrified screams of Roland Jr. as the nine-year-old boy was dragged down the hallway. *The bandits aren't content with loot—they're taking prisoners!*[2]

Soon a second group of bandits appeared to search the compartment for more valuables. After finding none, they motioned for Allen to leave the train. "I am *not* leaving my family!" he said, visibly shaking.

One of the bandits cocked his pistol and pointed the barrel at Allen's head. As Martha gasped, the major tried to appear calm even as he trembled with fear; he had never had the barrel of a gun pointed at his head before. To everyone's surprise, it was Bobby who spoke up. "Go with them, papa. I'll stay with mother."[3]

Before Allen could reply, the bandits grabbed Bobby and forced both him and his father down the corridor together. To the bandits, twelve-year-old boys were fair game. The degenerate Po-Po Liu even made it a point to recruit teenage boys (who were often orphans or the victims of his own kidnapping schemes) because their immaturity made them easier to entice or force into service. He placed them in frontline roles, those that carried a high risk of death or permanent injury. The bandits thus viewed Bobby not as a child entitled to any special treatment but as an adult who was subject to the same handling as the rest of the men.

Rather than wait in the carriage alone, Martha followed her son and husband down the corridor. In the carriage vestibule, an enclosed end of the car with doorways exiting on both sides, she stood barefoot in her nightgown, sobbing and pleading for her husband to take her along. "Martha, stay here!" he insisted. "It is far better for you to remain behind."

Robert and Bobby Allen were then pushed out of the train and onto the embankment. The last image that the major saw of his wife was her

standing in the dim gray light of the moonlit sky, weeping, while he and
Bobby were dragged away.[4]

As the Pinger family huddled in their compartment, the glass
window in the door to their stateroom was kicked in with a loud crash.
Once the flimsy door was unhinged and opened, a dozen bandits exploded
into the room brandishing swords, fists, and pistols. Major Pinger shouted
at the bandits to take everything.

"I'm an American! American!" Pinger pleaded, but the words, in English,
were meaningless to the bandits, who rummaged through handbags taking rings, bracelets, cameras, clothing, watches, thermos bottles, and bedsheets. Miriam's response was to show the bandits her bare fingers, which
lacked any rings or jewels. But the bandits figured she was hiding something and tried to frisk her for jewelry.

"No, you don't!" yelled Pinger, who was being manhandled himself. Furious, he pushed away the bandits and put up his fists in a hopeless attempt
to defend his wife. The bandits, momentarily caught off guard by this cou-
rageous stand, took a moment to respond before pouncing on him with
their rifle butts and tearing the back of his pajama top.

Startled but not seriously hurt, Pinger raised his palms in defeat. Yet he
had won something for his defiance—the bandits stopped groping Miriam.
But now one of them was grabbing Roland from under the bottom berth
and pulling the boy out the compartment door.

Pinger grabbed hold of the screaming child and yanked him in the opposite direction, but the bandits pulled harder, bending his arm around the
doorway, making it clear that they would break it if he didn't let the boy go.
Roland was then dragged barefoot down the glass-littered corridor.

As Miriam cried hysterically beside him, Pinger felt helpless. He wanted
to follow Roland, but he couldn't leave Miriam and his other boy, Edward,
unprotected. He worried that if he wasn't there, the bandits might try to
rape his wife. *You'll need to kill me first*, he thought.[5]

"They *will* kill you if you resist any more," Miriam said, as if reading her
husband's mind. The bandits had a half-dozen firearms pointed in his direction. "Let's all go out together," she reasoned. Whatever they would face,

it would be better to face it as one family. So down the corridor the Pingers went, barefoot and half-dressed. In the dark vestibule they found a desperate Martha Allen, cowering in the corner like a white-haired wraith in the hopes that she might be overlooked.[6]

"Take me with you!" Martha pleaded tearfully.

But the Pingers had no time to respond as they were hustled off the train by the bandits. Martha stumbled behind them. Major Pinger jumped to the ground through the shattered exterior door. He then reached back for three-year-old Edward, grabbing the child. Miriam jumped next. It wasn't until she hit the ground that she noticed the deep cuts in her bare feet caused by walking on broken glass and rough cinders. The pain caused her to slump to the ground. As Pinger bent to help his wife up, the bandits slammed the butt of their rifles against his back, forcing him to leave his wife behind to fend for herself on the embankment.

THE DERAILMENT HAD SIMPLY SEEMED LIKE A TERRIBLE ACCIDENT TO Victor Haimovitch and Alfred Zimmerman until they heard a chorus of rifle shots and broken glass.[7] Minutes later, six bandits burst into their first-class compartment, one of them hissing and screaming and waving a gun in Haimovitch's face. Haimovitch threw up his hands and pointed to their valuables and the stash of cash on the table. The bandits grabbed everything, including a banjo under the bottom berth. Zimmerman pleaded for them not to take his beloved instrument, but the bandit slapped his hands away. Then the bandits stepped out of the compartment, leaving the young men to wonder what would happen next. They heard the screams of women and children being dragged from the train.

"They are going to kill us," Zimmerman said. "We need to do something if we want to get out alive!" As they contemplated their next move, a lone bandit clambered through their window from outside the train. He seemed to be searching for more valuables, but the two cabinmates noticed that this bandit was unarmed—he must have left his weapon outside the train. They looked at each other: *This is our chance.*

Haimovitch then hit the bandit square on the jaw with every ounce of strength he had. The two men then jumped on the young bandit and tied his hands with their belts and gagged him with a necktie. "Let's go!" Hai-movitch said.

Zimmerman and Haimovitch gingerly climbed out the window and dropped about six feet to the track below. They slipped under the carriage and hid in the darkness between the tracks and wheels. After about thirty minutes, while the other passengers were being corralled on the embankment, they crawled from under the cars and ran into the fields of *kaoliang* (grain sorghum) on the west side of the track away from the bandits and hostages.

The rest of the Shanghai cousins weren't as lucky as Zimmerman and Haimovitch. Down the hall, the bandits rushed into their compartments and pushed them off the train. If they weren't so frightened by their dangerous predicament, the cousins probably would have found much comedy in their various states of undress. Freddie Elias was barefoot and wore only pajama bottoms and a sleeveless undershirt. Theo Saphiere had managed to put a shirt and jacket on but lacked trousers and socks. Emile Gensburger was fully dressed, as was Eddie Elias—except for his socks.

Freddie Elias and Gensburger were led in one direction, and Saphiere and Eddie Elias in another. Two guards dragged each of the cousins forward and forced them to walk about two hundred yards down the track, where they saw the bandits lined up and firing their weapons at the retreating train guards, who were running west into the fields. The bandits forced the men to walk down into a slight depression just in front of the firing party. The Shanghai cousins looked at each other. They thought they were about to be shot. But actually, the bandits seemed only to be separating the hostages and then assigning multiple, heavily armed guards to each group.

Eddie Elias watched as the bandits dragged a frail, older gentleman along the embankment as if he were a rag doll, his head and shoulders bumping the ground repeatedly. Eddie wanted to intervene but knew that might be a fatal mistake: multiple guns were trained in his direction. The man was William Smith, a sixty-five-year-old from Great Britain, who, earlier in the evening, Eddie had seen alone in a corner of the dining car glued to his guidebooks and maps, poring through the details of the historical sites he would visit. Smith had set out on an around-the-world trip seeking calm and relaxation on the advice of his doctors. He suffered from neurasthenia, a common but ill-defined diagnosis for such symptoms as dizziness, fainting, and weakness. The truth of the matter was that Smith was addicted to painkillers and sedatives, making him perpetually nervous. His doctors believed a trip to the Orient would be a chance to help wean him off the narcotics, and after months on the road, he actually had managed to kick his habit. But Smith now found himself being whisked away from the serenity of his luxurious train compartment by a horde of bandits in the middle of nowhere.

DRESSED BUT BAREFOOT, THE AUTOMOBILE DEALER LEON FRIEDMAN felt like there was a big target on his back. Among the other hostages gathered on the embankment, he stood out like a sore thumb. He was not only a large man but in excellent physical condition thanks to his frequent workouts at the Shanghai YMCA. His friends called him "Big Six"—auto industry parlance for the powerful inline six-cylinder engines of the day. But his size and strength also meant that he could look like a threat to the edgy, armed bandits. So Friedman stood there stoically and did exactly what the bandits told him to do. *Escape*, he thought, *is not a realistic option.*

At least he was surrounded by friendly faces. John Powell, Larry Lehrbas, and Marcel Berubé stood nearby, along with the other hostages, shivering in the cool early-morning air and marveling at the once-proud Peking Express, which was now jackknifed, with several carriages lying on their sides like some angry little boy's toy train.

Of the four men, the journalist Lehrbas was in the worst shape. He had been hiding under the bed in his stateroom when the bandits pulled him to his feet, struck him in the face with a rifle butt, and broke his knuckles. Then the bandits cleaned him out. "They even took my cigarettes and a letter home that was in my pocket,"[8] Lehrbas whispered to Powell.

As he was being hustled out of the train, Lehrbas noticed the body of a foreign passenger, apparently an Englishman, who had been shot point-blank in the face and lay dead in his sleeping compartment. Lehrbas said the bandits pointed to the corpse and then back to Lehrbas as if to say that, if he did not cooperate, he would suffer a similar fate. Then the bandits pushed him off the train like a sack of mail.[9]

Powell told Lehrbas to quiet down. The hostages were not allowed to talk to one another, and if they were seen opening their mouths, they would get slapped or have a gun jabbed in their face. Those captives who knew some Chinese tried to reason with the bandits. But communication was challenging, for the bandits spoke an array of regional dialects that were mutually unintelligible. While the passengers waited, the bandits looted the entire train, breaking open travel bags and ripping up the fixtures in the sleeping compartments, taking the mattresses and tearing up the rugs. One bandit even filled his pockets with electric lightbulbs, a seemingly pointless exercise because electricity was practically nonexistent in rural China.

At around five o'clock in the morning, the bandits hauled the captured passengers over to an adjoining grain field and began to mix foreign prisoners into larger groups with the Chinese captives. Powell did a quick count of the bandits—he could not believe how many there were: at least two or more guards for each passenger, not to mention the hundreds who were looting the train. Perhaps a thousand men in total. He watched as they dragged the last of their booty onto the embankment and wrapped everything up in giant, unwieldy sacks, which they hoisted on their shoulders.

May 8, 1923, headline of the Shanghai-based *China Press*. It was one of the major daily newspapers in Shanghai before 1949, cofounded by US journalist and publisher Thomas Millard in 1911. (RIHS)

At some point, Powell heard the shriek of the train whistle. It was time to move out. The bandits then began to push and shove the hostages eastward in single-file lines toward the mountains. It was a surreal, terrible sight. Without a common language, the bandits used their guns to direct traffic, gesturing and sometimes pressing their rifle barrels into the backs of hostages to push them along.

Of the three hundred passengers recorded on the manifest that evening, more than one hundred had been taken prisoner, including twenty-eight foreigners. Some of the remaining passengers had disembarked earlier under murky circumstances—like the Japanese businessmen—but the rest who managed to escape were largely third-class passengers who fled into the surrounding countryside in the mayhem of the attack, running to the vast fields on the west side of the train, away from the bandit horde.

As they fell in line, Powell and Berubé looked at each other in the gloomy dawn light and shook hands. It was a simple gesture, but it meant they would stick together and help each other to the end.

The march to Paotzuku Mountain had begun.

PART 2

FROM PASSENGERS TO HOSTAGES

CHAPTER 6

THE BANDITS OF PAOTZUKU MOUNTAIN

There were about twenty bandits in our convoy, each carrying a bundle that was in some instances bigger than the bandit himself, but above all the bundles, the bayonets glistened ominously.

—Lucy Aldrich, American tourist and hostage[1]

MAY 6, 1923, 5:30 A.M., EIGHT LI SOUTH OF LINCHENG

As the passengers were hustled across the grain fields and up the foothills, Powell looked back to see the silhouette of the locomotive. The electric lights in some of the rear coaches blinked eerily in the dark surrounding countryside. And he could see the heavily padlocked mail car behind the tender. It was off the tracks and lying on its side, but its contents seemed to be untouched.[2] *If robbery was the motive, why didn't they break into the mail car?* He looked ahead. They were heading east and climbing up. Powell could see a series of ever-steeper hills giving way to the cone-shaped mountains of Shantung.[3]

As they marched in the early-morning darkness, followed closely by their heavily armed guards, Powell and Berubé heard a crying child. It was the Pinger boy, barefoot and in his pajamas, calling for his father, who was lagging behind with a different group of bandits and captives. As the nine-year-old stumbled and fell, one of the young bandit guards approached the boy, cocked his gun, and pointed it at the terrified child. Without a moment of hesitation, Berubé raised his open palms and stepped between the boy and the bandit.[4]

"Don't do that!" Berubé snapped, and in one swift motion he lifted Roland onto his back and walked away toward the hills. Several of the older bandits rattled off a number of commands in Chinese directed at the trigger-happy young guard. The rebuked outlaw laughed and uncocked the hammer in his gun as Powell stared him down.[5]

Sunrise revealed the line of train passengers strung out for a half-mile up the side of the gradually rising landscape. Trailing behind were hundreds of overloaded bandits toiling under their plunder, including suitcases and trunks, crates and boxes, clothing and accessories, and mattresses and fixtures. All morning long, the hostages and their bandit guards trudged eastward.

AS THE MARCH BEGAN, A GROUP OF BANDITS HAD PULLED LUCY ALDRICH and Minnie MacFadden by their wrists down the track embankment and into the adjoining kaoliang fields. Kaoliang was a staple crop of the region; the stalks could be turned into fodder for animals or used for thatching, fuel, and brooms. In the cool, predawn air, the women inhaled the earthy scent of farm animals and freshly tilled soil. They could feel the long grass around their ankles, but the moonlight was too dim to make out much of the surroundings. They stayed together as they tripped and staggered through the fields. Aldrich supported her companion as they walked. MacFadden's loose, thin slippers kept sliding off and were no match for the uneven, hardened ground. She eventually tried to walk barefoot, but the pathway was an uninviting mix of rocky soil, wiry twigs, and roots.

MacFadden was not the only one having trouble; many of the foreign men were also walking barefoot as they were goaded across the fields. The next few hours were a nightmare, and it was almost a blessing that the bandits were weighed down by their loot, for it kept the pace slow.[6]

Mathilde Schoneberg, Aldrich's maid, soon caught up to the pair. She was dressed in multiple layers of clothing, including Aldrich's pale-blue velvet dressing gown trimmed with gray fur. She was one of few who had stockings and shoes. *Mathilde is getting by wonderfully, almost prancing along,* Aldrich thought. But the fur-lined wrapper Schoneberg was wearing was just too much for the occasion. "Dear, you look like the Queen of Sheba in that outfit, and much too conspicuous," Aldrich said with an air of seriousness. "You will end up attracting the unwanted attention of the bandits, so you better take it off!" As she removed the covering, Schoneberg whispered to MacFadden that she had concealed within her undergarments a sachet holding Aldrich's jewelry. She wanted to pass this on to either Aldrich or MacFadden. "Not now," MacFadden said, as a half-dozen bandit guards looked their way.

Because Schoneberg was wearing shoes, the bandits prodded her to walk faster and to catch up with Powell and Berubé's group. Soon she was separated from Aldrich and the limping MacFadden.[7] As dawn approached, the two women could make out the outline of hilltops and mountain peaks in the near distance.

Aldrich and MacFadden found the bandits more irritating than fearsome, and they actually took some pleasure in telling them to get lost every time they came near. But their imperious attitude toward the bandits changed after witnessing their cruelty toward the Chinese passengers. As Aldrich and MacFadden struggled along, those Chinese captives who could not keep up were beaten, bayoneted, or shot. The bandits demonstrated little respect for the well-off Chinese passengers, viewing them as supporters of the warlords who were causing the peasants and disbanded soldiers so much misery.[8] They were viewed as part of the comprador bourgeoisie (the Chinese interlocutors who represented foreign interests), who allied with the warlords in a system that benefited only them. Aldrich and MacFadden didn't fully understand the cultural reasons for the tension playing out in this cruelty toward the wealthier Chinese passengers. Yet in their global travels they had repeatedly witnessed the intense level of social conflict triggered by the gap between the rich and powerful and those who were neither.

Some of the Chinese captives were crying piteously, pleading with the bandits in Chinese, but the captors showed no mercy. One Chinese man in a silk tunic had been beaten so ferociously by the bandits that he could hardly open his eyes. A teenage boy sobbed in fear as the bandits shoved him along. When an older man walking beside him fell to the ground exhausted, the bandit guard dropped his bundle and shot him at point-blank range. Aldrich and MacFadden froze in horror.[9] "We are in the hands of men who are desperate," Aldrich whispered to MacFadden.

"Lucy, do not identify yourself," a shaken MacFadden replied.[10]

Aldrich nodded nervously in agreement. If the bandits knew who she was, she believed, they would put a very high price on her head and reduce whatever chance she had of getting out of this mess alive.

LEHRBAS PRESUMED THAT HE WAS THE LAST OF THE FOREIGN PASSEN-gers taken from the train: he could hear English speakers ahead of him but none behind him. Lehrbas came upon a group of bandits escorting Shang-hai lawyer Giuseppe Musso. Lehrbas knew that among all the passengers taken hostage, Musso was perhaps the biggest fish. One of the most in-fluential Italians in the Far East, Musso was commonly referred to as "Il Commendatore," an official title awarded by the president of Italy to indi-viduals of special honor. He had deep roots in Asia. His father had been both a successful merchant and the Italian government's consul general for the British Colony in Hong Kong.

Musso represented a colorful mix of spies, drug smugglers, gambling houses, gunrunners, underworld figures, and the tuchun of Kiangsu Prov-ince. He was a well-regarded lawyer and was in high demand by wealthy, and somewhat shady, clients. Musso himself had made his fortune as the lawyer for the Shanghai Opium Combine, which drove the opium trade before and after it became completely outlawed in 1917. The combine was formed in 1913 to control the importation and distribution of opium into China in response to the anticipated phasing out of legal imports, based upon an agreement reached with the Peking government that allowed for opium imports and sales to continue until 1917. The terms of the Interna-tional Opium Convention of 1912 required that drug smuggling into China be eliminated and that all opium retail shops and dens in the foreign-controlled areas be closed. In anticipation of this, the combine sought to control the price and thus corner the market during the limited window remaining for legal sales, and thus to maximize the financial return on imported opium. Between 1912 and 1916, the price of imported Indian opium had risen sixfold, and the combine and its merchants and distributors had prospered handsomely. With the impending deadline in 1917, the combine also, quite skillfully, negotiated a deal with the Peking government to sell its remaining stocks to the government at inflated prices, but under public pressure Peking was forced to destroy its opium stockpiles in 1919.[11]

Walking alongside Musso was his secretary, Alba Corelli. Musso was dressed in a nightshirt covered with a raincoat, and Corelli wore a light cotton shirt and laced bloomers that exposed most of her legs. Both were without shoes.

"Where do you think they're taking us?" Lehrbas asked Musso, who looked too tired to speak and just pointed in a direction toward the hills ahead. Then he raised his finger to his lips to signal to Lehrbas that speaking was forbidden. Almost immediately, the bandits pushed the three apart to block off further communication. The bandits pulled Corelli aside and led her down a different path. Musso pleaded with the guards as he was led away. "For God's sake, take care of Mademoiselle!"[12]

One of the bandits then struck the heavy-set Musso with his gun, grabbed him by the shoulder, and started to drag him forcibly onward. Lehrbas felt helpless and attempted to follow the group leading Corelli away, but he was hit across the back of the legs with a carbine. The distressed woman cried out to Musso, pleading with him not to leave her to the bandits. Corelli was sobbing. She begged in thickly accented English for Lehrbas to help her, but there was nothing that he could do as he was pulled away by his guards. The three captives were marched on different paths but all in the same eastward direction.

Lehrbas soon lost track of the two Italian hostages. He could hear the overloaded brigands dropping and juggling their plunder while hiking up the slight incline. The bundles were poorly packed, and every few steps something would tumble out, with the bandits stopping to retrieve it. Lehrbas's cluster of fumbling guards was falling behind the main group, and the voices of the marching passengers and captors became too faint to hear. Lehrbas then watched as one of his bandit guards, who was the last person in the entourage, placed his rifle on the ground to gather his spilled cargo. It just so happened that at this moment the two other guards near him had rushed ahead to assist a fellow bandit who had fallen face first to the ground and couldn't get out from under the load on top of him. *Now's my opportunity!* Lehrbas thought.

He leaped down a deep ravine and ran away from the bandits. After several hundred yards, he stopped and lay still in the kaoliang field, listening for the guards. This time of the year the kaoliang had not yet reached its maturity, and the stalks ranged from about three to four feet in height— tall enough to hide in if he crouched down. He scrambled along on hands and knees, making a wide detour through the grain fields in the direction of the train.[13] Crouching low, he ran as fast as he could without shoes.

Just when Lehrbas thought he had lost the bandits, rifle shots rang out above his head. The bandits were in pursuit, but they could not keep up with the athletic Lehrbas, who in college had been a medal-winning track-and-field star. After running for a few more paces, Lehrbas dropped to his stomach in the kaoliang fields and crawled. For twenty minutes, he inched along until he came to a series of crude graves—mounds of earth and stones that dotted the edge of the grain fields. It was likely a family burial site. With the protection of the stone cairns, Lehrbas hid from the roaming bandits until he was sure they had given up the chase. Then he ran back to the train.[14]

THE BANDITS BELIEVED THAT POWELL AND BERUBÉ WERE WALKING TOO slowly because of having to carry Roland, and they motioned for the men to stop. The bandits offered to give the boy two pairs of socks taken from the train so that he could walk on his own. The socks were heavy knitted wool and reached up to his knees. Because they weren't elasticized, Roland had to pull them up to avoid sagging.

"These won't last forever, but we'll encourage the guards to find you some shoes at the first opportunity," Berubé told the boy. "Stay close by and let us know if your feet begin to hurt." Roland nodded in agreement. All smiles, the bandit guards gave the boy thumbs up and were pleased that they could now go at a faster pace.

"Here, here," one of the guards said in English, giving Roland a red Chinese coat that was taken from the train. The coat was not only useful in the chilly morning dampness; Roland also saw it as a souvenir to show off to his family. Beaming, the boy put it on over his pajamas.

Standing nearby and looking back toward the line of hostages and bandits, Powell felt queasy. He hadn't slept, was hungry and thirsty, and had consumed too much alcohol in the drawing-room car the night before. *Hangover or no hangover*, Powell told himself, he needed to keep moving.

About two hours into the trek, Powell and Berubé came upon an assortment of donkeys, ponies, mules, and horses scattered across the open fields. These were farm animals used to power the stone grain mills and till the soil. Some were ponies from the northern Mongolian grasslands—short, sturdy, and shaggy. Powell persuaded the bandits to round up some of the grazing animals to carry Schoneberg and some of the other, frailer foreign hostages who were trailing behind them, including Aldrich, MacFadden, and the disoriented British tourist William Smith.[15]

With Powell and Berubé assisting, the bandits outfitted several animals with improvised saddles of bedding and rope stirrups, which were so short that the rider's leg was nearly at a right angle. This might have worked for the smaller Chinese villagers, but not for the taller and larger foreigners. There was no bridle, only a rope tether that guards would use to pull the animal forward. Without a real saddle and anything secure to hold on to, staying on the backs of the animals would be a challenge.

"You better go on a donkey, as you might have far to go and up a steep grade," Powell cautioned Schoneberg, pointing to the looming hillside ahead.[16] Schoneberg initially refused to mount the animals while they brayed and stirred around as they were being tied up with rope. She rightly feared that the pack animals were not accustomed to heavy, squirming human cargo. She also feared that she would be separated from the other foreign passengers on foot, especially the stronger men such as Powell and Berubé. But realizing that the uphill climb ahead was likely to be strenuous, she reluctantly agreed. The smallish Schoneberg mounted the donkey first, and then Berubé lifted Roland to sit in front of her. She wrapped her arms around the boy, and both of them then held fast to the donkey's short mane.

As the bandits continued to pester the local farmers to hand over their animals, Aldrich and MacFadden caught up to Powell's group. They, too, were initially reluctant to ride the animals but gave in as they looked at the approaching hills and mountain paths ahead.

It took several bandits to load the hefty Aldrich up on to a small, frisky pony that brayed and moved side to side in obvious disapproval under the weight. Even as an experienced equestrian, Aldrich found it difficult to stay on the uncooperative pack animal, but she did her best to avoid falling off. Aldrich could see that the trail cut a path through terraced farmland to the base of a mountain. Mile after mile, they went up and down gradually rising hills, and Aldrich slid up and down the animal with every precipitous ascent or descent.

The pajama-clad Smith had trouble staying on the donkey. When the animal stumbled, Smith fell down a fifteen-foot ravine lined with stones at the bottom. Somehow, he survived the fall. Although he was hurt and already black and blue from being dragged by the bandits from the train, he mustered the strength to climb out of the ravine with Powell's help. He then decided that walking was a safer option. Most of the able-bodied men, especially those wearing shoes, preferred to walk rather than ride. And almost all of the Chinese captives in their group walked as well because they were not given the option to ride. The bandits themselves had little experience with pack animals; Aldrich found herself repeatedly barking orders for them to properly guide her animal. She was constantly telling her guard to slow down or to choose the smoothest pathway to keep the pony from stumbling.[17]

Aldrich finally managed to catch up with Schoneberg, who waved her mistress to come closer. Schoneberg then quickly passed the sachet of jewelry to her. Although she projected a look of calm, the heiress was overjoyed that her jewels, many of them family heirlooms, were safe. She carefully hid the pouch inside her brassiere.

Aldrich and the others were now making their way through a valley of grain. She noted the beauty of this peaceful landscape and thought that the long stream of a thousand bandits and hostages marching four or five abreast, winding through the cultivated fields and rising hills, looked almost "biblical"—like Moses leading the Israelites to Canaan. Except that she knew they were not heading to some promised land.

The bandits and captives eventually reached the base of a steep, conical mountain. Here the bandits separated the foreign hostages into smaller groups. This way, they would not risk losing all of the foreigners if they were attacked by the pursuing army or train guards. The strongest and fastest among them would be the first up the mountain, taking a rocky and steep trail.

MAJOR PINGER WAS FOCUSED ON FINDING HIS SON ROLAND. HE HAD ALready lost contact with Miriam and their younger son, Edward. In the first hour of the march from the train, Pinger and Miriam had kept in touch by shouting to each other at regular intervals. She returned his call several times, but each reply sounded fainter than the last. Eventually, they lost touch. The major tried to slow his pace, crouching down to remove imaginary pebbles from between his toes, but his guards hit him on the back with their rifle butts.[18]

He prayed for the safety of his wife and younger son and hoped they would all be reunited when they finally reached their destination, wherever that was. Now, though, he walked faster to catch up with Roland, whom he believed was ahead of him in the dim morning light. It had been hours since they were separated on the train. From across a canyon, he could see a column of hostages ahead of him being divided into two groups. Half the prisoners were heading to the right and the other half to the left of the tabletop mountain peak.

Pinger feared that he and Roland would be taken in different directions if he didn't find the boy soon. Then, at about ten o'clock in the morning, he finally saw him, walking alongside a donkey. He was wearing a red, padded-silk, sleeveless Chinese coat over his pajamas and had on oversized socks that were obviously not his. Roland had dismounted the donkey and was helping to guide Schoneberg and her animal over the pathways. Pinger ran ahead toward his son, yelling his name.

"Daddy!" Roland shouted in response.

Basking in relief, Pinger couldn't help but grin at Roland's offbeat combination of clothing. He begged the guards to allow him to stay with his son. He also asked the bandits to fetch a donkey because the socks on Roland's feet had already been worn down on the rocky trail.

They brought over a donkey with a simple rope around its neck and nothing for a saddle. After Roland mounted the animal, the guards and Major Pinger guided the donkey forward while the boy held on to the short mane. This was hardly an ideal mode of transport. When the trail descended, he slipped down the donkey's neck. When the trail went uphill, he slid down to its rump. Both father and son nervously laughed as Roland seesawed his way up and down the mountainous terrain.[19]

As they approached the hills at daybreak, Eddie Elias and Theo Saphiere, who were hiking forward just behind the Pingers, witnessed the horrific murder of a small Chinese teenage boy who was unable to go farther. When Eddie tried to help the boy, two bandits pushed him aside and shot the boy in the head. Eddie and Theo then watched helplessly as another Chinese captive was dragged across the ground face down. To the bandit gang, the Chinese captives had little ransom value, so they were simply murdered if they proved troublesome or if the bandits wanted to make an example of them to keep their other hostages in line.

Such brutality sickened Eddie and Theo, but they could do nothing but continue to march forward. At about ten-thirty in the morning, the group came to a fortified village at the foot of a mountain. Here, Eddie found his brother Freddie, exhausted and sitting on the ground, his bare feet bleeding with cuts.

When Eddie tried to help his brother, his guard jammed a loaded revolver deep into his ribs, forcing him to move on. As they were pushed away, Eddie and Theo begged Freddie to stand up, for the bandits were shooting the Chinese passengers lagging behind. "You *must* find the strength to keep moving," Eddie pleaded.

Freddie just sat there listlessly as his brother and cousin trudged on. It looked to Eddie like he had just given up.[20]

CHAPTER 7

THE BLACK-HEARTED GENERAL HO

The sight of that caravan of people extending from valley to mountaintop, in the gray dawn, was like an old biblical picture—one that the movies would have given a million for.

—Minnie MacFadden, American tourist and hostage[1]

MAY 6, 1923, NOON, EAST OF THE DERAILED PEKING EXPRESS

Several hostages noticed something conspicuous about the rifles and pistols that the bandits carried: every one of them was made in Japan. This may have meant only that Japanese gunrunners were doing a lucrative business in Shantung Province.[2] But it might also have been evidence that the Japanese government had some connection to the bandit army and thus some advance knowledge of the attack on the Peking Express, if not a hand in organizing it.

Strangely absent from the train at the moment the bandits stormed aboard were any passengers from Japan. Not one. This was particularly odd, given that Japan and its companies still had sizable investments in this province. Several prominent Japanese officials, including the governor general of Japan's colony of Sakhalin and the president of the Hakodate Chamber of Commerce, had been reported to be on the Peking Express. Yet all the Japanese who had boarded the train in Shanghai with a destination of Peking or Tientsin disembarked when the train reached the town of Süchow, forty-two miles south of Lincheng, the last stop before the train was robbed.[3]

The Japanese passengers had purportedly received a mysterious telegram warning them of the affair, and they then exited the train. Although Tokyo denied any involvement, there was, from the earliest news of what became known as the Lincheng Incident onward, deep suspicion about Japan's complicity. Japan had a messy history in China, particularly in Shantung Province. At the end of the Great War, Japan acquired Germany's territorial claims to the coastal city of Tsingtao in 1918, following the Treaty of Versailles—which also gave Japan administrative authority over Shantung's east-west railroad between Tsingtao and Tsinan, resulting in effective control over the economic interests of the province. China vehemently protested this violation of its sovereignty and repeatedly demanded the return of its territory.[4]

With tensions rising between China and Japan, the United States tried to play the role of mediator. The Shantung question had to be addressed. In 1921 President Warren Harding took the initiative in calling the Washington Conference, also referred to as the Washington Disarmament Conference.[5] As outlined in treaty terms, Japan agreed, albeit begrudgingly, to return Tsingtao to China by the end of 1922, and also agreed to respect the sovereignty, independence, and territorial and administrative integrity of China. Just six months prior to the attack on the express train, China had finally regained control of Shantung and its railroads from Japan. The province had not been in Chinese hands since 1898, when it was originally seized by Germany.

AS THE BANDITS AND THEIR HOSTAGES TRUDGED TOWARD THE DISTANT mountain, word of the attack quickly reached the Lincheng garrison, which was commanded by the notorious General Ho Feng-yu. Cruel and corrupt, he was despised both by his own troops and by the peasants of the region, who called him "Black-Hearted General Ho."[6] Even by the woeful standards of warlord armies, his troops were particularly lawless. They plundered villages and sold their ammunition to the highest bidder, including the bandits. General Ho mostly looked the other way, but from time to time he shot a few of his wayward troops to create an air of order and obedience.

Ho spent much of his time fighting bandits. He would often entice tufei to surrender, making pledges that he would not harm them, and then renege as soon as they lowered their arms. One news account said that Ho had "decorated the roads between Tsaochuang and Lincheng with the heads of outlaws."[7]

Ho was considered a valuable deputy to the equally treacherous Shantung military governor—the provincial tuchun—General Tien Chung-yu. When Ho learned that Sun Mei-yao had the audacity to raid the Peking Express right under his nose, he feared he would be blamed for the attack. Ho ordered his troops to give chase, and soon they caught up with the rear end of the bandit force and the slow-footed hostages they were dragging toward the mountains. Ho wanted the bandits eliminated once and for all. "Do *whatever* it takes to bring me Sun Mei-yao's head," he told his troops.

As he clambered over the stony slopes, Powell could hear the distant gunfire from the direction of the train. He guessed that the shots came from nearby soldiers in hot pursuit. The sound came as a relief—because it meant that help was nearby—but it also made him worried about getting caught in the cross fire.

As the morning sun rose, they could see that the mountain was at least three thousand feet high, with upward trails as steep as stairways. The bandits forced the hostages to move forward quickly, poking their captives with their rifles and revolvers and yelling incessantly for them to climb faster. The gunfire was getting closer. In their lightly colored nightgowns and pajamas, the captives stuck out among the drab, dark-blue and gray clothing of the bandits. But this did not stop the pursuing soldiers from firing in their direction.

Chinese provincial army troops near Lincheng Station, Shantung Province, in pursuit of bandits and captives of the Peking Express, May 6, 1923. (SHSMO)

My God, that's close! Powell said to himself as bullets whistled over his head and struck the stones along the sides of the trail. He flinched as he heard them ricocheting off the rocks. Scanning below, Powell could see hundreds of men spread out in the vast countryside in their gray and tan uniforms, running in their direction. Some seemed to be overloaded with packs or bedrolls, as if they were prepared for a long-term military operation. All had long rifles, some topped with bayonets. Scattering like ants, the soldiers seemed relentless in their pursuit of the bandits.

Around noon, Powell and his group reached the summit of what was referred to as Huang Nuishan (Yellow Cow Mountain), seven miles east of the derailed train. They climbed over rough stones to enter a crude, crumbled, stone-walled fortification with ramparts and rifle rests all about. These crumbling forts were built during the Nien Rebellion, a mid-1800s peasant uprising against the Ch'ing Dynasty, which followed several environmental disasters, including the flooding of the Yellow River and the resulting famine. Now the makeshift forts of Yellow Cow Mountain were sheltering another generation of rebels.[8]

Powell did a head count of those in his group. Berubé, Major Allen and his son Bobby, Corelli, and Smith had all arrived just behind him. Each had nearly dropped from exhaustion while marching through the rising sun, and they were now resting and taking cover from the wild shooting by the troops below. In time, more prisoners and their guards began to arrive at the fort, including the car dealer Friedman, still struggling without shoes. MacFadden was the last of Powell's group to reach the top. Allen and Berubé helped MacFadden get comfortable on the ground and bound her injured feet with strips of cloth torn from the night garments.[9] Looking over the group, Powell noted that Smith was badly bruised and babbling incoherently, and Corelli was barely dressed and begging the bandits for a cigarette.

Powell began to realize that the bandits had split up the foreigners into separate camps, each of which was holed up in a different structure on one of the surrounding hilltops. As the bandits returned fire on the soldiers, Powell tried to explain to his fellow captives the situation as he saw it. But MacFadden was worried about her companions, Aldrich and Schoneberg.[10] "Do you think they were shot by the bandits?" Powell reassured her that Lucy and her maid were probably in another camp. They were too valuable to harm.

As the hostages sat around nursing their feet, one of the young, eager-to-please bandits arrived with kaoliang flour cakes wrapped in weathered cloth, which he offered to each of the hostages. One after another, the hungry prisoners took a cake and nodded in thanks at the smiling server. The cakes were tasteless, with the consistency of hardtack. Most of the foreign hostages didn't get beyond the first bite because the biscuits were not palatable without water. *This is like shoe leather!*, MacFadden thought.[11] However, Powell quickly put the rusk in his pocket, knowing that it might come in handy.

Later, several other bandits arrived with a basket of fresh eggs and kettles of warm tea (*ch'a*). One of the bandits taught the hostages to eat a raw egg by poking a hole in one end of the shell and sucking out the contents. Although squeamish at first, one after another they quickly ate several raw eggs, which greatly helped offset the fatigue from the morning march. They then soaked and washed down the kaoliang cakes with the tea passed around in a communal tin cup. This was the first real food and drink they had since the attack on the train some eight hours earlier.

As they rested in the fort structure, the hostages watched as the bandits played with their loot from the train. Powell noticed that the bandits had taken about twenty-five cameras, but none knew how to operate them. He watched as a bandit pried open the camera case with his bayonet, unrolling and exposing spools of film to the damaging sunlight. He then turned to Powell and Allen for help in showing him how the camera worked. "You ruined the film and broke the lenses," Allen said to the bandit, who just blinked uncomprehendingly. The bandit then shrugged his shoulders and tossed the damaged camera on the ground.

Powell then watched as one of the bandits arrived at the fort lugging his Corona typewriter case, thinking that it was full of valuables. When the bandit finally managed to open it, he expressed intense disgust upon finding only a typewriter and then beat it into a shapeless mass with his rifle butt.[12]

Powell pleaded with the bandits for clothing and shoes to protect the captives from the elements. The bandits who carried the loot up the mountain were reluctant to part with anything. But the bandit subchiefs intervened, sorting through the trove taken from the train and handing out clothing to the foreign hostages. Not everything fit, but occasionally the passengers recovered something of their own.

While this was happening, MacFadden took Powell aside and asked that he convince the bandits to search through the baggage to find proper attire for Corelli, who was dressed only in skimpy lingerie. Although she didn't seem to mind, several of the bandits (not to mention the male hostages) were noticeably staring at the young woman attired only in a thin cotton shirt and black, tight-fitting, sateen bloomers that came about halfway down to her knees. To MacFadden, this was an affront to propriety—even under the current conditions. Scrounging through the loot, Powell was able to locate a thick silk dressing gown in one of the bundles of clothing taken by the bandits. Corelli expressed her gratitude in voluble Italian.[13]

IN AN ADJOINING HILLTOP STRUCTURE, MAJOR PINGER FOUND HIMSELF with a mixed group of Chinese and foreign captives including the lawyer Musso, Aldrich's maid Schoneberg, a Brit by the name of Reginald

Rowlatt, a Mexican couple who were on their honeymoon when the train was attacked, and a Dane by the name of M. C. Jacobson.[14] In all, there were about three hundred people in the group, although most of them were bandits.

Pinger's group, like Powell's, started begging the bandits for clothing and shoes. One of the bandits gave Pinger, still in his pajamas, a pair of trousers looted from the train. The pants were made of thick wool and several sizes too large. Several of the hostages said that the major's high-riding, baggy pants made him look like Charlie Chaplin.[15]

Watching the bandits fiddle with the things stolen from the train provided the hostages with some much-needed comic relief. One bandit wore three shirts, a pair of gloves, and tan felt spatterdashes (spats), the stylish footwear accessory that buttoned around the ankle and protected the shoes and socks from mud and rain. A guard who looked to be no more than eleven years old wore a lady's brassiere under his dirty jacket in which he hid more of his precious loot.[16]

The bandits strutted around showing off their stolen rings, pins, clips, nail files, and brooches. They were equally excited by the useful items such as blankets, sheets, bedding, pillows, mattresses, pieces of carpet, and brass door handles knocked off from the railway coach. The captives were constantly asked to value certain stolen jewelry, so they purposefully devalued items to trick the bandits into thinking their loot was not as valuable as they believed it to be. They saw a boy using a silver powder box as a teacup and another using a cross-stitch tray cloth for a shade.[17]

The bandits even started eating some nonedible items such as cold cream, Mothersill's Seasick Remedy (which was widely popular during the days of transoceanic liner travel), ink, spirits of ammonia, and various medications such as the analgesic phenacetine (which could be dangerous if consumed in high quantities). Major Pinger tried to tell the bandits that the cold cream was not to be eaten but rubbed into the cheeks to protect the skin. If it wasn't edible, the bandits usually tossed it away. Hot-water bottles and toothpaste equally confused them.[18]

Pinger became very concerned when one of the bandits thought that a bottle of poisonous iodine was a beverage. He pointed at the skull and crossbones on the bottle, took an imaginary swig, and stiffened out in open-mouthed "rigor mortis" to show the bandit that the reddish-brown fluid was not for drinking. Despite Pinger's insistence, the bandit still believed it to be a beverage, and he viewed the story as a fabrication, thinking that Pinger wanted only to fool the bandit so he could have the potion for himself.[19] Pinger looked on as the young bandit grumbled and put the bottle of iodine in his vest pocket for a later day; he never knew what became of the bandit or the elixir.

One bandit discovered a pint of castor oil and quickly drank it. Although he found the soapy taste unpleasant, Pinger tried to reassure him that he would be fine, although the laxative qualities of the oil would lead to dehydration and a serious case of diarrhea.[20] One of the bandits who had seized Zimmerman's banjo from the train urged the foreigners to play for him, but they ignored the request because they either didn't know how or weren't in the mood.

Pinger noticed that a bandit was carrying his wife's green velvet bag and a woman's girdle around his waist to hold additional items. The major asked the bandit if he could take a look inside the bag, and he agreed. Pinger then saw his wife's watch and other possessions, which the bandit refused to return. Inside the girdle, though, Pinger found Miriam's ivory-handled shoehorn and buttonhook. After Pinger demonstrated the device, the bandit discarded it because of its apparent lack of utility.

But Pinger looked at Miriam's ivory-handled buttonhook as a potential weapon. When no one was looking, he used a rock to pound down and uncurl the hook to a straight point. He then ground down the dull point and filed the end until it was as sharp as an ice pick. *A jailhouse shiv of sorts*, he thought. He was prepared to use this for protection, if necessary.

It was becoming obvious to the hostages that the original derailment of the train was better organized than the bold, reckless, run-for-the-hills escape. Few of the captives had been dressed and prepared to climb the rocky mountain paths. Meanwhile, the bandits were caught off guard by how quickly the soldiers pursued them and how they fired indiscriminately at bandit and hostage alike. Sun's men had wasted most of their ammunition while storming the train, so little could be spared returning fire during the escape.

By mid-afternoon, the gunfire from General Ho's troops had become more intense. The captives, together with their guards, moved to one side of the fortress walls for shelter from the whizzing bullets flying well over their heads and arching over into the next valley. Many of the bandits were just boys, unable to appreciate how deadly the firearms that they held could be. Groups of three bandits spaced themselves out along the seven-foot wall. There were small footholds projecting from the wall that allowed a bandit to stand precariously on one foot. His two companions would then help prop up the bandit with the gun. They shouted for him to shoot quickly so that they could have their turn. But the strong recoil of the rifle caused the rifleman and his companions to tumble to the ground amid a salvo of laughter.[21]

As the hostages and tufei hunkered down at the large tabletop of Yellow Cow Mountain, Sun Mei-yao dispatched a messenger down the mountain to send a telegram to Peking demanding that all troops be withdrawn from southern Shantung. Sun wanted the message in English so the foreign legations in Peking were aware of his demands. At gunpoint, Powell wrote up the message; the names and nationalities of a number of the foreign hostages were included. Sun and Liu insisted that the deadline for withdrawal of the troops was twenty-four hours. If the troops weren't gone, the message stated, the hostages would be executed. The messenger left on horseback for the telegraph office in the early afternoon. He was expected to return by sundown, but he never made it back. It was later discovered that the messenger had been captured by General Ho's troops and shot in the head.[22]

CHAPTER 8

THE GAUNTLET

The Battle scene from "The Four Horsemen" had nothing on our little party. . . . Marching and climbing by night, and little sleep and an occasional shower of bullets by day.

—Jerome A. Henley, American traveling salesman and hostage[1]

MAY 6, 1923, MORNING,
TSINAN TRAIN STATION, SHANTUNG PROVINCE

It was supposed to be a grand, festive day for Paul Whitham, the president of the Asia Development Co., Ltd. Whitham, who lived in Shanghai but originally hailed from Seattle, was in the Shantung provincial capital of Tsinan for the ceremony commemorating the flood-control work that his company had performed on the Yellow River. This was also meant to be a celebration of America's ongoing friendship with China, in particular the US commitment to supporting China's infrastructure development and helping the country manage its resources and prepare against national catastrophes. For this project, the Asia Development Company hired more than twenty-three thousand laborers, some of whom had been part of the Chinese Labor Corps in France during the Great War, to build levees and construct a diversion dam of rocks and earth. They brought in a huge steam pile driver to complete a rail trestle across the river using Oregon pine timber. The trestle was then used to transport the rock for forming the dam.[2]

Whitham expected that scores of reporters and American and Chinese government officials would come to inspect the completion of his ambitious work to tame the river system, which had taken over a year to complete. On Sunday, May 6, Whitham went down to the Tsinan train station at seven o'clock in the morning to greet John Powell, the editor of the *Weekly Review*, and the other correspondents due in on the Peking Express. But when he arrived, he was met with unexpected news.

"The express train is delayed or possibly held up by bandits some distance south of Tsinan," said David Wiesenberg, an accountant for Whitham's company. Wiesenberg was already at the Tsinan train station with Ralph Naill, a project manager for the Asia Development Company. Naill was a former naval officer who had led a company of marines deep into Russia's Far East as part of the American Expeditionary Force Siberia after the 1917 revolution. Leaving the military at the conclusion of the Great War, Naill joined the Asia Development Company to help manage its infrastructure projects in China.[3] Wiesenberg was a US Army veteran who served in Tientsin before becoming an accountant for the company.

"The stationmaster is very concerned because the train is always on time," Naill explained. "He does not have many details."

Worried, Whitham walked over to the nearby American consulate to ask Vice Counsel Harvey Lee Milbourne if he had heard any news of trouble on the express train. Milbourne hadn't, but he telephoned the offices of both the military governor and the civil governor in Tsinan. They, too, had no information concerning any problems with the express train.[4]

With an increasing sense of alarm, Whitham returned to the train station and learned that a repair train was under preparation to be sent down to the town of Lincheng, just under five hours south of Tsinan. Something was going on. *You don't send a breakdown crane unless there's an accident*, he thought.

"We need to find out what happened to the reporters that were on the Peking Express." Whitham ordered Naill and Wiesenberg to go down to

Lincheng on the repair train, with instructions to report back to him on the situation. "Send a telegram once you have news. And be careful."

General Ho's soldiers continued their relentless assault on the bandits. With still no sign of the messenger, Sun Mei-yao decided to send a foreigner down the mountain to try to convince the soldiers to stop shooting.

Because the women were already slowing them down, the bandits decided to use a few of them to deliver the message. MacFadden and Corelli were chosen to descend the mountain bearing a "flag of truce" made from a ladies' white silk skirt. Their message to Ho was simple: the prisoners would be shot if he did not retreat. The conductor of the Peking Express, Liu Nan Ching, was sent along with the two women to be their guide, for he supposedly knew the way back to the derailed train. Sun also decided to send with the party a young Chinese boy and girl—thinking that the soldiers wouldn't dare shoot a group of women and children.[5]

As the party was setting out, Major Allen saw an opportunity to get his twelve-year-old son, Bobby, to safety. He asked MacFadden to take the boy with her. As she put her arm around him and started to walk away, one of the bandits forcefully snatched Bobby away and pointed his gun at MacFadden. She raised her hands, and Bobby walked back to be with his father.[6]

MacFadden's group set out on the north side of the mountain and found that going downhill was even worse than going up. Some places were so steep that MacFadden had to sit and slide across the rocky surface as best as she could to the next step down.[7] Conductor Liu was anxious to get back either to the derailed train or to the Lincheng station before nightfall. He pushed the ladies and children to move faster down the rocky hillside. The older woman rebelled against the conductor's pace. Rather than fight with her, the conductor began to drag along the sobbing Corelli, leaving behind MacFadden with the two young Chinese children. Liu was obviously using the white-faced foreign lady as a shield against possible attacks by either the bandits or the soldiers. Corelli broke away from Liu and stood behind MacFadden, who was now furious and yelling at Liu to slow down.

When they reached the valley below at sunset, a fast-moving storm system arrived, bringing heavy showers and pelting them with hailstones. As the thunderstorm cut its way across the countryside, they continued their trek without shelter or proper covering. Drenched, they eventually found themselves in a sort of no-man's land, wedged between the bandits and the soldiers, who continued their random firefights. They were moving northward, parallel to the train track but nowhere near the derailed train, which was much farther to the east.

When the storm stopped, the danger only increased, for now there was a bright moon that exposed the group and made it more likely they would be mistaken for an enemy by either side. Liu finally yielded to MacFadden, who was now firmly in command of the group. She led them into a ditch, where they huddled together to stay warm and waited for daylight as the wind gusts subsided and the storm blew through. While the others fell fast asleep, MacFadden stayed awake to listen for a train whistle in order to better gauge the direction they needed to take in the morning. As MacFadden held Corelli and the young Chinese girl, she looked suspiciously at Liu, who was dozing. She did not trust him. And in the morning, when he insisted on going in the opposite direction from where MacFadden had heard the train whistle, she told him firmly that he was on his own. "No, we are not following you," MacFadden said, pointing to a different path from where Liu intended to go. "The train station is in that direction."

Corelli and the two children followed the older woman, leaving Liu to fend for himself. It didn't take long for the grumbling man to fall in behind the rest of the group. Even if he thought they were headed in the wrong direction, he didn't want to risk being misidentified as a bandit and shot by the army troops.

MEANWHILE, MAJOR PINGER AND ROLAND COULD HEAR THE RIFLE shots coming from below. They were holed up on Yellow Cow Mountain with a handful of other foreign hostages, including the Italian lawyer Musso and Mathilde Schoneberg. Also here were a dozen Chinese hostages. There was no hope of escape. They were guarded by three hundred bandits and encircled by five hundred of General Ho's troops, who were struggling to overtake the bandits, firing upward as they climbed.

By mid-afternoon, the bandit subchief known as the Frenchman suggested that a foreign hostage volunteer go down to the soldiers' front line and tell them to stop shooting or all the foreigners would be executed. The Frenchman had seen several foreign women and a Chinese man head down the mountain from the adjacent camp, but because the soldiers were still shooting, he doubted they had made it through the army cordon.

Musso volunteered immediately, wanting the bandits to think that he was powerful and well-connected enough to make sure the soldiers would take him seriously. "I am the Italian Vice Consul to China, and I will personally go to Peking to make representations to the authorities and to help you to clear the country of soldiers," Musso boasted. But he said that he needed to go down the mountain in the company of a woman so it was clear to the soldiers that he was a hostage who posed no threat.[8]

Pinger pointed to Schoneberg. He was concerned about her frailty and pleaded to the bandits to send down "this worthless woman" because she had little ransom value. The Frenchman considered this but eventually allowed only Musso to go down, unaccompanied. The risk of getting shot made Musso visibly nervous, but he decided to take his chances. If the bandits discovered how rich he was, his freedom would come at a heavy price.

As soon as Musso showed his face outside the old fort, the soldiers intensified their shooting. Even though he was carrying a white flag and was scantily dressed, wearing a toga-like nightshirt with his legs exposed, Musso was taken for a bandit. Under a hail of bullets, he quickly retreated back to safety, visibly shaken by the close call.

The bandits saw that Musso had trouble walking, given that his feet were cut and bruised from the morning march. The Frenchman barked out a series of orders and told Musso to sit down—perhaps realizing this very heavy man was in no physical condition to run the gauntlet.

The Frenchman then looked around for another candidate fit enough to carry the message down the mountainside. Eventually, M. C. Jacobson volunteered for the dangerous task. Jacobson was an inspecting engineer for the British-American Tobacco Company who lived in Shanghai and was on his way to Peking for meetings.[9] He was a longtime resident of China who, unlike most of the foreign passengers, actually spoke Chinese. The tall, blond-headed Dane was one of the few hostages who was fully clothed and wearing shoes.

The bandits handed him Musso's flag, made out of a pair of men's underwear tied to a bamboo pole. Then off he went. The firing resumed with renewed intensity. *This is insane!*, thought Jacobson. *Can't they see I'm not a bandit?*

Jacobson ran as fast as he could and covered about two hundred yards downhill, with soldiers shooting all the time from two sides. He ran under a hail of bullets, stumbling under the cross fire.[10] As he fell, both the bandits and hostages gasped, fearing the worst had just happened. They could see far below that Jacobson was face down and not moving. The Frenchman sent two young bandits scurrying down to bring Jacobson back, if he was alive. Musso was right: *They needed to send a woman.*

Even the blond Jacobson was mistaken for a bandit in the salvo of gunfire. Either that or the troops were just shooting indiscriminately at whoever was exiting the fort. The Frenchman then barked an order for Schoneberg to head down the hill, alone. The subchief gave her another stick with white fabric attached to it.[11] A bandit guard shoved her out the gate, but she was immediately grazed on the cheek by either a bullet or stone fragments from the bullets hitting the rocks. She stood frozen with fear, her hand on her wounded cheek.

As soon as the guard popped his head out to check on Schoneberg, he took a bullet through the throat. He dropped to the ground, grasping his bleeding neck. Horrified, Schoneberg began running down the hill, waving the white flag frantically. Yet the firing went from bad to worse. Oblivious to the genuine danger ahead, she ran out of the enclosure, following the path Jacobson had taken, running and sliding down the face of the mountain. As she ran, Schoneberg did not stop to check on Jacobson, thinking that he was dead. Schoneberg ran for about twenty minutes, stumbling but miraculously never hit, until she reached a group of soldiers who seemed—finally—to see her white flag. One man signaled to her that it was safe to proceed.

Schoneberg rested momentarily. She could feel her cheek throbbing. The wound was bleeding. The adrenaline rushing through her body had effectively blocked the pain while she was running down the hill. As she sat panting and trying to regain her senses, Schoneberg felt a hand on her shoulder. It was the friendly soldier who had ushered her to safety. He pointed downhill and helped her along the rocky path as she slid from stone to stone. When they finally reached the valley, the soldiers offered to carry her, but seeing their heavy packs and guns on their backs, Schoneberg didn't want to add to their burden. So she just held their hands or sometimes their arms and kept walking.[12]

HAVING ESCAPED THE BANDITS BY RUNNING THROUGH THE KAOLIANG fields, Lehrbas made his way back to the derailed train. He approached with caution, thinking that there might still be bandits around. To be perfectly safe, he crawled under a car, straddling the wheel and resting his feet on two brake beams and his chin on another. Lehrbas clung to the undercarriage for about thirty minutes, but he could still hear that the train was being looted by either bandits or villagers. His broken knuckles throbbed in pain. After the looters finally departed, Lehrbas got out from under the carriage and started walking toward the front of the train. He noticed that the engine was still upright but that the wheels were off the rails. The coal tender had tipped over, and half the load was spilled to the ground. Villagers were picking through the scattered coal pieces. The baggage car was turned over completely on its side, but unopened.

Lehrbas noted that all of the coaches had been transformed into a massive pile of debris of broken glass and removed doors. Mattresses and personal effects littered the corridors and spilled outside of the train cars, and all the baggage in the rooms was slashed open and the contents scattered. Personal papers, books and other reading materials, and clothing were strewn about.

Lehrbas came across a small group of Chinese men and boys, fellow passengers on the train who had also escaped the raid. They were huddled together, wrapped in blankets inside one of the compartments. One well-dressed Chinese man told Lehrbas how he had escaped by taking his bandit guard aside and whispering to him that he had a large sum of cash inside his coat and that he would give the money solely to him. Convinced of the scheme, the greedy bandit—not wanting to share this good fortune—followed the man out the carriage door to a secluded spot on the west side of the train. Then, when the greedy bandit looked around to be sure that no one was watching them, the passenger knocked his captor squarely in the chin, sending him to the ground. He then turned and ran into the fields to the west, away from the rest of the party.[13]

One of the boys mentioned to Lehrbas that several foreigners had also escaped and were in one of the first-class compartments toward the back of the train. Hoping to find allies, Lehrbas hustled back through the train and came upon Victor Haimovitch and Alfred Zimmerman, who were tending to an apparently dead foreign passenger sprawled across a bloody floor. This was the dead passenger whom Lehrbas had seen at the time of the holdup. His face was terribly disfigured and blackened by gunpowder from a gunshot at a close distance, and he had also sustained a chest wound. Shaken by the extent of the injuries, the three then searched the body and baggage for identification and located a passport in the coat pocket. From a nearby briefcase in his compartment, they found other documents. "Joseph Rothman was his name," Lehrbas said later. "He was rather tall and quite well dressed."

They could see a teapot on the floor in the corner of the compartment, which appeared to have been thrown across the room. The bandits had just left Rothman where he fell and didn't take his baggage, the pile of paper money, or the silver coins he had won playing poker the night before. "He was the luckiest at the poker game," Lehrbas said. "But things didn't end well for him."

"Oh, my, look at this," said Zimmerman, finding several large boxes of ammunition in Rothman's baggage. They were surprised that the bandits had quickly moved on and didn't take the ammunition or the two pistols on the floor.

At around noon, the southbound relief train that carried Naill and Wiesenberg down from Tsinan to the Lincheng station arrived at the derailment site. Several railway staff and soldiers quickly fanned out to assess what had happened to the Peking Express.

Meanwhile, Zimmerman, Haimovitch, and Lehrbas boarded the relief train with the other foreign survivors and the wounded Chinese for the

Lincheng Train Station (1923), built by German contractors using cut stone. (Pinger)

short return trip to Lincheng station. Rothman's body was also loaded aboard the train. Haimovitch was worried about his cousins who were still missing: Eddie and Freddie Elias, Theo Saphiere, and Emile Gensburger. At Lincheng he sent a telegram to his uncle Henri Gensburger in Shanghai: "TRAIN WRECKED BY BANDITS. I ESCAPED. COUSINS WERE CAPTURED AND ARE HELD FOR RANSOM. I AM SAFE. LETTER FOLLOWS."[14]

AT THE LINCHENG STATION, NAILL AND WIESENBERG WERE RELIEVED to meet Haimovitch, Zimmerman, and Lehrbas as they came in on the relief train, as well as to see Martha Allen, Miriam Pinger, and young Edward Pinger. The two women and the child had been carried from the nearby station of Shakou—south of the derailment—on a rough wooden oxcart over a coarse, cratered dirt path. They were rattled after their harrowing morning and recounted how, after leaving the train, they were pushed and shoved through the fields by fifteen bandits or so, all carrying guns and bundles of loot. Without shoes, the walk was painful for Miriam, who carried the extra weight of her three-year-old son.[15] Because the bandits were getting nervous about the sluggish pace, they abandoned the women to catch up with the retreating band. In time, a group of the train guards "rescued" them—the same train guards whom the women recognized as the ones working on the train the night before who had lacked the courage to put up much of a fight during the initial onslaught. When under attack, the guards had simply run with their rifles to the west of the train, away from the horde of bandits. They knew that they would be held personally liable for their firearms, so it was better to run away with their precious rifles rather than to fight and lose either their lives or their weapons or both.

JACOBSON DIDN'T KNOW HOW LONG HE HAD BEEN UNCONSCIOUS, BUT HE knew that as he rushed down the rocky mountainside, he had stumbled to the ground and taken a sharp blow to his head. Dazed, he sensed that he was not alone. He slightly opened his eyes to find two bandits hovering over him and poking their rifles in his chest. They were apparently trying to drag him back up to the fort structure at the top of Yellow Cow Mountain. Feigning unconsciousness, Jacobson lay motionless as the bandits tried to revive him.

One of the bandits told the other to wait until Jacobson came to, and then he left to return to the old fort under sporadic gunfire from the army troops below. When the remaining bandit turned his back, Jacobson tackled him from behind and tossed his rifle over a ledge. In a fit of rage, Jacobson pummeled him senselessly with his fists and then with stones. The two men tumbled together to the ground. The bandit then set upon Jacobson and grabbed him by the throat. The two men wrestled, and eventually Jacobson got on top of the bandit and punched his face until the man couldn't open his eyes.[16] Jacobson continued pounding the young bandit until he was nearly lifeless. Stopping, Jacobson looked down and could see that the bandit's face was a bloody mess of tissue.

Jacobson had never beaten a man like this in his entire life. Fearful yet sickened, he pushed away from the gasping, bleeding young bandit, picked up the white underwear "flag," and started to run down the mountain. He knew that the bandit's comrades were not far away and would likely seek revenge once they discovered what he'd done. Jacobson ran and slid as fast as he could down the hillside and to the valley below until he met Chinese government soldiers, who let him pass.

Meanwhile, though Schoneberg had found a party of friendly soldiers, the walk to safety seemed endless.[17] And the soldiers gave her no opportunity to rest until they reached the entrance of what appeared to be a small camp of a dozen tents, busy with troops coming and going. She rested outside and was given some hot bean bouillon to drink, which she found refreshing.

A few minutes later, Jacobson arrived at the camp. Schoneberg noticed that he had a swollen "goose egg" on his forehead and his knuckles were bloodied. It was clear that he too had made an unlikely escape. One of the soldiers who brought Jacobson to the camp fetched a pony for Schoneberg to ride to a larger camp a few miles away. Jacobson walked the distance alongside the maid's pony. There, they met General Ho and his aide-de-camp. "General, you need to order your troops to stop firing or all the foreign passengers will be killed," said Schoneberg. Her plea was not altogether understood. But the general said through his translator that he had sent a message to the bandits to first release all foreigners, and *then* he would stop shooting.[18] After several years of fighting Sun Mei-yao and other bandits, Ho had no intention of letting up his pursuit of the bandit gang.

As they sat in a large-walled command tent, one of the soldiers provided the shivering Schoneberg with his coat, and she then sat down on some straw on the ground. The sky grew very dark, and a thunderstorm rolled in with full force. Rain and hail pelted the heavy oiled canvas tent, and they braced for a stormy night as the draft blew in through the seams and flaps of the sidewalls.

"We may thank God to have a roof over our heads as it is raining and hailing," Jacobson said. Before they turned in for the night, the aide-de-camp then offered to send out telegrams on their behalf to family or friends. Schoneberg asked the soldier to cable Socony's office in Shanghai: "ALDRICH PARTY MISSING. DO ALL POSSIBLE. SCHONEBERG."

She tried to sleep but was overcome with worry. That night, Schoneberg "prayed all the time." Jacobson also had trouble sleeping, haunted by the battered face of the young bandit. He kept telling himself that he had no choice and that what he did was a matter of personal survival, but the image of the bleeding outlaw with his eyes pounded shut would not leave his mind.

In the morning, the two joined General Ho for a bowl of bouillon and a biscuit. As they were eating, a scout arrived and reported to the general that during the night the bandits had fled Yellow Cow Mountain and taken the prisoners with them. Ho was livid and started yelling at his subordinates, who bowed their heads in disgrace. "He's been duped," said Jacobson, who was translating for Schoneberg. "Now he is blaming everyone. The bandits, the villagers, the foreigners, and his own troops."

This was not good news. The room went quiet as Ho, still steaming with rage, considered what to do next. Jacobson spoke up and offered to stay with the soldiers to assist with negotiations for the release of the prisoners. Ho objected loudly: "No, I don't want you here—you need to leave!"

Ho then ordered his men to take the foreigners to Lincheng. The last thing he needed was nosy outsiders snooping around his camp. As the sun rose, Jacobson and Schoneberg started out on horses with accompanying soldiers for the ride to the Lincheng station.

Around seven o'clock in the morning, exhausted and crippled by soreness from the journey, MacFadden, Corelli, the uncooperative conductor, and the two children finally reached the branch rail line several miles north of their location but two miles east of Lincheng. This spur line serviced the coal mines in the town of Tsaochuang. They walked a short distance along the line to the small station of Chee-tsun, where locals gave them tea and hard-boiled eggs to eat. MacFadden wolfed down six eggs and several cups of tea.

A mining train with a locomotive engine pulling an open carriage then took the group to the Lincheng station and the main line. At Lincheng, MacFadden was greeted by Naill and Wiesenberg from the Asia Development Company. "Are you Americans?" MacFadden called out to the two young men who were dodging the exiting Chinese passengers and looking for foreign passengers. When they said yes, she believed that she was finally rescued, not only from the bandits but also from that crazed conductor, whom she sneered at as he walked past her, shaking his head. *Good riddance*, she thought.

Naill and Wiesenberg helped the hobbling MacFadden off the train and into the station. "Have you seen Miss Aldrich?" the older woman asked.

Naill shook his head and then told MacFadden that he was unaware of the whereabouts of Lucy, but he promised to do what he could to find her: "As soon as I get you on the northbound train to Tsinan, I'll look for her. I promise you that."

Naill and MacFadden then went into the station's telegraph office and sent multiple cables to Socony's office in Shanghai, as well as to Naill's boss, Whitham, to relay the demands of the bandits to the government in Peking to withdraw the army.[19]

Nearby, Wiesenberg tried to listen to Corelli's dramatic yet unintelligible description of her ordeal—and just nodded approvingly as he fed her cigarette after cigarette. While MacFadden was sitting in the telegraph office, the stationmaster and a group of Chinese Catholic nuns from the Lincheng parish took her aside to wash her hands and face and cut off the dirty cloth wraps and bandages that were glued to her feet. The pain was excruciating, but she was glad to get the first layer of dirt off. They provided her with soft, slip-on Chinese shoes. MacFadden asked for a skirt, but there was none available, so the nuns brought MacFadden a pair of blue cotton Chinese trousers. With her legs now covered, she was quite grateful for the efforts of the nuns but chuckled when she saw how the pants didn't improve her appearance much.[20]

As MacFadden sat with Naill composing telegrams, Schoneberg and Jacobson arrived at the station on horseback. The two women were delighted to see each other but deeply alarmed when they realized that Miss Lucy was nowhere to be found. MacFadden hugged the sobbing maid, who prayed softly, asking the Lord to protect Miss Aldrich from harm. MacFadden then took a deep breath while feeling a tremendous sense of guilt for having "lost" her ward, the person whom she was supposed to keep safe. But much more than that, she dreaded having to explain what happened to Lucy's overprotective sister and the family matriarch, Abby Rockefeller.[21]

CHAPTER 9

DIAMOND IN THE ROUGH

My Dear Sister,

I suppose if I am ever going to write you about our adventure I'd better begin at once, as I am getting to the place where I want to put the whole thing out of my mind, for a while at least. Of course, for the rest of my life, when I am "stalled" conversationally, it will be a wonderful thing to fall back on: "Oh, I must tell you about the time I was captured by Chinese bandits."

—Lucy Aldrich, American tourist and hostage[1]

MAY 6, 1923, MORNING, SEAL HARBOR, MAINE

John D. Rockefeller Jr. was tending the garden at his summer house on a sunny morning when he was disturbed by an Associated Press reporter who showed up out of the blue and asked him to comment on the kidnapping of his sister-in-law, Lucy Aldrich, from a luxury train in rural China. Rockefeller, one of the wealthiest and most powerful men on the planet, did not appreciate hearing absurd rumors on his day off from a third-rate stringer. His company, Standard Oil, controlled most of the inland China market for kerosene and had sales agents in remote locations throughout the country.[2] His family had deep ties with the power brokers in China, and just two years earlier he was in Peking for the launching of the Rockefeller Foundation's flagship Union Medical College, which was the first medical school in China to introduce Western medical education. Half of the Peking government was in his pocket, not to mention the US State Department. If Lucy was in trouble, Rockefeller should have been the first to know. *What nonsense*, he thought. But just to be safe, he rang up the US secretary of state, Charles Evans Hughes, for an explanation. "There must be some mistake," Rockefeller told Hughes.[3] The secretary of state hadn't heard anything about a train heist in China, but he told Rockefeller that he'd look into the matter straightaway.

After a flurry of nervous telegrams, State Department officials in Washington confirmed that the rumor was true. And not only had Miss Aldrich been taken hostage, but so had dozens of other prominent American and European travelers. Hughes was stunned but had hardly any time to act on the news before the press ran with the story. Soon it was on the front page of the *New York Times*.[4]

Meanwhile, at the other end of Pennsylvania Avenue from Hughes's office in the State Department, Lucy's capture was reverberating through the halls of Congress. Aldrich wasn't just the sister-in-law of one of the world's richest men. She was also the daughter of the distinguished late Republican senator Nelson Aldrich and the sister of a current congressman from Rhode Island, Richard Aldrich. Now Representative Aldrich was also calling Hughes, demanding information on the whereabouts of his sister and inquiring about the White House's strategy for getting her released. Soon enough, President Harding would be on the line.

What the devil was going on in China? Hughes wondered. *And how had Miss Aldrich, of all people, gotten mixed up in it?*

LUCY WAS ATOP AN ILL-MANNERED MONGOLIAN PONY THAT SLOWLY clomped up a narrow trail leading to the top of a mountain plateau while surrounded by a dozen bandits and a like number of foreign and Chinese hostages.

Aldrich knew that her kidnapping story would not go down well with the family. Of course, there would be the inevitable headlines for her brother-in-law to contend with. She knew that he hated dealing with journalists but also knew how worried he would be once he learned about a family member getting kidnapped in a foreign land. But the real thing she worried about, if she even survived this mess, was facing her relatives' annoying lectures about how she was too frail, too fat, and too deaf to be gallivanting around the globe. That they were uneasy with her "lifestyle" was nothing new to her.[5]

The eldest daughter of Senator Aldrich, who was a self-made millionaire before he became a powerful politician, Lucy had been brought up in an atmosphere of privilege. In her youth she had been fetching—stately with a fair complexion. She was an expert equestrian and adventurous enough to accompany her father on transoceanic sailing trips to Europe. She never would settle down or marry. And she always demanded that her world extend further than the cosseted Rhode Island society of Providence and Warwick Neck, where her family had mansions. She had invested wisely and grown into a serious art collector and a free-thinking philanthropist. Some people found Aldrich's individualism refreshing, but her overbearing younger sister, Abby Rockefeller, was not one of them. Abby always pitied Lucy's spinsterhood and hired nurses and maids to keep a watchful eye on her.[6]

Yet no matter how hard Abby tried, Lucy couldn't be reined in. At age fifty-three, she was deemed overweight (she was five feet two and weighed 170 pounds) and had a weak heart, yet she still relished the excitement of foreign travel. She was now on her second circumnavigation of the globe. She had first traveled extensively through the Far East in 1919, spending six months in Japan, Korea, China, and the Philippines. Her latest trip had been an even greater immersion: India, Burma, and then a long tour of China. Lucy prized Chinese textiles, particularly silk embroidery and gold-wrapped silk tapestry weaves. That was why she had been on her way to Peking: to acquire more exquisite Ch'ing Dynasty court coats and other wearable art for her expanding collection.[7]

Now, on this unexpected march through the mountains of Shantung Province, Aldrich felt like she had stepped into one of her Chinese tapestries. Although she had a gun to her back, she could not help but appreciate this magnificent landscape: the mountains with saw-edged ridges of limestone and rocky karst pinnacles, the deep gorges and steep rock faces rising from the cultivated and grassy valleys and meadows. She would later compare the sweeping panorama to the peaks of the Dolomites in northeastern Italy.[8]

Aldrich was in a party of a few dozen hostages, some of them Chinese and some foreigners who were unknown to her. The shaggy pony that the bandits had given Aldrich to ride was now grunting and unsteady. She believed that he was on his last legs, and she held on to the pony's mane tightly.[9]

At the next turn, her group passed a small village of adobe brick houses with kettles of hot water and bean soup carefully laid out over glowing coal fires. This was refreshment that the peasants had left for the bandits, either from fear of them or loyalty to their cause. Yet the peasants themselves were nowhere to be seen. The only person she saw in the village was a tall, skeletal man who mutely stared at the procession of loot-laden captors and half-dressed hostages. His gaunt expression of indifference made it seem like the sight of this extraordinary caravan was "an everyday affair for him."

After slurping the soup and hot water, the bandits raided an onion patch and quickly stuffed their jackets with large, raw onions, which they ate like candy. *I shall never smell onions again without thinking of bandits*, Aldrich thought. *They all reek of them.*[10] As they set off again through the challenging terrain, Aldrich realized that her pony was in serious trouble. He stumbled for a few yards and then careened his neck in angst, nearly toppling over. Aldrich knew he had had enough, and she expertly dismounted. But once on her two feet, she felt less sure of herself. After the difficult ride, her legs buckled. The bandits tried to lift her back onto the exhausted animal, but neither the pony nor Aldrich would stand for it.

The bandits were growing impatient. They tried to push Aldrich along the mountain path, tugging her by the wrist to move her along. But she found scaling the rocky terrain "like trying to climb in a coal bin." Her arms were soon black and blue from the tight grip of her captors. She felt her chest pounding from exertion as she was dragged uphill. She tried to explain to the bandits that she had a weak heart. "I'll die if I go on at this rate," she said, grabbing her guard's dirty hand and placing it on her chest so he could feel her heart racing.[11]

The bandit's eyes widened, and he conveyed the situation to the others in the group by clapping his hands together rapidly and making booming sounds. They all laughed and then continued to push Aldrich forward, while allowing her more frequent rest stops. Aldrich winced as she trudged forward. Her journey was particularly arduous, not only because of her age and poor health but also because she was walking on her mother's emerald and diamond rings, which she had moved from her brassiere and hidden in a pouch inside the toe of her right slipper.

By noon, the sun was beating down on her bare head and fair skin. Most of the bandits were wearing hats stolen from the train, around which they wound their long-braided ponytails. When one of the bandits started to unfold an orange chiffon-silk scarf that he intended to cover his head with, Aldrich asked him for the scarf. To her surprise, he gave it up without complaint.

Then she saw that one of the bandits was wearing MacFadden's blue georgette hat with its feather "waving in the breeze like the plume on the helmet of Navarre." It was heartbreaking to be reminded of Minnie but also a little comic to see her hat on this "villainous Chinese," as Aldrich later put it. "I had spent hours over that hat, sitting on a hard chair in the little French milliner's, trying to decide if it was becoming, whether it was too heavy for her, and if the feather was the latest thing."[12]

Aldrich did find something to admire about the bandits' attire: the intricate fruit-pit and nut carvings that were attached to their belts and tobacco pouches. Worn to keep demons away, these amulets were made from the pits of peaches, walnuts, and almonds. They were part of a craft tradition that went all the way back to the Song Dynasty, in the tenth century. "I persuaded several to let me look at their things closely," said Aldrich, "and they were as pleased as Punch when I admired them."[13]

ALDRICH WAS EXHAUSTED, BUT SHE WAS SURVIVING. HER HEART, though strained, had not failed her. She missed her friends but expected to see them again, expected that this would all be over soon, that Socony and the Rockefeller family would intervene on her behalf. Once her party finally rested, she drifted off to sleep with a measure of hope. But after an hour, she was awakened and ordered down into the next valley. She noticed that she was the only foreign hostage in this party and had no idea why she was being taken from the group. Lucy surmised that the other foreign and Chinese hostages were separated into several groups atop the two adjoining mountain plateaus. *Perhaps they were scattering the foreigners to prevent a rescue by the pursuing soldiers?*

Aldrich was pulled along by her wrist and stumbled over the rocks. With every step she took, the rings dug deeper into her toes. It was stupid to endure this pain for the sake of holding on to rings that were of negligible value to a woman of her wealth, but something in her refused to give up her mother's jewels to the bandits.[14]

In the valley they came upon a small, peaceful village and sat down under a tree next to two old men and a woman who was grinding corn in a granite millstone. The villagers brought Aldrich a small stool to sit on, and she quickly became the center of attention. Nervous children came by to touch her and then quickly ran away to hide behind the adults. She gestured that she was thirsty, and they brought her some water, which she gulped down even though the bowl she was given was previously used for bean soup and its rim was still sticky.[15]

She was by now so tired and sore that she could hardly get up, but the bandits ordered her to keep moving. They found a chair and used poles to carry her on a makeshift sedan chair. But the poles were much too short, and the bandits found it difficult to maneuver up the hill over the rocks. Rifle shots rang out in the distance—the pursuing soldiers were getting closer, which spooked the bandits.

Like others in her social milieu, Aldrich was brought up with the poison of racial superiority, and she looked upon most of these poor Chinese bandits as little more than animals. The one who pushed the gun into her back reminded her of a "black leopard without the '*bien soigné*' look a leopard has." Another guard "growled like a tiger" when she didn't move fast enough. She would go so far as to mentally categorize the bandits into two kinds: "one type short, pale yellow, intelligent; another very tall, almost coal-black straggling hair around wild faces and thick queues flapping around their knees—the last more like animals than human beings."[16] Like many foreigners, Lucy was only expressing the prevalent negative attitudes and stereotypes that the West had toward Asian cultures.

After hours of marching, they came to some small, wooded hills with a large, flat hilltop used for grazing. Amid the sparse grass were several small stone huts used as shelters to protect shepherds and their flocks against the cold prevailing wind. Some of the bandits crawled into the shelters to escape the winds and the intense sun. Aldrich was left outside. She begged one of the bandits to use the bedding that he was sitting on (which had been looted from the train) to protect herself from the elements. It was a large, white, honeycombed counterpane. He reluctantly agreed but stood nearby, watching over her so he could retake his booty when she awoke. Exhausted, Aldrich settled on the ground, covered her head with her cape, and fell asleep.

A short time later, she was shaken awake by a group of bandits. They wanted to know the English words for the things they had stolen. With a pencil, Aldrich patiently wrote out a string of simple words. The effort quickly turned into an impromptu English lesson.

"G-U-N . . . GUN." Then she used her hand to pantomime firing a pistol. The bandits chuckled.

As she was sitting around with her admiring students, Sun Mei-yao himself approached the group. While Lucy likened most of the bandits to animals, she described their leader as the boy next door. He was an "awfully nice-looking young man" who was "neatly dressed, about twenty-five or thirty." He seemed to understand English, or at least pretended to, and unlike the other bandits, who became badly frightened when the soldiers came too near, he had a real flair for adventure and seemed to be having the time of his life.

Sun took an immediate interest in Aldrich, although he also seemed to be putting on a performance for his men. When Aldrich told him that she was cold, he took off his coat and, in chivalrous fashion, covered her shoulders and buttoned it under her chin. She was quite grateful for his politeness, but she worried that now *he* was unprotected from the sharp winds. She urged him to take it back. He sent one of his men to locate a coat taken from the train. When one of the bandits returned with the coat, she stood up and removed her cape to put it on. Yet she realized she was only wearing her nightgown and a thin pink satin wrapper and so was quite exposed to her Chinese audience. Sun, seeing Aldrich blush, took the cape and held it up as a dressing screen while she put on the heavy coat over her nightgown.

They sat back down again, and Sun pulled out of his pocket several items designed to impress her, including a toothbrush, which was not something the ordinary bandit found useful. Sun saw himself as more sophisticated than his underlings, and he wanted Aldrich to know it. He also pulled out his cigarette case and offered her a smoke. She declined. Then he offered her a cigar. Aldrich raised an eyebrow. "No, thank you," she said.

Sun also showed Aldrich a silver fifty-cent piece that was his good-luck charm. He explained to her in halting English that all of his men were former soldiers. Sun gestured and pointed to himself, saying, "Good man, no bad," and then pointed down the hillside to the pursuing troops: "Bad men, no good." The hearing-impaired Aldrich couldn't quite make out exactly what he was trying to tell her, but she got the message that the bandits considered themselves to be on the right side.

A mischievous look then appeared in Sun's eye. He reached for his revolver. Lucy gulped. But she was amazed when Sun turned the barrel of the gun and handed it to her. The bandit chief smiled as he watched her eyes widen. "Take it," he said.

Nervously, she dangled it a bit and gave it back to Sun, saying that it was "very heavy." All of the other bandits laughed in delight at Sun's boldness. He offered her the gun a second time, but she trembled and pushed it away.

Sensing her unease, Sun changed the subject and showed her the green jade ring he wore, with the stone turned inward to the palm of his hand. Aldrich looked at the piece with a sense of wonder, although part of her wanted to ask the chief whether it was stolen. Then Sun pointed to Aldrich, then back to his ring. He smiled. A true bandit, he was inquiring whether she had any jewelry of her own to "share." Aldrich shook her head sadly, waving her hand in the direction of the train. "All gone," she said dramatically, and then drew her feet tighter under her cape.

Yet this movement had the opposite effect that she desired, for Sun looked down at her slippers. He shook his head, implying her slippers were far too thin to walk in. He sent for a pair of Chinese shoes, but Aldrich, protecting her rings, begged him off by saying that Chinese foot sizes were much too small. But she knew this might sound suspicious. Her slippers were starting to wear out. And she did not want to break her trust with Sun. Thinking quickly, she noticed a rock at the bottom of a small wall with a crack down the middle that was about two inches wide and five inches deep. In front of the crack was a thin, diamond-shaped stone that could be used to mark the spot. It appeared to be a perfect location to hide the rings.[17]

A dozen bandits stood around Aldrich in a circle. That meant she would have to hide the rings under their noses. Very discreetly, she positioned her cape to cover her feet and the cracked stone, and then removed her slippers. She grabbed the sachet with her toes and then dangled it over the crack in the rock. When she thought she was in the right position, she dropped the pouch of jewels. It fell noiselessly into the opening. Relieved, Aldrich then stretched out her legs and told her bandits that she had reconsidered Sun's offer. She could not fit into Chinese shoes, but she would gladly take a pair of men's socks stolen from the train. Sun was happy to oblige.

The bandit chief stood up to leave. Aldrich, feeling safe with him, gestured if she could go with him. He smiled and gently shook his head no. A strange feeling came over her, a feeling that there was something noble in this outlaw. She said, "You're much too good, much too bright, for this kind of work." She couldn't tell whether Sun was confused or touched by her outpouring.[18] "Do you understand?" He bowed gravely. "You should come to America, start over." Now he smiled. She felt ashamed for making such an unrealistic suggestion. He turned and, as he walked down the hillside, waved his hand at Aldrich. She would never forget the expression of kindness on his face or her mixed feelings for the young man who had orchestrated her misery.

Bereft of her protector, Aldrich was more frightened than ever before. When would this madness end? As the bandits milled around her, something seemed to shift inside her mind. A sense of panic gripped her. She found a scrap of fabric to write on and quickly jotted a message to the Shanghai office of Standard Oil Company, describing where she was and that she needed help. Then she pleaded with the nearest guard to carry her message to the nearest telegraph station.

"*Mei foo!*" she screamed. "*Mei foo!*"[19] *Mei foo* literally meant "beautiful confidence," but Aldrich was referring to Standard Oil's common name and Chinese trademark for its kerosene lamps, so Aldrich hoped the bandits would catch on to her request. But they either didn't understand what she was saying or pretended not to know, and just tossed her note on the ground. Then they pulled Aldrich to her feet and pushed her down the next hill, continuing the interminable march. She looked back one more time at where she hid the sachet of jewels, not knowing whether she would ever see them again.

No matter how she tried, she could not keep up. One of the bandits then tried a new tack, hoisting Aldrich on his shoulders and carrying her piggyback style, only to trip and be flattened under Aldrich's weight. She was not the only one who could not manage at this pace. Directly in front of her she saw an exhausted Chinese hostage who was being dragged by two bandits. When he tumbled to the ground, one of his captors, frustrated by their slow progress and cracking under the constant sound of rifle fire from the pursuing troops, started ferociously beating the man with his cane. As the prisoner struggled to his feet, Aldrich saw his face "gleam white, impassive, for a moment."[20] Then the man fell again. She choked with fear at the sight of this helpless person, someone's father, someone's son. To her horror, the bandits shot him dead. All she could think of was whether her journey would end this way as well.

The guards had found a small donkey, which they loaded with looted blankets and coats from the train. At their insistence, she tried to mount the donkey, but having no saddle, stirrups, or bridle for support, she immediately fell to the ground. Then the same bandit who had beaten the man unconscious started to hit her with his cane. She wondered if she would ever stand again. But her coat and cape seemed to protect her from serious injury. And as she lay there absorbing the blows, her blood boiled. She suddenly rose up and started screaming at the bandit: "Stop this! Stop it at once!" To her surprise, he backed off.

A storm was coming. The sky was filled with copper-colored clouds slashed with lightning. She marched for an additional mile and then collapsed. Her mouth was as dry as sandpaper and ringed with a cottony film. She was *done*—she could go no farther. One of the bandits pointed to a distant village and told her to head in that direction.[21] Half asleep, delirious with exhaustion, a ghost of her former self, she drifted down the footpath, stumbling between paddy fields toward the village. It was now dusk and raining hard. She thought the others were following behind her, but at a certain point she realized that they were headed in the opposite direction. And she was completely alone.

Had she escaped? Or was she now, without the bandits to guide her, in an even more hopeless situation?

BY THE TIME ALDRICH REACHED THE GATES OF THE VILLAGE, THE DOWNpour was overwhelming. The village was surrounded by high, blank mudbrick walls and sealed by tall wooden doors suspended by chains. She looked through a crack in the gates and saw a donkey but no buildings, no people, "nothing beyond but blackness." She pounded and pounded with her fists on the closed doors and screamed at the top of her lungs for someone to let her in, but her screams were drowned out by the torrent of rain coming down in sheets that turned the dusty ground "into a sea of liquid mud in which I slipped and slid in my thin slippers."[22]

What Aldrich didn't realize was that the villagers could hear her but were terrified of the marauding bandits who regularly stole their donkeys, pigs, chickens, children, and anything of value. Caught in the cross fire between the bandits and warlords, peasant villages had become fortresses with thick walls, impregnable gates, and armed towers to ward off intruders. The villagers did not dare to venture outside the walls after dark for fear of kidnapping or robbery. Aldrich could hardly blame them—for the first time she began to truly understand the condition of the Chinese peasant, who lived in constant fear without any government to turn to for assistance.

Aldrich sunk to the ground by the gate and pulled her knees to her chest, trying to get some shelter from the driving rain. When hail started to fall and the temperature dropped, she crawled around the gate until she found a small, leaky shed-like structure nearby that was thatched with kaoliang stalks and had a bed of straw on the floor. Judging by the smell, it was most likely a doghouse. She was soaking wet and covered in mud. Desperate for water, she tried to gather hailstones to quench her thirst. Then she burrowed herself in the dog's bed of straw for warmth. She dozed off while shivering and slept for a few hours before waking, pounding on the door of the village again, sobbing, and then slinking back to her mud hut to wait until daybreak.

As she curled up in the doghouse, Aldrich imagined what her family would say if they saw her now. "I couldn't help chuckling to think that here was I, who am never allowed by my family to sleep without someone in the room next to me with the door open . . . alone in a hostile China, sleeping on the ground and 'getting away with it.'"[23] As she drifted off to sleep, little did she know that at this very moment her brother-in-law was about to be confronted by a journalist in his garden in Maine—a world away on the opposite side of the globe.

ALDRICH WOKE WITH A JERK, THINKING THAT SOMEONE HAD CALLED out to her. But there was no one there. Her throat burned with thirst. She noticed that the rain had stopped and the ferocious storm that rolled across the countryside had indeed passed. The morning was calm, quiet. Help- less, she crawled in the direction of the wooden gates. She hoped that in the light of day there would be someone inside the village who might take pity on her. She was about to pound on the wooden doors when she looked through a crack and gasped: she was gazing straight into the eyes of at least fifty Chinese men. "I have no idea how long they had been standing there— immovable, silent, waiting for the strange something that had been batter- ing at the gates in the night to materialize."[24]

Ever wary, the villagers at first refused to open the doors. She held up her hands to reassure them, but they wouldn't budge. Finally, after several minutes of begging, the wooden doors opened. Aldrich was in tatters. Her hair was caked with mud and straw, she smelled of the doghouse, the heavy men's overcoat she got from Sun Mei-yao was soaked and filthy, her pink crepe-de-chine nightgown was torn and stained, and the socks and green slippers that had concealed her family jewels had been reduced to piles of mud. She put herself at the mercy of the villagers.[25]

An old woman escorted her across a small courtyard to an adobe brick seat. The woman spoke only Chinese and sat down next to Aldrich and held her dirty hand. Aldrich was touched deeply by this gesture. She motioned for water to drink, and the old woman busily instructed others what to do. A hive of activity formed around her: "I was, in short, an 'event' in the village. Everybody came to see me, and all jabbered away interminably." She came to understand that the villagers had initially refused to help her only out of fear: of intruders, of the reprisals of local warlords or bandits. But in their hearts, Aldrich could see, these people were "good Samaritans."

As the day wore on, the men dispersed to work in their vegetable patches, but the village women and children encircled Aldrich. They touched her white skin and light-brown hair. They stroked her face, explored her palms, pulled up her nightgown to see her legs and ankles. It occurred to her that maybe they had never seen a Westerner before. The probing was acceptable at first, but Aldrich pushed back when one woman tried to pry open her mouth to see her gold crown.

It broke Aldrich's heart to see the condition the children were in. The young boys wore rags that were tattered and dirty, and almost all their faces were pitted with disfiguring, permanent scars from smallpox. As for the village women, Aldrich noticed that despite their poverty they looked "comparatively neat" and had "a look of being sewed into their clothes." Yet she was distressed to see how all the women—young and old—painfully hobbled as they walked along. They had all been permanently disabled by the practice of foot binding. For centuries, the three-inch "golden lotus" foot was desired by a majority of Chinese and seen as a symbol of beauty and elegance, although the excruciating process to obtain it led to lifelong disabilities.[26]

Aldrich appreciated the kind attention of the villagers, but she was dying for water—to wash with and above all to quench her thirst. A younger woman brought bean broth and a Chinese biscuit. But she could not think of eating solid food before having a drink. Finally, a very old woman brought hot water for tea. Yet before pouring the tea, the old woman inexplicably licked and slurped the spout of the teapot with her wilted lips and fissured tongue. She did so as a matter of kindness to test the temperature, looking upon Aldrich as a sickly child who needed to be mothered. Aldrich was repelled nonetheless, but her dehydration had reached a point of desperation. "I couldn't refuse to drink it—I was dying of thirst—but I had visions of coming down with all sorts of Oriental diseases if I ever got out." Then she ate the food she was provided gratefully, even though it tasted awful to her.[27]

The villagers ushered Aldrich out of the rising sun and inside a dark mudroom hut. She noticed a traditional *kang*—a heated elevated platform of brick and terracotta used as both a bed and seating. This kang took up about one-third of the space in the hut and was heated by an adjacent fireplace and covered with indigo-blue bedding. The only other object in the room was a single hen in a wicker basket off to the corner, scratching and pecking in the dirt.

As Aldrich lay down on the earthen platform and used her coat as a pillow, the Chinese women obligingly and tenderly tucked her in. As she closed her eyes to sleep, Aldrich sensed that the villagers didn't leave the room but stood there watching her. She purposely kept her eyes closed and pretended to be asleep to keep them from talking. But as the number of spectators in the room grew (including several of the village men), Aldrich motioned for one of the women to shoo them out so she could get some sleep.

As she started to drift off on the kang, she was suddenly moved by the kindness of these strangers who, despite the danger they faced, had taken her in. She knew that this was a famine district—with severe scarcity of food causing malnutrition and starvation—but could not have imagined a place where people survived "on so little." Yet they still shared what food they had with her. Aldrich realized that she had long admired the art and, to a narrow extent, the culture of China without understanding anything of the steady state of the place, of the people. She felt ashamed but also grateful for this experience that was, for all its danger, also a kind of education. And she wanted to help these poor women, whose daily lives seemed so barren and colorless that the arrival of a strange foreigner would be treated as a major event. Before she finally fell asleep, she resolved that if she ever made it out of here alive, she would bring them back something—not just food or money or religion but perhaps pictures or a collection of artwork, something beautiful to look at to brighten up their hardscrabble lives.

CHAPTER 10

THE SCANDAL

The Tuchun had decided that his best course was to attack the brigands strongly; that he was convinced . . . the brigands would not dare to harm their foreign prisoners.

—Berthold George Tours, consul general, British consulate, Tsinan[1]

MAY 6, 1923, MIDDAY, TSINAN, SHANTUNG PROVINCE

Berthold Tours knew very well that the man sitting across from him in the hotel dining room was a brutal warlord. Yet as Britain's leading diplomat in the region, Tours did not have the luxury to limit his contacts to the morally impeccable. He had to deal with those in power, which explained why he was having lunch with the military governor of Shantung Province, Tien Chung-yu.

Aging and somewhat sickly, General Tien had a long, thick black beard and spoke with a low, distinctive voice. He had been the tuchun of Shantung for thirteen years, growing extremely wealthy by running a protection racket directed at the coal-mining companies in southern Shantung and skimming state funds earmarked for infrastructure or famine relief. The lunch at the Hotel Trendel in Tsinan was routine, if a bit long. After the main courses were removed, the general and the diplomat ordered tea and the hotel's famous chestnut layer cake. Then they both enjoyed a smooth smoke from German-made porcelain pipes.

Just as they were getting ready to part company, the general turned to Consul Tours and let slip a piece of news. Four foreigners had apparently been attacked by brigands on the spur line that ran from Lincheng to the mining district of Tsaochuang. Tien said that the victims were probably mining engineers.

Tours barely raised an eyebrow. He knew there were no British citizens working for the mining operations in the vicinity of Lincheng, so he immediately filed away this bit of news as irrelevant. After all, bandit robberies, or "outrages" as they were called in the press, happened on an almost daily basis, and usually it was only Chinese merchants who were targeted. At this point in his career, it would take a lot more to startle him.

At fifty-two years of age, Tours was an old China hand, having held diplomatic positions throughout the country since 1897. He and his family had lived through the siege of Peking during the 1900 Boxer Rebellion, when he was stationed as the accountant at the British legation.[2] In his current role, Tours was Britain's top diplomat in the provincial capital of Tsinan. He typified the empire's colonial civil service with his carefully knotted bow tie, his oversized khaki-covered gentlemen's pith helmet, and the constant presence of a lit cigarette at the end of his black Bakelite cigarette holder. Tours was always impeccably dressed and sported a neatly trimmed walrus mustache. He was both cynical and opinionated, and he carried himself with a look of superiority over both the Chinese and fellow members of the diplomatic community.

Tours returned home from lunch with no idea of the mayhem that was already unfolding in the countryside near Lincheng. But later that evening, the US consul general at Tsinan, Harvey Milbourne, called on Tours at home and told him that he had received two telegrams from Lincheng reporting the attack on the express train. The telegrams were the first details of the incident to be received by any foreign government officials. Milbourne, a twenty-seven-year-old former US Army officer and career diplomat, explained that two staff members of the Asia Development Company, Ralph Naill and David Wiesenberg, had made a trip down to Lincheng and

were now on the scene. Their first telegram made it clear that the minor in-
cident that General Tien alluded to at lunch was actually a major disaster
in the making: "TWENTY-SIX FOREIGNERS HELD BY BANDITS.
POWELL IN HANDS OF THE BANDITS. LARRY LEHRBAS,
CHINA PRESS, ARRIVE TSINAN TONIGHT. ROTHMAN,
BRITISHER, KILLED. INFORMATION MEAGER. WILL STAY
HERE TILL TOMORROW."

A second telegram explained that the bandits had split into groups and
that a "small military force" was pursuing them. As if it wasn't already abun-
dantly clear, Wiesenberg and Naill cabled, "SITUATION SERIOUS."

Earlier that day at lunch, did General Tien really not know what had
happened? What was that nonsense about a robbery on the "spur line,"
which was something wholly different from the main line used by the
express train? Either he was hiding something or he was woefully misin-
formed about the situation.

On the morning of May 7, both Tours and Milbourne decided to pay
Tien a visit. They went to the military governor's large European-style
house in downtown Tsinan. It was immediately clear to Tours that the tuchun knew more than he was letting on. Tours impressed upon him the
gravity of the situation and asked what steps the Chinese government
would take to secure the release of the captured foreigners. Tien knew exactly what was going on and who was behind the heist. Rather than being
forthright, Tien informed the diplomats that the brigands were ex-soldiers
disbanded without pay and that he had received a message from the brigands stating that they would release their prisoners on receipt of one year's
pay. None of this was true.

Milbourne had no confidence in Tien and decided to simply go over his
head and take the issues directly to Marshal Tsao Kun, the northern warlord who held considerable power over Tien and the Peking government.
Milbourne had his superior, Jacob Schurman, the American minister in
China, telegraph Tsao, informing him of the incident and requesting that
he take measures for the immediate release of the captives. Tsao replied
to Schurman in a telegram expressing "great anxiety" and stated that he
had already telegraphed Tien, instructing him to secure the release of the
captives immediately and send down troops to deal with the bandits.[3]

Marshal Tsao Kun, the head of the northern Chihli Party, which had effective control over the Peking government in 1923. He later would become president after ousting President Li Yuan-hung. (Ulrico Hoepli)

Schurman replied that he expected Tsao to "press matters unremittingly and effectively" until the release of the captives was secured. Tours followed up with a letter to Tien, "urging upon him that the safety of the captured foreigners was a matter of first importance." The British consul also bluntly told the warlord that he would be held responsible for the rescue mission, including "devising means" to secure the hostages' release, even if that meant "the meeting of the brigands' demands."

Yet willfully or not, Tien ignored Tours and misinterpreted Tsao's instructions, thinking that his order "to pursue" the bandits gave him permission to destroy them by any means necessary. This unnecessarily created aggressive hostilities that continued to endanger the lives of the hostages.[4]

Milbourne asked Tien's office to arrange a special train to take foreign doctors and medical supplies to Lincheng. Milbourne called the Shantung Christian University Hospital in Tsinan to request medical support and supplies. Two British doctors were assigned to support the rescue effort. Milbourne personally took the doctors to the railway station in his motorcar, and after some delay in getting the special train prepared, they got on the train, which left for Lincheng at three-thirty in the afternoon.[5]

In the meantime, Naill had sent two more telegrams explaining that the foreigners were "in grave danger" and that "American authorities must act immediately." Naill noted that the bandits had been surrounded and that with the army constantly firing, they were putting the captives in the cross-hairs. He suggested that somebody be sent to negotiate with the bandits.[6]

As they arrived in Tsinan from Lincheng, Milbourne greeted those hostages who had already been liberated. Among them were MacFadden and Schoneberg, who both had to be carried from the train and taken to a hospital.[7] MacFadden handed Milbourne a note from Powell scrawled on a scrap of Chinese paper. It was dated the day before, May 6, at five-thirty in the afternoon. It stated that the Peking Express passengers were being held prisoner on the top of a mountain east of the railroad and requested that the Shantung military governor "remove his forces which are surrounding the district." Powell's letter went on: "We wish to impress upon you the fact that most of the foreigners are without sufficient clothing, being clad in night clothes, and being threatened with death from firing on both sides and we therefore wish to impress on you the urgency of attending to this matter and relieve the situation immediately."[8]

Powell's letter only intensified the efforts of the American diplomats. The next morning, May 8, Minister Schurman and Consul Milbourne called upon General Tien at his headquarters to inquire what he was doing to bring about a release of the foreign captives. Schurman again pleaded with the military authorities to order the soldiers pursuing the bandits to back off: all they were doing was "driving the bandits further and further into the hills and causing great hardship" for the captives.[9]

The Americans' patience with Tien was wearing thin. Yet the wily old general did not back down. "My plan," he said, speaking cautiously, "is to surround the bandits, and after I have the bandits under my control, I will then force them to negotiate for the release of the foreigners. I have *more* than enough troops on the scene for this purpose."

The general had decided that his best course was to attack the brigands with force. He was convinced that the bandits' demand to withdraw the troops was "only a ruse" to allow them the opportunity to escape with the hostages farther into the mountainside. Schurman was livid with Tien's insistence on a military operation when the hostages' lives were at risk. "So, your current policy consists of the application of force?" he asked with skepticism.[10]

"Yes!" said Tien as he stared at the diplomats. Fuming, he then asked Schurman for *his* suggestions on how best to resolve the impasse.

"Let me be clear to you, once again," said Minister Schurman, "that the position of the United States government is that we make no suggestions— *none whatsoever*—regarding the methods you should adopt to secure the release of the foreigners." This was the same message that British consul Tours gave to Tien. "It's your call," Schurman went on, "but let me also emphasize that the prompt and safe release of the captives is critical and that we expect the continuation of energetic action on your part—and on the part of the *entire* Chinese government—until that result has been brought about."[11]

"Understood," said Tien politely. Schurman had made it clear that US policy was one of nonintervention, and that included giving advice to warlords on how to run their country.

Yet the next set of messages from Naill in Lincheng, which arrived early that evening after the meeting, revealed no change in tactics or evidence that the use of force of arms was working. "Military doesn't want to negotiate with bandits," he cabled. "Foreigners almost dead due to long marches and no food. Within three days all foreigners will die unless negotiation is effected. For God's sake do something."[12]

With a crisis in the making, Minister Schurman then ordered a number of his diplomatic staff to Lincheng to represent US interests, with Nanking consul John K. Davis taking the lead. After four years in the position, Davis was very familiar with the conditions in the southern Shantung district. He was a career diplomat and had been born and raised in China by missionary parents in Soochow. He previously held diplomatic posts in Shanghai, Canton, Chefoo, and Antung. Schurman instructed him "to report to the Legation any information he can obtain regarding captured Americans and to take steps he may consider advisable towards obtaining their release." Schurman also instructed Major Wallace Copeland ("Cope") Philoon, the assistant military attaché at the legation, and Major Lloyd P. Horsfall, an interpreter, to travel to Lincheng.[13]

US minister Dr. Jacob Gould Schurman, nominated by President Warren Harding on May 17, 1921, to be the minister to the Republic of China. He was the president of Cornell University from 1892 to 1920, and he also served as commissioner to the Philippine Islands in 1920-1921. (Library of Congress)

IN THE PREDAWN HOURS OF MONDAY, MAY 7, A MESSENGER FROM THE Wai-Chiao Pu—the Foreign Ministry—came pounding on the door to Roy Scott Anderson's courtyard home in Peking, arousing the tall American from his sleep. *Something serious was happening for someone to be awakening me at this hour,* Anderson thought.

"Come quickly," the messenger said. "The Peking Express was robbed by bandits, and many foreign and Chinese passengers were captured." The messenger told Anderson that the holdup had happened just south of Lincheng in southern Shantung.

Anderson, a political adviser to both the Chinese and American governments, was a go-between for the warlords, who could always trust him even though they never trusted one another. Born and raised in China by missionary parents, he was a native Chinese speaker, fluent in several dialects. His friends called him "Admiral" because he commanded the room with his imposing presence and booming voice. Anderson was highly respected for his candor and easygoing, affable nature.

The American fixer had revolutionary credentials, having taken an active part in the first Chinese revolution, serving in the revolutionary army of

Sun Yat-sen and helping to bring about the fall of the Manchus. At the age of forty, Anderson thrived on China's endless bedlam, and he characterized the country as "comparable to Europe at the close of the Middle Ages." He was a personal confidant of strongman Marshal Tsao Kun, the head of the Chihli Party and the real power broker behind the Peking government.

But now even the unflappable Anderson was worried. He expected that the Shantung provincial warlord and the Peking authorities would make a mess of the situation. He knew quite well how warlords operated and what motivated them—and that, in the case of Tien Chung-yu, the military governor of Shantung Province, he rarely acted ethically or logically. Tien always looked out for his own interests and would likely exacerbate tensions with the bandits in his refusal to accept any level of culpability for the incident or make any concessions. Anderson was also aware that the national government in Peking was beset with chaos and run by a mix of politicians who argued incessantly and agreed on little. There was no time to waste. He quickly got dressed and walked briskly to the Foreign Ministry to get more details on the identities of the foreign captives and to find out if the Peking authorities had an action plan.

Marshal Tsao briefed Anderson on what information was known and convinced the American to head down to Lincheng to provide him with a neutral assessment of the situation. He also wanted Anderson to lead negotiations with the bandits, but he warned him that General Tien might jockey for control of the discussions.[14] Anderson knew he was walking into a volatile situation that would not be resolved quickly and would require much finesse. Yet Anderson, as always, was up for the challenge.

Anderson left his home in Peking in the early-morning hours of May 8, heading southward by train. The American fixer had packed for the long haul.

REPORTS OF WHAT WAS SOON TO BE CALLED THE LINCHENG INCIDENT set off a flurry of activity in Peking diplomatic circles.[15] On the morning of May 8, José Batalha de Freitas, Portugal's minister and a senior member of the foreign diplomatic corps, stormed unannounced into a private meeting of Premier Chang Shao-ts'eng—ostensibly the second-most-powerful

official in Peking—and the Chinese cabinet at the Cabinet Office Building.
The stunned officials offered Minister de Freitas a chair, but he refused to
sit and angrily insisted that the cabinet members rise to their feet and stand
to hear his demands concerning the crisis. Deferential to the senior diplomat yet feeling humiliated, one by one the cabinet members slowly rose to
their feet to hear de Freitas's diplomatic protest:

> In the name of the Diplomatic Body and in the name of those of my Col-
> leagues who have their nationals in the hands of the bandits, I come today
> to protest most solemnly against the recent outrage committed by brigands,
> on the morning of May 6, against the foreign passengers on the Pukow-
> Tientsin train near Lincheng. The Diplomatic Body holds the Chinese
> Government responsible for the lives of those foreigners who are still in the
> hands of the brigands.[16]

De Freitas requested that the Chinese government suspend all military
operations against the bandits and pay any ransom demanded, while still
leaving the question of how to deal with the bandits to a later date after
the hostages were released. Premier Chang appeared to be much moved
by the emissary's emotional appeal. He assured him that he was doing
his best to save the foreigners and that he deeply regretted the incident.
Premier Chang implored de Freitas to reassure his legation colleagues that
every precaution was being taken to prevent a recurrence of the outrage.[17]
Wu Yu-lin, the minister of communications, advised de Freitas that the
government had summarily dismissed the commander of the railway police—who was off celebrating his birthday on the night of the attack. Then
some in the cabinet speculated that hostile factions actually instigated the
heist on the Peking Express as a plot to discredit the current leadership in
Peking. But de Freitas had heard enough and departed the meeting at full
tilt as Premier Chang tried to reassure him that his government had the
situation under control.

Behind this mask of calm resolve, the Chinese cabinet was, in fact, in
a state of sheer panic. An assault on the rail system was an attack on one
of the most critical parts of the nation's infrastructure. If Peking couldn't
control the trains, they couldn't hope to maintain a semblance of order over

the divisive political factions that made up the Republic. Although Premier Chang deplored having a foreign diplomat interrupt his cabinet meeting, he knew that this outrage was a consequence of failed policies of disbanding troops without a safety net and of warlords' brutal bandit-suppression campaigns, which only fueled the flames of unrest.

A more stable country could withstand this crisis, but a protracted hostage standoff with prominent foreign prisoners caught between an army of bandits and a rebellious warlord was more than enough to push the weak Peking government to the brink of collapse.[18]

PART 3

SURVIVAL

CHAPTER 11

THE DRUMBEAT

Now and then, we heard the weird beating of a wooden drum—probably a friendly signal—in the black distance. Then we were mystified by the appearance of a long line of lights far off ahead of us, like the lights of a city, and suddenly from them flashed the straight beam of a searchlight and swept across the clouds.

—Major Robert Allen, American tourist and hostage[1]

MAY 6, 1923, 5:30 P.M., YELLOW COW MOUNTAIN

For a handful of hostages, the ordeal was or would soon be over. But for most of the hostages and bandits, the saga was just beginning. Back at Yellow Cow Mountain, Sun Mei-yao and Po-Po Liu were getting restless. It had now been fifteen hours since the train was derailed, and the hostages and the huge gang of bandits were only seven miles east of the train atop a group of steep mountain plateaus. The bandits had taken heavy casualties in combat with the army troops, and the valuable hostages were at risk of getting shot. Sun knew they needed to keep moving until the army got the message to stand down. The dead and wounded bandits were left behind as the troops continued in close pursuit. Sun assumed, rightly, that any bandits captured by General Ho's troops would be tortured, beaten, and then shot.

Sun hoped that the foreigners and Chinese hostages sent down the mountain—Jacobson, MacFadden, Corelli, Schoneberg, and the conductor Liu Nan Ching—would be able to persuade the troops to withdraw or at least to negotiate a ceasefire. Regardless, they needed to move as quickly as possible to their more secure mountain stronghold—Paotzuku—some thirty miles away. A strong gust of wind caught Sun's attention as he almost lost his hat, and that is when he noticed dark clouds accumulating far away on the northeast horizon. Smiling, Sun saw an opportunity.

There could be no further delays. The order was to rest by day and march by night. Captives who could not keep up would be either left to fend for themselves or, if troublesome, shot. The two young foreign boys, Bobby and Roland, would be spared for the moment if they could manage the trek. Sun ordered his deputies to treat the boys well to avoid triggering any confrontations with their fathers, Pinger and Allen, whom Sun regarded as among his most important hostages.

Before setting out on the trek to Paotzuku, the bandit chief met with the last foreign woman among the hostages, the thirty-five-year-old Mexican Teresa Verea, who almost passed as a man because she was wearing a pair of trousers and a men's coat given to her by the bandits.[2] Sun told her that she would be released and taken by escort back to the derailed train. But Verea refused to leave her husband, Manuel Verea. She and Manuel, the scion of a wealthy old Mexican family from Guadalajara, had just gotten married a month before and had been in the middle of an around-the-world honeymoon when they were taken prisoner. Manuel was one of the largest paper manufacturers and publishers in Mexico. He was no stranger to banditry, having been kidnapped and ransomed by Mexican banditos the previous year. But the Vereas understood Mexico's form of banditry as more of a business transaction—there it was about money and less about politics.

"How could I leave my husband when a bride?" Teresa asked, begging the bandit chief. She believed his chances of survival were better if she remained with him. She was also concerned about what her captors might do to her, as the lone woman in the group, if she were separated from her husband. "I beg you to let me stay with my husband," she pleaded.

"OK, you can stay," Sun said, grinning. "But you are no longer on a holiday!"[3]

For the march, the first group included Powell, Friedman, Eddie Elias, and Musso. In the second group were Berubé, Pinger and his son Roland, Rowlatt, Smith, and the American businessman Lee Solomon. The third group included Allen and his son Bobby, traveling salesman Jerome Henley, and the rest of the Shanghai cousins: Gensburger, Freddie Elias, and Saphiere. The fourth and final group consisted only of Manuel and Teresa Verea. Each group of foreigners was again mixed with Chinese captives and bandit guards to shield the valuable foreign hostages from rescue efforts. Sun, Powell said, coveted his hostages like "golden eggs." He knew that they were his only chance of survival.

As dusk set in, the mood of the bandits darkened. Black clouds appeared, with flashes of lightning and low rumbles of thunder. The atmosphere was tense and menacing.[4] But Sun was pleased because the storm gave him cover to evade General Ho's pursuing troops. This was his chance for escape! At about seven o'clock in the evening, the captives were commanded to march down the back of Yellow Cow Mountain, despite the pouring rain. From a neighboring mountaintop, Powell could see groups of hostages and their guards moving down as well. The plan was for the four groups to meet in the valley below. Together, they would then move northeast in a single file across a vast plain, with the prisoners dispersed throughout the line.

Major Pinger helped Roland mount a small pony for the march. Pinger ignored the shrill protest of one of the young bandits, who seemed to have reserved the pony for himself and his pile of loot. The major was in no mood to debate and gestured at him to go away. With the use of a sharp stone, Pinger tore a hole in the center of a train blanket to make a serape-like poncho for Roland to wear. It would help keep him somewhat dry and warm with the approaching storm. "Not a moment too soon," Pinger said to his son as the roar of the thunder reverberated from hill to hill. *This is a real "King Lear" storm-scene of Jove's artillery*, he thought.[5]

The skies unleashed piercing rain and hailstones upon their unprotected heads. As they set out down the hillside littered with boulders, Pinger

grasped the corded edge of the saddlecloth as best as he could and led Roland's pony down the hill. The heavy downpour lasted for several hours,
making walking extremely difficult, especially in the dark: the rocks were
slippery, and the mud was clinging to their shoes.[6] They stumbled over the
rough ground and made their way across the valley floor, trudging northward as the rain stopped. Soon they started to hear a distant, intermittent
drumbeat, a low-pitched and muffled thumping. The bandits seemed to be
heading in the direction of the drumbeat in the inky darkness.

"Hear that?" Major Allen asked his son as his group stopped to listen.
It sounded like the beating of a wooden drum—a signal.[7] As they walked,
the sound got louder. At about nine o'clock in the evening, the group approached the branch line that ran from Lincheng to the Tsaochuang coal
mines to the east. Because this was the logical place for General Ho's troops
to intercept them, they stopped for several minutes to listen for soldiers.
They squatted in the fields until the bandits realized the coast was clear
and told them to cross the rail bed.

To their right, they could see a powerful searchlight several miles away
scanning the dark horizon. They were mystified by the appearance of a long
line of lights far off ahead of them, like the lights of a city, and suddenly
there was a flash. A straight beam of light swept across the clouds.[8] *Were
the American naval forces already moving to rescue the hostages?* For a moment
Allen imagined that gunboats were flashing their searchlights through the
darkness, looking for them. But then he realized there was no navigable
river or ocean in the area.

Within minutes, from across the tracks a tapping sound of a cartridge on
a rifle stock signaled that it was safe to cross the rail line. "*Tsou, tsou—go,
go!*" the bandits whispered loudly as they crossed the shining rails and were
submerged again in the blackness on the other side. The group moved on in
silence, everybody intently watching the distant searchlight.

After crossing the rails, Eddie Elias came upon Musso riding on the back
of a Mongolian pony and noticed that he was swaying precariously on the
animal's back. Apparently, Musso had earlier fallen off the pony, seriously
injuring his back. He was in excruciating pain; the bouncing motion of the
pony only irritated his condition. "Let me help you," Elias said, as he used
his hands to keep Musso from falling off.

"For God's sake, kill me. I cannot stand this any longer!" Musso groaned as he grasped Elias's hands.[9] Elias called out to the bandits to find a stretcher or sedan chair to carry the incapacitated man. But the guards pushed Eddie away and left Musso to manage on his own.

Not far away, as the aggressive storm system passed through southern Shantung, Minnie MacFadden and Alba Corelli were huddled together in a ditch with the two Chinese children and the annoying train conductor. Mathilde Schoneberg and M. C. Jacobson were sleeping in an army tent, compliments of General Ho. And poor Lucy Aldrich was very much alone, cramped in a doghouse outside the gates of a rural Shantung village.

After walking north several miles beyond the spur line, they could no longer see the searchlight. They continued marching in the dark, shivering from the wet and cold. Around midnight, they arrived at the first of several dark villages—the hostages had been marching for hours without much food, drink, or rest. Here, the bandits forced the villagers to build fires out of kaoliang reeds. The fires brought warmth but also a pungent smoke that was almost suffocating.[10] They were provided hot water and rested for two hours, and then were forced to march again in the darkness.

They hiked all night and arrived at another village, with the silhouette of its gates and walls against the faint, amber-colored dawn sky. Each of the foreign captives was placed in huts and animal stables—guarded by six to eight bandits per captive. Meanwhile, the Chinese captives were huddled together in the unsheltered courtyards, unfed and shivering.

Aided by one of the bandits, Pinger prepared a bed of straw by the stove, wrapped Roland in a blanket, and placed him on the floor. Then the men coiled up on mats without any covering. Roland instantly fell fast asleep. Pinger was dressed in a soaking wet pajama top and shaking from the cold. Searching about, he found a dirty, padded cotton shawl from the cantle of a pony saddle and used it to cover himself. Only then did he finally doze off.[11]

At about ten o'clock in the morning, May 7, Pinger awoke and joined the other captives and guards by a warm fireplace. The villagers offered them unseasoned hot millet gruel in an unwashed bowl with some tea. There was one clay bowl for every three people, and everyone slurped and shared the bland, grainy broth. When Roland woke up, he joined his father and the others around the fire. Offered the village fare, Roland refused to eat anything, which worried Pinger. Seeing chickens scratching around the hut, he gestured to the villagers by making an egg-shaped sign with his thumb and fingers, and they soon had several hard-boiled eggs to eat. This was a welcome relief, and the major and his son were most grateful to the peasants for their precious gift. The villagers always sold their eggs rather than eating them because a single egg was worth one-tenth of a man's daily wages.

While seated around the morning fire, Allen noticed a brash young bandit whom the prisoners would soon nickname "Straw Hat." Nicknames became common between the captives and the bandits because most of the bandits, except for the top leaders, refused to give their real names or used multiple aliases. Straw Hat was wearing multiple layers of stolen clothing from the train, as well as Allen's own spectacles. As Straw Hat approached the captives, Allen gestured that the glasses belonged to him. The bandit passed them on to Allen to inspect but insisted on taking them back afterward. It occurred to Allen that Straw Hat thought of eyeglasses "as an ornament like a piece of jewelry or perhaps as a symbol of learning and aristocracy."

Allen had noticed that several other bandits were proudly squinting through stolen eyeglasses. When the young bandit persisted in demanding that Allen return his own glasses, Powell intervened and shouted at the young brigand to back off. Clearly embarrassed, the bandit gave back the glasses but flashed a canny smile that let the group know that he was not letting the issue go away.

At midday, the "Tsou! Tsou!" call came to march once again. Allen found that his swollen, blistered feet made it difficult to put on his shoes. He hobbled along as best as he could, but every step was torture. Bobby was also very sore, and his gait was slow and pained. They made their way up a steep, rocky hill—an exhausting climb, especially under the hot sun. Sun Mei-yao ordered two of the groups—Powell's and Allen's groups—to head to higher ground to a steep plateau that overlooked the valley floor, while the others stayed at the base of a mountain.

Hot and fatigued, Bobby Allen stopped partway up the hill to remove his heavy wool coat. While he was trying to tie the coat sleeves around his waist, his guard, a boy bandit not much older than Bobby, started yanking his arm to get him to move along. Bobby instantaneously flared up in anger and clocked the guard with his flat, open palm. "Back off!" Bobby yelled.

Shocked, the youthful bandit conceded and allowed Bobby to fix the coat around his waist. Alarmed at first, Major Allen and the other foreigners quietly cheered the boy on for his nerves and true mettle.

When they reached the plateau, they discovered remains of crude walls that at one time were apparently used for defensive purposes, including one wall overlooking the valley from the edge of the sheer precipice that appeared to be part of an ancient, now roofless temple. The foreigners scouted the surface for shelter from the intense sunlight. The shade was meager, and the ground was so stony that it was difficult to find a place big enough to lie down, but they made themselves as comfortable as possible. While the hostages rested, the bandits went to select lookout points with a view down to the deep valley below. They heard shots in the distance, but to avoid revealing their position the bandits did not return fire.

After sleeping for about an hour at the tabletop, an order came down to the group: they had to head back down the mountain to the very same village they had just come from. This news was not received well by the foreigners, who had struggled mightily to climb up to this spot. Powell was enraged and began to harangue the bandits in English. They did not understand a word, but his tone and gesture made his feelings clear enough. To quell the protests, the bandits began to carry the hostages piggyback style down the mountain. For Powell, this lasted just a few minutes as he realized the grunting bandit carrying him was struggling to keep his balance on the unstable surface. "OK, OK, I will walk myself," said Powell as he got back on his own feet. "Just don't rush me down the hillside, for God's sake." Powell looked on as one of the larger, stronger bandits continued to carry the smiling, portly Friedman down the mountain.

When they arrived back at the village, Powell vowed to himself he would not travel another inch at the behest of these incompetent bandits, who were just going around in circles. *I am done rambling around the countryside,* he decided.

SOME TEN MILES AWAY, LUCY ALDRICH WAS SLEEPING PEACEFULLY UNder the watchful eye of the village women. She was awakened in the early afternoon by a man wearing an old and torn uniform. She didn't move and tried to fall back to sleep in the hopes that he would just go away. Aldrich was quite comfortable on the warm kang and did not want to leave. The villagers then began to vigorously shake her awake, for they themselves seemed anxious for her to depart. Bleary-eyed, she left the hut and instantly recognized the uniformed man as the bandit who the night before had directed her to the village. He signaled her to follow him, but Aldrich was afraid of leaving the relative safety of the village and rejoining the bandits. The man made it clear that she had no choice.

When she exited the wooden gates of the village, she realized that the bandits and soldiers from the night before had moved on. All was peaceful and quiet. The sky was clear, and there was no indication of the previous night's storm, except for some shallow puddles of rainwater and a slight sheen of slippery wet mud covering the ground. Her bandit escort smiled, showing his brown teeth. "Come, come," he said, gesturing toward a small donkey. He then knelt nervously on one knee to help her climb aboard.

She rode on just a blanket while the bandit pulled the animal forward. Aldrich had difficulty getting a grip, so after a few hundred yards the bandit recruited a young boy in a nearby rice field to pull the donkey while he supported her. He whipped the animal's rump with a strip of rope to keep it moving. The bandit-soldier was in a great hurry, and at times he had the beast in a full gallop as he and the boy ran alongside. After many miles, the trio came upon another gated village.

In the ramparts over the gates, there stood a group of ten to fifteen armed men, all with defensive if not menacing looks on their faces, who aimed their weapons in the direction of Aldrich's party. She had no idea if the people in this village were friend or foe. She sat patiently on the donkey as the bandit argued to be let in. After much discussion, one of the guards came down and opened the gate. But they refused to let the party inside. Instead, a well-dressed regal gentleman greeted them outside the gate and, looking all around, poured them each a cup of tea.

Aldrich dismounted the beast to stretch her legs and to drink her tea. After thanking the villager, the bandit-soldier helped Aldrich remount the donkey, and then they rode on. After several miles, they came to yet another village. Here, the bandit-soldier abandoned the donkey and rounded up a few older men to bring out a chair to create a palanquin, a sedan-chair-type conveyance carried on two poles over the shoulders of two or more bearers. He quickly realized that the two older gentlemen did not have the strength to carry Aldrich, so he commandeered a large wheelbarrow and driver instead.

Unlike a Western-style wheelbarrow, the conveyance had a single large centrally mounted wheel that a driver pushed from behind while the passengers sat on either side of the wood lattice-covered wheel. This wheelbarrow was adapted for the narrow country footpaths and could hold up to six human passengers or could be heavily laden and piled high with cargo. Aldrich sat on one side of the wheelbarrow and the bandit-soldier on the other. They bumped over the stones so fast that she felt as though her teeth and eyes would drop out of her head. She tried to make the driver slow down and avoid the potholes, but he just laughed and went faster.[12]

Aldrich could see that they were approaching a larger town, spotting the smoking chimneys and campfires off in the distance. As they got closer, the bandit-soldier pulled out a money purse and showed her some money. She interpreted this, as well as the scheming grin on his face and the bashful look in his eyes, to mean that he was hoping to receive a reward for his efforts. Aldrich never thought she was in the hands of a rescuer and so ignored his overtures, and he eventually put the money pouch away without pressing the issue. Soon they arrived at a small railway station, where they were immediately swarmed by hordes of excited soldiers and railroad workers. This was the same station, Chee-tsun, that MacFadden had passed through earlier in the day. Aldrich realized that she had been liberated only when she met the six-foot-tall, blue-eyed Ralph Naill of the Asia Development Company.

ALDRICH IMMEDIATELY TOOK A LIKING TO NAILL, WHO HELPED HER TO her feet and walked her into the station. She described him as an "ideal rescuer—handsome, cheerful, executive, and having the time of his life." She sighed with relief as the stationmaster brought her tea and eggs, and his wife and daughter bathed Aldrich's face and feet and fitted her with

Chinese trousers and stockings. When they removed her socks and slippers, they found that her feet were raw, blistered, and cut by the jewelry that she had been carrying. Embarrassed, she also realized how ragged she looked with her clothing streaked in dirt, her nose and face sunburned, and her tangled hair caked with mud and straw.[13] Naill told Aldrich that her companions, MacFadden and Schoneberg, had escaped from the bandits and were on their way to Tsinan: "We took good care of them and put them on an earlier train north, and they should have arrived in Tsinan by now." This was a huge relief.

As dusk neared, Aldrich and Naill quickly climbed into an open mail car attached to a locomotive and headed to the Lincheng main station a few miles away. At the Lincheng station, Aldrich was greeted by Wiesenberg and Father Wilhelm Lenfers, a German Catholic priest who served the local Lincheng community and was known to the Chinese as Ling Sun-fu. Aldrich characterized Lenfers as "a big man with a beard [who] beamed with sympathy and kindness." Lenfers and Wiesenberg offered to carry Aldrich from one train to the other, but she walked on her own. She warmly gave Naill a hug good-bye.

Aldrich boarded the empty express train, having the entire carriage to herself. She was provided a first-class sleeping compartment, and she propped herself up on the lower berth with the food trays on the compartment's table. While she was having a bite to eat as the train sped northward, her bandit-soldier and "rescuer" appeared at her compartment door. He looked at her food and nibbled at his fingers ruefully to indicate that he wanted something to eat. Then he vanished as Wiesenberg came down the hallway. "Ma'am, are you OK?" Wiesenberg asked, noticing the unsettled look on Aldrich's face.

"My bandit was just here begging for food," she said. "You know, the one that brought me to the train station?"

"It probably was just one of the soldiers guarding the train, pacing up and down the corridors," assured Wiesenberg, thinking that Aldrich was just imagining things. But when Wiesenberg stepped out, the bandit-soldier appeared again, peering around the corner like the Cheshire Cat, she thought, and begging for food.[14] She then filled his hands with sliced bread and meats, and, squatting down, he ferociously started eating.

"By Jove, it *is* your bandit!" said Wiesenberg upon returning to her compartment. Wiesenberg then called out for the train guards, who quickly came down the hallway and grabbed hold of the hungry stowaway. "What shall we do with him?" Wiesenberg asked.

"Feed him up!" Aldrich said, as the train guards ushered him out of the compartment and down the hallway.[15] She trailed them into the corridor to ensure that they gave him food and money but watched with unease at the bullying by the train guards.

The train pulled into Tsinan at about midnight, and Aldrich was greeted by US vice counsel Milbourne and Joseph Babcock of the Tsinan office of the Standard Oil Company.[16] Babcock noted later that Aldrich arrived in tatters, half-dressed in Chinese clothes and shoes, but that she seemed to be in good spirits and was quite able to walk to the motorcar. He reported to Socony that she was not in serious condition but should remain in Tsinan for rest and observation at the Shantung Christian University Hospital.

Aldrich alerted Babcock to the pouch of jewelry that she had concealed under the rocks and provided him with a map and description of its whereabouts. Before she was taken to the hospital to greet her companions, Aldrich was asked once again by Wiesenberg what she wanted to do with "her bandit." Because she didn't want him to go hungry or want him to return to banditry, Aldrich asked that Socony give him a job. Quietly annoyed, Babcock took the bandit to his office to figure out what to do next. He needed directions from Socony headquarters in Shanghai and cabled, "Miss Aldrich brought back with her one of the bandits. We understand this man, who is an ignorant coolie in soldier dress, rescued her at the risk of his life and guided her about ten miles back to the railway. What should be done?"[17]

"Do what Miss Aldrich says!" the Shanghai office responded.

Solving two issues, Babcock enlisted Lucy's bandit as a guide to comb the countryside to locate Aldrich's stash of jewelry, tucked away in a crevice someplace southeast of Lincheng. Babcock wasn't thrilled, for all he had to work with was her hand-drawn diagram, and rock piles of the kind she described were all over the rural countryside. He offered the bandit a reward if he could help retrace Aldrich's steps to narrow down the search. The man was eager to please, and he agreed to lead the hunt. The next day, Babcock and the bandit would travel south to Lincheng to search for the

Aldrich family jewelry. Amazingly, after combing the countryside for several days, the pair successfully recovered the jewels and returned them to a delighted Lucy.[18] Not long after, the bandit returned to the hills to rejoin Sun Mei-yao.

Lucy went on to Peking on May 9 and thereafter to Japan with McFadden and Schoneberg, before sailing onward to San Francisco and taking the transcontinental railroad back to New York. She found the experience with Sun and his gang of bandits "most dangerous" yet "thrilling and extremely amusing at times."[19]

Less than an hour had elapsed since Powell's group arrived back in the village after their pointless hike up the mountain when the dreaded words "Tsou! Tsou!" were called out. It was time to march once again. "Go ahead and shoot me," shouted Powell. "I can't go another goddamn step!"

Thoroughly drained, Powell and several other foreigners sank to their knees in exhaustion. Powell refused to move until the bandits provided donkeys or ponies. Because the bandit chiefs were aware that Powell was the ringleader in what was fast becoming a "sit-down strike," one of them approached him and, drawing a revolver, threatened to shoot. Knowing that he was too valuable to be shot, Powell taunted the bandits to pull the trigger and even bared his chest by opening his shirt in a gesture of bravado. Then one of the bandits pointed a cocked revolver at his head and held it there while six of his companion bandits severely beat him over the back and shoulders with clubs and rifle butts. Powell tried to explain his exhausted condition by pointing to his swollen and blistered feet.[20]

Pinger was stunned, expecting that Powell would be shot on the spot. But, instead, there was only a volley of dull thuds as the young, cocky bandit Straw Hat—whom Powell had previously embarrassed in the spat over Major Allen's spectacles—now took his revenge by viciously thrashing Powell with a heavy pole. Tempers flared. Even as Straw Hat beat him, Powell still refused to budge. Several of the younger bandits looked upon the situation as fine sport.

As Powell yelled and the bandits pounded away, two of the English-speaking Chinese captives tried to intervene by calmly telling the bandits that this was an unfortunate miscommunication—this angry foreigner was saying only that he was in pain and exhausted. Neither interpreter translated verbatim Powell's raucous cavalcade of expletives; rather, they massaged the message to avoid confrontation and maintain face for all. The bandits then retreated. Everyone sighed in relief. Friedman then helped the badly bruised Powell up off the ground.

"There's nothing like a good beating to revive the faint-hearted," Powell said. "But it was worth it, as the bandits realized we were in earnest." Powell thanked the two interpreters: a university professor, Hung Shi-chi, who just days before had been enjoying drinks with the Shanghai cousins in the drawing-room car of the Peking Express, and the more reserved and soft-spoken banker, Koon Chi Cheng. Chi Cheng, who worked with the China Merchants Steamship Company in Shanghai, spoke English like a native, having spent a decade in Britain as a young man, including at Cambridge.[21]

From the start, several of the Chinese captives who were educated overseas and fluent in English quickly realized that they would have a better chance of making it out alive if they threw their lots in with the foreign captives. As they marched across the countryside, they let every Western hostage know that they could speak English and offered, if not begged, to act as translators. These captives stuck by the foreigners faithfully, often at great peril to themselves.[22]

Powell would carry the black-and-blue marks of his beating on his back and shoulders for weeks. But the protest had worked. The bandits located pack animals for the foreign hostages to ride.[23] As for the Chinese captives, they were given the choice of walking or getting shot. With little sunlight left, they began to march once again.

This time they made a wide detour to the west, avoiding the previously climbed mountain peak and instead marching up a valley past another hilltop with a fortified group of mud hovels. They hiked up and over a low mountain pass and then eastward again to another village, arriving at about nine o'clock on the evening of May 7. The groups of foreigners were spread out in huts, which they shared with farm animals. Matting was spread on the floor. Using their coats for pillows, all the hostages lay down to sleep. It was a terrible night. No one could move without disturbing the person next to him. Nearby barn animals were separated only by a flimsy rope and freely roamed about, loudly grunting, sniffing, and braying at the presence of the unwanted guests.[24]

At dawn, the hostages were given hot soybean soup, kaoliang cakes, boiled eggs, and tea prepared by two women from the village. One of the bandits also gave them some kind of boiled poultry—maybe chicken, maybe not. They ate a bit of it but tossed the rest: it was mostly inedible cartilage, and they feared it was undercooked. Without proper refrigeration or suitable cooking equipment, they decided, it was not worth the risk of eating.

After breakfast, they set out again after the bandits ordered them to march. Leaving the village, they hiked directly north and ascended another high ridge that revealed sweeping views of the countryside. They remained on the ridge most of the day, sweltering under the intense sun. With the troops in sight, the bandit chiefs reorganized the four groups of captives and assigned senior guards who, in general, were much more friendly and mature than the younger, trigger-happy bandits. Pinger's group was assigned to Russky. The Frenchman was assigned to Allen's group. They trekked onward in a northeastern direction across the countryside.

At sunset, Powell, Friedman, and other hostages in their group arrived at what was referred to as the Dragon Door Temple, surrounded by nearby villages. They entered the temple compound as the Buddhist monks were closing the gates. The foreign hostages were herded together in one small structure within the temple compound and the Chinese prisoners in another. Exhausted and hungry, they were served tea and some sort of grain-based gruel. As they readied their bedding for the night, they heard a commotion outside as the monks and several bandit guards reopened the compound door. A group of bandits had dropped a large object at the doorway and gone away. Leon Friedman peered outside to investigate: "It's Musso, and I think he's dead!"[25]

Musso wasn't quite dead, but he was badly hurt and unable to walk. He had been carried in an eight-man palanquin to the temple door. He was dressed only in a nightshirt and sprawled over the seat and footrests of the sedan chair. Given Musso's weight, it took twice the number of bearers than usual. Powell, Eddie Elias, and several of the guards rushed out to help Friedman carry Musso into the temple building.[26] "He had quite a spill yesterday, falling off a horse and down a ravine," said Elias. "And the constant pounding of the trail ride was just making it worse."[27]

Musso appeared to be unconscious when Friedman and Elias splashed water in his face to revive him. They also tried to get him to drink some hot tea. Musso briefly awakened, but after a few minutes he again relapsed into unconsciousness for the rest of the night.

The guards hovering over the injured man told the captives that Sun Mei-yao had briefly contemplated executing Musso to get the soldiers to withdraw. The plan was to dump his body at the military lines and then lay the blame for his death on the wayward shots of the pursuing troops. The bandits figured that Musso was so seriously injured that he would slow down the rest of the group. But the bandit known as the Frenchman intervened, telling Sun that he had spoken to Musso himself in French earlier in the day and learned that the Italian was a powerful lawyer with major political connections. After Sun realized Musso's value, the bandit chief backed down. The Frenchman had saved Musso's life.

Meanwhile, Pinger's group crossed a small stream and reached a walled village with gates closed for the night, a short distance from the Dragon Door Temple. A bandit the captives would call "Big Bill" let out a yell in his deep baritone voice and demanded the villagers provide food and other items to the group. The bandit knew that the villagers were not obligated to open the gate at night but that sending provisions to outside visitors, even bandits, was expected. In a short time, over the wall came hard-boiled eggs, pots of tea, and a large quantity of straw for bedding. Pinger used his buttonhook to sew together two blankets as a sleeping bag and placed it on a thick layer of straw.

With Roland sleeping, Pinger propped himself up and noticed the bandits building a large campfire of kaoliang stalks under the clear, bright stars. Solomon, Smith, Berubé, and Rowlatt, each busy making a bed for the night with straw, looked on as well as the campfire flamed upward with a loud whoosh sound followed by intense crackling. Big Bill's group of about fifty men were in a cheery mood, partly because of Bill's gregarious personality but also because they believed that they had beaten the odds by escaping from the pursuing soldiers.

The gang decided that tonight was the night to sing and celebrate. Things commenced with a soloist singing a cappella, with the group joining in the chorus at intervals. Whoever concluded his song on the highest, thinnest, and most quavering note brought the loudest clapping and cheering. What the foreigners were hearing were traditional folk songs describing daily life in the villages, sung in the ancient Chinese scale of five tones. The main event that night was a performance by Russky, who had adapted Russian love songs into traditional Chinese folk-music form. Russky had a naturally high and even falsetto tenor voice, and he sang a repertoire of colorful Russian barracks-room ballads. Even the Russian-speaking Lee Solomon found Russky's songs impressive. Bandits as well as foreign captives clapped and gave him a rousing ovation.[28]

When they noticed that the foreigners were also watching, Big Bill started to good-naturedly heckle Pinger. He sprang to his feet to mimic Pinger's futile effort to communicate with his wife when they were separated the night of the train robbery. "*Meerreeam, Meerreeam*," brought howls from his bandit audience.[29]

"Oh, pipe down," Major Pinger said with a smile.

"At least we know they have a sense of humor," Solomon said.

Big Bill then started to impersonate the way that Pinger put up his dukes in a boxing stance on the night of the attack when he was defending his wife in their train compartment. This also got big laughs from all the other bandits. Pinger just rolled over to sleep.

As the fire died down, it began to get chilly. The captives and bandits settled into their bedrolls and straw. Before doing so, the bandits, especially the older ones, lit up their brass pipes for a dose of tranquility. The strong smell of burning opium hovered over the camp.

When you lacked all, Pinger thought, as he tried to fall asleep, *opium was food, drink, shelter, raiment, wife, children, and any other good thing.*[30] He remained awake, wondering what new dread tomorrow would bring.

CHAPTER 12

THE MONGREL FEAST

Lack of food was our chief problem on the long march. One day they brought us some fresh meat which they said was "young cow." Later, we were informed that our veal stew was Shantung dog, a particularly tough type of mangy cur.

—John B. Powell, American publisher and hostage[1]

MAY 9, 1923, SUNRISE, DRAGON DOOR TEMPLE

Initial media reports had indicated that Major Pinger had been seriously injured in the melee back at the train and was suffering from a gunshot wound. If Pinger was indeed wounded, the medical missionary doctors whom US consul Harvey Milbourne had sent down to Lincheng on a special relief train were ready to treat him. Their intent was to locate Pinger and evacuate him, if possible, to Tsinan for treatment.[2] Yet the reports were not accurate; Pinger was indeed fine, though exhausted after three days of schlepping across the countryside. At sunrise on the third morning after the holdup, he was sound asleep on the ground outside the gates of a hamlet somewhere in rural Shantung, waking to a rooster crowing and the sounds of the village coming to life.

On the morning of May 9, Pinger, his son Roland, and the other captives in his group walked through the open gates of the walled village searching for breakfast. They all noticed a general scarcity of men, except for a few who were very old. Word came that they would not be moving again for a while and that the hostages would be staying put in the vicinity of the Dragon Door Temple compound, which was nestled in the tree-covered foothills just below a steep plateau of white rocky cliffs. The complex included the connecting villages, which supported the temple. This was a welcome relief, even if the villages seemed mired in abject poverty. Protected by the mountain backdrop, the bandits and their prisoners were sheltered from the growing army presence at the military lines several miles to the south.

Pinger scanned the surroundings and noticed that there was hardly any traffic, save for a boy leading a team of small oxen and donkeys that carried wicker panniers filled with manure and night soil to be dumped in the community fertilizer reservoir. The stench of the fecal sludge pit was overpowering and attracted swarms of flies. Pinger winced with revulsion and watched Roland pull up his coat to cover his nose and mouth. Nearby, a younger woman with a sad, bored look on her face held a toddler who was covered in sores and was trying to wiggle out of her grip. Her gloomy expression contrasted with the cheerful mood of an old woman who sat beside her, preparing a meal on a smoky wood and coal fire.

Big Bill greeted the older matron as if she were his own grandmother. She showed him a big cauldron (goa) filled with boiling kaoliang gruel. When Roland Jr. refused the thin, grainy soup, the major gestured and said "Cluck, cluck, cluck" to the old woman in the hope of getting some fresh eggs to eat. She burst out laughing at Pinger's chicken impersonation. She then handed him two eggs and was prepared to toss them into the bubbling goa.

"No, no, Grandma. Give them to me, and I'll show you something." The major then cracked open the two eggs into a large metal ladle and stirred them with Miriam's shoehorn. As the scrambled eggs were cooked, the old woman smiled and eagerly pulled out a hollowed-out gourd filled with black salt, which got its color from the soot falling from the roofs of caves where the homemade seasoning was cultivated from boiling brine. The salt on the scrambled eggs indeed made a big difference; young Roland gobbled them up with much pleasure.

"Grandma" took a liking to Major Pinger and with needle and thread mended the rip in his pajama top without taking it off his back. She then started her daily chores of spinning cotton yarn that would eventually be weaved and dyed into fabric for "coolie-blue" summer garments. Roland was fascinated by the spinning wheel, which created a fine, even thread of yarn from combed cotton fibers. Water was brought into the hut so that the foreigners could take a cold bath from the waist up. The villagers watched with curiosity as the foreigners one by one stripped and sponged themselves clean.

The foreign captives had little to do throughout the day other than to rest and watch the daily activities of the villagers. The villagers also took an interest in their visitors.[3] The sad-faced younger woman gave Roland a hard, brown-colored cake that had the texture and firmness of teething cookies. It was intended to be lunch, but the Pingers found it inedible. When they couldn't finish the cake, the major tossed it into a nearby pig's trough, which contained scraps of food dumped throughout the morning. This ended up being a most terrible faux pas. Before the pig could pounce on the morsel, the young woman retrieved the priceless bit of rare dessert, washed it off, and gave it to her little son, who enjoyed it immensely although he had no visible teeth.

At about four o'clock, Pinger heard a great commotion coming from outside the village walls. One of the bandits came in and grabbed him by the wrist shouting, "Tsou, tsou!" As Pinger and the other prisoners were led outside the walls, one bandit with pursed lips immediately gave him a smart, figure-four salute, and then another with an awkward grin fumbled with his firearm and gave the major a rifle salute. One after another, the ragtag band of brigands saluted Pinger with much hilarity. Why they were saluting him was a bit of a mystery to Pinger because he was in civilian clothing and he assumed that his identity as a US Army officer was a secret. "What's the big idea?" Pinger called out to Rowlatt among the swarm of captives, bandits, and villagers.

"There's a written message for you," shouted Rowlatt over the cackle of voices, "and it's addressed to *Major* Pinger!" Pinger groaned and immediately felt a sense of unease now that his military affiliation was known.

MEANWHILE, BRITISH CONSUL BERTHOLD TOURS HAD BEEN ORDERED by the Foreign Office to proceed at once from Tsinan to Lincheng.[4] The diplomat didn't have much information to work with, but he knew that at least one British subject was dead and several more had been taken hostage. Before leaving Tsinan for Lincheng, Tours needed to draft a report concerning the death of Joseph Rothman. The local magistrate in Lincheng conducted an initial examination but later passed on the corpse to the British consulate in Tsinan for consular examination and burial. The body had arrived in Tsinan from Lincheng and been stored temporarily at the Shantung Christian University's hospital morgue. An inquest was required by law in the case of a sudden, unnatural death of a British subject.

Rothman's body had been wrapped in an assortment of bedsheets and blankets taken from the train. The corpse had been unrefrigerated for days and subjected to the balmy spring temperatures, so when the orderlies at the morgue began cutting and peeling away the layers of linen wrapping Rothman's head, Tours had to cover his mouth and nose with a handkerchief. The smell was awful. The inquest ended almost as soon as it began. Tours and the attending Chinese officials had seen enough. It was apparent that Rothman had been shot in the face at very close range. Tours simply stated in his report that the "body was too decomposed for examination."[5] A passport in Rothman's coat and papers in his briefcase established identification. At Tours's request, Rothman was buried in the Tsinan foreign cemetery that afternoon.

Tours would now be on his way to Lincheng to represent His Majesty's interests. He hoped for the best but feared that this would not be the last death report he had to write concerning the Lincheng Incident.

LATER IN THE DAY, ONE OF THE BANDITS CAME INTO THE COMPOUND AND presented Powell with a two-pound chunk of warm, bloody meat that they pressed into his appreciative but squeamish hands. Apparently, the bandits had killed some kind of animal and divided up the carcass between the camps—saying that it was a "young cow." Elated, Powell and Friedman busily chopped and seasoned the meat and boiled it, bones and all, in a large goa.[6] For their efforts, they found the meat to be unique and gamy but tasteful, and everyone in their group had a hearty bowlful.

"Not bad," both Powell and Friedman agreed, complimenting each other for their rural, do-it-yourself meal preparation. Later, one of the bandits told banker Chi Cheng that the "veal" that was passed around to each of the camps was actually Shantung dog, a somewhat domesticated mutt foraging in packs inside and outside of village compounds. In rural Shantung, dogs were primarily used for herding or as sentries and not frequently consumed as food. But in famine-stricken regions of China, and when the need arose, the starvation diet had no bounds. Mongrel or veal, the meat gave them the energy to live another day.

SOMEWHERE IN THE CROWD WAS A MESSAGE FOR PINGER, BUT ALL THE locals were clamoring to see and touch the all-important letter being passed around, so it was difficult for the major to get his hands on it. He saw Chi Cheng, and could tell by the nervous look on his face that he had already translated it for the bandits.

"What is good for one to know is good for *all* to know," shouted Big Bill, who had sensed Pinger's outrage that his private mail was shared with the masses. A very-nervous-looking Chinese houseboy dressed in a long-sleeved blue gown and black cap had delivered the mysterious letter to the bandit camp and told the group that it was given to him by two medical missionaries.

Attached to the message was a name card for Colonel Chang Chou, Shantung Army, 6th Brigade, which the messenger used as a pass through the military lines. The name card alone raised alarm with Big Bill. There was something about this foreigner, a US military man who supposedly received special treatment by the Shantung government troops. After all, Colonel Chang was their enemy.

This letter clearly made Pinger a big fish. But Rowlatt thought the letter was a fraud and cautioned the major about responding; it might have come from a competing bandit faction trying to get involved with the action by having their own prisoner. Pinger began to realize that it was unlikely that he would be freed but that this might be the opportunity to have Roland released. He pleaded with his guards to bring the matter to the attention of the bandit chiefs. Big Bill agreed and asked Russky to take Pinger to find Sun Mei-yao or Po-Po Liu. Professor Hung joined as the translator.

Russky led the group through a maze of narrow, winding alleys that opened up into a courtyard with a farmhouse in the center guarded by a "neatly clothed, well-armed straw-hatted bandit sentry with a bandoleer full of cartridges over his shoulder." Hung spoke in Chinese to the two watchmen at the gate. While one remained on guard out front, the other went into the shadowy, sepulcher-like entrance of the house. As he waited, Pinger could smell the sweet, overwhelming vapors of burning opium drifting from the interior. After a few minutes, a balding, mustached man came out from the entrance—bony with pale yellow skin and lazy eyes. This was Po-Po Liu, bandit chief number two. Pinger was finally meeting the old bandit face-to-face after watching Liu's evil brutality from a distance the past three days. The major felt uneasy, but he approached Liu with a sense of determination given the important task at hand.

"Tell him that *this* message has come to me from the outside world, and I deemed it my *duty* to bring it to his attention *immediately*." Hung translated both Pinger's comments and the letter, which appeared to seek the release of a supposedly wounded Pinger to two medical missionaries waiting at Lincheng station. Hung handed the letter to Liu, who studied the paper and foreign handwriting, although he obviously did not read English. Liu paused to either think or wake up, or both.

"You *cannot* go," grumbled the bandit chief.

"To be sure, *I* cannot go," Pinger said. "But this is a wonderful opportunity for *you* to tell the outside world the meaning of this matter, and your terms for our release." Pinger explained that he would write a letter that emphasized the need for the government troops to stand down, lest the captives continue to be at risk.

"I would like to answer the message, and to send my son out with the reply," Pinger then went on, as he proudly put his arm on Roland's shoulder. Liu appeared to be struggling to grasp this foreigner's request and went back inside the house to retrieve his outer coat and shoes. When he returned, he slowly led the group to an open courtyard crammed with villagers and bandits milling around with other prisoners—including the Shanghai cousins. Liu called out for stools and a large pot of tea. As the chairs were arranged and refreshments brought, Pinger had a chance to quietly coach Roland on how to ingratiate himself to the bandit chief. "Play up to the old man—it may mean your release!"

Roland stood up, straightened his red silk coat, smiled, then walked over to the aging bandit. Liu was most impressed with the boy's coolness. Liu set Roland on his knee like a kid visiting Santa Claus, admired his fair hair, and, with Hung interpreting, asked what his age was, patting him in an affectionate manner. Liu then began to talk.

Liu agreed that the letter from the two doctors to Major Pinger presented an opportunity. Liu knew that the messages to the Chinese soldiers carried by other released hostages had not succeeded in getting the troops to stand down. He also believed that a military officer's response would certainly help in gaining the attention of the US government as leverage against the deceitful Chinese warlords.[7] Liu then paused in reflection, and, lifting Roland off his knee as if to hasten his departure, he ordered, "The boy can go!"

Glory, Hallelujah! the major thought, clasping his hands together and slightly bowing to Liu in a gesture of gratitude and respect.

Po-Po Liu gave Pinger a piece of paper to write the letter that Roland would take back with him. With Hung translating, Liu asked Pinger to write that "all hostages would be shot in three days if the troops were not withdrawn." Pinger flinched at the wording dictated by Liu, thinking of how Miriam and his family back in the United States would react if this letter were printed in the newspapers. Pinger toned down the language and simply wrote that the bandits had "threatened the worst." A short deadline of three days was quite unreasonable, too, given the time that it would take to deliver the letter to the authorities and thereafter to deliver the instructions to the troops to withdraw. Liu also instructed Major Pinger to write that the government troops have "burned our villages and killed our men," but Pinger simply wrote that the brigands had "suffered at the hands of the troops."[8]

On a read-back, the bandit chief told Hung that he was not satisfied with the letter and angrily ordered Pinger to "tell your friends that we mean business," or at least that was how Hung translated Liu's threatening language. Hung realized that Pinger may have wanted to shun the menacing language, but Hung also wanted to avoid angering Liu in order to ensure that Roland would be allowed to leave. So, without changing the original letter, Hung asked Pinger to add a few forceful lines that may have slightly stretched the truth. Hung told Liu that this language would make it clear to the outside world the seriousness of the situation.[9]

The key message of Pinger's letter was to urge the government troops to withdraw. Pinger added in a final sentence about the need for Western food; the only thing the prisoners could eat in the villages appeared to be eggs, watery gruel, and Shantung dog. During the drawn-out wordsmithing, several of the Shanghai cousins repeatedly shouted out to Pinger to be sure that twelve-year-old Bobby Allen went along with the younger Roland.[10]

"Keep your shirts on," yelled back Pinger.

Pinger was concerned that if he asked too much, Liu would renege on the whole idea. Pinger also could see that the bandit chief was getting anxious to return to his opium, so it was important to get him first to agree to the language of the letter. After some reflection, Liu audibly grumbled but finally agreed. Hung smiled as he translated back Liu's consent, and Pinger breathed a big sigh of relief. Before Liu got up, Pinger pitched the idea that it was necessary for Bobby to accompany Roland on the journey down the mountain. Liu wavered and ran his hand through his mustache overhanging his upper lip. "How old is this other boy?" Liu asked.

"He's about twelve years," said the major, thinking that the bandit chief might not believe him, for Bobby was taller than him, and probably heavier.

"Very well," said Liu, "take your guard and go back to your village. I shall send for the other boy and his father. When they arrive, *both* boys will go out together."[11]

"Just a moment," Pinger said, although the meeting with Liu had obviously ended. "The night is *very* dark—*both* boys are small. Will you not send with the lads five or six of your most trusted followers?"

"Have no fear for your son!" Liu angrily shouted back. Pinger hesitated but decided to not push the issue, knowing that it was too risky. Pinger then noticed that Liu immediately regretted the harshness of his tone, realizing that the major was only trying to protect the boys. "Have you no coat?" Liu calmly asked, changing the subject.

"No," said Pinger, standing before Liu in his ridiculously oversized pants and pajama top. "This large garment must serve both as trousers and as waist-coat."

Liu smiled at the badly dressed foreigner and then ordered one of his subordinates to produce a coat; in a moment Liu was back with "a parting gift" for Pinger—a fine dinner coat which had been looted from the train. Pinger then thanked Liu for his generosity as the bandit walked back inside his house.

The major gave Roland the letter, kissed him good-bye, and told him that if—God willing—Miriam and Edward had made it to safety, he should take care of his mother and younger brother. Pinger, Hung, and their guards returned to the village compound from the bandit chief's house as dusk approached. Pinger walked in a haze, feeling a deep sense of worry about his decision to leave young Roland in the hands of the bandits. He would never forgive himself if something happened to his first child. He nonetheless believed that his choices were limited. His captivity was likely to be a long, drawn-out process, and there was much risk that the boys would be shot in the cross fire. The major also thought that if he needed to risk an escape, he was better off without the boys present. Further, Pinger believed the assurances of the bandit chief. "When old Po-Po Liu said, 'Have no fear for your son!' I knew that I was dealing with a man who would have shot *both* of us *if necessary*, but he meant just what he said," Pinger told Hung.[12]

AT TWO O'CLOCK IN THE MORNING OF MAY 10, ROLAND AND BOBBY SET out down the valley on two donkeys, moving at a brisk pace across the moonlit countryside. Accompanying the boys were several of Liu's bandit guards and several Chinese captives, including one of the captured train guards, who were being released by the bandits so they could guide the boys through the maze of villages and past the army cordon.[13]

When they reached the bandit army's front lines, the escorts pointed in the direction of what looked like the lights of a nearby town. The bandits, turning northward in the direction of their camp, then disappeared into the darkness. The boys headed toward the light, reaching the military line around dawn. The Chinese captives in their party called out to the soldiers to identify themselves, and the group was granted safe passage through the lines. As they got closer to the town lights, they could see a searchlight on a high tower scanning the horizon. At seven o'clock in the morning, as the sun was rising, the boys arrived outside the heavily fortified mining compound of Tsaochuang, which would soon become the de facto command center for the military and diplomatic efforts to rescue the hostages taken from the Peking Express.

CHAPTER 13

DIPLOMACY IN ACTION

The mining company maintains an armed force of eight hundred men for protection. They have several machine guns and howitzers. All night a strong searchlight is played on all of the approaches to Tsaochuang and especially on the roads and paths leading from Paotzuku.

—Carl Crow, publisher and the chief of the American Rescue Mission[1]

MAY 10, 1923, 7:00 A.M., TSAOCHUANG MINING COMPOUND

Located nineteen miles east of Lincheng, the Tsaochuang mining compound was owned and operated by the Chung Hsing Mining Company, one of the first Chinese-owned mining operations without foreign interests. Still, it was as disconnected from the lives of ordinary Chinese peasants as the foreign-held mines had been. Although equipped with sophisticated, foreign-made mining technology, the compound was situated in one of the poorest regions of China. There were no roads beyond the mines other than simple country paths. Given the proximity to bandit country and a restive peasant population, all the mining company's senior managers lived inside the safety of the compound's high walls in comfortable European-styled houses. The mining company employees did not dare venture more than a

mile from the walls for fear of being captured and held for ransom.[2] Inside
the grounds' twenty-five acres were the coal-mine pit head, a power plant, a
small railway station, a rail yard, and a large administrative building.

For protection, the company had a private security force of eight hundred men armed with high-powered rifles, machine guns, howitzers, and
75 mm artillery capable of firing up to twenty-four rounds per minute. The
compound was a fortress; the walls were topped with an electric fence and
multiple guard towers. Outside the walls was a moat and barbed-wire en-
tanglements. The security services operated a powerful sixty-inch General
Electric searchlight that constantly scanned the countryside for potential
bandit attacks. All throughout the night, the searchlight illuminated the
footpaths and roads leading to Tsaochuang.[3] This had been the strange finger of light the hostages saw as they marched across the countryside a few
nights earlier.

Since the Lincheng Incident had begun, the Peking government had sent
about thirty railcars to Tsaochuang to serve as sleeping quarters for the
consular representatives and support staff who were descending upon the
fortress. The American diplomats, among them Consul John Davis, Assistant Military Attaché Wallace Philoon, and Language Officer Lloyd Horsfall, were the first to arrive and were followed by Raffaele Ferrajolo, the
vice consul from the Italian consulate in Shanghai, and Pierre Jean Crépin,
the general consul of the French consulate in Shanghai. Soon more people
came: distraught family members of the hostages, soldiers from both Chinese and foreign militaries, as well as nosy local curiosity seekers. British
consul Berthold Tours was late to the party, for he had remained in Tsinan
to conduct the inquest concerning Rothman's death and arrived in Tsaochuang at ten o'clock on the evening of May 13.[4]

In addition to the diplomats, Tsaochuang had also become a destination
for newspapermen, who started to camp out in the compound to cover the
latest developments of the crisis. The former hostage Larry Lehrbas of the
China Press arrived in Tsaochuang after an overnight trip down to Shanghai to get a new set of clothes. The *Chicago Tribune*'s Peking correspondent,
Charles A. Dailey, was there, as well as the esteemed "girl reporter" Edna
Lee Booker, a stringer for the International News Service. Foreign correspondents were urged to spare no expense to cable the news as it happened,

but many US newspaper correspondents complained to Minister Schurman that their telegrams were delayed or not being sent or received by the telegraph operators. According to the correspondents, the operators were instructed by the Chinese Telegraph Administration to chuck or delay transmissions from foreign media to suppress news about the Peking Express.

Chinese officials also pressured reporters to publish "nothing unfriendly" about the government's handling of the crisis. But the international press escaped the censors by sending runners with handwritten stories to the treaty ports outside the Chinese Telegraph Administration's jurisdiction, and these articles were then forwarded by the wire services to every corner of the planet.[5]

EARLY IN THE MORNING ON MAY 10, THE FOREIGN DIPLOMATS AND scores of people living and working within the mining compound started to make their way to the canteen for breakfast. At the gates, the tower guards were surprised to see two light-haired boys and several Chinese men waving their hands over their heads and walking toward the north gate of the mining compound in the dawn light. As a precaution, the guards trained their rifles on the strangers.

After realizing they did not pose a threat, the guards opened the massive doors to let the group into the stone-walled compound, while another guard sprinted to the two-story office building, which the foreign diplomats and government officials had turned into their headquarters. Within minutes, a large, jubilant group had gathered just inside the gate to welcome the boys. They were greeted by US diplomats, including Major Horsfall, Major Philoon, and Consul John Davis. Horsfall asked Roland if his father was injured and in need of medical care. "He's fine, but his feet are blistered and bruised," the boy said. "But so is everyone else's!"

Relieved, Horsfall explained that the initial reports were that Roland's father had been shot, so the two doctors had been sent to provide medical treatment. The boys handed Horsfall and Davis the letter from Po-Po Liu drafted by Major Pinger. The key message, the diplomats quickly discerned, was that the troops needed to cease firing and stand down.[6]

Roland Pinger Jr. and Bobby Allen with journalist Larry Lehrbas at Tsaochuang upon their release from captivity on May 10. Major Lloyd Horsfall (in background) is preparing to take the boys to their mothers waiting in Tientsin. (Pinger)

While Philoon and Horsfall debriefed the two American boys, Father Wilhelm Lenfers, whom Lucy Aldrich had met a few days earlier at the Lincheng station, talked with the Chinese captives who accompanied Roland and Bobby. They gave the priest a description of the villages and the temple where the hostages were located. Given his knowledge of the region, the well-traveled priest immediately knew that the hostages were being held in the vicinity of the Dragon Door Temple, which was located in the Taihuanpeng Mountains, roughly five miles north of Tsaochuang. Lenfers approached the diplomats and offered to go meet with the bandit chiefs to determine the conditions for their release. The aging priest set out to find the missing passengers on his own.

AFTER LEAVING TSAOCHUANG WITH MAJOR HORSFALL, BOBBY AND Roland slept soundly on the train ride from Lincheng northward to Tientsin, where their mothers were waiting.[7] When they woke up, they went to the dining car and were quickly surrounded by a group of passengers who were riveted by the stories of their time in captivity. The reporter Edna Lee Booker rode the train specifically to get an exclusive in-depth account of the boys' ordeal. The worst part of the adventure, the boys said, was the long, forced marches and the filthy sleeping quarters. When asked how they were treated, they announced that the bandit chiefs liked them. "The bandits were good to us," Bobby explained. "Every day the bandit chief played with us and called to his men to look at our hair and eyes. They liked to ruffle our light hair."

When asked if they were afraid of getting shot, the boys were quick to dismiss the outlaws' marksmanship skills. "I wasn't afraid of the bandits— Why? They can't shoot. Every time they shoot, they aim and turn their head around and close their eyes when they fire," said Roland to the laughs of his audience.

"We can shoot better than they can," boasted Bobby Allen. "The bandit that followed me around just wore an old soldier uniform and carried a gun and had a goofy grin." They both laughed when they described the silly antics of the bandits in playing the musical instruments acquired from the train. With the attention of an admiring audience, the boys started to embellish their stories for color.

"We looked into a cave one morning and there were piles and piles of silver dollars—hundreds and hundreds of them—and rolls of paper bills," said Bobby, with an air of mystery.

"I also saw lots of rings and bracelets and watches," added Roland. When Booker started to sense that the boys' cave and treasure story matched some of the features of *The Adventures of Tom Sawyer*, she asked if they were brave like the book's namesake character.

"Tom Sawyer? Why he only lived in Missouri," said Bobby, "while Roland and I were kidnapped in China. Gee, Tom Sawyer hasn't anything on us!"

"No, and I guess Huck Finn hasn't either," added Roland.[8] For all their boyish bravado, they didn't talk about the murders and beatings they witnessed, and they didn't admit how they feared never seeing their fathers again. The excitement of their adventure masked the trauma of what they had lived through.

When the plucky youngsters arrived at Tientsin—where the US Army maintained a permanent garrison—they were smothered by their mothers as they stepped off the train.[9] Even the toddler Edward hugged his brother Roland in excitement. Major Horsfall told the waiting US military and medical personnel—standing by to provide support for the boys—that he believed the boys were in fine shape despite the ordeal. Haggard from the experience, both Miriam Pinger and Martha Allen thanked Horsfall for escorting the boys, but they remained disappointed about the lack of progress on the hostage situation and were deeply worried about the safety of their husbands.

Father Lenfers left Tsaochuang around midday on May 10 for the five-mile hike up to the Dragon Door Temple. Lenfers was a member of the Society of the Divine Word, known by its Latin abbreviation SVD (*Societas Verbi Divini*). Originally from Münster, Germany, Lenfers was fifty years of age. Shantung had become his home; he arrived in the province in 1898. He lived and worked at the large Lincheng Catholic Church complex, within walking distance of the Lincheng train station on the Tientsin-Pukow rail line.[10]

Lenfers was committed to an ascetic lifestyle. Indeed, he wanted to live the same simple life as the Chinese peasant. He dressed in a long, pale white *changshan*—a Chinese-styled gown—and wore soft Chinese shoes made of cloth. He was tall and had a long, unkempt beard that was streaked with gray. To guard against the hot sun, Lenfers wore a white pith helmet, and he used a cane to navigate the rough paths and stones of the rural countryside. For food, he carried a loaf of bread and dry sausage, and instead of riding a horse, he walked everywhere. Lenfers had strong Chinese-language skills and had built the trust of the Lincheng community.

Whenever Lenfers was in the presence of bandits, many of the outlaws hid in shame because they respected him and were embarrassed by their activities. Several of the bandits were Catholic converts and attended Mass at the Lincheng parish church. Even the non-Catholics would ask the old priest for his blessings and prayers as he traveled from village to village. The bandits sought shelter and medical assistance from local missionaries, and they often relied on the missionaries to help settle disputes between rival factions. The old priest was not judgmental, realizing that most of the men who became bandits did so out of desperation.

On the morning of the train robbery, Lenfers was preparing for Sunday Mass when a parishioner came to the sacristy and told him that the express train had been derailed just south of Lincheng and more than a thousand bandits had dragged away hundreds of foreign and Chinese men, women, and children. Lenfers immediately understood the gravity of the situation. He had seen warlords like General Tien destroy scores of villages in the area as payback for giving shelter and support to the bandits. He expected that the military would only intensify its campaign now that foreigners had become captives, and he feared that many lives would be lost.

To try to mediate the crisis, Lenfers now believed that it was best to head to the Dragon Door Temple in an effort to locate the hostages and speak with the bandit chiefs. Leaving Tsaochuang, he walked through the porous military lines without being stopped by the provincial troops. Lenfers stayed overnight in a hamlet just below the villages surrounding the temple. His hope was to meet the bandit chiefs to determine the condition of the prisoners and terms of release.[11] When he arrived at the Dragon Door Temple, Lenfers was led into a small but clean room with a table and four benches, and was given the place of honor at the table. There he met with Sun Mei-yao, who was well acquainted with him. Lenfers noticed that Sun looked more like a university student than a bandit chief—he was clean-cut and well dressed and wore eyeglasses. He had a quiet voice, and his cordial and friendly tone belied his rather grim message: "We are not bandits but have been deprived of our livelihood when we were dismissed as soldiers, unpaid."

The bandit chief emphasized that they were desperate and believed that the wholesale kidnapping of foreigners was the only way to force Peking to take their demands seriously. Sun emphasized that he was not interested in money. Rather, they wanted, first and foremost, that the Chinese troops be withdrawn and to cease their relentless attacks on the bandits and the neighboring villages. Second, Sun insisted that the bandits be re-enlisted into the military forces. He also wanted a guarantee that should they come to terms and cease hostilities, there would be no reprisals in any form against the bandits and their leaders. "We are prepared to slaughter the prisoners if our demands are not accepted," Sun warned, his voice as soft as a whisper.

Sun set the deadline for forty-eight hours. Lenfers talked with him for more than an hour, but the priest was unable to get him to soften his position. The bandit chief also told Lenfers that statements of the Chinese officials, especially the hated General Tien, meant nothing to the bandits and that a commitment by the foreign governments must be given—Chinese promises alone were not sufficient: "Our demands include guarantees from the foreign diplomats, since we are unwilling to accept any pledges from Chinese officials."

This did not surprise Lenfers. He knew that the warlords dominated the country with unrelenting violence and corruption, which had affected Sun's faith in his own government's ability to keep its word.

Lenfers agreed to take the message to the government representatives at Tsaochuang. The priest then pleaded with Sun to allow him to see the captives. They first brought in Leon Friedman, a physically imposing figure in comparison to the bandits. Friedman looked like he was in good health despite the long trek. Friedman told the priest about the march, the condition of the captives, and the need for food and clothing. He also told the priest that he was unaware of the exact demands of the bandits but was informed repeatedly that ransom was not important. Friedman then called in Eddie Elias, who was fluent in German, Lenfers's native language. Lenfers found Eddie to be sunburned but otherwise in good condition. The priest told Elias that press reports indicated that both Haimovitch and Zimmerman escaped when the train was first seized and that they had safely arrived in Tientsin. This was a huge relief for the Shanghai cousins.

Lenfers next met with Saphiere, who had to be carried into the room because his right foot, lacerated during the shoeless trek, had swelled to twice its normal size. Lenfers found the young man's condition serious and asked the bandits to release him for treatment. Sun refused this request but assured Lenfers that they planned to summon a foreign doctor to treat both Saphiere and Musso.[12]

Next, Major Allen was brought in. Lenfers grasped Allen's hand, his voice shaking with emotion.[13] Lenfers told Allen that Bobby and Roland Jr.

had arrived safely at Tsaochuang and were on their way to Tientsin to meet their mothers. Allen breathed a huge sigh of relief.

After meeting them individually, Lenfers addressed this group of foreign captives and informed them of the demands of Sun Mei-yao. The priest also mentioned the growing contingent of foreign consular representatives and officials at the Tsaochuang mining compound in support of a rescue effort. All were very concerned about the short time they had to meet the bandits' demands. Before departing, Lenfers went back to Sun and again pleaded with him to extend the deadline. Sun and Liu discussed the matter and eventually agreed to extend the time period from two to three days. But Sun absolutely refused to give any more time and told Lenfers in a calm voice that he would kill all the hostages if Peking did not give in.

Lenfers took Sun aside and calmly spoke to him in Chinese. "You are too smart, too intelligent, to shoot these innocent people," he said.[14]

"Do not deceive yourself or believe me soft!" Sun warned. "What I threaten I will carry out exactly as I promise."[15] Just then they heard distant gunfire coming from the south, where General Tien's troops had amassed. Sun's face flashed with anger. "If they don't keep their promises, we won't keep ours."

The old priest assured him he would "walk the whole night, sore feet and all, to carry out your message."[16]

Major Allen, not understanding Chinese, asked the priest if they would be released soon. "No, they will not release you," Lenfers replied. "And they say if the Chinese troops do not withdraw within three days you all will be shot."[17]

Lenfers, speaking in English in a low voice, told the hostages that he still thought that Sun would not carry out the threat, given that the bandits needed them alive in order to achieve their objectives. But this was hardly reassuring to the hostages.

Before Lenfers left the village, the captives wrote out letters to family and friends. The Shanghai cousins quickly prepared a letter to their families stating that they were receiving "good treatment"—"all well, don't worry, expecting release." Friedman drafted a general statement to the diplomatic corps, which was signed by all of the captives.[18] As they were writing the statement, Lenfers requested to see the Italian lawyer Musso, but

German Catholic priest Wilhelm Lenfers and unknown Chinese government official at the Tsaochuang mining compound rail yard after walking down from the bandit camps. Lenfers proved to be a valuable interlocutor between the captives, the bandits, and the foreign government representatives at Tsaochuang. (SHSMO)

the bandits declined his request, stating that Musso was in poor health and being kept a good distance away.

The priest left the hostages with a basket of food, including bread and other baked goods, Chinese ham, and vegetables from the missionary gardens. For reading materials, the priest left behind the only thing readily available, several copies of the Bible. While the captives were quite grateful, Leon Friedman couldn't help but laugh: "What is a good Jew boy going to do in the circumstances? We starve and they send us a ham! We have nothing to read, and they send us the New Testament!"[19]

LENFERS WAS WORRIED ABOUT THE SHORT DEADLINE IMPOSED BY THE bandits. He walked down the valley as fast as his legs could take him. It was difficult for the old priest to travel so quickly through the deep ravines and rocky roads. As Lenfers hobbled toward the military lines, shots rang out, causing him to drop to his knees. Unlike the day before when he merely walked through the military lines, the troops at the cordon now saw him as a threat. His drab dress, worn and dirtied from the day's arduous travel, also made him look like more of a peasant than a foreigner. He raised his hands in surrender as Tien's soldiers surrounded him.

Lenfers was clearly unarmed, but the soldiers nevertheless pushed him to the ground, looking for weapons under his changshan as he tried to explain that he had a message for the foreign consular representatives in Tsao-chuang. After searching him, the soldiers pushed him away and let him continue. Lenfers trembled as he walked past the angry, armed men. As he proceeded behind the lines, he saw several medics treating soldiers who had fresh gunshot wounds from firefights with the bandits. The fighting had been raging all day. *This is truly a valley of the shadow of death*, he thought, hurrying toward Tsaochuang. Lenfers was relieved when the mining compound was in sight and the heavy gates began to open.

Almost immediately, a crowd swarmed the exhausted old priest. They gave him a chair and some water. Catching his breath, Lenfers told the audience that the release of the passengers would not come easily. The militant position of both the bandits and the army troops was not encouraging. He was not optimistic for a quick resolution. Lenfers handed to US consul John Davis the initial demands of the bandits prepared by Sun Mei-yao, as well as the captives' collective statement prepared by Leon Friedman.[20]

The handwritten letter of the "Self-Governed Army for the Establishment of the Country" stated that the brigands were former soldiers who were defeated and disbanded after battles in neighboring Honan Province and who then returned to Shantung to live their lives as farmers. But the Shantung provincial army operating in the region saw them as a threat and began hunting them down. They had no choice, they said, but to gather their men in the mountains in order to wage a war for peace.

"During the past few years, the people in the adjacent villages have been greatly oppressed," Consul Davis said, reading the bandit chief's letter out loud. "While the troops ostensibly were sent to suppress the bandits, they have robbed the people of their money and have carried away their cattle and horses. The people, on account of their inability to live in peace, have joined us in large numbers."

The key demand of the bandits, Lenfers added, was to end the siege of Paotzuku Mountain. This needed to occur *before* any negotiations for the release of the foreigners.

The letter went on to make a clear threat against the foreign captives. "The foreign captives are all here," Davis continued. "It is desired at present that all troops which surround us be *immediately withdrawn* to the provincial capital. We will then discuss our other demands. If the troops are not withdrawn in two days, all foreigners will be shot and not one will be spared. The military officers should take action accordingly."

As the letter was being read, General Tien approached the group. The warlord had arrived with a large contingent of bodyguards just a few hours before. He announced that he would remain in Tsaochuang until the hostages were released. Sensing that he would be held responsible if the Lincheng Incident resulted in a bloodbath, Tien had earlier offered to resign from office, but the Peking authorities declined and implored him to continue his efforts to obtain the release of the captives.[21]

This vote of confidence from Peking seemed to embolden Tien. He was now in no mood to negotiate with the bandits. "Tear up this nonsense!" Tien shouted at Davis. Then Tien turned to Lenfers: "*You* had *no* authority to be in communication with the brigands, and you were not sanctioned to cross the military lines to go up to the bandit camps." But the foreign diplomats gave the priest a reassuring nod to ignore the angry general. As Tien walked away in a huff, the reporters clamored around Lenfers to learn more about the bandit chief and the health and morale of the hostages, whose fates hung in the balance.

"I advise you to print in large letters that *there's no hope of the prisoners being released in short time*," the old priest said as General Tien walked away. "Who thinks otherwise is ignorant of the ways of mountain outlaws."[22]

No one was surprised when Shanghai publisher and ad man Carl Crow volunteered to lead a relief mission after hearing that prominent members in the Shanghai expatriate community had been taken hostage by bandits.[23] Polished and with a good-natured smile, Crow loved to shoot the breeze with friends and clients about the latest advertising trends in the booming China market. He was extraordinarily perceptive and understood the China game better than most. Crow was also chairman of the Shanghai chapter of the American Red Cross and was prepared to carry the American Red Cross flag to Tsaochuang.

Crow not only had the requisite sense of adventure; he also felt a professional obligation to ensure that the rescue efforts came off successfully. Since 1913, he had written and published the leading guidebook of China for Western tourists, business travelers, and missionaries. Now in its third edition, *The Travelers' Handbook for China* was already a classic. Crow peddled the idea that travel in China was safe and that the bandits were harmless, their presence adding only "zest rather than danger to the journey." But now that those same bandits were threatening to kill dozens of foreign travelers, Crow believed that his credibility, as well as China's reputation as a safe destination for travelers, was at stake. What's more, his best friend, John Powell, was one of the hostages, and Crow knew that Martha Powell was quite fearful about her husband's well-being. Besides, why let J. B. have all the fun and attention?

Crow arrived at Tsaochuang from Shanghai with a half-dozen suitcases of food and clothing to establish what he called the "American Rescue Mission," even though it was not sanctioned by the US government. He set himself up in a used railroad carriage in the walled mining compound, next door to the American diplomats. Within days, the American Rescue Mission enlisted local peasants to carry supplies to the bandits' stronghold for use by the hostages. The supply line quickly became known as the "Coolie Express."

CHAPTER 14

THE AMERICAN FIXER

The Chinese soon found that this tall, heavy bodied giant of a man not only knew their own language better than they knew it but that they could trust him with their most important secrets. They also learned that no Chinese had a deeper love for China than his. In China, wherever Roy sat, that was the head of the table.

—Carl Crow, publisher and the chief of the American Rescue Mission[1]

MAY 12, 1923, TSAOCHUANG MINING COMPOUND AND DRAGON DOOR TEMPLE

While officials in Peking squabbled over the right way to resolve the hostage standoff, Marshal Tsao Kun, the northern warlord to whom General Tien reported, was making decisions unilaterally. He was beginning to understand that the bandits lacked faith in Tien, who was at least nominally under his command. To mediate a resolution to the crisis, he needed a neutral interlocutor—someone who would be respected by all parties. There was only one man for the job: Roy Anderson.[2]

Anderson had arrived at Tsaochuang with Carl Crow, Consul Davis, and other US diplomats on the evening of May 9, each finding sleeping quarters

American fixer Roy Scott Anderson at the Tsaochuang mining compound. (SHSMO)

in a dilapidated train car in the rail yard of the walled mining compound. Throughout the day, they huddled together—smoking and drinking—trying to figure out the objectives of the bandit chiefs and the Chinese military and to come up with a possible way out of the predicament. Anderson warned Crow that his six suitcases of food and provisions wouldn't last the weekend, prompting the ad man to send a telegram to Shanghai seeking additional donations from the American Red Cross and the business community.

Anderson's timing was fortuitous. At the bandit camp, Sun Mei-yao needed someone to go down to Tsaochuang and request that a medical doctor be sent up to attend to Musso and Saphiere—valuable captives who couldn't be allowed to die. All Sun had to do was read the newspaper reports to know how important, and how wealthy, these hostages were. Whereas several days ago he had almost gotten shot for slowing the bandits down as they fled to higher ground, Musso was now regarded by the chieftain as his "prize captive"—so the newspapers said.

Sun also needed someone to request provisions because they were running out of food and the local village fare was not working for the finicky foreigners. At the same time, he thought that this would be an opportunity to get someone to carry their message, once again, that the troops needed to stand down. Sun's impression was that captive Jerome Henley was the least valuable and least useful of the captives. Sun had noticed that Henley was ostracized by the other captives because of his constant gabbing and overweening, which was getting on everyone's nerves.

On May 11 Sun ordered Henley's release on condition that he return to the camp by Sunday night, May 13. Henley, a traveling salesman originally from San Francisco, was allowed to pass through the military lines on a smallish donkey wearing only his pajamas, his lanky legs dangling almost to the ground. Sun gave Henley explicit instructions to return to the camp as instructed, or the remainder of the captives would be shot.

Henley made his way down the mountain, and as with the arrival of the two white boys the day before, the tower guards were surprised to see an oddly dressed foreigner coming toward the gate waving his hands and flopping on the back of a donkey. As Henley came through the gate, a menagerie of reporters, foreign consuls, Anderson, Crow, and Chinese government officials immediately surrounded him.

While Henley rambled about how sore he was from riding the donkey, the onlookers were more interested in receiving information about the captives and their well-being. Henley informed the consuls that fifteen foreign men and one woman, Teresa Verea, were held by the bandits, as were close to one hundred Chinese, many of them prominent or wealthy. All captives were well, said Henley, except for Musso and Saphiere. Yet food was scarce, and certain items like blankets and army cots were needed immediately.

Anderson believed that Henley's obligation to return to the camp was an opportunity to open the door for negotiations. Crow saw an opportunity, too; he chirped up and said that he would send back with Henley a squad of coolie carriers and a first round of supplies.

Anderson made it to the bandit camp on the morning of May 12, the sixth day of captivity. Given Anderson's imposing stature, it took a crew of four coolies to carry him in a sedan chair up through the military lines to the bandit camp at the Dragon Door Temple. Sun had been expecting Anderson; runners had alerted him of the slow-moving, shaded sedan chair coming up the slight grade carrying in Cleopatrian fashion a large white man wearing a pith helmet.

Anderson was escorted to one of the temple's large structures and seated across from Sun and Po-Po Liu. They began by drinking tea and exchanging pleasantries. But soon the bandits lapsed into elaborate formal speeches that had no real purpose other than venting their frustration. Anderson knew this was coming and carefully listened, allowing Sun to rationalize his position. He saw that this was just the opening of negotiations, and he was trying to build trust. He didn't want to get too aggressive with the bandits until he knew exactly what they wanted, as well as what the Chinese government was willing to offer. Anderson also wanted to understand the dynamics between the various bandit chiefs and subchiefs. He could see that there were not just ex-soldiers among their ranks but also drug addicts, hardened criminals, and starving peasants. Money wasn't irrelevant to these men, but it didn't seem to be the primary goal of their leaders. The bandits wanted something more. However, their most urgent demand was that Tien's men stand down.

"You have my word," Anderson said. "I will take your message to the army to raise the siege and withdraw the troops as a first step." This was essentially the same message that had already been conveyed by the hostage messengers and that was brought down to Tsaochuang by Father Lenfers. Yet Anderson hoped that he could succeed where they had so far failed.

Even if he couldn't get Tien to stand down, Anderson believed that this meeting had been productive, that he had generated a rapport with Sun, and that the door was now open for further negotiations. "I will return in the next day or so," he said. "Until then, I would like to suggest that you release the two older, grey-haired captives." He meant British tourist William Smith and Major Allen. "They don't have the stamina, and their health is fragile." Anderson knew the request was a long shot, but he told Sun that releasing these men would also show the waiting diplomats down at the mining compound that the bandits were willing to be reasonable. But Sun had no intention of releasing anyone until some of his demands were met. Besides, he had already released a score of foreign captives over the past few days, including the Pinger and Allen boys, to send messages that, so far, seemed to have fallen on deaf ears.

BACK IN WASHINGTON, D.C., ON MAY 12, PRESIDENT WARREN HARDing summoned Chinese minister Shih Chao-chi—known in the English-speaking world as Dr. Alfred Sze—to the White House to lodge his concerns over the bandit outrage. Since 1921, Dr. Sze had been the head of China's legation in Washington, and he had a good relationship with the US president. Harding was now well aware of the Lincheng Incident from reports from the State Department. He expressed grave concerns about the kidnapping of innocent civilians and pointed out that press reports of the Lincheng Incident continued to make front-page headlines. It was good news that Rockefeller's sister-in-law had been released, but the American people were now actively following the story in the daily press reports and were greatly alarmed that some of their compatriots were still being held hostage.

Minister Sze assured the president that his government was doing everything possible to win the release of the hostages. He claimed that definitive results would likely be obtained "in the next twelve hours." When President Harding asked him who was behind the affair, Sze deflected all blame and claimed that foreign gunrunners—most likely the Japanese—had played a role in arming the bandits: "The bandits were equipped with automatic firearms that could only have been obtained in violation of the general agreement among the powers that no arms would be permitted to reach lawless bands in China." He then insisted that the Peking government should not be held entirely responsible and that "the foreign governments should take greater pains to enforce their pledge against arms shipments."[3]

Harding scoffed at Sze's response. He was in no mood to debate the responsibility of foreign governments in the affair, especially because the Chinese themselves controlled both Shantung Province and the Tientsin-Pukow Railway. The president reminded Sze that—following Harding's own efforts at calling the Washington Conference—the Chinese were now in possession of Tsingtao and the rest of Shantung. It had been five months

since the takeover, and the Peking government should have already taken
control of the province.

Not unsurprisingly, the Japanese media had been quick to compare the
Lincheng Incident with the Boxer uprising in 1900 and argued that such
lawlessness proved that it was necessary for the stationing of foreign troops
in the municipal centers of China. There was no better way to prove to the
world that Japan should recover resource-rich Shantung than to trigger a
political crisis that would lead to international military intervention. Then
Japan would naturally be able to contribute a contingent to the international force on the basis that its interests were affected and, in doing so,
retake control, in whole or in part, of Tsingtao and Shantung Province.[4]
Harding wanted to prevent this from happening, but the Peking government needed to take decisive action to solve the hostage crisis without delay.

ANDERSON DEPARTED TSAOCHUANG FOR A SECOND ROUND OF NEGOTIA-
tions with the bandits on the morning of May 13.[5] As he rode the sedan
chair up to the camps, Anderson was startled to hear sporadic gunshots as
he passed the military lines up to the camps. *The troops should've backed off
by now,* he thought. When Anderson arrived at the camp, he immediately
realized that the mood of the chiefs had soured since the previous day's visit.

Sun was riled, and he was growing angrier. He chided Anderson for the
troops' continued presence. Government snipers had apparently shot and
killed a number of their sentries, forcing them to retreat to higher ground.
"Withdrawal of the troops was first and foremost the key to any negotiations!" the bandit chief repeated.

Anderson was contrite. He tried to calm the bandit leader down by telling him that General Tien himself, to his face, had assured him that the
troops had been ordered to withdraw. But Anderson immediately realized
that merely mentioning the name of the Shantung military governor was
not prudent. Sun was seething: "General Tien is a dishonest man who can't
be trusted."

Anderson knew that government troops had encircled the bandits, but
he was not aware that snipers were picking off the bandit sentries, a provocative move that impeded any attempt at negotiations. Anderson could see

that Sun was angry, but he wanted to continue to build a rapport. "I will take this issue directly to Marshal Tsao Kun," Anderson said. This, at least, seemed to have a calming effect on Sun. Then Anderson delicately asked Sun for his terms and conditions. "What would it take to have the hostages released?"

The bandit chief shook his head in feigned disgust, as if he did not want to even begin negotiations until the troops had withdrawn. Sun took a deep breath and let out a heavy sigh. Anderson could sense that the young bandit chief had a talent for high drama and knew that it was best to let him play the victim. Sun then began to state the conditions for the release of the foreign captives, including the complete withdrawal of the surrounding government troops and the formation of two brigades of eight thousand men, taken from the bandit ranks. Anderson caught on to Sun's game quickly. He knew quite well that Sun did not have eight thousand men at his disposal but that he hoped to cobble together his own larger army from the bandit ranks of nearby districts and provinces.

The Chinese government would also need to recognize the bandit brigades as separate and independent, and to be garrisoned in three districts of southern Shantung. Sun would be appointed as commander of this army. Sun also demanded back pay, and he asked that food, clothing, arms, and ammunition be sent daily to the bandits during negotiations. Most importantly, he wanted any agreement that he hashed out with the Peking government to be guaranteed and signed by the foreign countries whose citizens were among Sun's hostages: Britain, France, Italy, Mexico, and the United States.[6]

Anderson thought Sun was mad. There was not a chance in Hell, he said to himself, that Peking would allow "a group of bandits, revolutionaries, mutineers, insurrectionists, or whatever, to form their own army in a carved-out section of the country." The Republican government was just then struggling to reunify China and demilitarize and disband its excessive number of troops. Empowering a bandit army in a breakaway region did not exactly advance its strategic goals.

Anderson wanted to reply to these demands with a firm but measured response, although he knew that Sun could be volatile and was likely to respond indignantly to any lecture that Anderson had in store for him. So

he simply nodded to say that he understood and that he would take his demands to the government authorities. It was getting late in the afternoon,
and Anderson needed to head back down to Tsaochuang before dark.

Before leaving the camp, Anderson walked over to a group of the foreign
captives, who could tell that the discussions weren't going well. "You look
seriously peeved," Major Allen said to him.

"Yeah, there's a hitch in the proceedings, and the chiefs are asking for too
much," Anderson said. "Hang in there until I get back."

Anderson returned to Tsaochuang that evening at about ten o'clock, tired
and sore from the journey and carrying the demands of the bandits. General Tien immediately summoned him to hear the latest demands. Anderson
thought that Tien had no business ordering him around. He answered only
to Marshal Kun and viewed Tien as the bandits' foremost antagonist, the
man who was possibly responsible for the entire affair. Yet, in the spirit of
cooperation, he decided to give the general a short, late-night debriefing on
the events of the day.

Anderson told Tien he found the bandit leaders to be receptive to a resolution, but negotiations would take time and challenges remained, given
the lack of trust between the Chinese government and the bandits. Anderson confirmed that the villagers were in league with the bandits, and
although the villagers may have feared the tufei, they also feared the soldiers who were supposed to protect them. Anderson told the general that
his soldiers were only making his work harder.[7] He explained that he was
trying to build rapport with the chiefs and planned to return to the camp
for further discussions. But his progress depended on the quick withdrawal
of the troops. "If the troops do not stand down, nothing can be negotiated,"
Anderson stressed to the warlord.

ON MONDAY, MAY 14, ALMOST TEN DAYS AFTER THE INITIAL TRAIN ROB-
bery, Minister Schurman gave the keynote address at a general meeting
of the American Chamber of Commerce in Shanghai. The turnout had
been large and included representatives of the tight-knit American business
community, educational institutions, and missionary interests. With the
Peking Express on everyone's mind, the crowd was deeply anxious. Most

attendees were friends or acquaintances of the American hostages from Shanghai: Friedman, Powell, and Solomon.

Schurman commenced by applauding the efforts of the chamber in financially supporting the American Rescue Mission, as well as the efforts of Paul Whitham and his staff at the Asia Development Company for their work at Lincheng and Tsaochuang. He proudly noted that it was the US contingent—and specifically Carl Crow—that was providing supplies of food and clothing to the foreign and Chinese captives. But then Schurman was almost immediately peppered with a litany of questions from members of the audience adamant that the United States should do more to protect the lives and property of American citizens in China.

How soon will the hostages be released?
Should we be sending in the US armed forces?
What will the United States do to prevent further outrages like this from happening in the future?

Question after question came from the audience. Schurman tried to persuade his fellow Americans that the disorder in China needed to be fixed by the Chinese people and that foreign military intervention would not be effective, but the emotional crowd remained unconvinced. He did not have all the answers, he explained, but was optimistic that a resolution was forthcoming and that the hostages would soon be home. He assured them he had mobilized the best resources of the US government in China—Consul Davis, Major Philoon, and Major Horsfall—and that the legation and consulate staff, as a whole, was focused on doing everything possible to hasten the release of the hostages as well as to ensure the protection of the persons and property of US citizens. "As painful as it is," Schurman said, "the community needs to be patient."

Little did he know that the hostage situation was about to escalate. At the very moment that Schurman stood before the American community in Shanghai, the hostages and bandits were on the march once again, this time to Paotzuku Mountain.

CHAPTER 15

THE MOUNTAIN STRONGHOLD

We moved again, still going east, crossed over another pass in the hills and there saw not far off the huge mass of Paotzuku. . . . It is far away from any human habitations, in a cul-de-sac of the hills, with steep natural rock walls on three sides and a man-built wall on the fourth side.

—Major Robert A. Allen, American tourist and hostage[1]

MAY 13, 1923, SUNSET, DRAGON DOOR TEMPLE

After a full week in captivity, the hostages had reconciled themselves to life at the Dragon Door Temple and neighboring villages. Food and clothing were being sent up to the camp, and they could bathe in the clean, clear water of the nearby stream. The captives were also allowed to freely move from camp to camp, and they were all reassured by the presence of American fixer Roy Anderson. Freedom, they assumed, was just a matter of time.

But they also started to hear more than the usual shooting and firefights coming up from the south. They knew that the government troops had not withdrawn as promised. Every day, the troops were getting closer. The bandits grew more agitated as the army snipers cut down their comrades. Dead and seriously wounded young bandits were dragged up to the temple compound for all to view.

On almost a nightly basis, Chinese government troops clashed with groups of bandits who were headed to the Dragon Door Temple to consolidate their forces with those of Sun Mei-yao. The government feared that brigands in nearby provinces viewed the Lincheng Incident as an opportunity to address their own grievances, and General Tien was not going to allow the bandit ranks to swell any further. In a series of fierce firefights, Tien's men pushed the would-be recruits back and managed to contain Sun's army.

By nightfall on May 13, Sun believed that his position was vulnerable. His meeting with Anderson had convinced him of that, knowing that it was uncertain whether the American fixer would be able to convince the Chinese army to stand down. He decided to take the hostages and flee to the superior safety and security of Paotzuku Mountain, the principal bandit stronghold in southern Shantung. They would march ten miles under the cover of darkness and take shelter in the Temple of the Clouds at the foothills of Paotzuku.[2] The strategy was to use the captives as cover and to fight or bribe their way through military lines.

At the same time, they would also initiate a number of attacks as diversionary tactics to allow them to clear a path as they made their way to Paotzuku Mountain. Sun sent small contingents of bandits to attack two coal trains on the spur line near Tsaochuang, drawing troops away from the military lines. To make matters worse for the government, the five hundred soldiers who had been guarding the coal trains put up no resistance—they had not received their salaries for more than a year and refused to fight the bandits.[3] Meanwhile, Sun's allies attacked the railroad station at Shakou—ten miles south of Lincheng—seizing the local stationmaster and demanding ransom. The raid was eventually repelled by the government troops after a fierce firefight, although it was a success, given Sun's aims: it distracted the attention of the troops away from the main bandit army.

When word of the attack on the coal trains and on the Shakou station reached Tsaochuang, the foreign diplomatic corps and relief workers began to fear that they were in imminent danger of an attack on the fortified mining compound.[4] Sun's army had attracted nearby bandits, and their combined force now numbered over two thousand, with the ranks still growing. The Peking government feared—not without justification—that China was witnessing a full-scale revolution led by disgruntled ex-soldiers.

At two o'clock in the morning of May 14, the captives heard the dreaded words "Tsou, tsou" rousing them from their sleep. They packed the latest provisions on horses and donkeys and set out toward the east. The night was dark, but the moon and stars provided enough light to show the path forward. They marched seven miles up the valley.

At daybreak, the hostages and their guards arrived at a small, gritty village set at the foot of a rocky hill. The village looked like it had been heavily bombarded. It was completely deserted, and most of the buildings had been burned to the ground by passing troops months earlier—part of General Tien's scorched-earth strategy to rout the bandits at whatever cost. At least half of the remaining structures were roofless. *This village is all but dead. No cattle, sheep, or goats—not even a chicken*, Major Allen thought.[5]

As the bandits and hostages fled, two Chinese captives managed to escape to Tsaochuang, where they were greeted by a throng of foreign consuls, correspondents, and military officials. One of the men had been a train guard. He explained to the inquisitive crowd that the bandits and hostages were on the march again, and this time to a place the bandits called Paotzuku. Tien—seeking to control the information flow—hustled the two former captives away from the prying foreign consular representatives who sought information on the movements of their nationals. Cutting them off, he warned the two escapees in Chinese not to speak to the foreign reporters or diplomats.[6]

"General, what is going on, where are the hostages?" called out Consul Davis.

"As I warned you, the bandits have escaped with the hostages to their mountain stronghold," Tien said, seeming almost to revel in this latest bit of bad news.

Anderson and the foreign diplomats turned away with a great sense of unease as Tien stormed off. They didn't want to waste their time arguing

with the warlord: he was convinced that he should have been given free rein
to use force against the bandits. "If he had his way," said Anderson, "we
would have nothing but dead hostages." They all agreed that the only reason the bandits absconded further into the countryside was because they
were tired of fending off the government troops that Tien refused to withdraw. He and his generals were squarely to blame.

AFTER AN ALL-NIGHT HIKE, THE CAPTIVES SAT DOWN FOR A BREAKFAST
of tinned sardines, crackers, boiled eggs, and tea. They were about two-
thirds of the way to Paotzuku Mountain. They then rested for several hours
before starting off again. While savoring their grub from the Coolie Express, they realized that the outlaws had no food. Although they scrounged
around for local fare, there was nothing in the destroyed villages for the
bandits to eat. The captives grinned at one another, taking clever delight in
enjoying their meal as the hungry bandits looked on. Some of the bandits
helped themselves to the canned sardines and milk, whereas others waited
politely to be offered food by the hostages. Eventually, the hostages gave
them about half of their bread and crackers.[7]

A group of bandit scouts interrupted the meal with news that Tien's
troops had been spotted nearby. The bandit guards consulted with one another, trying to plot a path forward that avoided combat with the army.
Eventually, after the scouts thought that the coast was clear, the captives
and bandits continued on across the broad valley heading northeast. They
forded a shallow, gravel-bottomed river (the Tenli), then at sunset arrived at yet another partially destroyed village, which the bandits called
Pei Chuang. The hostages were sheltered here in old temple structures or
stables. At night, the field mice had the run of the place, scampering over
the prisoners as they lay down. Despite the miserable accommodations,
the hostages were so exhausted after their twenty-hour hike that they all
quickly fell asleep.[8]

At dawn, Major Allen lay awake, watching a mud swallow build its cup-
shaped nest, tucked into the rafters of the partially open roof. He had been
awakened by the gentle flutter and flapping of the very active bird, which
was a skillful carpenter. It would fly in with a mouthful of mud, which it

would carefully lay on the growing wall of its habitation, chirping softly to itself as it positioned the moist clay into place; then away it would fly to get another mouthful. Springtime was breeding time for the swallows, and they were very busy racing in and out of the structures, carrying mud and grass for nesting materials. The swallow kept up its efforts, unconcerned about the humans sleeping on the floor below. For Allen, watching this act of nature brought a brief respite of peace before the next day's march.

After breakfast, several of the captives went down to the river and washed their clothes in the clear, cold mountain water. In the afternoon, they started out once again to the northeast. They crossed over a gap in the hills and could see in the distance a huge, cone-shaped rock mass with a skirt of lush green forests around its lower half. When this very distinctive mountain came into full view, the young bandits pointed and began to shout in unison: "Paotzuku! Paotzuku!" The bandits had made it home. The distant mountain was indeed stunning.

Located twelve miles northeast of Tsaochuang, Paotzuku was accessible by only one narrow pass. The outlaws had long used this *shanzhai* (mountain stronghold) as a rendezvous and sanctuary far away from official interference and control. They stored at its summit a large quantity of provisions, water, and weapons. They were not headed to the very top of Paotzuku—at least not yet—but to the Taoist retreat of San Ch'ing Temple (the Three Gods Temple), which the hostages would call the Temple of the Clouds. It was situated in a well-fortified walled compound that was tucked into a canyon on the west side of the mountain. From here, Sun Mei-yao knew that he could safely and securely imprison the hostages while negotiations proceeded.

Paotzuku had a long history as a haven for outlaws.[9] In the mid-1800s, it was the final refuge for the remainder of the Nien rebels who had carried out a peasant uprising directed against the Manchu Ch'ing Dynasty. Then, months before the Lincheng Incident, the suppression campaign by government troops placed a siege around Paotzuku to lock down and snuff out the bandit gang.

Paotzuku was a beautiful, quiet place, carpeted with a densely wooded deciduous forest, teeming with wildlife and thick flora. The karst pinnacle of Paotzuku towered above the surrounding foothills. The mountain was composed of sharp limestone surfaces at its upper echelon and shale and sandstone at its lower slopes. The topography of the region was dotted with caves, vertical shafts, and cascades of rock formations. Inside the many caves were intricate wall carvings of deities made centuries before.

As they approached the mountain, the captives couldn't help but contrast the lush surroundings to the devastation of the many villages they had passed. The temple had plenty of shade and a view down to the valley below. It was surrounded by hills, with steep natural rock walls on three sides and a man-made wall on the fourth side with a circular gate.[10]

As the bandit army and the hostages arrived at the Temple of the Clouds, they passed under the "moon gate." This circular passageway was thought to bring luck. It represented the continuous cycle of birth and death, as symbolized by the rising and falling of the moon. In the temple's inner courtyard was a ginkgo biloba tree that was said to be more than nine hundred years old and that was cultivated as an important source of traditional herbal medicines and food. The tree had lush branches and was adorned with red flags and streamers at the lower branches. At the top of the tree, large iridescent black-and-white Chinese magpies—an auspicious bird that symbolized happiness and good fortune—chattered in their large nests.

The four temple buildings were all made from cut stone and topped with exquisite, faded gray-blue tile. The roof edges were adorned by Chinese zodiac and mythological figures and by symbols for good health, wealth, and longevity. Each of the temple structures had high ceilings with rafters held up by large, roughly cut logs.

Inside, the floors were made of rough compressed earth, and the back wall held an altar with a shrine featuring four- to six-feet-high painted terracotta statues of Taoist deities. The Temple of the Clouds was an active place of worship used by the bandits and villagers alike, and the presence of the newcomers did not impede temple activities. The captives watched as the bandits themselves displayed a sense of reverence as they bowed before the temple shrines.

With nighttime coming, the foreign captives split up into groups and took shelter in the temples. With no beds in sight, the captives found discarded doors, propped them up on bricks, and lay directly upon them,

British captive Reginald Rowlatt and banker Chi Cheng in a temple structure at the Temple of the Clouds in the foothills of Paotzuku Mountain that served as their sleeping quarters. (Pinger)

having no straw to soften their bedding. Sleeping was difficult on the unforgiving wood doors, and the captives were not prepared for the drop in temperatures inside the damp canyon walls or for the bugs that overran the complex. Major Pinger tied his trouser legs at the bottoms to keep his feet warm and wrapped his blanket around him.[11]

Sleep was also tenuous because the bandit guards—away from the combat zone—were in a jubilant mood, smoking opium and drinking *samshu*, playing mahjong and laughing and quarrelling late into the night. Their voices echoed off the canyon walls and kept the weary captives from sleeping. Someone in authority finally arrived at an early hour in the morning and gave the intoxicated guards a tongue-lashing. After that, peace generally reigned, and the captives were able to get some sleep, at least until the change of guard at the moon gate, which was supposed to happen every two hours. The guard on duty was not allowed to leave his post and had to yell for his relief, who could be asleep as far as two courtyards away in the temple compound. Both bandits would often scream back and forth at each other about the time, for neither had a watch and neither wanted to man the post. Each change of guard involved at least ten minutes of loud shouting about who was on duty.[12]

THE AMERICAN RESCUE MISSION'S COOLIE EXPRESS INITIALLY COM-
prised seventeen men and two guides. The caches of supplies would leave
Tsaochuang daily at five o'clock in the morning. Thirty to forty coolie
loads were sent out to the bandit camps each day.[13] After the bandits
and captives moved from the Dragon Door Temple to the Temple of the
Clouds, the coolies would then need to walk a round trip of twenty-four
miles a day, yet the additional distance did not cause any decrease in
the loads they carried or disturb the regularity of the daily trips. Each
day, the Coolie Express made its shipments, with each worker carrying
the standard weight of one *picul*—equivalent to 133 pounds, which was
traditionally thought to be the weight that could be carried on a man's
shoulder.

As time went on, the requests from the captives changed from the basic
necessities of food and clothing to camp cots and cooking utensils, reading
materials, cameras, and other items to reduce boredom. Carl Crow, who led
the effort, was concerned that a stalemate could result if negotiations broke
down, which might result in the porters being unable to reach the camps,
thereby cutting off the captives' supply of food and fresh water. So he tried
to send up a surplus of food and especially bottled water.[14] Crow provided
each of the captives with a traveling kit and emergency rations to be used in
the event of a forced march (or an escape attempt). Each of the captives also
received a personal medicine kit containing drugs for dysentery, iodine for
wounds, bandages, and other first-aid supplies.

The remoteness of Tsaochuang made it difficult to secure ample supplies,
especially foreign canned foods and other items. Crow bought out the two
local shops' supply of foreign goods in short order. He sent out a constant
flow of telegrams requisitioning supplies from the nearest possible point.
The food supplies included oatmeal, sugar, salt, potatoes, onions, bread and
biscuits, canned fruit, raisins, cheese, jam, butter, lime juice, grape juice,
distilled water, brandy, coffee, tea, rice, candy, and canned corned beef, sardines, salmon, and other meats. Given the climate and time of year, Crow
had trouble obtaining fresh vegetables beyond onions and potatoes. He
also found it difficult to deliver a sufficient amount of bottled water to meet
the captives' needs.[15]

Major Wallace Copeland "Cope" Philoon, US Army military attaché at the Tsaochuang mining compound, with two coolie workers for the American Rescue Mission preparing supplies for the trek up to the Dragon Door Temple and later to the Temple of the Clouds in the foothills of Paotzuku Mountain. (SHSMO)

In addition to food and water, Crow's team sent up other items of necessity, including toothbrushes, eating and cooking utensils, razors, underwear, toothpaste, bars of laundry soap, gallons of Jeyes and Lysol disinfectant fluid, bedding materials, mosquito nets, kerosene, sterno, toilet paper, candles, towels, and a complete lady's outfit for Teresa Verea, the sole remaining female hostage, who had been wearing the same men's clothing since the day of the train robbery.[16] They also sent up cigars, pipe tobacco, cigarettes, and writing supplies. For the bandits, the American Rescue Mission provided more than a hundred thousand cheap cigarettes and a thousand pounds of rice to be distributed among them to keep the bandits from appropriating the food sent to the prisoners.

Family members also started to send their detained relatives articles of clothing. The recovering Musso had not been able to find any clothing to fit him and continued to wear a long nightshirt until the Coolie Express sent him clothing given by his family. In the meantime, his fellow captives jokingly called him "the Roman senator" because he hobbled around the camp in what appeared to be a toga. The wives of Pinger and Allen started sending clothing, books, letters, newspapers, and other items to their husbands. The extended family of the Shanghai cousins and Friedman's brother in Shanghai did the same.

Crow quickly realized that feeding the sixteen foreign captives and scores of Chinese captives took serious funding, not just what could be drummed up from the foreign business community in Shanghai, Tientsin, and Peking. One day, Crow casually mentioned to Roy Anderson that he was just about out of money and would have to return to Shanghai for more. "Don't bother to do that," the American fixer said. "I'll go over to the other train and dig some cash out of the civil governor of Shantung."

Anderson returned a few minutes later and handed Crow a stack of bills too large to be rolled or folded. The pile contained bills of large denominations. Wide-eyed with amazement, Crow asked Roy how much was there. "I don't know," Anderson said. "I just told the governor you needed a hell of a lot of money." Crow counted out $7,000—more than enough to keep the rescue mission in business for the time being.[17]

At the request of family and the Italian consulate, Musso's personal physician, Dr. Paul Mertens, arrived at Tsaochuang the morning of May 17. Father Lenfers volunteered to escort Dr. Mertens to the Temple of the Clouds. As they approached the camp on horseback just south of the temple grounds, Lenfers and Mertens heard a signal shot and saw bandit guards stationed along the mountain ridges closely watching them as they made their way toward the temple. They continued cautiously until they were halted at the outer camp of the outlaws. The bandit chiefs had strong words for Lenfers, feeling cheated and deceived because the troops had still not withdrawn as promised. The army troops were now only four miles away and continued to engage in firefights.[18] After much persuasion, however, the bandit chiefs allowed Lenfers and Mertens to walk up to the temple grounds to visit Musso.

Mertens had arrived none too soon, for he brought to the camps much-needed surgical instruments and medicine. Prior to his arrival, Major Allen had provided medical treatment to several of the hostages, including the interpreter Hung, who was unable to sleep on account of the pain in his foot, which was badly swollen because of an abscess. Lacking surgical equipment, the only thing that Allen could do was to take an old safety-razor blade and affix it to a piece of wood, creating a makeshift scalpel. A young Chinese prisoner who worked for a Shanghai doctor assisted him. Allen boiled up a razor blade and a pair of hemostats and drained the abscess.[19]

Mertens directed his attention to Musso, who was the worst of the lot, having an injured back and frail heart. He tended to other captives who needed medical attention, including Saphiere, who, like Hung, had a severely infected foot.[20]

With the hostages' basic needs covered, life at the Temple of the Clouds began to normalize, and the captives settled in for the long haul. Pinger and Allen received from Major Philoon four of the latest editions of the *Army & Navy Journal*—a luxury read for bored US military officers interested in catching up with the latest army gossip. The rescue mission also sent in some much-needed carbolic soap—for removing the lice that had infested their clothing.[21] Morale improved as supplies increased. Solomon and Major Pinger received cameras from their wives—something that they thought would come in handy. Initially, they kept the instruments hidden from the bandits to avoid the risk of confiscation. In time, the bandits became more comfortable with posing and invited Solomon and Pinger to take their photos.

Meanwhile, Allen, Friedman, Solomon, and Pinger played bridge together in the temple courtyard to pass the time in the fine spring weather. The jollity and merriment of the Shanghai cousins, nicknamed the FEET Club—Freddie, Eddie, Emile, and Theo—brought levity to the camp with their endless impromptu performances throughout the day. They also exchanged news clippings received in the mail, and the cousins were especially delighted that Bobby and Roland had their story printed in worldwide newspapers, photo and all. They were in a good mood, and their letters to family reflected that they had adjusted well to their surroundings.

In addition to supplying provisions, the American Rescue Mission managed a mail service that Carl Crow called the "Bandit Post," which operated daily. At daylight, a fast-running coolie would leave Tsaochuang with letters and small packages and return the same day with outgoing mail. The

Shanghai publisher and community leader Carl Crow at the Tsaochuang mining compound in the American Rescue Mission's train car. (SHSMO)

system worked with the regularity and precision of a postal service. The mission's mail carriers were provided with heavy canvas mailbags, which were locked with a padlock—these the bandits allowed through the military lines without interference. One key was kept at the American Rescue Mission, and the other was sent up to Powell to be used by the camps. At first this service carried only a few letters a day, but as friends from Shanghai and elsewhere began writing to the captives and as they began replying to all the letters received, the Bandit Post was soon handling from fifty to one hundred letters a day each way.[22]

The train car used by the American Rescue Mission included a simple post office box. Not only did the relatives and friends of the captives use the Bandit Post, but the foreign and Chinese officials also used it in their communications to the chiefs. Even the bandits used the Bandit Post system to communicate with Tsaochuang. The twice-daily arrival of the mail from the bandit camp was considered the biggest event of the day. All of Tsaochuang gathered around the incoming mailbags to learn how the hostages were coping or to get an idea of the bandit chiefs' stance on negotiations. This fed the hungry correspondents with the daily coverage they needed to generate buzz for the newswires.

Relief packages from relatives and friends increasingly grew larger. One item that started to take a toll on the service was books and other materials sent by the friends and relatives of the captives. But the Bandit Post continued to deliver everything on time.

One afternoon, Crow came across a ramshackle lithographer shop in the little village surrounding the Tsaochuang mining compound. In order to help raise the captives' morale, he came up with the idea of designing mock postage stamps to affix to their mail.[23] With the old Chinese gentleman running the shop, Crow drew up a crude design for two stamps using sketches on paper. He then sent the finished stamps up to the captives with a humorous letter telling them that "we had been carrying mail free long enough and that hereafter all letters would have to be stamped."

The whole thing may have only started as a joke, designed to while away a tedious afternoon, but the stamps were a hit with the captives, and they used them on letters coming down from the bandit camp. In time, the stamps would adorn hundreds of outbound letters to family and friends around the world. Interestingly, one Shanghai newspaper was hoodwinked into believing that the bandit chief himself, Sun Mei-yao, had issued the stamps. This triggered the interest of collectors and philatelic dealers, who started sending telegrams and letters to Crow requesting stamps at any price, even though the stamps had no real value and were not recognized by the Chinese postal authorities.

With the daily mail service, everyone wrote home about his or her dirty appearance, ragged clothing, growing whiskers, and general outlook. "We are a queer lot with our wonderful assortment of garments and our unshaven faces," said Rowlatt, the British prisoner. "We look more like bandits than the bandits themselves." In one letter to the American Club in Shanghai, Leon Friedman poked fun at himself as "Schlemihl the Jew Bandit," using the Yiddish word for an "unlucky person."[24]

Powell also tried to laugh at his predicament: "I have associated so long and intimately with these Chinese bandits that I am getting to be like one of them from the standpoint of procrastination and time doesn't mean much up here on Paotzuku." He also used comedy to tell Martha that he missed her: "One thing you may feel certain [of is] that I have been absolutely true and virtuous to you since I left home—and now I suppose you will say 'through necessity' because the only thing of the female gender that has been near our camp is a female donkey—so there you are!"[25]

LEON FRIEDMAN WAS A COMMITTED BACHELOR WHO LIKED TO COOK FOR himself. Although he was wealthy enough to have chefs catering to his mealtime needs during his busy workweek in Shanghai, he was a connoisseur of fine cuisine and took on the role as the camp cook at the Temple of the Clouds.[26] With Powell's help, Friedman constructed a brick stove that used coal from the Tsaochuang mines. Their dining room was inside one of the temple structures and composed of temple doors elevated on bricks and rocks. In lieu of chairs, everyone sat on the wooden crates used to transport bottles of distilled water. Until the Coolie Express sent up utensils, they used their hands or makeshift chopsticks.

Friedman's favorite dishes included French toast, broiled pork leg stew in garlic, and a pudding made from a mixture of oatmeal, local cherries, and raisins supplied by the relief mission. Itinerant cherry peddlers occasionally passed through the bandit camp, trading their harvests for cigarettes from the captives. The main courses usually involved canned meats—bully beef, pork sausage, poultry, and tuna—but Friedman also prepared lighter, vegetable-based dishes such as potato and onion soup and recipes with canned fruits and vegetables.

One of the most interesting delicacies perfected by Friedman was called a scorpion roll. Scorpions were plentiful in the local mountains, and fried scorpions were a regional delicacy. Friedman watched the locals boil the bodies and remove the stingers and shells. They would then chop up the shrimp-like tail meat with red peppers and garlic, rolling the mixture into kaoliang flour cakes. Finicky at first, the captives eventually found this mountain specialty to be quite tasty, though very spicy.

THE FOREIGN CAPTIVES AND VISITING PHYSICIANS FREQUENTLY TOOK the opportunity to help the wounded or injured bandits—not just for humanitarian reasons but also to win their hearts and minds. *Acts of kindness might keep us alive*, thought Major Allen, who frequently dressed the wounds of the bandits. One unfortunate young bandit had sustained a gunshot wound during the initial firefights with the pursuing troops, and it shattered the entire length of his left forearm. In time his dangling, wounded arm festered with infection. His comrades fed him opium to dull the pain, although his situation was viewed as hopeless. The foreign captives pitied him and tried to help by cleaning and bandaging his wound.[27] Proper medical care for the severely wounded bandit could be administered only at the infirmaries in Tsaochuang or by nearby missionary groups, but this required that he get past the military lines and surrender—a certain death sentence. He shuffled about the temple grounds for several weeks and then disappeared. The captives never learned of his fate but assumed he succumbed to gangrene.

Another young bandit, nicknamed "Big Lip," suffered from a serious mouth injury caused by the recoil of an improperly held rifle. His torn lips, broken teeth, and bruised cheeks put him in excruciating pain. With a few sutures, Allen and Mertens stitched his lips, which aided the healing process. As he recovered, Big Lip started working for Friedman as a kitchen assistant, eager to please by retrieving water and running errands. This was an opportunity to be rewarded with food, cigarettes, and other niceties that the foreigners received from the rescue mission. Friedman was also impressed by the young bandit's hard work and life story. Big Lip claimed that he was a farmer who lived near the rail line and was press-ganged into the army. He eventually deserted and walked home to southern Shantung, where he joined Sun Mei-yao's group to defend his local village.

MUSSO AND FRIEDMAN WERE THE CENTER OF MOST OF THE INTENSE DIScussions and debates on politics, these lasting late into the night, a place where well-read men could converse on a host of geopolitical topics. Powell, Allen, Pinger, Rowlatt, and Solomon would join in. Professor Hung and Chi Cheng would listen intently to the debates and chirp up frequently to give the educated Chinese viewpoint. And the elderly Smith would sit quietly on the periphery, consumed in his own thoughts yet eager to listen in to the learned discussions. This was not just a group of adolescents at a Boy Scout campout but powerful and influential journalists, businessmen, and military officers who helped shape the views of the West regarding China and its place in the world.

Musso loved to talk about global politics. He had a long history in Asia and a strong command of the political whims and institutions of China.

Musso lamented the persistent lack of leadership. Six months earlier, he had met with Mussolini, the fascist dictator of Italy, and thought China could benefit from a similar kind of strongman. "The people of Italy had much faith in Fascist rule," said Musso, "and I believe that Mussolini is level-headed, patriotic and sincere, and someone like him would be good for the Chinese people." Because of Mussolini, he told his campfire audience, Italy was no longer at risk of the Bolshevik epidemic causing upheavals throughout Europe and Russia.[28]

"Would that be someone like Marshal Tsao Kun? Or Sun Yat-sen?" Friedman asked. "With so many warlords and Tuchuns, it's hard to see who that leader may be."

Musso grew thoughtful. At present, there was much chaos, but out of that chaos order will eventually evolve, he said. Musso was convinced that China would awake to a great future: "I am persuaded that such a man, if not already in evidence, will be forthcoming." But China's success, he believed, hinged not only on a charismatic leader but also on developing strong commercial ties with trading partners in Asia and around the world. Musso, of course, would have much to gain if China thrived economically, given his financial interests in real estate, Shanghai's modern tramway system with its more than three hundred tramcars servicing fourteen routes, and various newspapers such as the *South China Morning Post*—as well as the still-flourishing underground opium trade: "In trade and commerce lies her surest hope of redemption, because when trade is good, the people are prosperous and satisfied, and people who are satisfied have no time to waste on, nor ears to hear, frothy demagogues spouting out their self-interested vaporing."

Meanwhile, the Vereas, still technically on their honeymoon, avoided the political debates and preferred to stroll through the surrounding forests together after dinner, finding some peace and romance in the land of banditry.

EARLY IN THE EVENING OF MAY 17, PROFESSOR HUNG TOLD THE GROUP that he had just heard the discouraging news that the bandit chiefs had called off all negotiations because General Tien's troops had been spotted less than a mile south of the temple complex. The foreign captives viewed Hung as a "very shrewd and tactful" go-between who was able to secure invaluable information concerning the thinking and strategy of the bandit chiefs. Solomon and Friedman called a meeting to compile a list of things they thought they would need for a long siege, namely more army cots and bedding. They also talked about how the bandit chiefs were moving supplies to the top of Paotzuku. "I wonder if they plan to force us up to the summit?" Major Allen asked his companions. "That is not a pleasant thought."

The Temple of the Clouds was remote enough to begin with, yet a climb to the top of the mountain meant further isolation. Then, as the captives were huddled around a campfire, Powell arrived at the temple courtyard with Lenfers. The two men were winded. "You won't believe what I saw," said Powell, catching his breath. "It will really make your flesh creep."[29]

CHAPTER 16

THE CHILDREN

If the spectacle of a group of little children in a semi-starved and diseased condition at the top of a bandit stronghold dying one by one does not arouse human compassion, then nothing will.

—Carl Crow, publisher and the chief of the American Rescue Mission[1]

MAY 17, 1923, EARLY AFTERNOON, TEMPLE OF THE CLOUDS

As it turned out, the passengers from the Peking Express were not the only hostages on Paotzuku. Earlier in the day, when Father Lenfers saw John Powell unpacking crates of food sent up by the Coolie Express, the old priest motioned him aside for a private conversation: "One of the local gentry told me that a group of the bandits has been kidnapping children from wealthy families, and that the gang was holding the children for ransom right above us at the top of Paotzuku Mountain." Clearly alarmed, Powell listened closely as Lenfers continued. "During the siege of Paotzuku several months ago, the bandits apparently pushed dozens of the children to their deaths over the sides of the mountain, and all because they lacked sufficient food and water."

"Terrible," Powell said. "How many children remain at the top?"

"It is uncertain the number that survived, but some have been held for years."

"We need to find out," Powell said. He then asked the Frenchman if he and the priest could have an escort, claiming they wished to hike around the west side of the mountain. The bandits were never worried that any of the foreign captives would escape because it was difficult to get through the military lines down the valley without a pass. But it required considerable diplomacy, in addition to several packages of cigarettes, before the bandits granted permission for the men to leave the immediate area of the temple grounds.[2] The plan was to hike around the forest area, but Powell and Lenfers would then need to somehow ditch the guards to reach the summit, where the children were supposedly being held hostage.

Lenfers, being more familiar with the habits of the bandits, told Powell to fill an army canteen with brandy. They climbed briskly for about an hour until they reached the base of the cliff, which rose almost perpendicularly to the summit, perhaps a thousand feet straight up above the surrounding land.[3] Sweating and out of breath, Powell, Lenfers, and the two guards sat down on a rock in the sun. With a wink at the priest, Powell handed the guards the canteen containing a full quart of home-brewed brandy. The two guards gulped down the concoction like milk and after a few minutes were stretched out asleep on the rock.

Lenfers and Powell then left the dozing guards behind and continued along a narrow path to the base of the cliff, where they came upon a crude ladder made of handholds chiseled into the limestone rock. There were small landings every fifty feet. When they looked down, they could still see the sleeping guards on the rock below. Powell led the way, with Lenfers following a few steps behind, his robe tucked up under his belt to give him freedom of movement.[4]

At one of the landings, the old priest could not go any farther on account of what he said was a weak heart. Knowing that time was limited, Powell hurried to the top of the summit and continued alone up the difficult and dangerous climb.

THE FINAL STAGE OF THE CLIMB TO THE SUMMIT OF PAOTZUKU WAS PAR-ticularly perilous, for it required going up the face of a nearly vertical granite cliff, in which the bandits had chiseled crude handholds or driven pegs into crevices. *Paotzuku* means the "Calf Carrying Hill." It earned this name because the sheer path up was so steep that grown oxen could not make the climb. So farmers, wishing to cultivate the plateau, had to carry up baby calves on their backs, which they would then graze on the mountaintop until they reached maturity and could be used as beasts of burden. It was a one-way trip to the top for a calf that would spend its entire life tilling the soil.

When he finally reached the summit, Powell saw a huge, unguarded wooden gate. The plateau was fairly level, and the bandits had built stone and earth defenses about the rim. The view of the surrounding countryside was extraordinary; even the Tenli River, three miles away, was visible. He noticed that practically all the surrounding mountains were terraced and farmed nearly to the tops, but few farmers were in the fields because of the presence of the bandits and the Chinese army.

On the top of Paotzuku, Powell noticed several stone huts covered with thatch and several large cisterns cut in the stone to catch rainwater.[5] Other tanks were filled and stored with grain and fuel. It seemed that the bandits had stocked the summit with food, water, firewood, and cooking utensils. If negotiations collapsed and the bandits were besieged, this is where they would make their last stand, dragging the hostages to the top of Paotzuku. *The bandits could hold out here almost indefinitely*, he thought.

When Powell heard noises coming from one of the large structures, he approached and pulled aside its straw-matting curtain. It was even worse than Lenfers had feared. The room was filled with children, little boys and one girl ranging in ages from eight to twelve years. The stench was suffocating. Powell counted about twenty-three children. Most of them were dressed in rags. A few wore the remnants of silk or satin robes, mute testimonials to the wealth of their families. He could tell that they were all suffering from diseases and on the brink of starvation.[6] At first, some of the children were frightened by the appearance of a tall white man and hid in the corner of the hut. But others warmed up to the stranger, whom they could see was very different from the bandit guards. Several of the boys approached Powell, touching his clothing and arms while speaking softly in Chinese, which he did not fully understand. Thinking that a foreigner had come to rescue them, their faces lit up with joy.

Little do they know that I, too, am a captive in a camp farther down the mountain.

POWELL WOULD LATER LEARN THAT MORE THAN A YEAR BEFORE THE EXpress train was held up, a subgroup of the bandits led by Po-Po Liu had been capturing and confining Chinese children from around the country, holding them for ransom from their parents. Kidnapping the children of wealthy merchants had been a chief enterprise of this gang for several years.

During the siege of Paotzuku in February, the bandits had ordered the murder of several of the children. Running low on water and food, and besieged by government soldiers, Liu reasoned that he had no choice but to order some of the children to be hurled off the mountaintop, which the bandits considered a more humane fate than letting them starve to death. In the two months just before the Lincheng Incident, forty-seven children had been thrown over the side of the cliff.[7]

THE CHATTERING CHILDREN ATTRACTED THE ATTENTION OF ONE OF THE bandit guards on the summit, who was startled to see a foreigner and instinctively swung his rifle in the direction of the intruder. Powell was unarmed, so all he could do was smile and greet him with a friendly gesture: "He understood the gesture, for I was holding out toward him a package of cigarettes."

After appeasing the guard, Powell quickly descended the summit to meet Lenfers. Together, they headed back down to the Temple of the Clouds, where they met with the other captives to inform them of what they had found.

PART 4

ALL OR NONE

CHAPTER 17

THE DEADLINE

In the Absence of strong specific instructions from the Peking Government, and with the knowledge that Tuchun Tien has no real control over this portion of his territory, it is open to any Chinese official to butt in and try his hand at arranging a settlement. Hence the number of Chinese officials now assembled here.

—Berthold G. Tours, Esq., consul general, British consulate, Tsinan[1]

MAY 18, 1923, THE WHITE HOUSE, WASHINGTON, D.C.

The Lincheng Incident became the subject of President Warren Harding's cabinet meetings and daily briefings, as well as his weekly poker games. As they played cards in a cloud of cigar smoke, Harding's advisers hashed out the political issues in China, the future of US-China relations, and whether Minister Schurman's strategy was working.[2] US commercial interests and investments were at stake, and a huge corps of missionaries, medical doctors, and charity workers and their families—living in the hinterland— were at personal risk. Harding was intrigued by the description of Paotzuku, seeking to get an idea of what the American hostages were up against. Secretary of State Charles Hughes showed him photographs of

southern Shantung Province, giving him a feel for the terrain and countryside.[3] In addition to his concern for the American nationals in China,
Harding was deeply worried about the tensions between China and Japan,
and Tokyo's incessant grumbling over the instability of its neighbor.[4]

It was becoming increasingly clear to Harding that China couldn't govern itself under the current chaotic warlord system. Yet, as Hughes told
the president, "Mr. Schurman's policy is 'to keep hammering' at the Chinese Government for the immediate and safe release of our nationals and to
hold up to them their exclusive responsibility."[5]

The calls for foreign military intervention increased daily. The pressure
came from the family, friends, and business associates of the hostages, as
well as from government officials and even the Vatican. The United States
needed to stay the course and not allow emotions to drive its policy, and to
avoid falling into a trap of using its military to intervene. The risk of doing
so would effectively weaken the Peking government—which was exactly
what the bandits wanted—and possibly fuel further bloodletting in a country already beset by violence.

This is China's problem, Hughes would regularly emphasize to President
Harding, *and the Chinese people need to resolve it.*

This same smoke-filled scene wasn't happening just in Washington but
also in other capitals of the world—especially in London, Paris, and Rome,
where heads of state were deeply concerned about the well-being of their
own citizens held captive at Paotzuku Mountain. The Lincheng Incident
had indeed rocked the world.

ON THE MORNING OF MAY 18, GENERAL TIEN CALLED A MEETING OF THE
foreign consular representatives to discuss the status of negotiations. Tien
first announced that, pursuant to the Chinese government's decision to
meet the demands of the brigands, his troops besieging Paotzuku had
withdrawn 20 li (6.2 miles) from the mountain fortress. The foreign consular representatives knew that this was a boldfaced lie. Then Tien began
to fret over the next phase of negotiations and told the consular representatives that he had decided to take matters into his own hands—effectively

pushing aside Roy Anderson, at least for the time being. This, of course, was contrary to the instructions of Marshal Tsao Kun.

Apparently, Tien had summoned local landowners who, he claimed, were on good terms with the bandit chiefs and would act as mediators. He instructed them to go up to the bandit camp at the Temple of the Clouds for discussions. Realizing that the bandits needed a guarantee of safety, Tien had encouraged the local gentry to act as personal guarantors.[6] Several landowners in Shantung Province promised that they would offer the bandits their own homes, farms, and other property as collateral, ensuring the good faith of the Chinese government in upholding any agreement made with the bandits.

Although he was highly skeptical, Anderson kept quiet, knowing that it was unlikely that Sun would play ball. *The bandits were smart enough to realize that their personal safety couldn't be protected by the gentry's property,* Anderson thought. Pleased with himself, Tien ended the meeting by advising the foreign consular representatives that he would keep them informed of the gentry's progress.

Three local landowners left that morning in their sedan chairs to meet the bandit chiefs at Paotzuku Mountain. Yet as soon as they came within sight of the bandits, guards fired several volleys, causing them to dive out of their sedan chairs and seek cover.[7] Terrified, they pleaded with the sentries to allow them to pass safely to meet with the chiefs for discussions. They were then searched and brought up to camp to meet with Sun Mei-yao and Po-Po Liu. Upon arrival, the local nobles received a harsh dressing down by the bandit chiefs, who scolded them for aligning themselves with General Tien.

Raging with emotion, Sun and Liu threatened to shoot them for their betrayal of loyalty. The gentry pleaded with the bandit chiefs that they were only trying to bring peace to the district and were not taking sides. As expected, the bandits rejected the local gentry's offer and were not interested in their property as a form of guarantee. Before sending them back down the mountain empty-handed, the bandits seized the sedan chairs and forced the gentry to walk the twelve miles back to Tsaochuang. When they arrived back at the mining compound, General Tien was livid after hearing how the bandits responded. *I hate to say I told you so,* Anderson thought.

The next day, two senior government officials arrived at Tsaochuang to support the negotiations: Wu Yu-lin, the minister of communications, whose agency was responsible for the supervision of the railroads, and General Yang I-teh, the chief of Tientsin police. Wu suggested an offer that each bandit with a rifle be received into the army but that, in view of the importance of foreign relations, the hostages needed to be released *first*. Wu and Yang further offered themselves in exchange for the release of the foreigners as a performance guarantee.[8] Anderson saw this as nothing more than a political stunt that would be unacceptable to the bandits.

Even General Tien questioned the plan, but only because he believed Wu and Yang were out to usurp his authority as the military governor of Shantung. Tien worried that they would eventually receive the credit for the release of the captives. Tien nevertheless sent a messenger to the bandit camp with this new offer. But it was rejected as quickly as the one before. The bandits simply did not trust any element of the Chinese government and rejected the precondition that the captives first be released. Sun knew how often bandits and ex-soldiers had been tricked by warlords into surrendering, only to be slaughtered.

Tien was furious about the lack of progress, and he blamed the impasse on the foreign governments, who were resistant to use force against the bandits because it put the hostages at risk. Meanwhile, the foreign consular representatives were hopeful that Tien would soon finally realize that the troops needed to stand down or no progress would be made. Otherwise, the diplomats could see that this affair might go on indefinitely. The lack of a single, unified strategy among the Chinese officials was as counterproductive as it was maddening.

ALTHOUGH HUGHES WAS URGING DIPLOMACY, THE WESTERN DIPLOMATS in Peking were asking for battleships. Words had failed them, and they wanted to send a forceful message to the Chinese government that their patience was running thin. They began to make plans for the naval ships in the area to conduct joint exercises. Sending in the floating artillery would hopefully boost the morale of the prisoners and indicate to China that the lives of these foreign nationals must be protected—or else.[9]

A provocative place was chosen to conduct this show of force: off the coast from the Taku Forts, an imperial military fortress largely destroyed by the forces of the Eight-Nation Alliance during the Boxer Rebellion, just two decades before. At the time, the Battle of Taku Forts had effectively pushed the Manchu government to support the Boxers, as well as to order the Imperial Chinese Army to attack all foreign military forces within Chinese territory. The result was the eventual defeat of the Chinese forces and humiliation for China by way of the imposition of the Boxer Protocol, which provided for the execution of government officials who supported the Boxers and a huge monetary indemnity to be paid over thirty-nine years.[10]

The British, French, Italian, and American governments all discussed the proposal with their respective senior naval officers. If agreed, the plan was for the powers to not advise the Chinese government that the ships were coming. In addition, there would be "no visits of courtesy to Chinese officials by foreign vessels and no salutes to the Chinese flag."[11]

There were plenty of warships nearby—including a US Navy fleet with three divisions of destroyers off the Chinese coast—but Minister Schurman eventually decided that showy naval maneuvers were not the right way to put pressure on Peking. After all, foreign pressure was *exactly* what the bandits wanted.

Schurman believed that a naval demonstration would only delay the release of the captives because it would exaggerate in the minds of the bandits—who actively followed the news of the crisis—the value of their hostages and induce them to demand higher terms for their release.[12] If the foreign governments discredited the Chinese government, they would only weaken its ability to deal with the bandits. Schurman was convincing: the British minister would eventually agree with him and back down on the naval maneuvers. But even as Schurman publicly urged patience, in the back of his mind he knew that military intervention was on the horizon if a deal couldn't be worked out in short order.

It had now been twelve days since the attack on the train. Sixteen foreign hostages and about sixty Chinese captives remained in the grip of the bandits, all languishing at the Temple of the Clouds as the days passed. Sidelined by General Tien the week before, Roy Anderson watched with dismay as various Chinese officials and local gentry paraded up to the bandit camp in a desperate attempt to cut a deal with Sun Mei-yao. All failed miserably.

Anderson could sense the frustration mounting, not only among the bandits and Tien but also for the diplomats, who had hoped for a speedy release of their citizens. As if on cue, he watched a slew of adventurers and opportunists scramble on stage to offer rescue schemes, ransom offers, and bold but unrealistic plans to save the hostages.

This included Major Alan Hilton-Johnson, the former head of the Shanghai Municipal Police and a British veteran of the Great War. Hilton-Johnson claimed to have deep contacts with Chinese soldiers and criminals, and he proposed to recruit several Shantung mercenaries to rescue the hostages. Shanghai British consul Sir Sidney Barton sent a telegram to British minister Sir Ronald Macleay stating that in his opinion Hilton-Johnson was "eminently qualified to assist," but Macleay believed that it was "neither necessary nor desirable" for the British government to encourage what might be perceived as foreign intervention, even by private citizens. Macleay was uneasy about sending soldiers of fortune to a combat zone, which might not end well for the hostages caught in the middle: "When I require Major Hilton-Johnson's assistance, I will ask for it."[13]

Then there was British businessman James Stewart of Tientsin, who proposed to the British government employing the services of his good friend Wang Yung-hsiang, a former bandit chief from Shantung. Wang's plan was to pay a ransom of $50,000 for each of the British captives—and never mind the other captives.[14] Stewart, who was known in the expat community as an outlier, had been friends with Wang for twenty years and guaranteed that he was "alright." Minister Macleay dismissed the scheme outright as opportunistic: "I am inclined to suspect that Wang's offer is motivated by the hope of sharing in profits of kidnapping and that he has no real knowledge of the situation or the brigand's terms." As well, "We can leave James Stewart and his brigand friend to their own devices."[15]

Minister Macleay fielded a number of similarly outlandish ideas from British citizens throughout China, often generated or encouraged by his own consulate staff. Herbert Goffe, the British consul in Hankow, sent a cryptic telegram to Macleay that created much alarm: *Secret. A young En-glish aviator here has been commissioned to organize an air force to attack the bandits.* Macleay hit the ceiling. "By whom is he commissioned and against which group of bandits is the air force to be used? You will of course take every measure to prevent unauthorized British subjects from taking part in aerial or military operations."[16]

Yet the British weren't the only ones with harebrained rescue schemes. Secretary of State Hughes was approached by a US company suggesting that two aviators fly biplanes with twenty-passenger capacity to Paotzuku to rescue the captives. But the idea was not well conceived for several reasons, including the absence of landing facilities in the mountainous region of Shantung. And even the proponents of the plan stated that the "practicability of rescuing prisoners is limited to landing facilities at place of detention."[17] Assuming that the aviators could land the aircraft, then what? Two pilots would never be able to neutralize the bandit army. The State Department rejected the idea.

There was also no shortage of wealthy family members ready to individually pay ransoms. The Mexican legation passed on a message to the Chinese government that the relatives of the Vereas "are ready to pay any ransom demanded in order to obtain their release." The Peking diplomatic corps objected to this suggestion because it was contrary to the position that the Chinese government was solely responsible for the payment of whatever ransom might be necessary and that they should not accept funds from any private sources to secure the release of select hostages.[18]

Where cash or rescue schemes didn't work, the Vatican tried to use its moral authority to win the release of Musso. Cardinal Pietro Gasparri, the secretary of state for the Holy See and assistant to Pope Pius XI, ordered the Roman Catholic priests in Lincheng, including Lenfers, to appeal with a sense of urgency on behalf of the Holy See to obtain Musso's unconditional release on humanitarian grounds, given his poor health. Lenfers was also ordered to remain by Musso's side at the camp to tend to his spiritual needs. But the entreaties of the Vatican and the fawning attention given to Musso only reinforced the perception among the bandits that the Italian lawyer was an important man. Musso was not going anywhere, sick or healthy, and was likely to be one of the last hostages released. "Musso must be a remarkable individual to cause the intervention of the Pope in this affair!"[19] observed Macleay.

The only scheme that was successful in achieving the release of a foreign hostage was carried out by the French. In the afternoon of May 18, after several well-dressed Chinese gentlemen mysteriously appeared at the Temple of the Clouds for meetings with the bandit chiefs, Marcel Berubé was unexpectedly and quietly released.[20] Berubé had been respected by the captives for his friendly spirit and always-helpful attitude, but many objected to his preferential treatment in getting liberated. The other hostages looked on with stunned silence and disappointment that they weren't included. Why did Berubé get to go free?

As it turned out, Berubé's freedom had been secured by Huang Chin-jung, the leading Chinese detective of the Sûreté, the French Concession Police. The police force was effectively an arm of the French government and existed to serve the interests of Paris in China, especially its Shanghai

French national Marcel Oliver Berubé, an official with China's salt monopoly administration, was released under suspicious circumstances after the intervention of notorious Shanghai underworld figures. (SHSMO)

concession. Known as "Pockmarked Chin," Chin was also the notorious boss of Shanghai's organized-crime syndicate, the Green Gang. Chin met with Sun Mei-yao on several occasions to broker the release of Berubé. He used his underworld connections to secure safe passage for Berubé through the military lines.[21]

Berubé's freedom was bought, and it remains a mystery who paid for it—or why. Berubé had no known connections to the Chinese underworld, yet it made sense that an organized-crime figure would have a back channel to the bandits. The French government might have paid Chin to secure Berubé's freedom, even if it meant leaving the other hostages to their fates.

Chin created the impression that Berubé had been released only on "parole" and that Berubé was heading to Peking to carry a message to President Li Yuan-hung and would thereafter return to the bandit camp at the Temple of the Clouds. Supposedly, Berubé's return was guaranteed with the lives of Powell and Musso, who would be shot if Berubé failed to return. Of course, none of this turned out to be true. Berubé never returned.

When the foreign diplomats caught wind of Berubé's release, they were outraged. This would only complicate life for the remaining hostages by creating an "every man for himself" precedent. When cornered by his fellow consular representatives, French consul Crépin claimed ignorance of the gangster's role in Berubé's release. But his counterparts were skeptical and found it hard to believe that Crépin was unaware of what Pockmarked Chin was up to, given his high-profile position with the Sûreté. "I imagine [Chin's] services were brought from Shanghai with a promise of reward if he could get the French prisoners out," Tours told his American and Italian diplomat colleagues. "And, in true Chinese fashion, any method is good enough for him."[22]

Although Chin's story about Berubé returning to the bandit camp after delivering his message turned out to be nonsense, the liberated Frenchman was indeed carrying an important message from Sun Mei-yao. It was an ultimatum that he delivered to the officials and diplomats at Tsaochuang. If the government troops did not withdraw from the vicinity of Paotzuku by Tuesday, May 22, the bandits would execute two foreigners, one American and one British.[23] The clock was ticking.

DESPITE THE FACT THAT SUCH TACTICS HAD FAILED IN THE PAST, ON THE morning of May 20, General Tien once again sent a delegation to the Temple of the Clouds with an offer to enlist the bandits into the army on the precondition that the hostages be released. The proposal was rejected outright.[24] Sun was so irritated that he treated the envoys as outcasts by not offering them chairs or the customary tea, and threatened to destroy their sedan chairs and force them to walk back to Tsaochuang. Although he allowed the Chinese officials to depart safely, Sun's bandits began firing their weapons in the air, spooking the servants carrying the chairs, who began running down the hillside, causing the envoys to bounce and flop about.

"And take the Mexican lady with you!" ordered Sun. The bandits and prisoners no longer wanted the responsibility of taking care of the camp's only woman. After much pressure from both her husband and the bandit chiefs, she finally agreed to leave her husband's side. Along with the envoys, Verea left the bandit camp at seven o'clock in the evening and arrived at Tsaochuang at two o'clock in the morning. Upon her arrival, Verea met with American consul Davis, military attaché Philoon, and Anderson. She was distraught about the lack of progress and the tension at the camp, and she informed the diplomats and Anderson that three Americans—Allen, Pinger, and Solomon—were being readied to be taken to the top of Paotzuku Mountain. "Others will be going to the top as well," she said with much concern.[25]

ON THE MORNING OF MAY 21, GENERAL TIEN CALLED YET ANOTHER meeting of the foreign diplomats to express his frustration. The bandits, he explained, had rejected the latest offer and had done so despite the fact that he had withdrawn his troops, as he emphatically claimed. Tien then argued that standing down was exactly what the bandits wanted so they could move the captives to their strongholds even deeper in the mountains.

In response, the foreign consuls countered Tien's narrative. They knew that his troops were closing in on Sun and that his snipers were shooting the bandit sentries. Several foreign witnesses who had been to the camps— including Lenfers and Berubé—had confirmed this. "It is quite clear that you never intended to relax your hold on the brigands," said Tours.[26]

Frustrated, Tien asked the foreign diplomats what they would do in his place. Tours refused to take the bait. Neither did the other consular representatives. "We are not here in an advisory capacity, but to observe what is being done by the Chinese authorities to cope with the situation, and to keep the Legations informed," Tours said.[27] The message was clear: "This is not our responsibility, so don't ask us for recommendations."

Tien, dramatically throwing up his hands, said that he was in an impossible situation and that unless somebody could come up with a better strategy, he planned to leave Tsaochuang at once and plead his case in Peking. He would ask permission to declare war on the brigands and crush them by force, regardless of the impact on the hostages. Tien added that it was a mistake for the foreign government representatives to be on site at Tsaochuang. Having the foreign powers present "puffed up" the bandits and increased their leverage over the Chinese government.

The foreign consuls at Tsaochuang could see that Tien was under significant pressure. The old warlord seemed to become increasingly paranoid. He made up irrational and delusional conspiracy theories to deflect responsibility or lay the blame on competing warlords or the foreign governments. Tien then began reciting his personal woes—how he was having trouble sleeping and was suffering from headaches, stomachaches, and other bodily pains. *He is getting to a pitch of strain where nobody would be surprised if he did something foolish in sheer desperation,* Tours thought.[28]

Not unexpectedly, at the close of the briefing, Tien and his entire retinue and bodyguards walked to his train car and headed to Peking. After his departure, various other Peking and Shantung officials also fled the scene. Anderson saw this as a good thing, but he also needed to get in touch with Marshal Tsao Kun to be sure that any request by Tien for authorization to engage in the use of force against the bandits—along with the hostages—be rejected. The diplomatic corps delivered a message to the Chinese Foreign Ministry stating that "the deadlock in the negotiations between the Chinese officials and the delegates of the brigands is due to the fact that the troops surrounding the brigand's camps have not, in spite of the repeated assurances of the Chinese Government, been withdrawn."[29]

In addition to the failure to withdraw, they argued, the competition by various factions of Chinese officials to take credit for the release of the hostages created much delay and confusion. American Minister Schurman feared that the number of officials engaged in negotiations was complicating the situation.[30]

Major Philoon described the scene like a bad movie: "Officials of every grade from cabinet minister and Tuchun to the most menial underling appeared on the screen, all, almost without exception, playing politics with only their own private interests in their thoughts, their only concern as to foreign captives being, how best they might be capitalized to their own advantage."[31]

The exodus of General Tien and other officials created much tension among the Chinese troops stationed at Tsaochuang. Just a few days before, on May 19, a massive brawl erupted on the grounds of Tsaochuang between two Chinese army brigades. It involved more than one hundred troops who fought one another with rifle barrels, poles, and knives. Although no gunshots were fired, several soldiers were injured in the melee, including one soldier who was stabbed in the abdomen with a bayonet.[32] With so many angry soldiers but no commanding officers around to enforce discipline, the foreigners in the compound began to fear for their own safety.

Disregarding his orders from Peking, on his departure General Tien directed three brigades of his troops to make a wide circle around the

US Army major Wallace Philoon at Tsaochuang with Chinese Army troops, many of them undisciplined and of questionable loyalty, given that the soldiers hadn't received their pay for months and were reportedly selling ammunition and equipment to the bandits. (Philoon)

bandit encampment, cutting off the outlaws' communications in an effort to isolate the gangs holding the hostages. Tien intended to "dig the bandits out" of their hiding place with machine guns. As his plan unfolded, skirmishes broke out, resulting in fatalities on both sides. Although some of Tien's troops were shooting the bandits, others were helping them. Many of the general's soldiers hadn't been paid for months and were reportedly selling ammunition to the bandits, as well as saddles, horses, and mules—resupplying the very enemy they were trying to vanquish. Morale among the troops was low, and the line between soldier and bandit seemed to be blurring. Even if he would never admit it, Tien knew that many of his troops were disloyal. That is why before he left for Peking, he had called in a large contingent of personal bodyguards from Tsinan. But in a sign of the lawlessness that reigned among his troops, one of General Tien's bodyguards had his rifle purloined from him in plain daylight.[33]

FEARING THAT NEGOTIATIONS WOULD COLLAPSE, THE US MILITARY AT-taché on the scene, Major Philoon, decided he might need to act. He wrote out a private note to Major Pinger and John Powell, which he carefully folded and hid in a package of raisins that was being sent up with other supplies to the Temple of the Clouds.[34] Philoon wanted to see whether the captives would be in favor of an armed rescue mission led by US troops stationed at Tientsin. The plan was to covertly bring to Tsaochuang a fifty-man contingent of US soldiers and marines. The troops would arrive in small groups dressed in civilian clothes to avoid attracting attention. Meanwhile, Philoon would smuggle up to the camp revolvers and ammunition hidden in parcels carried by the Coolie Express. When the designated day came, the hostages would take their weapons and barricade themselves in a cave behind the temple structures as the US troops attacked the bandit compound.

The stakes were incredibly high, Powell said when presenting the plan to his fellow captives, but it just might work. The American and British hostages gave their guarded endorsement. Both of the Chinese interpreters, Hung and Chi Cheng, also signed on. Major Pinger was one of the strongest advocates for the plot. "Civilize 'em with Krags is my motto," he said,

Bandits and captives at the Temple of the Clouds at the base of Paotzuku Mountain. *From left to right:* notorious child bandit Straw Hat (adopted son of Po-Po Liu) with rifle, Chinese captive and interpreter "Chang" in background, bandit chief Po-Po Liu, banker and returning Cambridge student Chi Cheng in front, friendly bandit Russky in background, Lee Solomon with cigarette, and unknown child bandit fully armed. (SHSMO)

referring to the Norwegian-designed Krag-Jørgensen rifle, which was the US Army's weapon of choice during the Boxer Rebellion.[35]

Yet everyone was worried. They knew that once provoked, the bandits could offer fierce resistance. Powell wrote back to Major Philoon a measured report on the reactions of the hostages to the proposal. They all realized what would happen if the plan failed.[36]

CHAPTER 18

THE SAP CLUB

The view is like an artist's map. But it serves to emphasize our squalid surroundings here. While down below everything seemed blessed with a Sabbath peace and calm, our immediate surroundings suggested only the wickedness of man to man.

—Major Roland W. Pinger, American tourist and hostage[1]

MAY 19, 1923, MIDDAY, TEMPLE OF THE CLOUDS/PAOTZUKU SUMMIT

A commotion had broken out in the temple courtyard. The bandits announced that because of the threatening movement of General Tien's troops, who were creeping ever farther up the valley, three of the most valuable hostages were to be moved to the top of Paotzuku: the businessman Lee Solomon and the US Army majors Allen and Pinger, who were soon to be collectively known as the SAP Club, with the title formed from the first letter of each man's surname. Sun chose to maroon these three Americans as an insurance policy. Rescuing them from the top of the mountain would be a practical impossibility, and he calculated that the move would ratchet up the pressure on the Chinese to negotiate a good-faith resolution to the crisis.[2]

Sun also believed that he was running out of both time and options. Only three days remained until his May 22 deadline. If Tien's troops did not completely withdraw before then, he would be forced to execute two of the hostages, one British and the other American. Yet it seemed like, if anything, Tien's troops were advancing, not retreating.

With Russky as their escort, Pinger, Allen, and Solomon set out for the summit. Coolies carried the supplies, thus freeing the three Americans to use all four limbs to climb the precipice. It was a steep climb; they stopped frequently to catch their breath, dangling from handholds that had been chiseled in the rock. "This climb is hell," Solomon said to Pinger. "It's like scaling the Woolworth building."[3]

On the way up, the three Americans could smell the stench of the decaying remains of the children who had been hurled off the northern parapet months earlier. A few small bodies lay among the rocky crags about halfway down.[4] *Powell and the old priest were right*, the three Americans said to one another. Pinger could feel his eyes well up with the thought that this could have been his own children. He tried to pray, but his anger overwhelmed any sense of charity he had.

When they got to the top, they noticed a large wooden door riddled with bullets and supported by a waist-high wall of sandbags. It was a guardhouse of some sort that contained a small, ancient cannon similar to the swivel gun (*lantaka*) commonly used in Southeast Asia.

About fifty feet from the guardhouse, they were ushered into a low mud-and-stone house that had a strong stench of human waste. As they surveyed their surroundings, looking for a cleaner place to sleep, the three Americans also assessed their escape options. Besides the extremely steep slope on the northwest corner that they had climbed on the way up, there was no other way to get off the mountaintop. "We threw a rock—counted the seconds—heard and saw no impact—and were discouraged," Pinger recalled.

The three Americans could see dozens of dugout structures that were not in use, some of them small and others quite roomy. All of the dugouts showed evidence of having once been occupied at some point: broken pieces of pottery, remnants of clothing, reed mats, campfire residue, teapots, and water jars. They guessed there must have been more than three hundred people on the mountaintop at one time. While looking around, they found a dugout that was fairly clean, though small. This would be their new home.[5]

The dugout had no windows, and the door was only three to four feet high, meaning they had to stoop to enter. After walking through the door, they had to jump down three feet to the dugout floor. The roof was made from wood and thatch covered with soil, and the four walls were rough-cut stone. Inside, wicker matting covered the stone walls for further insulation.

The dugout was a traditional dwelling for humans and livestock that was favored in northern China for its natural insulation capabilities—cool in the hot summers and warm in the cold winters. Though not perfect, it was livable. After the captives shoveled out the rubbish and debris, they proceeded to set up their cots. It was dark by the time they finally moved in. Under candlelight, the captives got busy writing notes and letters describing the day.

Russky set up his bedroll inside and near the entrance of the dugout. For whatever reason, Russky seemed to trust the Americans more than the other bandits did. He not only slept with them in the dugout but would also leave his rifle and bandolier there. They did not sleep well the first night: all three Americans woke up constantly, scratching their faces. Something was irritating them. In the candlelight they could see that their faces were caked in a film of dirt, which they thought had fallen from the ceiling. But this was not the cause of the horrible itching.

In the morning they quickly discovered that in the darkness the night before, they had all washed their faces in contaminated water. Given the scarcity of water on the plateau, the old man who acted as the caretaker at the summit had collected used water into a large jar.[6] Going forward, the three Americans demanded pure water for consumption *and* washing.

As the days passed, the members of the SAP Club set to work improving their surroundings. They developed a sanitary cooking and washing operation, aided by a clay-lined five-gallon Standard Oil can stove that burned the coke they received from the mining company. They employed two such stoves and kept them burning all day long, one for cooking and one for cleaning. The old caretaker looked aghast at the fuel consumption by the foreigners, but sanitation was paramount.

Major Pinger made a SAP Club sign fashioned from a hammered-flat milk can with extruded holes, pierced and punched through by using his handy buttonhook. He kept busy with various creative tasks. He carved clothespins from discarded pieces of wood, and he made envelopes from old magazine advertisements, using rice pudding as glue to seal the seams. Lee Solomon took the initiative to do all the cooking. Dinner was baked beans, canned corned beef, potatoes, and onions. The two army officers did the dishes.

After dinner on the first night, Major Allen operated on Solomon's blistered feet using a sterilized razor blade and Chinese brandy for anesthesia. Killing time, the two majors together made a rough-pegged cribbage board out of discarded wood planking and sticks. Major Allen taught Pinger how to play "crib," giving them a variation from the usual card games.

As the sun went down, the three Americans started singing by the warmth of their coke stove under the starry night sky. They sang old college songs, to the enjoyment of the bandit guards who gathered about the campfire.[7] Even Russky joined in, singing Russian and Chinese ballads in his falsetto voice. The camaraderie of the four was genuine. "You are a decent and intelligent chap," Major Allen said to Russky, "and very musical."

ALTHOUGH THE SAP CLUB TRIED TO MAKE THE BEST OF THEIR MOUNtaintop isolation, they could not look away from the children who were also being held on the summit. The three Americans went to the dank hut where the children were kept and saw the bored guards yelling at the kids to stay inside. There were more than twenty children still alive, most of them under ten years old, but they were not well. The children were scabby and listless, covered in sores. Two particularly emaciated children looked to Allen to be wasting away from tuberculosis or some intestinal infection. One child was blind in one eye. Another had skeletal ribs that looked like the spokes of a hamster wheel.

The men had never seen such a wretched sight. All the youth and vitality had been drained from these children. *They're crouched on their straw with the utter dejection of hopeless, hungry little old men*, Pinger thought.[8]

All were boys except one girl of about nine years old, whom the Americans viewed as particularly vulnerable. The Americans noticed, as Powell had, the children's tattered but once fine clothing, indicating their wealthy origins. They had all been on Paotzuku for at least a year, and one of the oldest had apparently been confined for five years. The bandits ransomed the children, forcing their families to make monthly payments. If the payments stopped, the children would either be killed or be raised as bandits.[9]

One morning, Solomon made a hefty pot of rice pudding, which the three Americans dished out to the children. It was highly sweetened and enriched with milk and raisins, so the youngsters gulped it down hungrily. The Americans wanted to be sure that their handouts were going to those who needed it the most. Pinger repeatedly demanded that the old caretaker bring out the "little living skeleton," the child with the protruding ribs, to allow the Americans to feed him some oatmeal, fearing that the bandit guards and caretaker were taking the food for themselves. "The way he wolfed down the porridge convinces me that while he may have tuberculosis or worse, there is nothing wrong with his appetite—he was simply *starving*," Pinger told Allen.[10]

They received from the rescue mission a large tin of biscuits and Chinese candy that they gave to the children. Although having food and clean water for the children was a priority, Allen had also requested from the Coolie Express medical supplies and soap, which he used to clean and disinfect the children's festering sores as best as he could.

The SAP Club also kept the children busy with projects that alleviated some of the boredom and gave them much-needed exercise. One project involved putting down gravel along the path that everyone in the camp used to go to the latrine. During heavy rains this path became "a mass of gumbo," in Pinger's words. The Americans located a pile of granite-like chips that were chiseled out from the rocky plateau. As they worked, the children began singing songs they remembered from school or their families. It touched the SAP Club to see a bit of joy brought back into the lives of the kidnapped children. "Our coming was a Godsend to these little ones," Pinger said. "At least a temporary one."

AT NIGHT, THE SAP CLUB FREQUENTLY SAW CAMPFIRES AND LIGHTS IN the valleys below. And on one clear evening, the three Americans noticed the strong beam of the searchlight from the Tsaochuang mining compound. In a letter to Philoon, Major Pinger had described their position at the top of Paotzuku. Several days later, the powerful searchlight pierced through the sky and illuminated the top of the mountain like a spotlight in a theater.[11]

Every night thereafter, the three Americans started to notice that the searchlight at Tsaochuang was flashing some sort of message in Morse code. The code proved too difficult to decipher, which the trio explained via letters sent down to Tsaochuang. So the people in the mining compound began to use the searchlight in a semaphore fashion, flashing an alphabetic code. The signals came every night for several nights in a row.

Pinger wrote a letter to Philoon, delivered by the Bandit Post, telling him that the beams of the searchlight were right "on the nose." In his reply, Philoon explained that he wanted to establish communications so he could rapidly warn them if the military decided to mount a rescue mission. More and more, it seemed like there would be a bloody end to the Lincheng Incident, especially if Tien's troops continued their siege.[12] Every night thereafter, the three Americans started to closely watch the searchlight on the horizon to decode the incoming messages.

GENERAL TIEN ARRIVED IN PEKING ON MAY 22. HE WENT IMMEDIATELY to Marshal Tsao Kun, expecting to receive authorization to launch a full-scale attack against the bandits. But Anderson had beat him to it and sent a telegraph to Tsao pleading with him to order Tien to stand down. Tien tried to persuade Tsao to use overwhelming force of arms to wipe the bandits off the face of Shantung. Tien was unwavering in his position. He was convinced that once the military cordon was relaxed, allies of the bandits would pour in from adjoining provinces: "I can either fight the bandits at the risk of the lives of the foreigners or withdraw my troops to points designated by the bandits and risk the influx of allied marauding bands driving in from the surrounding countryside to take full possession of southern Shantung."

Tsao had heard enough. Tien had been given ample opportunity to solve this crisis through military maneuvers, and he had failed. Tsao was also aware that the Shantung Provincial Assembly—the legislative body of the province—had sent a telegram to President Li Yuan-hung calling for the ouster of Tien because of his abject failure to deal effectively with the bandit situation. The assembly found that only a single district out of 107 in Shantung Province was without banditry and that the well-funded Shantung army, which received 70 percent of the annual revenues of the province, had proven wholly incapable of dealing with the growing insurgency.[13]

Now, Tsao decided, it was Roy Anderson's turn. Although Tsao had dispatched Anderson two weeks before, he knew that the American's efforts at mediating had been hamstrung by Tien's two-faced strategy of fighting and making empty promises. Tsao ordered Tien to stand down. General Cheng Shih-chi, the assistant military governor of Shantung, would take his place commanding the troops in Tsaochuang, who were now there only to support Anderson.

Anderson agreed to restart negotiations, but he wanted full authorization to cut a deal with the brigands. Tsao agreed. Yet Anderson still faced formidable challenges. He would have to find a way for the bandits to accept a deal without the guarantee of the foreign governments, which he knew was a nonstarter for the American and European diplomats.

Meanwhile, Minister Schurman had no objection to Anderson leading the negotiations, provided that the Chinese government and the bandits understood that Anderson was acting independently and did not represent the US government. The other diplomats responded with suspicion, expecting that Anderson would first try to get his own nationals released, at the expense of the British, French, and Italian captives.[14] But they were still willing to give him a chance to break the impasse.

CHAPTER 19

POWELL'S CHARGE

There is great danger constantly, as the bandits are drinking heavily and are getting in an ugly mood at times and something serious may happen if they are provoked.

—Leon Friedman, American hostage and Shanghai automobile dealer[1]

MAY 22, 1923, AFTERNOON, TEMPLE OF THE CLOUDS

The hostages had now been in captivity for sixteen days, negotiations were at a standstill, and the morale at the Temple of the Clouds had fallen to a new low. The sheer number of foreign and Chinese captives living in close quarters created appalling sanitary conditions. During a community dinner at the temple, Musso went ballistic when news reports published overly optimistic coverage about the progress of negotiations. At least from the hostages' perspective, nothing could be further from the truth. Sun Mei-yao repeatedly threatened that all the captives would soon need to make the treacherous climb to the top of the mountain to join the SAP Club. Meanwhile, the bandits had begun to drink heavily and to pick fights with the hostages.[2]

Powell got into a scuffle with one of the younger bandits, who struck him in the back for no apparent reason. Powell generally tried to be diplomatic with the bandits, but some of the younger bandits were immature troublemakers who thought it was funny to do things like throw manure into the captives' food. If the hostages objected to their treatment, these undisciplined juveniles would point their weapons and threaten to shoot. On a nightly basis, bandits would try to rob the captives of the clothing and supplies that were sent up from the relief mission. One of the bandits tried to take the plain wooden box that Rowlatt used to store his personal belongings. When Rowlatt protested, the bandit pulled out his revolver, cocked it, and pointed it at Rowlatt's head. The greedy bandit was on the point of shooting Rowlatt when he was forcibly dragged away by three of his comrades. If the treatment of the foreign hostages was bad, the Chinese captives continued to have it much worse. In plain view of the foreigners, the bandits executed five Chinese hostages who either refused to obey an order or did not do so quickly enough.[3]

The tension was becoming intolerable for British tourist William Smith, who had come to the Orient in the hopes of recovering from his addiction to painkillers and sleeping pills. Dr. Mertens, Musso's physician who visited the temple grounds, started to supply Smith with the barbiturate Veronal to calm his nerves and help cure his insomnia. But it wasn't enough for him. Smith wrote a letter to Carl Crow, pleading for him to send up even more sedatives. He was so keyed up that he would often wander around outside the camp aimlessly, irritating the guards and causing his fellow captives to send out search parties to bring him back.[4]

SUN MEI-YAO HAD THREATENED TO KILL TWO OF THE FOREIGN hostages—one American and one British—if his demand for a withdrawal of the troops was not met by May 22. Even though General Tien had left for Peking on May 20, three of his brigades were still in place, on his orders. So on the afternoon of May 22, all the foreign captives were told to gather in the temple courtyard. They were silent. They knew that the fateful hour had come. After weeks of captivity, having seen multiple deadlines come and go without action, the hostages thought that this time Sun had meant what he said. The foreigners knew, from the treatment of the Chinese captives, that the bandits had no fear of spilling blood.[5]

They looked at one another, nervously, silently. And then, suddenly, in that intense moment, a strange thing happened. Someone in the camp started to sing, "Hail, Hail the Gang's All Here!," a popular song from *The Pirates of Penzance*:

> *Hail, hail the gang's all here,*
> *What the heck do we care,*
> *What the heck do we care,*
> *Hail, hail, the gang's all here,*
> *What the heck do we care now!*

All the hostages joined the singing, one voice after another. The Shanghai cousins were the loudest. Even the aloof Smith chimed in. Like a rollicking band of pirates performing in a light opera, they all leaped to their feet to join the chorus in the courtyard. No contemporary production of the Gilbert and Sullivan musical ever reached this level of collective emotional intensity. The sound of the hearty voices echoed off the canyon walls, and the guards and Chinese captives alike all came out to see what the commotion was.

There was a sense of defiance, of protest. "Look at them," Smith said to his fellow hostages, "the bandits are nonplussed by our pluck and *sang-froid*."[6]

Verse after verse they sang. They swung their arms with clenched fists. They yelled out the words while looking up to the sky so that their three American comrades isolated at the top of Paotzuku could hear the courage and solidarity in their voices. The SAP Club actually heard them. And in their camps the bandit chiefs Sun Mei-yao and Po-Po Liu heard them too.

The last thing Sun and his gang wanted was an open revolt by the foreign captives. He knew, hearing the sheer tenacity in their voices, that executing one member of their ranks carried such a risk. The message was clear: the hostages of the Peking Express were sticking together till the end. The day came and went without any of them being harmed.

EMBOLDENED BY THE COURAGE THEIR FELLOW HOSTAGES HAD SHOWN BY facing down Sun's deadline, Friedman and Powell called a meeting of both the foreign and the English-speaking Chinese captives to discuss their situation and come up with a strategy to end the deadlock.[7] Professor Hung suggested that they take matters into their own hands. They should meet with the bandit chiefs and attempt to negotiate their own way out of captivity—or at least help the bandits resolve the stalemate with the Peking government.

On the evening of May 23 at about seven o'clock, the bandit chiefs arrived at the Temple of the Clouds for discussions. Friedman was appointed by the captives to be the chairman, and Powell would serve as secretary. Friedman was the perfect person to speak on everyone's behalf. He had the charisma and charm of an entertainer, the persuasion of a car salesman, and the aura of a confident corporate kingpin. Whenever he walked into a room, his deep, eloquent voice and steady demeanor captured the attention of the audience.[8]

With Hung interpreting, Friedman told the bandit leaders that he understood their situation and wanted to help them find a way to settle the standoff. "But we can't do anything to help you until we know your terms," Friedman explained. "Just what do you want?"

After some hesitation, each of the bandit leaders began to talk at length and with much passion about past injustices. All of the captives listened intently without interruption or judgment, although they had heard many of these demands before: the withdrawal of the troops that were besieging Shantung; army commissions for the ragtag bandits, with back pay, weapons, food, and clothing; and a guarantee from the foreign powers to prevent any double-crossing by the Chinese government.

Like Anderson, the captives knew that many of these demands were impossible. But Friedman and Powell were pleased that the chiefs were articulating what they wanted. Still, they had no idea how to encourage the bandits to genuinely restart negotiations and tone down their demands. They needed to give the bandits a reality check.

Friedman diplomatically emphasized to the chiefs that they were running out of time. Peking was under increasing pressure to resort to a military solution to the crisis, which would almost certainly lead to the annihilation of both the bandits and the captives. Any sympathy that the bandits hoped to receive for their cause from the foreign community was waning as the days of captivity wore on. Both Friedman and Powell mentioned that they had received many letters from family and friends, and the messages were uniformly in favor of using foreign troops to secure the release of the hostages.

As the discussions continued, the captives began to earn Sun's trust. The bandit chief seemed charmed by Powell in particular. He was impressed that Powell had attended the 1922 Washington Conference, where the Japanese were forced to leave Tsingtao and Shantung. Jokingly or not, Sun called Powell the "savior of Shantung," even though all he had done at the conference was take notes as a journalist. Sun agreed that it was time to cut a deal. He decided to send Powell down to Tsaochuang with a message that the bandits wanted to reopen negotiations.[9]

ON THE MORNING OF MAY 24, POWELL MOUNTED A MULE AND DE-scended the mountain with a guard of about 150 mounted bandits. They were not for his protection—if anything they made him a bigger target—but to demonstrate his importance as the official emissary of the bandit army.[10] The thunder of hooves echoed off the canyon walls and gave the impression that Sun Mei-yao's troops were a force to be reckoned with. The mounted bandit guards turned back at the military lines, leaving Powell to make the rest of the trip alone. The ride down the mountain to Tsao-chuang took most of the day. He reached the mining compound at about five o'clock in the afternoon, where he was welcomed by Anderson, the American consul Davis, and General Cheng Shih-chi, the Chinese military leader who had replaced General Tien.

General Cheng would not provide Powell with a written reply to the bandits' demands, but he offered to meet and negotiate with the chiefs if they would be willing to send representatives down to Tsaochuang. Cheng also guaranteed the absolute safety of any negotiators who came to Tsaochuang, putting this commitment in writing for Powell to take back to the chieftains.

Powell used the opportunity to bathe, shave, and change clothes—a welcome relief after almost three weeks in the same filthy outfit. He also had his first hot meal that wasn't cooked over a campfire. For the first time, Powell realized that he was safe and free from the grip of the bandits. Absorbed by thoughts of his wife and children, Powell was tempted to not return to the bandit camp. But a refusal to return meant the almost certain death of one or more of his waiting comrades. The two American army officers would likely be the first to get shot. Or they could target his friends Friedman and Solomon. He just couldn't do this to them. The bonds formed over the past weeks in captivity were too strong. He had to return for their sake, even at his own personal risk. Something also told him that the assurances of General Cheng, and the fact that Anderson was now in the lead, meant that real negotiations would finally begin.

The next morning, Powell returned to the bandit camp. Sun Mei-yao agreed to Cheng's offer to meet in Tsaochuang and designated as representatives two subchiefs, Kuo Chih-tsai and Chou Tien-sung, to return with Powell to begin the negotiations at once.

Mid-morning on May 26, Powell and the two envoys prepared to depart. Kuo and Chou changed from their bandit gear to traditional *changshan* gowns emblematic of the Chinese scholar class—outfits they had likely stolen from the Peking Express. Kuo was considered the diplomat of the group, whereas Chou was the man of the people, having come from peasant stock. Kuo and Chou carried hand fans for show and thus earned the nickname "fan-bandits" from the captives.[11] Po-Po Liu also asked his adopted son, the smug and pretentious Straw Hat, to accompany Powell and the fan-bandits down to Tsaochuang. Straw Hat was viewed as a miscreant by the hostages. He always carried a heavy, oversized revolver under his silk jacket and sometimes pointed his massive revolver with his childlike hands at one of the foreigners, grinning menacingly with his grayish-black teeth and silly laugh.

Just before the group's departure, Sun, while looking directly at Powell, drew his revolver and pressed the barrel of his gun into the chest of multiple foreign captives. In this manner, Sun indicated that one or possibly all of the captives would be killed if Powell failed to carry out the mission or attempted to double-cross the bandits by allowing their envoys to be captured by the army.[12] This terrified the captives. Then, as Powell mounted, Sun broke the tension by clapping his hands and cheering. Everybody followed suit so enthusiastically that the noise scared the mules, which bolted down the valley at a gallop.

Powell, the fan-bandits, and Straw Hat rode all day, and when they reached the military lines, the accompanying mounted escorts left the four riders to proceed on their own. They entered a mile-wide "no man's land" between the bandit lines and the military outposts. Powell noticed that Kuo and Chou were getting increasingly nervous, being outside of the protection of their fellow bandits and in the realm now of the unforgiving government troops. As darkness fell, they approached the lights of the walled compound of Tsaochuang. At the gate, a sentry shouted out an order, and suddenly the bright searchlight came beaming down on them, illuminating the four travelers.

Panicked, the three Chinese riders abruptly turned their mounts and dashed across an adjoining field. While the sentry trained the spotlight on the fleeing riders, Powell gave chase, shouting reassurances that their safety was guaranteed. Powell feared that Kuo and Chou had lost their courage and were about to return to Paotzuku. After exhausting his limited supply of Chinese obscenities, he succeeded in overtaking the bandits and finally got them to turn around and head back toward the gate. Powell, the two nervous fan-bandits, and Straw Hat cautiously walked their panting mounts forward under the bright glare of the compound's searchlight. It wasn't until he heard the loud clang of the door of the compound's gate that Powell heaved a sigh of relief.[13]

POWELL AND THE TWO FAN-BANDITS WERE IMMEDIATELY WHISKED AWAY to the railway coach of US consul Davis, and there they met with the foreign consular representatives, Anderson, Crow, and Philoon. There was great excitement when they arrived and enormous curiosity regarding the two bandit envoys whom Powell had brought with him.

Anderson took the fan-bandits to meet with General Cheng, who received them with all the formality of a high government dignitary. The bandits presented the general with their list of demands and immediately engaged in a dialogue. In true Chinese style, where pride was always an overriding concern, General Cheng said this to the fan-bandits: "This

The negotiations begin. *From left to right:* American fixer Roy Scott Anderson, fan-bandits Chou Tien-sung and Kuo Chih-tsai, US major Wallace Philoon, US consul John K. Davis, and Wen Shih-tsung, commissioner of foreign affairs, Nanking, Kiangsu Province, during negotiations at Tsaochuang. (Philoon)

situation has caused the officials of the province to lose much face. It has caused the people of China to lose much face. It has caused the bandits themselves to lose face. Therefore, *we might as well eliminate the subject of face altogether and get down to business!"*[14]

The brigand chiefs and the Shantung officials retired to a private conference and began discussions that went on until midnight. Although no formal settlement was reached, Cheng agreed to incorporate one thousand bandits into the army if each of the recruits had a rifle in his possession. The government also agreed to pay one month's salary to men who enlisted and to issue rations to them. The question of the foreign government guarantee was not discussed. This proposal was not satisfactory to Kuo and Chou, but they did agree to share the offer with Sun Mei-yao and continue discussions.[15]

Powell slipped away from the negotiations and met with his friends Crow and Anderson in their railcar, where he was served dinner and stayed awake past midnight discussing the situation, even though the grueling mule ride down the mountain had exhausted him. Powell, Crow, and Anderson were all clubmen and chatted, drank, and smoked as if they were at the bar of the exclusive Shanghai Club on the Bund. Powell wanted to know from Anderson and Crow what the warlords planned to do to end the affair; Anderson wanted to know from Powell the mind-set of Sun Mei-yao and Po-Po Liu.[16] Powell explained that Liu could be satisfied solely with a bag of silver, but Sun wanted much more—his own army. This unapologetic boldness made the three Americans laugh. They also laughed at the silly "costumes" of the fan-bandits, who just days before had been dressed like gritty outlaws. All three men were troubled by the demand for some form of security guarantee for the bandits. Without it, there would be no deal and no freedom for the captives.

Given the hour, it was decided that they would stay the night at Tsao-chuang and return to Paotzuku in the morning. Consul Davis offered to host Kuo and Chou in his own carriage. Straw Hat would be Powell's responsibility.

The French representative, Consul Crépin, had informed his fellow dip-lomats that fan-bandit Kuo Chih-tsai was actually a notorious Shanghai underworld figure named Fang Yao, who was wanted by the police in the French Concession for various crimes, including extortion, arson, and kid-napping. Kuo had previously lived in Shanghai, where he ran an extortion-ist racket with his brother. The two earned a living by threatening to bomb the homes of wealthy Chinese businessmen if they did not pay up. Kuo also maintained a number of bordellos and opium dens in Shanghai and other cities, where he invested his ill-gotten gains. The police in the French Concession of Shanghai had six months earlier arrested Kuo's brother and sentenced him to five years' imprisonment. Kuo was on the run. Crépin as-sured the other foreign consuls that when all was resolved with the bandits, the French police would demand the arrest of "Kuo," who would be impris-oned in Shanghai.[17]

Anderson believed that the checkered past of the bandit subchiefs was irrelevant to the settlement discussions and that this was an issue for the French to take up after, and *only* after, the hostages were released. He made it clear that Kuo—or Fang Yao as the French claimed him to be—was not to be threatened or confronted until the negotiations were settled. After Berubé was released in suspicious circumstances, the French, in Anderson's eyes, had followed their own agenda to the detriment of their fellow diplo-mats' efforts, rendering their credibility questionable. The American fixer wanted the French sidelined from the negotiations.

When he returned to his assigned sleeping compartment after long hours of conversation, Powell was surprised to see Straw Hat waiting for him. The boy bandit looked sickly. Apparently, he had been given an extravagant dinner and eaten so much cake and candy that he was on the point of exploding.[18] Straw Hat had also smoked a cigar, inhaling the thick and intense smoke into his lungs as if it were a cigarette. Powell was able to get him outside just in time for him to throw up the entire contents of his stomach. The boy returned to the sleeping compartment stinking of vomit. He then insisted on sprawling out on the floor next to Powell's berth. He was so used to sleeping on the ground that he spurned the bed. Powell opened the windows and covered his nose, but he still had difficulty sleeping because of the smell.

IN THE MORNING, THERE WAS A CONFERENCE AMONG GENERAL CHENG, Davis, Philoon, Anderson, and Powell, in which Cheng informed the Americans that he was ready to negotiate with the bandit leaders directly.[19] The plan was that each side would be represented by an equal number of principals and guards, with Anderson taking the lead in mediating the discussion. Anderson asked Powell for his advice on how the Chinese and foreign governments should proceed. "Keep the military pressure on the bandits," Powell said. "Tighten the cordon without bloodshed. Any further skirmishes between the outlaws and the government troops could be fatal to all."

General Cheng wrote out his proposal for the next step in discussions and handed this to Powell to take back with him. Anderson emphasized to the fan-bandits that Sun Mei-yao needed to resolve any differences between the various bandit chiefs, for time was indeed limited and there was much talk of foreign military intervention. Sun had to reply to Cheng's proposal within two days.

Cheng showered dignity on the two bandit emissaries as if they were an official party and, in lieu of a mule ride, provided them (as well as Powell and Straw Hat) with sedan chairs for the return journey up to Paotzuku.[20] As they left the mining compound and were a safe distance from the gate, the boy bandit had the coolies carrying his sedan chair jog up alongside

Powell's chair. After getting Powell's attention, he giddily pulled up his jacket to show him that he had "acquired" a large army revolver, which he kept in a holster strapped to his chest. In true bandit fashion, Straw Hat had taken the liberty to steal the weapon from the mining compound while he was a guest. *This kid is truly incorrigible and hopeless*, thought Powell, clicking his tongue and shaking his head.

After traveling for about four hours through the heat of the day, they reached the military lines. The Chinese soldiers on guard refused to allow them passage through the cordon of soldiers without the formality of a written *huchow* (permit to pass). Powell's cavalcade had no option but to return to Tsaochuang to obtain the required document from General Cheng.

Upon their arrival back at the mining compound, Cheng profusely apologized and expressed regret at the actions of the guards at the military line. He mentioned to Powell that he had received orders to tighten up the military lines that morning but forgot to issue passes for Powell and the fan-bandits. This sounded like a reasonable excuse to Powell. After the huchows were issued, they set out again. As they passed the American Rescue Mission's railcar, Powell met a laughing Roy Anderson. "Powell, that was a dirty trick to play on you." Anderson smiled. "But the old *Pang-pan* has certainly impressed those bandits with the strength of his military lines," he went on, using a term of respect to refer to General Cheng.[21]

General Cheng's trick was indeed a clear message to the bandits that the military cordon was strong and that, unlike General Tien, he had full control over his troops. The two fan-bandits realized that they were indeed encircled. Cheng had subtly gotten his point across that the government was ready to negotiate but that a military solution was still very much on the table.

Kuo and Chou now understood, with more urgency than anything General Cheng or Anderson might have said to them, that the Chinese and foreign governments were losing patience and the window of opportunity to negotiate a deal was closing. The Peking politicians had gone home, and the only remaining government officials at Tsaochuang were Roy Anderson, who had been appointed by Marshal Tsao Kun, and General Cheng.

THE BANDITS WERE GROWING MORE AND MORE DISTURBED BY THE noticeable nighttime searchlight communications between Tsaochuang and the three American captives at the top of Paotzuku. Night after night, they had watched the searchlight aimlessly wave its long beam across the sky, but this was the first time the bright rays had been focused on the top of Paotzuku Mountain. It had become obvious that the officials down at the mining compound were using the searchlight to send signals to the captives.

Then, on the night of May 29, the tenth day the SAP Club had spent at the top of Paotzuku and after almost four weeks in captivity, the three Americans decoded a searchlight message that read, "Parley begins tomorrow! Hopeful of results!"[22]

CHAPTER 20

THE BREAKTHROUGH

My impression is that the brigands realize that their game is up, but that they are holding out till the eleventh hour in hopes of obtaining a maximum of security for themselves.

—Berthold George Tours, consul general, British consulate, Tsinan[1]

MAY 30, 1923, MORNING, TEMPLE OF THE CLOUDS

Early in the morning, Powell raced back down the mountain to Tsao-chuang with the news that the bandit chiefs had agreed to General Cheng's offer. They would meet and negotiate with the Chinese government's chosen representative and mediator, Roy Anderson. The meeting would take place later that day in a small village just below the Temple of the Clouds.[2]

The meeting room chosen was packed to suffocation with the negotiators, bodyguards, and various hangers-on. Anderson was in charge. He quickly realized that in the two weeks since he last spoke to the bandit leaders, strong differences had emerged between them. Po-Po Liu had lost all faith in negotiations and had become more defiant as the crisis wore on. He wanted any settlement to include a sizable ransom payment. Liu, unlike

Sun Mei-yao, had no interest in enlisting in the army. He claimed that all
the foreigners, including Anderson and the hostages, had "crooked hearts"
and should be killed. But Liu was clearly in the minority; the majority of
the bandits desired a settlement whereby they could join the government
army. It would mean steady pay and respect for men (and boys) who had
had neither for much of their lives.

Anderson could tell that these discussions would take time. He knew he
had to be patient and be prepared to cajole, manipulate, and even kowtow
to achieve the results he wanted. With General Tien out of the way, he
finally had control of the negotiations. He opened with a risky gambit: an
attempt at shaming the bandits.

"Let me start by saying that I have personally lost much face as a result of the lies about me that have been perpetuated and circulated by
the bandits," said Anderson, aware of the rumors circulating about how
the American fixer was just as evil and double-crossing as the warlords he
served. Anderson said that this was not true and that he had exhausted
himself making the difficult journeys to the bandit camp. He felt pity for
China, the country where he was born. He said that every day that this
highly publicized hostage crisis continued only added "to China's shame."
As an American, he was saddened that the Chinese were mistreating their
friends by taking American citizens hostage. After all, the United States
had recently helped China recover Shantung from Japan at the Washington Conference.[3]

Although he had just restarted negotiations, Anderson gambled that his
best approach would be to convince the bandits that he was already out of
patience and on the brink of giving up: "So, my brothers, now is the time
to act, and if you wish for me to continue to play a mediator role, you need
to act immediately or I would just as soon pack up and leave and return to
Peking and advise Marshal Tsao that I have failed to negotiate a deal." The
bandit chiefs sat quietly as Anderson's words sank in. He had made an impression on them.

Anderson then realized that it was a good moment to ask for something.
As a sign of "good faith," he pressed the bandit chiefs to immediately release William Smith and Major Allen, as he had also attempted to do more
than two weeks before. He argued that the two older men were in fragile

health. Allen was actually younger and in better condition than Musso, but the major's gleaming white hair was looked upon as a sign of old age. Anderson explained that if anything happened to these venerable foreigners, international public opinion would turn decidedly against them. The bandit chiefs said they would review the request and quickly went into the first of many sidebar discussions.

As the bandits stepped out of the one-story building to engage in private discussions, Anderson took Powell aside and told him to ride up to the temple compound and tell Smith and Allen to prepare for release. Anderson believed that the chiefs would soon come back to the table and, with much fanfare, agree to release the two white-haired captives. He wanted the men to get off the mountain before the bandits changed their minds. Powell immediately headed up the canyon to the Temple of the Clouds to break the news.[4]

As Anderson expected, the bandits returned to the table and formally agreed to unconditionally release Smith and Allen, who had by that point been in captivity for twenty-five days.[5] *Now we're getting somewhere*, thought Anderson.

Pinger and Solomon were also allowed to come down from the Paotzuku summit, where they, along with Allen, had spent the last eleven days. As they descended the pinnacle, the SAP Club looked toward the hut holding the children, and each vowed to do something to rescue them from their horrendous predicament.

Sedan chairs were prepared, and the two graying captives set out for Tsaochuang with Anderson. The release of Allen and Smith reduced the number of foreign captives to twelve.[6]

Most of the remaining hostages were relieved to see Smith go. "The poor old chap was fast losing his mental balance," said Rowlatt, as he watched Smith depart. "I am so glad he was released."[7]

The consular representative from Italy, Raffaele Ferrajolo, complained that Musso, who was in fact older than Major Allen, should also be released because of his poor health. But Anderson knew that the bandit chiefs believed Musso to be valuable and would hold on to him as long as possible. Fuming, Ferrajolo protested to General Cheng, demanding that he "make immediate arrangements for the release of Mr. Musso on account

Renowned Shanghai lawyer G. D. Musso, who represented the Shanghai Opium Combine, with Straw Hat (the adopted son of bandit chief Po-Po Liu) to his right and "Chang" (a Chinese captive who was a returning student and acted as a translator) to his left, at the Temple of the Clouds. (SHSMO)

of his illness" and claimed that the release of Smith and Allen was based upon a "question of nationality without regard for the health of the respective captives."[8]

Cheng and Anderson simply ignored the request of the Italians. Musso was not going anywhere, sick or healthy, and was likely to be held captive until the end. It was unreasonable, they thought, to believe otherwise. If the bandits wouldn't yield to the plea of the pope, they certainly wouldn't listen to Anderson. Even Rowlatt had told British counsel Tours in a letter that the bandits "will probably keep Musso."[9]

There seemed to be something about Musso that excited the bandits, something more than just his wealth or the fact that his clients were opium smugglers and operators of bawdy houses. As it turned out, Musso was also a gunrunner. He had served as the legal representative for a Shanghai arms merchant named Bacei, who had made a deal with the northern warlord Chang Tso-lin for the supply of a large quantity of firearms and ammunition. Chang advanced a deposit into a Shanghai bank account, but when the transaction collapsed after his defeat in battle, the former warlord demanded the return of the funds. Musso objected to the reimbursement on the grounds that it was a nonrefundable deposit, and he took the matter to court in Shanghai, with Italian consul Ferrajolo as a foreign assessor, acting as both an observer and advocate for Musso. Musso, of course, prevailed in the court case and was allowed to keep the funds. Chang sent an officer to seek the support of the French consulate for the return of his money, but the French government refused to take sides. French consul Crépin conveyed this story to British consul Tours; Crépin believed that Chang had engineered the whole Lincheng Incident in order to ransom Musso and get his money back. When the bandits first attacked the train, they supposedly asked many of the train staff if a foreign passenger named Musso was on board the train.

Crépin raised the gunrunning case with Ferrajolo, who strongly denied having any knowledge of the matter.[10] When Crépin pushed the issue, Ferrajolo stormed off in a huff. True or not, the gunrunning story led to a falling out among the four diplomats, with much bickering and finger-pointing in all directions.

With the hostage crisis extending into a full month, the tension among the four diplomats increased. "We are as happy a family as can be under the circumstances," said Consul Tours as he called out his fellow diplomats. "America suspects France; Italy suspects America; France suspects America and Italy over the Musso arms deal; and I suspect the whole lot. I am the only one who has made no attempt to send spies into the brigands' camp. The result is that all three take me into their confidences as against the remaining twain. It is rather like an old ladies' tea-party, with myself as grandmamma."[11]

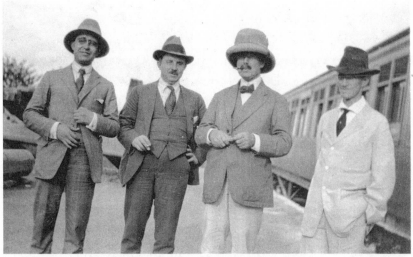

Left to right: Consuls from Italy (Raffaele Ferrajolo), France (Pierre Jean Crépin), Britain (Berthold George Tours), and the United States (John Kerr Davis) at the Tsaochuang mining compound during the standoff and the negotiations. The infighting among the consuls over the priority release of their nationals would lead to tension during negotiations, but the American fixer Roy Anderson would ultimately get them to stand down in order to effect the release of all the foreign captives. (SHSMO)

THE ONE THING THAT THE FOREIGN CAPTIVES COULD NOT GET OUT OF their minds was the Paotzuku children, the bedraggled tiny souls still languishing at the top of the pinnacle. It also led to a heated debate in the camp. Although he didn't agree with the tactics, Professor Hung believed that the children were not necessarily the victims of kidnapping but rather of financial misfortune or a financial arrangement. A parent or clan may have sent the child to the bandit camp as security for payment of a debt. A failure to pay meant that the bandits could do what they wanted to do with the children. It may have been true that the children were sold to pay debts, the foreign captives said in response, yet murder is still murder. "How can they be so horribly unconscionable—so unspeakably depraved—so utterly inhumane?" questioned Major Pinger.[12]

Hung shrugged his shoulders and didn't offer an explanation other than to say that this had always been the way that things were done in China. The foreign captives saw this as ethical corruption at its core. *China needs to make changes from the sordid and rigid past*, they all believed.[13] The foreign hostages understood that their mission was now more complicated: they needed not only to find a way to free themselves but also to rescue these helpless children.

OVER THE NEXT WEEK, ANDERSON MADE MULTIPLE TRIPS UP TO THE bandit camps for negotiations. There was much haggling over the actual number of bandits who would be enlisted in the army, the amount of back pay they would receive, and whether a bandit would be required to have a weapon to be given a uniform. As word spread through the province that the government was preparing to pay bandits to enlist, local villagers were pushing their sons and husbands, young and old, to join up. During these difficult times, an army commission meant one fewer mouth to feed. But the government had no interest in enrolling starving villagers. It also didn't want to empower Sun Mei-yao by putting even more people under his command.

Originally, the government took the position that if a bandit could not supply a rifle, there would be no uniform. But eventually this demand was relaxed, and bandits who had pistols or revolvers would be admitted as well. This concession was significant and increased the number of potential enlistees, but it also had the effect of encouraging the holders of multiple weapons to sell or barter their superfluous firearms to those without.

The financial terms were clearly not important to Sun Mei-yao. His endgame was to be the commanding officer—a brigadier general—of his own brigade of troops. With legitimate soldiers under his authority, he would be able to solidify his command and control over the southern Shantung region. By effectively ousting General Tien's troops, he would become his own minor warlord. Under Sun, fan-bandits Kuo and Chou would become colonels, and the rest of the subchiefs would also become officers.

The intractable Po-Po Liu would not join the new brigade, but he would still be protected by Sun. However, Liu was more concerned about money and a pardon, and he had no interest in joining the army. Consul Davis observed that Liu and his men were "congenital bandits" who had "no ambitions beyond being allowed indefinitely to prey upon the people." Sun, himself a savvy negotiator, persuaded Liu and three hundred of his men to accept a pardon, cash, and the protection of his soon-to-be-established brigade.[14]

Because Anderson had gotten the bandits their army commissions and back pay, he now demanded, in return, that more of the remaining captives be released. Anderson focused on the "black-haired young men" from Shanghai. He pretended that they were "worthless and troublesome," and claimed that they lacked the prestige of the other captives. Anderson also tried to get Manuel Verea released at the same time. He said Verea came from Mexico, a country that had thousands of its own bandits and thus "could not be expected to have any interest in those of countries from across the sea." Sun was aware that there was no consular representative from Mexico at Tsaochuang, so this was interpreted as a sign that the Mexican government was indifferent to Verea's capture. Anderson added that Jerome Henley, the least liked of the foreign captives and more of a disruption in the camp, should also be released.

After long, tense negotiations, the bandits agreed to release four additional captives: Eddie Elias, Theo Saphiere, Jerome Henley, and Manuel Verea.[15] This was good news for Anderson, but he kept pressing the chiefs to release more of the captives, or at least explain why he still needed to hold on to so many hostages when most of his demands had been met.

"Why do you need eight captives?" Anderson asked the chiefs.

The bandits paused and looked at one another. "We keep the last ones we like the best!" said Sun. This brought howls of laughter from the bandits.

Anderson tried to look amused; he wasn't entirely satisfied, but he thought that things were moving in the right direction. He asked Powell to head up to the Temple of the Clouds with sedan chairs to take the four captives to their freedom.[16]

Anderson stepped out of the room to have a smoke. He counted up the remaining eight foreign hostages: Powell, Friedman, Musso, Freddie Elias, Solomon, Gensburger, Rowlatt, and Pinger.[17] Anderson knew that even if he could squeeze a few more hostages from Sun, the bandit would keep at least one hostage representing each of the major foreign powers—the Americans, the French, the British, and the Italians—as collateral until he was satisfied that the Chinese would hold up their end of the bargain. Anderson was, first and foremost, focused on gaining the freedom of the foreign captives, yet Powell reminded him of the plight of the Chinese, especially Professor Hung and Chi Cheng. "In good time," Anderson reassured Powell, although even Anderson knew that he was unlikely to have much impact on the fate of the Chinese hostages. The reality was that the foreign captives took priority for geopolitical reasons—Marshal Tsao Kun himself prioritized the release of the foreigners first because he didn't want to have to listen to the grumbling of the foreign diplomatic corps in Peking. The Chinese government could deal with the bandits and Chinese captives later, without so much scrutiny.

Anderson needed a backup plan in the event that discussions went south. While outside, he watched Powell and the Frenchman organize a train of sedan chairs. "Come with me," Anderson said as he approached Powell and the Frenchman. "I have an idea that might just work."

On June 7, Sun Mei-yao went to the Temple of the Clouds to announce that a tentative agreement had been reached. Sun informed the eight remaining captives that as soon as confirmation was received from Marshal Tsao Kun, they expected Anderson to come up to the camp with various officials to sign the deal.

"We keep the last ones we like the best!" said bandit Sun Mei-yao. Photo taken by Major Roland Pinger on the final day of captivity. *Front row, left to right*: John B. Powell, Freddie Elias, and Emile Gensburger. *Middle row*: captive and interpreter known as "Chang," banker and returning Cambridge student Chi Cheng, and Reginald Rowlatt. *Back row*: Leon Friedman, Lee Solomon, and G. D. Musso. Not shown are Professor Hung Shi-chi and Major Roland Pinger. (Pinger)

The official enrollers of the army had arrived with paper, ink, and brushes, along with many boxes of uniforms and food for the new brigade. The process of enrollment would take several days to complete. Until then, said Sun, the remaining captives needed to sit tight. The only contentious issue that remained was the guarantee of the foreign governments. Though pleased with the news, the captives became quickly impatient that their freedom was so close but was delayed because of paperwork.

Sun then mentioned that there was also talk that the bandits might keep only three of the high-value captives, pointing to Pinger, Rowlatt, and Gensburger. They would thus be releasing five additional captives, including the sickly Musso. This way they would continue to hold an American, British, and French citizen as a guarantee. The bandits knew that Pinger, Rowlatt, and Gensburger were in good enough shape that they could be pushed to a remote hideout on a moment's notice if the deal collapsed or the bandits were betrayed.

They would be Sun's insurance policy; Musso, despite his powerful connections, was no longer seen as valuable because he couldn't be easily moved.

"How long?" Rowlatt asked Sun.

"Oh, maybe a week, maybe a *month or so!*" Sun said sarcastically. Then he left the temple courtyard.

He can't be serious, Major Pinger thought.

"Oh boy," Rowlatt said with a sigh, looking at the concerned faces of Pinger and Gensburger.

"In the long months to come they want healthy, agreeable, *mobile*, youngish hostages—not people that they might have to shoot for their inability to run," Pinger said.[18]

They all also feared that the more desperate element of the outlaw band, those who were unfit for army discipline, would seize the remaining three and flee deeper into the mountains.

"They have *no* intention *whatsoever* of releasing the last three," said Solomon, saying out loud what everyone was thinking.

"We are not leaving anyone behind!" Friedman said with authority. All of them nodded and then shouted out in agreement.

Even Musso, who would be one of those released and who was physically on his last leg, could not in good conscience cut and run on his fellow prisoners. They had all stood together through thick and thin.

"Nothing doing—eight or none!" they instantly said.[19] With that, the captives instructed Powell to pass on a message to Anderson that they had made a collective decision that a partial release was wholly unacceptable.

"All eight," they shouted, "or none!"

CHAPTER 21

FREEDOM

We are willing to be "called and pacified" and organized into a national army. From this time on, we will be permanently loyal to the country and commit nothing that will disturb the order of the army or hurt the reputation of soldiers.

—Bandits of Paotzuku Mountain[1]

JUNE 8, 1923, MORNING, TEMPLE OF THE CLOUDS

The captives and bandits watched overhead as a wood-and-canvas biplane flew up the valley and circled Paotzuku. The loud whir of the engine broke the morning calm, echoing off the canyon walls. This was one of two British-made Avro scout biplanes that Marshal Tsao Kun had sent down to Lincheng in special railcars a week earlier.

He wanted to start aerial observation of the bandits to monitor their strength and position, and to watch for any attempt to escape northward to the more mountainous regions of central Shantung. Although the airplanes were armed with machine guns and could drop small bombs, this plane was just dropping leaflets that urged the bandits to accept peaceful terms.[2]

Yet the bandits did not respond peacefully. Instead, they trained their rifles on the plane and began shooting wildly, although the aircraft was much too high and fast for their bullets.[3] The bandits saw the government spy plane as a bad omen—their enemies now had eyes on them from above— and thought it meant that a large-scale attack was imminent, perhaps with the support of the foreign powers.

Unlike the bandits, the hostages saw the plane as a good sign. "This is better than the grandstand at the county fair," laughed Friedman, recalling his barnstorming days.

Anderson was aware that the cordon of troops was getting tighter and tighter. He was also aware of the aircraft sorties and the increased presence of foreign military officers at Tsaochuang and at military lines. The officers were part of a commission organized by the foreign powers to investigate the military situation arising from the Lincheng Incident. The Chinese government wasn't happy with the commission but begrudgingly accepted it. However, the investigation, like the planes overhead, raised the stakes for everyone: hostages, bandits, and the government in Peking.[4] Anderson needed to play these cards to his advantage.

ANDERSON CONTINUED NEGOTIATING WITH THE BANDIT CHIEFS OVER the next three days. The sticking point remained the same: the guarantee of the foreign governments. For the bandits, this was, as always, nonnegotiable—they wanted some trustworthy outsider to certify that the deal they made with the Chinese government was binding and wouldn't just be ignored once the hostage standoff was resolved. Anderson knew he couldn't get the French, Italian, American, or British governments to offer a guarantee, so he proposed an audacious alternative.

Would Sun and his fellow bandit chiefs be willing to accept a *personal* guarantee from Anderson for the performance of the Chinese government? Anderson could see that the bandits were getting spooked by the biplanes. For all the tough talk by Sun and his cohorts, there was a sense that the sooner they were in the army and the hostages released, the better.

Anderson said that he would not make such a guarantee on faith alone. Rather, he would ask for a written pledge from the Peking government, which he would receive by telegram from Marshal Tsao Kun. Although Anderson placed his trust in Tsao, he was no stranger to the frequent shenanigans of the mercurial tuchuns—double-crossing your friends was a warlord tradition. But the telegram gave him the go-ahead that he needed to close the deal.

Although hesitant, the bandits decided to take a chance on Anderson.[5] He was known and respected by all the power brokers in China, and as an American he was also an outsider who was perceived as uncorrupted. Such a diplomatic solution to the crisis had no precedent in the history of China. Never before had a private foreign citizen been given the authority to guarantee the performance of the Chinese government. Anderson was accustomed to advising cutthroat warlords who fought each other to the death, but this was the first time that he felt a deep sense of concern for his personal safety during a negotiation. It would be his name on the performance guarantee of a very unstable government.

Anderson's word helped settle the matter of the guarantee, yet the bandit chiefs continued to debate whether to hold on to a few hostages for leverage. Anderson had gotten the "all or none" message from the captives; he had no intention now of leaving anyone behind. So he had to somehow force the bandit chiefs to come to final terms. If they waffled, there was a risk that a dissenting group of bandits would take the eight remaining captives and go their own way.

With that in mind, Anderson had cut a side deal with the Frenchman, who, with a group of his allies, would protect the hostages should the deal go south.[6] This was the conversation Anderson had had with the Frenchman and Powell earlier in the week when he had negotiated the release of Eddie Elias, Theo Saphiere, Jerome Henley, and Manuel Verea. As one of the leading subchiefs, the Frenchman spent a lot of time at the Temple of the Clouds. Powell and Musso had gotten to know him well. His time in Europe during the Great War allied him to the foreigners more than could be said of the other bandits. Powell and Pinger had told Anderson that not only could the Frenchman be trusted; he also had a mind of his own and would turn against Sun Mei-yao and Po-Po Liu if the situation called for it.

If negotiations collapsed and they had to send in the military to rescue the hostages, the Frenchman agreed to protect the eight foreign captives, using his loyal men to form a protective cushion around them inside the Temple of the Clouds. He would then barricade the hostages in limestone caves behind the temple compound until they were all liberated. In exchange for this, the Frenchman and his allies would be given preferential treatment, including immunity and commissions in the Republican Army.

It was a bargain within a bargain, but it gave Anderson the edge he needed to play hardball with the bandits. Anderson intended to have one final meeting with Sun and Liu. He would give them what they wanted when it came to enlistment and back pay, on the nonnegotiable condition that all foreign hostages had to be released immediately. If talks failed, Anderson planned to withdraw from the discussions and advise the government troops to attack immediately.

THE FINAL, DRAMATIC SCENE OF NEGOTIATIONS TOOK PLACE ON JUNE 12, the thirty-seventh day of captivity, in a decrepit rural village by the Tenli River, two miles down the mountainside from the Temple of the Clouds— well within the bandit lines. A run-down barn served as the conference room, with old, weathered doors and planks propped up on posts to serve as a makeshift table.

Anderson had sent a letter to the bandits stating that all the preparations were made. Their uniforms and money were ready. All they had to do was agree to release the hostages and sign on the dotted line. Anderson also signaled to the chiefs that he was in no mood for further stalling. He said that he had important business to attend to in Hong Kong and that if a deal could not be reached that day, he wouldn't be around tomorrow to continue talking.[7]

To a full room, Anderson started with a lengthy speech about the traditional friendship between China and the United States, emphasizing his personal sacrifice to mediate and resolve the issues between the bandits and the Chinese government. "After you, my brethren, have submitted, you shall, for the sake of your country and fellow citizens, be loyal to your country and keep the order of the army, so that the whole nation, seeing that you are serving the country, will praise your spirit of sacrifice," Anderson said, speaking slowly in Chinese and reading off the written guarantee. He directed his comments mainly to Sun Mei-yao, who beamed with a sense of accomplishment and honor.[8] Po-Po Liu, on the other hand, looked away in a trance of disillusionment.

Anderson then produced a large, scroll-like Chinese-language document two feet wide and three feet long, outlining the terms and conditions. Each of the bandits would be pardoned, and 2,700 of the bandits would be enrolled into the Chinese army, forming the "New Brigade." Each soldier would receive a small cash payment along with uniforms and provisions. In addition, the Peking government would direct funds to rebuild the villages of southern Shantung that were damaged or destroyed by the Chinese troops.

In truth, the amount of silver dollars that was hauled up to the negotiations was a pittance compared to the reparations demanded by the bandits. But Anderson's strategy was to use the chests of shiny coins to dazzle the bandits and create the impression that the Chinese authorities would make good on their promises. Included in the written agreement was a stipulation that the remaining eight foreign hostages *must be immediately released*.

The room became silent after Anderson read off the terms of the agreement, which later became known as the Lincheng Accords. Anderson was prepared to unleash a harangue if the bandits quibbled with the deal, but he hesitated. He did not want to provoke another sidebar discussion, which would give the bandits the chance to pause and endlessly bargain. He decided that it was better to allow Sun Mei-yao to save face and to capture the moment as the leader of the New Brigade.

Anderson turned to Sun and offered him the floor, referring to the bandit chief for the first time as General Sun Mei-yao. All eyes were now on the bandit chief turned brigadier general. Sun knew that this was his cue and rose to his feet and gave a rousing speech about friendship and comradeship. He pledged the allegiance of his brigade—his so-called Self-Governed Army for the Establishment of the Country—to the Chinese government and declared that it was both an honor and a privilege for him and his allies to serve the Chinese people.

The room erupted in cheers from all quarters.

Several of Sun's underlings stood up and bowed toward Anderson in a sign of reverence—including the fan-bandits, Kuo and Chou, looking regal in their scholarly attire. Others came up to the tall American fixer or reached across the table to shake his hand. Anderson then looked around the room and invited the bandit leaders to sign the guarantee to conclude the settlement agreement between the New Brigade and the Chinese government.

Powell watched as Sun, "with a grand flourish," stepped up to the table and signed the document. Then Liu and the other bandit chiefs added their signatures, followed by those of Anderson and the Shantung authorities.[9]

Anderson turned to Powell as the room once again erupted in noisy applause: "It is a fine kettle of fish when a foreigner has to sign a document guaranteeing the good faith of the Republic of China."[10] The two men were amazed at the turn of events, but there wasn't much time to chat, for they both wanted to get all the hostages down to Tsaochuang as quickly as possible. From the corner of his eye, Anderson could see that the old bandit chief Liu was silently fuming over the outcome. This worried Anderson.

While both the other bandit chiefs and the representatives from the Chinese side exchanged handshakes and accolades, Anderson signaled to Powell to ride up to the temple and prepare the remaining hostages to leave.[11] Anderson feared that a renegade band led by Liu would disrupt the release of the foreigners. To ensure the quick evacuation, Anderson had readied eight two-man sedan chairs with plenty of coolie reliefs.

On their way down the mountain from the Temple of the Clouds, the remaining eight foreign hostages stopped to bid farewell to an exultant Sun and the fan-bandits. They wanted to take photographs and to drink one last celebratory shot of samshu together. Pinger, Friedman, Rowlatt, Solomon, and even Musso welcomed the opportunity for a final drink with these "gentlemen of the hills."

Anderson did not. Neither did Professor Hung and Chi Cheng, who looked on as they wondered about their own uncertain predicament. Anderson tried to usher the foreign captives back in the sedan chairs and out of bandit territory. He was a calm man, but he had no more patience for clowning around. He desperately wanted to get the hostages past the

Bandit chief Sun Mei-yao with hostage Lee Solomon, bandit chief Po-Po Liu, and Liu's bodyguards. (Pinger)

military lines before sunset. "Don't you want to be liberated?" Anderson called out loudly. He was dumbfounded that such camaraderie should exist between the hostages and the bandits. "Let's get the hell out of here."[12]

They all got the message and with much haste said their good-byes to the bandit chiefs.

But then Major Pinger noticed that Hung and Chi Cheng were not provided sedan chairs, so he decided to join them on foot. Pinger could tell that they were very anxious because they were not sure if they were allowed to go. "Just consider yourself one of us—walk with us—we'll take care of you somehow," said Major Pinger.[13]

No sooner were they on the move than Po-Po Liu caught up to them and stopped the procession of sedan chairs. He then yelled at the two interpreters in Chinese.

"He says I must go back," said Chi Cheng.

"Pay no attention to him, Cheng," said Pinger. Liu didn't even have his firearm with him.

Musso then intervened in Chinese and told the old bandit chief that a special arrangement had been worked out so that the departing foreigners were entitled to two interpreters up to the military lines. At the military lines, the interpreters would go back up the mountain. If he didn't believe them, Musso suggested that escorts accompany them to the military lines to find out. None of this was true, of course. Liu called Musso's bluff; he ordered a few of his trusted henchmen to follow the interpreters to make sure they didn't flee with the foreign hostages.

Yet as soon as they arrived at the military lines, the half-dozen bandit escorts sent by Liu found themselves facing down the rifles of two companies of Chinese soldiers. Seeing that the bandits were outgunned, the foreigners started yelling in unison for Hung and Cheng to run past the military lines with them to safety. The two interpreters sprinted to freedom.[14] Realizing that they had been hoodwinked, the bandit escorts simply smiled, turned, and galloped back to the hills. The foreigners cheered. "It was all or none!" they shouted in agreement.

AROUND EIGHT O'CLOCK THAT EVENING, THIRTY-SEVEN DAYS AFTER THE start of their ordeal, the last eight foreign hostages from the Peking Express arrived at Tsaochuang.[15] A crowd of friendly and curious faces—Chinese and foreign, soldiers and onlookers—greeted the bedraggled men as they entered the mining compound. After more than five weeks in captivity, all had unshaven faces, unkempt hair, and grubby clothes. The grunting, sweating coolies carefully lowered the sedan chairs to the ground.

Left to right: Major Roland Pinger, Lee Solomon, G. D. Musso (in sedan chair), and John B. Powell realizing that they are finally free as they depart the Temple of the Clouds for the Tsaochuang mining compound after 37 days of captivity. (Pinger)

Italian consul Ferrajolo and Dr. Mertens greeted the ailing Musso, helping to lift him out of the sedan chair and onto his feet. French consul Crépin
approached the younger Gensburger, a French protégé, handing him clothes
and letters from his family. Tours took aside Rowlatt, his fellow Brit, offering him a cigarette. American diplomats Davis and Philoon joined the
larger crowd of American ex-captives as they cheered Anderson and Powell
for brokering their release. Despite their earlier bickering, the other diplomats—Tours, Crépin, and Ferrajolo—all thanked Anderson for his efforts
on behalf of their citizens. Davis was also highly complimentary of Anderson, finding that he "displayed fearlessness, resourcefulness, impartiality,
and a thorough knowledge of Chinese character" and that "the Chinese officials looked to him for leadership and, together with the bandits themselves,
have evidenced the strongest belief in his ability and good faith."[16]

The captives took turns bathing in the sole bathtub at the mining
company—a bit of modern luxury in the middle of nowhere. A hot bath
and a shave did wonders for their appearances and spirits. They also
changed into a fresh set of clothes previously sent to Tsaochuang by their
families—most of the items hung from their bodies because everyone had
lost weight during the weeks in captivity.

The diplomats hosted the former captives—plus Hung and Cheng—
with their first real dinner since the holdup. They admired the savory meal
cooked in the mining company's kitchen, as well as the dishes, silverware,
and linen that adorned the tables. They joked about how nobody was eating
out of a tin can, cooking over a campfire, or having "local critter cuisine."
Nor did they worry that one of the bandits would come over and pilfer their
grub. They expressed much gratitude toward Carl Crow and the American
Rescue Mission for having kept them all remarkably well fed and connected
with loved ones, thanks to the Coolie Express and its mail service.

It was Powell who reminded the group that their job wasn't over. Although they were now enjoying freedom, something must be done for the
remaining Chinese captives and, even more urgently, for the kidnapped
children who were languishing at the top of Paotzuku. They all agreed.
Anderson vowed to raise the issue with Marshal Tsao Kun. Powell and
Crow said that they would not only publicize the plight of Chinese captives
in the media but would also rally business leaders to call for the release

of the remaining hostages. Cheng also offered to garner support from his colleagues at China Merchants and from the larger Shanghai business community.[17]

About midnight, after much drinking and eating, the former hostages all headed for a single sleeper car in the mining compound's rail yard to get a few hours of rest. Powell took an upper bunk in the carriage, much as he had on the night of the derailment. As he stared at the ceiling, it finally dawned on him that he was no longer in a bandit camp. There would be no further beatings. No more gunfire from pursuing troops. No more marching across the countryside. Never again would he have to worry about the menacing Straw Hat or other trigger-happy teen bandits. But, in a strange way, he knew he would also miss the comradeship of his fellow hostages, not to mention the friendlier bandits and the moments of unforgettable entertainment they provided, including Russky's Russian ballads. He grinned as he thought about his cowboy-like mule rides up and down the mountain—Friedman had called him a "hero" at dinner, but he didn't see himself that way.

Powell heaved a sigh of relief. He knew he had lived through what would be the most unforgettable experience of his life. Paotzuku Mountain, for all the hell he endured there, was indeed one of the prettiest places he had ever seen. His eyes welled up with emotion as he considered how close he had come to death. It was a miracle that he survived. As he slowly dozed off, he thought of nothing but his family in Shanghai and how badly he wanted to be reunited with them.

At four o'clock in the morning, a mine-engine locomotive hooked up to the sleeper car with a noticeable thump. It barely woke Powell and the other exhausted ex-hostages. The locomotive and carriage then lurched forward through the rail yard and the compound's open railway gates, which clanged shut as it passed. Despite the jolts and motion of the train, Powell turned over to sleep again for the thirty-minute ride from Tsaochuang to Lincheng. There he would catch the early-morning train south to Shanghai. Finally, he was going home.

CHAPTER 22

A PALACE COUP

The Lincheng Incident has served to bring strongly to the attention of the civilized world the utter collapse of government in China. Failure to read aright the handwriting on the wall will inevitably lead to the occurrence of some further and greater tragedy that will shock the world.

—John K. Davis, American consul, June 12, 1923[1]

JUNE 13, 1923, SHANGHAI-NANKING RAILWAY STATION TO TIENTSIN CENTRAL STATION

The crowd of thousands that greeted the former captives in Shanghai was the largest the city had ever seen. As the train drew into the Shanghai-Nanking Railway Station—the same station from which they started their journey on May 5—the Russian Cadet Band, courtesy of Shanghai's prestigious Astor House Hotel, played Handel's "See, the Conqu'ring Hero Comes!" A sea of well-wishers washed over the blue-steel train as it slowly came into the bay platform with its steam brakes hissing.[2] Photographers held aloft dozens of T-shaped flash lamps to illuminate the scene for both the still and motion-picture cameras that were registering every move of the former captives. The intense brilliant light of the magnesium flash powder gave off a loud whoosh of white smoke and vapor, delighting the celebratory crowds. Ex-captive Larry Lehrbas had come out to meet the train, as had dozens of other journalists eager to get the story.

Powell was greeted by his wife, Martha; four-year-old son, John William; and nine-year-old daughter, Martha. His sister Margaret, who had taken the reins of the *Weekly Review* during his captivity, was also waiting at the station. To the delight of his family, Powell was quickly pulled away and hoisted on the shoulders of friends. His efforts to broker a deal had been well documented in the press.

The entire Italian community of Shanghai came out to greet their favored son Musso, their *capitano d'industria—Il Commendatore*. Musso had lost much weight and looked aged, worn, and ragged, with gray patches of stubble on his face. He wanted to show his comrades that he could walk on his own, and he did so with the aid of crutches, all the while smiling for well-wishers.

Eddie Elias, Victor Haimovitch, Alfred Zimmerman, and Theo Saphiere were there to meet Freddie Elias and Emile Gensburger as they stepped off the train. The Shanghai cousins were back together again. Leon Friedman emerged from the train to find the complete staff of China Motors waiting for him. They had arrived at the station in multiple fancy motorcars—knowing that Friedman would approve of this opportunity to show off the inventory. Friedman was clean-shaven, and he looked his usual "hale and cheerful self," according to the pressmen. As he tried to get his arms around one of several beautiful women who were in his welcoming party, a reporter asked Friedman how the bandits had treated him. "They feared me," he said jokingly as he smiled, stood tall, and puffed out his chest—more to impress the women than the newspapermen calling out questions.[3]

WHEREAS POWELL, FRIEDMAN, MUSSO, AND OTHERS TRAVELED SOUTH to reach their homes in Shanghai, Pinger, Anderson, and Rowlatt headed north. Anderson's destination was his home in Peking, and Rowlatt lived in Tientsin. Pinger was on his way to Tientsin as well to reunite with his family and Allen's family, who were together waiting for him there.

Left to right: Reginald Rowlatt and Roland Pinger after their release from captivity on June 13, 1923, at a stopover at the Tsinan train station on their way northward to Tientsin. (Pinger)

Unlike in Shanghai, there were no large crowds, musical bands, or reporters to greet the released hostages as they arrived at Tientsin. But the scene at the Central Station was no less chaotic. There was great commotion on one of the adjoining sidetracks. Army troops had surrounded a train car. "That's President Li's train car," said Anderson. "Something serious is happening."

Anderson had been so far away from Peking, and so busy with negotiations, that he had no idea that a political crisis was underway. The president of the Republic, Li Yuan-Hung, was effectively under siege. His entire cabinet had resigned. Several factors contributed to the downfall of Li's government, including economic instability, massive student-led street demonstrations, and threats from various warlords. But the Lincheng Incident was the proverbial straw that broke the camel's back.[4] As the bandit outrage unfolded, the Li government had struggled to come up with a cohesive and decisive strategy to secure the release of the captives.[5] President Li looked both incompetent and weak in the eyes of Chinese power players for failing to stand up to the foreign powers who persistently dictated ultimatums and threats about the safe return of the hostages. The politically embattled President Li had to face the reality that his primary supporter, Marshal Tsao Kun, was demanding his resignation. In fact, Tsao had engineered a coup to give himself the opportunity to replace Li. As Li departed Peking on June 12, he sent a letter to the diplomatic corps stating that he was leaving for Tientsin because he could not "freely exercise" his functions as president.[6] It was unclear if this meant that he had given up his power.

As their train stopped, Pinger and Rowlatt did not stick around to watch this presidential crisis unfold. Instead, they raced out to see their families and friends and were quickly whisked away in motorcars. After bidding the men farewell, Anderson mulled around the station waiting for the train to take him home to Peking. He took the opportunity to approach several soldiers on the platform. "Why are you holding President Li?" he asked.

"He's a fugitive," replied one soldier.

On the orders of Tsao, Li had been detained in his private train car for twelve hours by a cordon of troops. Tsao wanted his hands on the official seals of the presidential office—which had gone missing. Only the holder of the seals could exercise the powers of the presidency.[7] Evidently, Li's wife had concealed the presidential seals under her dress while she was hiding at a French hospital in Peking. Li had left the official presidential seals in Madame Li's custody with strict instructions not to deliver them to anyone without his authorization.

In the end, a deal was made to release Li's train in exchange for the presidential seals. When President Li reached his private residence in the foreign concession of Tientsin at four-thirty in the morning, he dispatched several telegrams confirming his resignation. Li's wife then released the seals in the early-morning hours of June 14.[8] Tsao's allies took control of the seals and informed the press that they were exercising the powers of the presidency.[9] The coup was completed.

Anderson felt a deep sense of unease, the weight of his personal commitment to the bandit chiefs on his mind. The warlord intrigue dominating

Peking was baffling. The only consolation he had was that his benefactor, Tsao, still nominally held the reins of the government. But Anderson knew better than anyone that Tsao could be scheming and volatile. Something told him that he needed to watch his back in the months ahead.

Despite the fact that the remaining eight foreigners and two interpreters had been released, scores of Chinese prisoners remained in captivity. The remaining Chinese prisoners were purportedly of financial means, and the professional bandits led by Po-Po Liu continued to hold them in the hope of receiving ransom payments. "Now that the foreigners have been let go," wrote one Chinese captive, "nobody bothers any more about us." Led by the former foreign captives, loud protests were made to the military and civilian governors of Shantung and to Tsao, demanding immediate action to effect the release of the remaining prisoners at Paotzuku. After almost two months of captivity, the Chinese passengers of the Peking Express were released on June 25 under a deal brokered by a local magistrate. Several months later, and as a result of the media attention and public outcry, the Paotzuku children were eventually removed from the top of the mountain by the Catholic and Presbyterian missionaries and either returned to their families if they could be located or placed in the care of mission schools.[10]

CHAPTER 23

BETRAYAL

Sun Mei-yao was a notorious bandit leader. He was responsible for the Lincheng outrage, in connection with which Chinese and foreigners were kidnapped to bring pressure to bear upon the Government. No robbers in history have done so much harm to the country as Sun Mei-yao. The dishonor and loss of dignity suffered by the country fills one with indignation.

—Proclamation, Shantung military, December 20, 1923[1]

JUNE–DECEMBER 1923, LINCHENG, SHANTUNG PROVINCE

Following the signing of the Lincheng Accords in June, 2,700 members of the Paotzuku bandit gang were incorporated into the New Brigade, with Sun Mei-yao as brigadier general and with the fan-bandits Chou and Kuo as colonels and commanders of two regiments. The New Brigade was stationed in Lincheng and tasked with keeping order and security in the region.

General Cheng Shih-chi, the military governor of Shantung who replaced the much-hated General Tien and who was also at the table during the final rounds of negotiations, was piqued from the start by the brash Sun and quietly plotted revenge against the bandit chief.[2] Cheng's strategy was to keep Sun and his associates on a short leash and then look for the first excuse to disband the New Brigade and punish its members.

The sins of Lincheng had been too great to ignore. The highly publicized hostage standoff had been a stain upon China's national honor. And its military was humiliated by having to enroll thousands of bandits into the army. Cheng was determined to take steps to provoke Sun to commit offenses that could give him a pretext to have the ex-bandit arrested.[3] A trusted ally of Cheng, Colonel Wu K'o-chang, was stationed at Tsaochuang to keep an eye on Sun and the New Brigade. Sun despised Wu, knowing full well that he was Cheng's spy.

Almost immediately after the New Brigade was formed, there were several incidents that justified Sun's removal. To begin with, he refused to surrender captured firearms to the local government armory. He snubbed this request, believing that the weapons were recovered by the New Brigade under his leadership and should be kept in his control. Sun also refused to engage in suppression operations against bandit groups south of Tsaochuang at the Kiangsu-Shantung border; he would not lead attacks against men who had formerly been his brothers in arms. Worse, Sun had difficulty controlling his own troops, who began harassing the local villagers—eating their food and running roughshod over their homes.[4] Many in Sun's brigade were extorting from the farmers and the merchants just as they had done before—the very same tactics employed by General Tien's troops.

Wu viewed Sun's actions as "an intention to rebel" and reported this mutinous activity to Cheng, who, in turn, issued a secret order for the capture of Sun and the disbandment of the irredeemable New Brigade. As soon as the tall kaoliang was cut to reduce the hiding places in the fields, Cheng planned to send in his troops to wipe out this gang of soldier-bandits. In early December, he quietly moved seven thousand troops into Lincheng and Tsaochuang, under the command of the loyal commander Chang P'ei-jung. The idea was to surround the New Brigade with such a massive show of force that it would have no choice but to surrender.

In the meantime, the fan-bandits, Chou and Kuo, could see that Sun was being unnecessarily antagonistic toward Wu, creating problems for himself and the New Brigade. They realized that Sun was a target and that it was in their best interest to distance themselves from him and maintain a cordial relationship with Wu.

To save their own skins, Chou and Kuo agreed to cooperate with Chang and Wu and to offer no resistance to a planned arrest of Sun and the disbandment of their two regiments. For their cooperation, Chou and Kuo would retain their positions as colonels and eventually be promoted to the position of inspectors by the government forces.

ON DECEMBER 19, CHANG INVITED SUN AND OTHER SENIOR OFFICERS OF the New Brigade to dinner at the Tsaochuang mining compound. The ruse was an opportunity to meet and discuss the security situation in the district.

As they gathered in the dining room at Tsaochuang's administrative building, Sun began to brief the visiting Chang on the New Brigade's activities and also to report, from his perspective, the challenges he was having with Wu. After listening to Sun's iteration of his efforts, Chang bluntly asked Sun why he refused to take orders to suppress bandit activity in the region. Sun balked at the idea of arresting and executing the local bandits, for many of them were from nearby communities and had been his supporters during the Lincheng Incident.[5]

Chang scoffed at Sun's self-serving comments. As Chang and Sun debated the efforts of the New Brigade, Colonel Wu sat quietly. Sun could see that Wu had obviously been conniving against him and that he had gone behind Sun's back to report the events in the district in a manner that made Sun look undisciplined. As expected, Chang took Sun's defiance as an act of mutiny: the excuse that the Shantung authorities needed to act against him and his band. Chang waited for Sun to end his tirade and then let out a deep sigh. "No, sir, your ongoing lawless acts have disturbed the peace of the district and, by taking foreigners hostage, you have brought great harm and dishonor to the Chinese people in the eyes of the world," Chang said, slowly and deliberately. "You, as the ringleader, yesterday and today, are to be held accountable."[6]

Sun scoffed at Chang's lecturing, but he must have begun to see the direction of the conversation. *Why was he bringing up the Lincheng Incident again? Was I not pardoned?* Sun wondered.

As he looked around the table and dining hall, Sun could see that the room was lined with armed troops, guns readied. Kuo and Chou, seated at the table, never spoke up to offer support and never looked at Sun directly. *This is all a setup*, Sun realized.

As he slowly stood up from the table, Sun and his bodyguards seated nearby were immediately surrounded and disarmed by the regular troops. Sun didn't even have a chance to unholster his sidearm. Word spread within the Tsaochuang mining compound, and the regular troops quickly encircled and neutralized scores of Sun's followers who were eating dinner in a separate canteen. The troops dragged ten members of Sun's entourage who showed resistance to the courtyard and summarily shot them in the back of the head.

Sun could hear the screams of his compatriots. He stood before Chang, begging for a chance to explain himself, as the troops tied his arms behind his back. He even begged to talk with the American fixer, Roy Anderson, who had guaranteed his safety. The troops then forced a strip of cloth in Sun's mouth, gagging him as they tightly tied it behind his head. His face became deep red from the struggle.

All talk was over. There was nothing to discuss. Sun was hauled out into the compound courtyard in full view of Kuo and Chou, who were standing idle and, as he could see, not under guard. They said nothing. "Traitors! Traitors!" Sun kept trying to yell out, but only a muffled noise was heard. Once in the courtyard, Sun saw on the ground the lifeless, freshly bleeding bodies of his bodyguard and fellow comrades at arms. As he moved across the courtyard, he came face to face with Wu.

Sun was then forced down to his knees, arms behind his back. The blood drained rapidly from his face. Bound and gagged, he let out muffled yells and screams to no avail. As the troops stepped away, all he could do was stare straight ahead, biting on the now-soaked cloth gag. His eyes welled with tears.

He knew exactly what was coming. Wu, stepping to the side, swiftly beheaded the kneeling Sun using his officer's sword.

As Sun's body and still-gagged severed head hit the ground, silence fell over the courtyard—until a voice pierced through the quiet. "Let this be a warning to all. Acts of lawlessness will never go unpunished," Chang said.

Sun's severed head was rolled in dirt to congeal the blood and was then placed in a basket for transport to Tsinan for public exhibition in the provincial capital. The other dead New Brigade members were propped up against a wall. Photographers were on hand to document the executions.

Kuo and Chou would order the troops under their command to peacefully surrender. In a deal cut beforehand, the soldiers of the fan-bandits' regiments would receive three months' pay and an additional amount for each rifle surrendered. The bandit-soldiers were further required to produce documentation from guarantors, including members of the gentry or family members, to demonstrate that, once disbanded, they would find work and not break the law. Those who could not produce sufficient documentation were imprisoned. Anyone who resisted the disbandment was summarily executed—a number that was reported to exceed six hundred soldier-bandits.[7]

A proclamation was posted on the city gates and railway stations on December 20, which was evidently drawn up for the purpose of justifying Sun's execution.[8] Some members of the New Brigade surrendered; others fled. Sun's younger brother, Sun Mei-sung, a battalion commander, had disappeared along with three New Brigade commanders. On January 7, 1924, district magistrates in southern Shantung ordered warrants for their arrests.

After Sun's execution, the professional bandits working the Paotzuku district had nowhere to hide and no one to protect them. Their key ally had been executed. Liu and other professional bandits under Sun's protection knew that it was time to run.

Roy Anderson became physically sick when he was told about the trickery that led to the execution of Sun and hundreds of his bandit army.[9] He had staked his name when he signed the agreement, guaranteeing that the Chinese government would uphold its end of the bargain. But that guarantee had turned into a blood-drenched sham. After decades of being a trusted adviser to warlords and foreign governments alike, Anderson thought that his life's work in China, along with his credibility, had been violated. It was his name on the guarantee, not Tsao Kun's. Anderson felt a sense of betrayal by his purported ally and now the new leader of the country.

The American fixer began to think that this had all been a game, that he had been used by Tsao to cut a deal with the bandits for the release of the foreign hostages only to discredit the leadership of President Li Yuan-Hung so that Tsao could oust him from office. In time, Tsao's own duplicity would be his undoing. Sure enough, Tsao would last only one year in office as president until rival factions turned against him. He was imprisoned by one of his own generals.

The betrayal of the bandits also put Anderson's safety at risk. Shortly after the death of Sun, an attempt was made on Anderson's life as he slept in a compartment on a train from Nanking to Shanghai. Several unknown men tried to strangle him, but Anderson was able to fight them off and call for help. The assailants were never identified or caught, but Anderson's enemies were many. Rumors reflected a connection to the disgraced warlord Tien. Others thought that the assailants were remnants of Sun's gang. Shaken yet mostly unharmed, Anderson never reported the incident for fear that it would tarnish his reputation as an impartial mediator in Chinese politics. He and his wife decided to spend a few months in America, hoping that things would cool off. Anderson returned to China in 1924 and resumed his business activities. Yet the attack on the train from Nanking to Shanghai proved to be prescient of what was to come.

On March 12, 1925, Anderson died unexpectedly at St. Michael's Hospital in Peking under suspicious circumstances. He was just forty-two years old and apparently in good health. The cause of death was cited as "from the effects of pneumonia," but he had not been ill, and his death was never fully explained. His wife suspected foul play, believing that he had been assassinated by some powerful person in China who either sought revenge for some past action by Anderson or viewed his influence as a threat. "His life was not in danger from illness but from enemies in China," Julia Anderson insisted.[10]

The American legation ordered its staff to enter Anderson's home in Peking and gather five parcels of Anderson's papers, which were sealed and taken into custody. Although no reason was given, Anderson's role as an adviser to the United States and to various Chinese warlords and governments meant that he likely had many secrets worth protecting.

COMMANDER CHANG SENT EACH OF THE EX-HOSTAGES WHO LIVED IN China a photograph showing the sprawled and bloody bodies of the New Brigade members all propped up against the walls of Tsaochuang.[11] Chang thought that the ex-hostages would be pleased to see the photographs, but the former captives were repelled and horrified. This was not the outcome they had envisioned. They had lived with the bandits for six weeks and developed a level of respect and empathy for at least some of their captors, whose circumstances and living conditions were pitiful. But the ex-hostages' feelings, and those of Anderson, had no bearing on Chang's course.

By February 1924, all of the leaders of the New Brigade had been captured and neutralized. And many of the bandits who had not joined the army were also rounded up. Liu Shou-t'ing—the infamous Po-Po Liu— tried to escape from the Lincheng area but was captured in late December by the Chinese Army along with two other bandit subchiefs.[12] After a hasty military trial, they were all sentenced to death by the sword.

Though not contesting his death sentence, Liu begged Chang to allow him to die by gunshot or hanging rather than beheading, stating that he was a soldier and deserved to die with dignity. Decapitation was viewed as the most disgraceful kind of death because the head, which is the principal part of a man, was separated from the body, and the body was not consigned to the grave whole, as at the time of birth.

Chang bluntly denied the old bandit chief's request, and Liu and his associates were executed on January 21. The severed heads were sent to the district seat for public exhibition, and the bodies were thrown into a ditch to be scattered by marauding dogs and the elements—the law having deemed them unworthy of regular funeral rites.[13]

Justice had been served. Warlord justice.

EPILOGUE: THE MYTH AND MEMORY OF LINCHENG

It took more than one man to change my name to Shanghai Lily.

—Marlene Dietrich, *Shanghai Express* (1932)

AFTER 1923

Many more years would pass—and much more blood would be spilled—before the lawlessness, corruption, and disorder that had led to the Lincheng Incident would finally subside in China. Warlords continued to plunder the countryside and massacre one another.[1] And there would be more bold and ruthless bandit outrages, even if none ever captured the world's attention quite like the raid on the Peking Express.[2] In the years to come, the presence of foreign interests in China continued to be an imperfect, if not self-serving, attempt at bringing about some level of order and stability through education, religion, infrastructure, technology, information, and commercial investments. But foreign intervention and control, real or perceived, had the effect of placing strain on China's sovereignty and self-determination as a nation-state.

After forcing the removal of President Li Yuan-hung, Tsao Kun was overthrown as president in 1924 in a coup manipulated by his former ally General Feng Yu-hsiang, the "Christian General." Tsao was imprisoned until Feng's forces were driven out of Peking in April 1926. In the meantime, Sun Yat-sen courted the support of the Soviet Union but passed away from cancer in 1925 while en route to Peking to strike an alliance with the Manchurian warlord, Chang Tso-Lin, to overthrow the Chihli clique of Tsao and Feng. The revolving door of militarist rulers all contending for power continued, and once again the central government ceased to exist until prevailing military leaders could fill the gap. The Kuomintang forces of Chiang Kai-shek's Nationalist Party advanced northward, marching toward Peking, in the summer of 1926. Chiang Kai-shek seized the leadership of the Kuomintang, cut off ties with the Soviet Union in 1927, and ultimately captured Peking in 1928, ushering in a brief period of stability before the Japanese invasion in 1937—referred to as the "Nanking Decade."

One of the people closely following the Lincheng Incident was the young Chinese communist leader Mao Tse-tung. In one of his first public speeches, at the Hunan Peasant Congress in December 1926, Mao specifically cited the event as an example of "starving peasants rioting" against the imperialists, warlords, and feudal classes. Mao relied upon the peasant class for his rise to power. And although he admired Sun Mei-yao's ability to mobilize the people, he viewed the organizers of the Lincheng Incident as having lacked a unifying political strategy, which, he argued, is why they could never achieve anything of great significance. What was needed was a true political party to "dig up the political foundations of the warlords and develop the organization of the masses" in order to lead the peasant revolution.[3]

The Lincheng Incident has become a mere footnote in history, having been overwhelmed by the sweeping tides of the Japanese invasion of China, World War II, the Chinese Civil War and Communist takeover, the Cold War, the Cultural Revolution, and China's opening to the West.[4] But the Lincheng Incident still has lessons for the present. The deep economic divide in the years before and after the holdup of the Peking Express made it possible for those in power to take advantage of the poor and for corruption to take root. Today, economic inequality and systemic corruption continue to bedevil the leadership in power, just as in 1923. China's contemporary warlords, up and down the government and state-sector hierarchy, continue to plunder the country's wealth and opportunities at the expense of the powerless, notwithstanding the periodic—yet politically driven—reforms and crackdowns on corruption.

One of the first significant casualties of the Lincheng Incident was the postponement of talks to abolish the system of extraterritoriality in China. This was an important issue for Chinese people of all political persuasions given that the continued imposition of extraterritoriality, whereby foreign subjects were exempt from local jurisdiction, was perceived as an egregious infringement of sovereignty. This vestige of colonialism, many thought, had to go. Just days before the Lincheng Incident, the foreign powers and China had agreed upon the date of November 1, 1923, for a meeting in Peking of the Commission on Extraterritoriality in China to move forward with abolishment. Further delay would be demoralizing, yet there was strong opposition given the ongoing negotiations to release the Lincheng hostages. As US minister Schurman wrote at the time, "The opinion of the foreign community in China is overwhelmingly, I believe unanimously, opposed to the coming of the Commission at the present time and the Lincheng outrage has strengthened their opposition."[5]

One view was that China was a battlefield of military factions, incapable of securing the countryside and developing and enforcing a predictable rule of law. Others claimed that the Chinese embryonic legal institutions could not be trusted and that the horrors of Chinese prisons, torture, and punishment were too vivid to ignore. The Chinese government pushed back on the postponement, insisting that the relinquishment of extraterritorial privileges was distinct from the Lincheng Incident and that "the citizens of China expect an early restoration of the rights of extraterritoriality." Peking believed that the commission should move forward consistent with treaty obligations and that "even if one or two powers refuse to talk about giving up extraterritoriality, the Chinese people must exert all the more efforts to secure it and the equality it represents."[6] The work of the Commission on Extraterritoriality was postponed repeatedly, and not until almost twenty

years after the Lincheng Incident, in January of 1943, did the foreign powers formally abandon the system—and only after compelled to do so with
the world in a state of war.[7]

Successive Chinese governments struggled with how best to address and
pay for the monetary claims lodged by the victims of the Lincheng Incident.
Many commentators believed that the Chinese government should not be
held responsible, for this was not an act by the state but by criminals.[8] At
the same time, the claimants and foreign governments believed that the
Chinese government, including at the national and provincial levels, was to
blame because the bandits had largely come from the ranks of the military
and were uncompensated, disgruntled former soldiers. On February 23,
1925, the Chinese government relented, paying a sum of $351,568 to settle
the demands of the foreign claimants.[9]

WHETHER OR NOT THE JAPANESE GOVERNMENT HAD AN ACTUAL HAND
in the robbery of the Peking Express has never been conclusively established. Although there was evidence that Japanese passengers were somehow aware of the train robbery in advance and many signs that Japan stood
to gain politically from the affair, even the US State Department saw such
a plot by the Japanese as "unlikely."[10] Yet Japan continued to nurse territorial ambitions in East Asia. In 1936 the Japanese refused further partic-
ipation in the arms-limitations agreements that had been signed during
the Washington Conference. Shortly thereafter, Japan invaded China and
other parts of the Asia-Pacific, committing unspeakable atrocities on both
the native populations and the many foreigners who had come to China to
live and work.

MOST OF THE BANDIT CHIEFS AND SUBCHIEFS—OTHER THAN THE CON-
niving fan-bandits Kuo and Chou—met the same grisly fate as Sun Mei-
Yao and Po-Po Liu. Yet some escaped. A few were actually offered jobs by
their former hostages. Russky, the singing bandit, traded his rifle for a horse
and then headed to Shanghai to work for former captive Lee Solomon.[11]
Shortly thereafter, he was recognized in Shanghai by the British authorities

and arrested and charged with murder and banditry. Solomon and other American friends worked to have him released. Russky eventually married a Russian woman and had two children with her.

The bandit Big Lip snuck through the military cordon and, with money from Leon Friedman, made his way down to Shanghai to work for Friedman's China Motors Company. Friedman took a liking to the hardworking young bandit, who had proved himself by running errands for Friedman while Friedman was in captivity. There was something in Big Lip's work ethic that Friedman viewed as a reflection of his own upbringing. The former bandit remained in the employ of Friedman for almost two decades.

The Frenchman—the independent-minded bandit subchief—was not interested in joining Sun Mei-yao's army or continuing the life of a bandit, and he disappeared into the night on the final day of negotiations. Although it's unknown where he went, the former captives speculate that he made his way to France to build a new life for himself.

THE PRISONERS, INTERLOCUTORS, AND RESCUERS WENT ON WITH THEIR lives. Some wrote and talked about their experiences, whereas others chose not to relive the situation.[12]

John B. Powell returned to his office at the *Weekly Review* (which was later renamed the *China Weekly Review*) at 4 Avenue Edward VII, Shanghai. He wrote extensively about the Lincheng Incident and its impact on China's relationship with the world. Powell was the keynote speaker at the annual dinner of the American Chamber of Commerce in Shanghai on June 29, 1923, and used the opportunity to thank the chamber for supporting the American Rescue Mission on behalf of all the captives. Powell was well connected with the nationalist government leadership and even received an invitation to attend the wedding of General Chiang Kai-shek to May-ling Soong on December 1, 1927, at the storied Majestic Hotel in Shanghai.

In 1937 the Japanese invaded Shanghai. Powell, who had written scathing editorials decrying Japanese aggression, earning him the moniker of "Public Enemy No. 1," was captured in 1941 and so badly tortured by the Japanese in prison that both his feet eventually had to be amputated. While

Journalist and publisher John B. Powell in his Shanghai office after his release from captivity in June 1923. He is holding the headlines of the *Chicago Daily Tribune* from May 17, 1923. (SHSMO)

behind bars in the infamous Bridge House prison in Shanghai, Powell recognized one of the other prisoners—Eddie Elias—a fellow hostage from the Peking Express twenty years earlier. Powell extended his hand to him, saying, "I prefer Chinese bandits to these scoundrels."[13] When finally released by the Japanese in 1942, Powell weighed just 75 pounds. He provided testimony of his treatment at the hands of the Japanese to the US War Crimes Office in February 1945. Powell wrote a book about his experiences in China titled *My Twenty-Five Years in China*, published in 1945.

Lucy Aldrich left China shortly after her release and wrote about her experience at Lincheng in "A Week-End with Chinese Bandits," which was published in the November 1923 issue of the *Atlantic Monthly*.[14] Minnie MacFadden and Mathilde Schoneberg prepared detailed first-person accounts of their thrilling capture and release by the bandits. For decades thereafter, the two loyal women remained in the employ of Aldrich as she traveled around the world seeking adventure and treasured artwork.

Roy Scott Anderson, who led the negotiations for the release of the captives, was celebrated for his efforts at a luncheon at the Shanghai Union Club on August 19, 1923.[15] After Anderson's death, in 1925, the former Lincheng captives raised funds for the construction of a memorial monument at Anderson's grave in Peking. Leon Friedman acted as the treasurer for the fund-raising and used his China Motors branch offices to generate and collect funds from the community. The former captives showered Anderson with much praise and accolades. Major Allen wrote to Secretary of State Hughes about "the debt and praise and gratitude which we owe to that splendid American, Roy Anderson, who obtained our release from captivity."[16]

Carl Crow returned to his advertising business in Shanghai after the hostages were released. Many of the ex-hostages expressed their gratitude for Crow's crucial volunteer efforts with the American Rescue Mission and presented him with a silver shield at an event at the Union Club in Shanghai, presided over by John Powell.[17] Crow's Paotzuku bandit postage stamps, which were popular with the captives and adorned the hundreds of outbound letters to family and friends around the world, became a serious collector's item.[18] When Reginald Rowlatt, while still in captivity, requested that the British legation on his behalf send a telegram to King George V on his birthday (June 3), British minister Macleay suggested that they send the king some of the bandit stamps: "It occurred to me that the King might be interested, as a philatelist, in having specimens of the brigand mail stamps, although they are not official. If Tours can't get any more I have one which I could spare."[19] Someplace in King George V's archives might actually be one of the Paotzuku bandit postage stamps. On August 14, 1937, also known as Bloody Saturday, Crow was blown out of his chair when Japanese aircraft bombed the Bund in Shanghai. Crow survived the bombing but was placed on Japan's Most Wanted List. He thought it best to leave China after twenty-five years, returning to the United States.[20]

Leon Friedman continued to operate China Motors Federal in Shanghai. Following his release from captivity, one of Leon's first acts was to send contributions to Father Wilhelm Lenfers and local Presbyterian missionaries for their unselfish support and care during the incident. Leon sold off his China assets before the Communist takeover in 1949 and moved to Los Gatos, California, "and became somewhat of a gentleman rancher," owning a house with an orchard full of fruit trees.[21] From his barnstorming days and time in China, including his time in captivity at Paotzuku, Friedman kept a trove of newspaper clippings and other materials, giving much color to his extraordinary life.

After his escape, Lloyd "Larry" Lehrbas was on assignment at Tsao-chuang for the duration of the affair, writing extensively about the march to Paotzuku, troop movements, and life for the captives in the bandit camps. Lehrbas remained a journalist in China and worked later for the Associated Press and the International News Service as a foreign correspondent serving in Europe, Asia, New York, and Washington. Lehrbas covered the Sino-Japanese War and traveled to Warsaw, arriving just in time to report on the first German air raid.[22] In February of 1942 he received a commission as a lieutenant colonel in the army and was appointed as General Douglas MacArthur's aide-de-camp and public relations adviser. Lehrbas would be immortalized in a legendary photo with MacArthur wading ashore on his return to the Philippines during World War II.

Father Wilhelm Lenfers continued to serve the Lincheng community until, in 1927, he left China after thirty-one years.[23] The former captives collectively donated money to Lenfers's church as a token of their appreciation for the work of the Catholic mission.

After a quarter-century in China, Giuseppe Domenico Musso left Shanghai for Italy in 1926 and with his eldest son produced propaganda films for the fascist regime of Benito Mussolini. In 1926 he published a well-recognized two-volume treatise, *La Cina Ed I Cinesi: Loro Leggi E Costumi* (China and the Chinese: Their Laws and Customs), which he had been writing at the time of the holdup of the express train, including a description of Sun Mei-yao and his bandit gang.

Roland W. Pinger and his family moved to the Bay Area after his release. He worked in the office of ordnance in the War Department in Washington and was promoted to colonel, serving in World War II. Colonel Pinger retired from the army in 1944 and returned to the University of California as a professor of engineering. Over the years, Pinger would write a detailed memoir of his thirty-seven days of captivity, providing an exhaustive insider's recollection of the events and daily life at the bandit camps. He also kept the SAP Club sign, Miriam's ivory-handled button-hook, Roland's red-silk padded Chinese coat, the brass-and-bone-handled knife given to him by bandit Russky, and a custom-made tapestry carpet depicting scenes from the Lincheng Incident that he had made in Peking after his release from captivity. Roland Pinger Jr., who was nine years old at the time of the train robbery, would later in life tell his own young children the story of his remarkable journey through the countryside in the land of the Chinese bandits.

Major Robert Allen returned to the United States with his wife and son, left the army, and resumed the practice of medicine. He wrote a diary of his twenty-five days in captivity, giving his candid assessment of the personalities, qualities, and character flaws of certain fellow captives and the bandits who held them hostage.

The Shanghai cousins continued to thrive in China—until the Japanese invasion.[24] Edward (Eddie) Elias would later become a British undercover agent of the Oriental Mission of the British Special Operations Executive in Shanghai. In January 1942 he was arrested by the Japanese forces and imprisoned in the infamous Bridge House prison and interrogation center in Shanghai, where he was tortured and where he ran into his old friend John Powell. Eddie was finally released in October 1943. Frederick "Freddie" Elias returned to Shanghai and, together with his brother and his father, Reuben, developed Haig Court, a luxury apartment block on Haig Avenue in Shanghai, where they lived until leaving Shanghai. Freddie had a reputation for high living and socializing and was a successful racehorse owner. Emile Gensburger, Theo Saphiere, Victor Haimovitch, and Alfred Zimmerman would all thrive in China until World War II forced them to emigrate across the globe. Each of the Shanghai cousins prepared detailed accounts of their experiences from the time of the train holdup until their release or escape from captivity.

The interpreter Hung Shi-chi returned to his position as a language professor at Nanking University and continued to socialize with his foreign friends in Shanghai. Koon Chi Cheng returned to China Merchants in Shanghai. At a dinner in Shanghai sponsored by the French consulate on July 2, 1923, to honor those who had supported the captives, including Professor Hung and Cheng, the two men were recognized for "the risks they took to support the captives as translators, negotiators, and in general as go-betweens with the bandit chiefs on behalf of the foreign hostages."[25]

Lee Solomon returned to Shanghai and continued to operate a company that produced mahjong sets for export to the United States.[26] Solomon was very protective of former bandit Russky, giving him a job in his company. One can only imagine that after a few shots of vodka, the two of them would be singing Russian ballads and traditional Chinese folk songs as they did together at the top of Paotzuku Mountain.

RECOGNIZING THE ENTERTAINMENT VALUE OF A TRAIN ROBBERY BY BAN-dits set in "exotic" China, Hollywood released a movie very loosely based upon the Lincheng Incident—the 1932 film *Shanghai Express*, starring Marlene Dietrich, Clive Brook, and Anna May Wong. The screenwriters fiddled with many of the details of the historical event. The express train in the film is going southward from Peking to Shanghai, and it is seized not by bandits but by the rebel forces of a powerful warlord. There is never any march to the mountains. Yet the essential story remains the same, and *Shanghai Express* became the highest-grossing film of 1932 and was nominated for the Best Picture and Best Director awards.

Screenwriter Harry Hervey, who was considered an expert on Asian themes, wrote the script. In 1923 Hervey worked as a cruise-ship director, traveling throughout Asia, and was inspired by the day-by-day media coverage surrounding the Lincheng Incident. It was during his time cruising the waters of Asia that he developed the characters for the movie. Dietrich's most famous line, "It took more than one man to change my name to Shanghai Lily," was never attributed to anyone involved in the actual Lincheng Incident. Though purely fictional, the film industry's ode to the Lincheng Incident is part of the quintessential lore surrounding this historical affair.

AFTERWORD: THE JOURNEY OF THE PEKING EXPRESS

My path to writing *The Peking Express* is rooted in three decades of work as a lawyer and adviser in China, helping people navigate the political and legal complexities in the second-largest economy in the world. While I watched as China made tremendous strides economically, I also witnessed how the legal system had become more and more politicized. Over my career, I was repeatedly reminded that the law serves the politics and that detention is just another tool in the toolbox.

Looking for historical patterns and lessons in the past on the use of detention for political reasons, I found myself in Chinese and foreign archives. I became fascinated by records concerning Republican-era suppression campaigns against groups of people—always branded as bandits—who engaged in kidnapping and other criminal activities for economic and political purposes. The Lincheng Incident stood out as a historical event that was both forgotten and never critically reviewed or fully understood.

I started to learn more about the context surrounding this colorful episode. I immediately saw that it was more than a train robbery by disgruntled, unpaid soldiers. It struck me as a story in which cultures, history, and circumstances collided. I did not set out to conduct an academic study or to write a white paper to encourage policy changes. Rather, I viewed the Lincheng Incident as a human story, where lives were affected for generations and events became watershed moments that changed the course of history.

To get deeper into the characters and circumstances, I set out to experience the environment and conditions that the characters in the Lincheng Incident lived through a hundred years ago. Over the course of several years, this led to an odyssey of train rides, trekking across the countryside for miles on end. Living in Beijing and just under three hours by high-speed rail from the Lincheng area, I frequently found myself climbing mountains, exploring temples, and meeting wary government officials suspicious about inquiries into Shandong's checkered past.

I discovered that many of the key landmarks of the story still exist today. I walked the streets and haunts of various characters who lived and worked in the foreign concessions of Shanghai, Beijing, and Tianjin. This included John B. Powell's office at the Great Northern Telegraph Company's former building on 4 Avenue Edward VII (34 Yan'an East Road, Wai Tan, Huangpu Qu), which is now the Shanghai Telecom Museum (上海电信博物馆), and Leon Friedman's China Motors Building at 125 Bubbling Well Road (702 Nanjing West Road), near the People's Park. In Beijing I explored what remains of the Tsing Tsung-pu Hutong (Xizongbu Hutong or 东城区西总布胡同), where Roy Anderson lived.

No train story in China is complete without first visiting the former Shanghai-Nanking Railway Station, which is now the Shanghai Railway Museum (上海铁路博物馆). This is where the Peking Express passengers started their journey. A feature of the museum is an all-steel passenger car made by the venerable Pressed Steel Car Company of the United States, the supplier of the all-steel express train cars of the Tientsin-Pukow line. Riding the rails to Nanjing, I explored the Pukow Railway Station (浦口火车) on the north bank of the Yangtze River across from the city of Nanjing, where the passengers crossed the river by ferry to the waiting sleeper cars bound for the north.

I explored the old Lincheng Train Station—built with cut stone and German technology in 1912—which is still standing strong and preserved at the Zaozhuang West Railway Station (枣庄西站) in Shandong Province. Lincheng is a subdistrict of the Yuecheng District, Zaozhuang City. Zaozhuang, which is the pinyin spelling for Tsaochuang, boasts a new train station that is serviced by the Beijing-Shanghai high-speed-rail network. Today, a trip on the high-speed train between Shanghai and Beijing takes just under five hours to complete. Those who take the high-speed option from Shanghai to Beijing nonchalantly pass through Lincheng and Tsaochuang (Zaozhuang City) without knowing the significance of the turbulent events that happened in the region a century ago.

Nearby, I visited the large Lincheng Catholic church and complex, where Father Lenfers lived and worked, which was heavily damaged during the Cultural Revolution and is in crumbling condition on the grounds of the current Church of the Holy Spirit in Lincheng (枣庄市薛城区北临城天主堂). The Catholic priests at the compound maintain a number of books and photographs about Lenfers and his fellow European priests, who were well-known community figures in the early twentieth century. I visited the cut-stone building of the Presbyterian Mission run by the Reverend Carroll Yerkes, who provided material support to the bandit camp, in nearby Yishien. It continues to operate as a Christian church. Yishien is now the Yicheng District of Zaozhuang City.

I combed the countryside eight li south of Lincheng on the old railroad line and walked the embankment and adjoining fields where the bandits derailed the train and started the trek eastward. Hiking around the site of the derailment on an active rail line, I heeded the good-natured warning of a railway guard to stay off the tracks as he photographed my every move. Getting into the weeds, I stumbled upon remnants of the ganger houses (rail-worker dwellings) and farm structures and the toppled-over millstones and grave mounds dotting the fields along the train tracks. Looking eastward, I walked in the direction the hostages took to the so-called Yellow Cow Mountain, where the bandits ran for the hills with booty and prisoners, which is actually two separate adjoining mountain tableaus referred to today as the DaFu (big blessing) mountains, 大福山, and the Apricot mountains, 杏子峪山.

I followed the spur line twelve miles east of Lincheng to the Tsaochuang mining compound of the Chung Hsing Mining Company. Still in operation today, it is known as the Zaozhuang Xin Zhong Xing Industrial Co., Ltd., Zaozhuang City (枣庄新中兴实业有限责任公司). The compound and mines sustained heavy damage during World War II and China's civil war but are in remarkable condition today. Most of the compound walls and rail yards are gone, but the original office building used as the headquarters of the American Rescue Mission and the diplomatic representatives still exists. The mining company operates a small museum at the premises, but there is no mention of the Lincheng Incident or the fact that its grounds were used as the execution site for Sun Mei-yao and his gang.

From Tsaochuang, I followed the path northward five miles to the so-called Dragon Door Temple (Kan Ch'üan or Ganquan Temple, 甘泉禅寺), which continues to operate as a Buddhist temple. It is surrounded by the villages where the hostages were held for their first nine days of captivity, little changed from when they had their mongrel feast and where the singing bandit Russky held his impromptu concert.

Traversing the hilly countryside between Tsaochuang and Paotzuku, I followed the arduous paths and could only admire Powell's horsemanship as he made the hard ride back and forth to push the negotiations forward. I also marveled at the daily efforts of those extraordinary workers—whom the captives called "coolies"—who hauled the hefty Roy Anderson in a sedan chair and gave the hostages a lifeline of provisions and mail twice daily from the American Rescue Mission in Tsaochuang. I even walked the five miles from the Dragon Door Temple to Tsaochuang, following the same path as Bobby Allen and Roland Pinger, no small feat for those young boys to accomplish in the middle of the night through military lines.

Taking rural country roads east for ten or so miles, I gasped when Paotzuku Mountain came into view (part of the Baodugu National Forest Park, or 抱犊崮国家森林公园). I repeatedly climbed the Paotzuku summit, which was very much in the same condition it was in 1923. The Temple of the Clouds (San ch'ing Temple or Temple of the Three Pure Ones, or 三清观) continues to operate as a Taoist temple in the foothills below Paotzuku Mountain. Because of the temple's isolation, the buildings, the courtyard, and the ancient ginkgo tree are in relatively the same condition as in 1923, with the icons and statuary intact and still adorning the temple altars. I sat for hours in the small temple structures to get a feel of where Musso, Friedman, Powell, Rowlatt, Henley, Hung, Chi Cheng, Pinger, Allen, Solomon, the Shanghai cousins, the Vereas, and the others slept for weeks. I stood under and touched the thousand-year-old ginkgo tree, still thriving in much the way that it was in 1923. There in the temple courtyard, I interviewed the locals who are perhaps the descendants of Paotzuku bandits, speaking regional dialects through interpreters. There, too, I sat with the granddaughter of Major Pinger and daughter of Roland Pinger Jr., Candace Pinger Smith, reflecting on the many stories she was told by her grandfather and father.

Baodugu National Forest Park is a relatively unknown tourist attraction with a rickety cable car that, on demand and winds permitting, takes hikers to the conical base of the sugar-loaf mountain for a steep climb to the top of "Calf Carrying Hill." The mountain caves that dot the landscape, from centuries before, contain scores of rock carvings of religious icons that the hostages wrote about in their diaries. There is no mention of the Lincheng Incident in any of the signage or brochures of Baodugu, although on the climb to the summit one finds a reflective, if not a somber, statement of the past carved into the rock:

自性起一念恶, 灭万劫善因; 自性起一念善, 得恒沙恶尽[1]
To think of all the evil things is to generate evil practices;
to think of all the good things is to generate good practices.

FOR ALL THOSE WHO TRAVERSED THE COUNTRYSIDE OF LINCHENG WITH me experiencing the magic and mysticism of the region as we followed the steps of Sun Mei-yao and his captives—I welcome you back. For those who have not been to China's bandit country but wish to do so, I look forward to enjoying the sunset at the top of Paotzuku Mountain with you—whenever you get here.

MAJOR CHARACTERS

PROMINENT PASSENGERS OF THE PEKING EXPRESS

Lucy Aldrich (US)

Major Robert Allen (US)

Martha Allen (US)

Robert (Bobby) Allen Jr. (US)

Marcel Berubé (France)

Koon Chi Cheng (China)

Alba Corelli (Italy)

Thomas Hyatt Day (US)

Edward (Eddie) Leopold Elias (GB)

Frederick (Freddie) Sassoon Elias (GB)

Leon Friedman (US)

Emile Gensburger (France)

Victor Haimovitch (US)

Carl Heinz (Germany)

Jerome Henley (US)

Hung Shi-chi (China)

M. C. Jacobson (Denmark)

Kang Tung-yi (China)

Lloyd (Larry) Lehrbas (US)

Minnie MacFadden (US)

Giuseppe D. Musso (Italy)

Major Roland W. Pinger (US)

Miriam Blacker Pinger (US)

Roland Pinger Jr. (US)

Edward Pinger (US)

John Benjamin Powell (US)

Joseph Rothman (GB)

Reginald Rowlatt (GB)

Theodore (Theo) Saphiere (GB)

Mathilde Schoneberg (US)

William Smith (GB)

Levi (Lee) Solomon (US)

Manuel Ancira Verea (Mexico)

Teresa Verea (Mexico)

Yang Yü-hsun (China)

Alfred Lionel Zimmerman (US)

COMMUNITY SUPPORT

Roy Scott Anderson (US)

Joseph Babcock (US)

Carl Crow (US)

Dr. LeRoy F. Heimburger (US)

Dr. Laurence M. Ingle (GB)

Fr. Wilhelm Lenfers (Germany)

Robert McCann (US)

Dr. Paul Mertens (Germany)

Ralph Naill (US)

Dr. Ernest B. Struthers (GB)

Paul Whitham (US)

David Wiesenberg (US)

Reverend Carroll Yerkes (US)

FOREIGN DIPLOMATIC SUPPORT

Pierre Crépin, consul general,
  French consulate,
  Shanghai

John Davis, consul, US
  consulate, Nanking

Raffaele Ferrajolo, M.C., captain,
  vice consul, Italian consulate,
  Shanghai

Lloyd Horsfall, major, language
  officer, American legation,
  Peking

Sir Ronald Macleay, minister,
  British legation, Peking

Harvey Milbourne, vice consul,
  US consulate, Tsinan

Wallace Philoon, major, assistant
  military attaché, American
  legation

Jacob Schurman, minister,
  American legation, Peking

Berthold Tours, Esq., British
  consul, Tsinan

CHINESE GOVERNMENT OFFICIALS

Chang Wen-t'ang, general,
  commander of the Tientsin-
  Pukow Railway Police

Chen Tiao-yuan, general,
  defense commissioner, Süchow,
  Kiangsu Province

Cheng Shih-chi, general,
  assistant military governor,
  Shantung Province

Ch'i Hsieh-yuan, military
  governor, Kiangsu Province

Ho Feng-yu, general, defense
  commissioner, Yenchow,
  Shantung Province

Li Yuan-hung, president,
  Republic of China (1916–1917,
  1922–1923)

Tien Chung-yu, military
  governor, Shantung Province

Tsao Kun, marshal, Chihli
  Party; president, Republic of
  China (1923–1924)

Wen Shih-tsung, commissioner
  of foreign affairs, Nanking,
  Kiangsu Province

Wu Yu-lin, minister of
  communications

Yang Ih, police commissioner,
  Tientsin

LEADERS OF THE SELF-GOVERNED ARMY FOR THE ESTABLISHMENT OF THE COUNTRY (AKA THE BANDITS)

Sun Mei-yao

Liu Shou-t'ing (aka Po-Po Liu)

Wang Feng-wu

Sun Kwei-chih

Sun Mei-sung

Chou Tien-sung

Kuo Chih-tsai (Fang Yao)

The Frenchman

Big Bill

Russky

ACKNOWLEDGMENTS

Probably the most significant contribution to this writing project came from the private records of the families and descendants of the various hostages and participants. Around the world, I tracked down the descendants of the people involved in this story. This led me to a trove of unpublished diaries, statements, affidavits, notes, letters, and photographs that helped relive and reconstruct the experience from the perspective of those who were there. Many families told me that the Lincheng Incident was deeply embedded in their family lore, with stories passed down for generations. For one, the Pinger family records not only contained Major Pinger's diaries, photos, and letters from the Lincheng Incident; they also had the SAP Club sign hammered out from a tin can by their grandfather, the buttonhook that Major Pinger used as his weapon and all-purpose tool, and the Chinese coat given to Roland Pinger Jr. by the bandits. They also have the brass-and-bone-handled knife given by the bandit Russky to Major Pinger on the final day of captivity. After almost a hundred years, it was an amazing feeling, knowing that this knife was not only used during the Lincheng Incident but was also carried by the bandit Russky during his sojourns across the vast Siberian continent. I am very grateful to the Colonel and Mrs. Pinger family for their time and friendship during this writing project (Sharon Dowsett, Steven Pinger, Candace Pinger Smith, and Bruce Riordan).

One of the most remarkable discoveries was finding the original guarantee signed by Roy Anderson and the bandit chiefs in the Anderson family records in a rural country house in western Massachusetts. Included in the files was the original telegram from Marshal Tsao Kun to Roy Anderson authorizing the American fixer to sign the guarantee with the bandits on behalf of the central government. Without that telegram from Tsao, Anderson would not have been vested with authority to close the deal, the Lincheng hostages would not have been released, and the whole story could have ended on a very different note. For this, I am most grateful to the Roy Scott Anderson family (grandniece Lucy Anderson).

I also wish to thank Bradley Friedman, the grandnephew of Leon Friedman, for his access to a treasure trove of news clippings, photographs, and correspondence reflecting the incredible lives of Leon and Max Friedman, ranging from their days as barnstorming promoters to their automobile dealership days in China and years beyond.

I also wish to thank a host of other family members who shared photos, letters, and other materials, including the Philoon family (Sara Kurensky, Steven Philoon, Alan Philoon); the Horsfall family (Larry Horsfall, Dan Graves); the Dr. LeRoy F. Heimberger family (Dr. Doug Heimberger, Jane McDowell); the Babcock family (Christopher Berg); the Solomon family (Dee Halpin); and the Wiesenberg family (Arnold "Arnie" Wiesenberg). All of the family members provided startling records, photographs, and their family history, for which I am very grateful.

I want to thank the researchers and staff at a variety of institutions around the world who assisted in granting access to various facilities, records, photographs, and historical materials used in the research of this book. These include the Rhode Island Historical Society; Yale Divinity School Library, Special Collections; the State Historical Society of Missouri Manuscript Collection, SHSMO Research Center, Columbia, Missouri; Hoover Institution Library & Archives, Stanford University; Hong Kong University Library, Archives; the Church of the Holy Spirit, Xuecheng (Lincheng), Bei Lin Cheng Xue Cheng Area, Zaozhuang City; Yicheng (Yihsien) Presbyterian Church, Yicheng District of Zaozhuang City; Zaozhuang West Railway Station (Lincheng Railway Station) in Shandong Province; the Zaozhuang Xin Zhong Xing Industrial Co., Ltd., and Chung Hsing (Tsaochuang) Mining Company, Zaozhuang City; Beijing National Library; Mill Hill School Foundation, Mill Hill Village, London; National Postal Museum Library, Smithsonian Institution, Washington, D.C.; Shanghai

Xujiahui Library (Bibliotheca Siccawei); Society of the Divine Word (Societas Verbi Divini [SVD]); Shanghai Railway Museum; Second Historical Archives of China (SHAC) in Nanjing; and the Wisconsin Veterans Museum, Madison, Wisconsin.

I am also grateful and thoroughly indebted for the research assistance of those in China, including Fan Jiang for her tireless research and logistics assistance with Chinese Catholic Church records in southern Shandong, various resources in Zaozhuang (Tsaochuang), and the Beijing National Library; Jiamu Sun for her review and research regarding Chinese-language materials, especially the archival materials in traditional characters; Kai Chi (Elvis) Li for his research at Hong Kong University Library; and Xinlan Liu and Denise Zhou for their research at the Second Historical Archives of China (SHAC) in Nanjing.

Outside of China, much thanks to Ariane Finn for her research at the National Archives, United Kingdom; Raymond Hyser for his research at the US National Archives & Records Administration; Baasil Wilder, branch librarian, National Postal Museum Library, Smithsonian Institution; Samantha Wolf, reference archivist, Wisconsin Veterans Museum, Madison, Wisconsin; Nicolas (Nico) Cian Ospina for his research regarding resources and records in Italy; Wolfgang Baldus regarding the history and market for the Paotzuku bandit postage stamps; Maria Crespo for her research regarding sources and records in Mexico; Laura R. Jolley and Heather Richmond of SHSMO Research Center; Kevin Crawford of Yale Divinity School Library, Special Collections; Phoebe S. Bean, librarian, and J. D. Kay, reproductions and rights manager, of the Rhode Island Historical Society; Dean of Students Jean Gaspardo of the Loyola University of Chicago Law School for tracking down resources in Italy for G. D. Musso; and my daughter Jocelyn R. Zimmerman for her research at the Library of Congress.

I would also like to extend my sincere thanks to all those who reviewed, edited, and commented upon the project proposal and various drafts of the manuscript, as well as providing much encouragement, including Stephen Heyman, Jane Perlez, Jill Marsal, Eric Jay Dolan, James Palmer, Kristina DaCosta, Fred McClintock, Marie Finn, my wife Ellen Zimmerman, and my daughters Jocelyn, Michaela, and Elise.

I would like to express my deepest appreciation to my extraordinary literary agents, Peter and Amy Bernstein of the Bernstein Literary Agency, who guided me through the process with patience, creativity, and a profound belief in my work. Finally, I have also had the great pleasure of working with the team at PublicAffairs Books and the Hachette Book Group, including the legendary executive editor Clive Priddle and his extraordinary team, including Katy O'Donnell, Kiyo Saso, Shena Redmond, Donald Pharr, Melissa Raymond, Olivia Loperfido, Jenny Mandel, Tracy Williams, Amy Quinn, and a host of folks who helped get this to print.

To all of you, I am most grateful.

NOTES

PROLOGUE

1. J. B. Powell, "The Bandits' 'Golden Eggs' Depart," *Asia*, December 1923, 914, 958.

2. See generally Jerome Ch'en, "Defining Chinese Warlords and Their Factions," *Bulletin of the School of Oriental and African Studies* 31, no. 3 (1968): 563–600; "1,200,000 Chinese Under Arms; Peking Controls Only Tenth," *Evening Star*, May 8, 1923, 1; "New Chinese Alliance Against Wu-Pei-Fu: Sun Yat-sen Unites Forces with Chang Tsao-lin, Governor of Manchuria," *New York Times*, April 18, 1922.

3. In 1923 there were ninety-two separate outrages involving foreign hostages in Shantung Province alone, and the ransoms demanded equaled the province's total tax revenues for the year. See Phil Billingsley, *Bandits in Republican China* (Stanford, CA: Stanford University Press, 1988), 173. See also "Brigand Outrages in Ichang District," *North-China Herald*, April 7, 1923, 19; "Bandits' Awful Toll at Yingchowfu," *North-China Herald*, April 21, 1923, 154; "Bandits Swarm in China as Nation's Distress Grows," *New York Times*, May 13, 1923, 1; "Brigands Overrun Shantung: Withdrawal of Japanese and Wu Pei-fu's Victory Resulted in Chaos," *New York Times*, May 9, 1923, 2; "Honan's Soldier Bandits," *North-China Herald*, May 5, 1923, 295; "The Wolf in Sheep's Clothing: Bandits Last Winter Now Regular Soldiers," *North-China Herald*, May 5, 1923, 297; "Honan Still Beset by Bandits," *North-China Herald*, April 21, 1923, 153; "Only Priests Exempt from Bandit Raids," *North-China Herald*, April 7, 1923, 23; and Xu Youwei and Philip Billingsley, "When Worlds Collide: Chinese Bandits and Their 'Foreign Tickets,'" *Modern China* 26, no. 1 (January 2000): 38–78.

CHAPTER 1: ALL ABOARD!

1. Carl Crow, *The Travelers' Handbook for China*, 3rd ed. (Shanghai: Carl Crow, 1921), 26.

2. "Dr. Schurman to Visit Yellow River Repair Enterprise," *Weekly Review*, May 5, 1923, 338.

3. See generally R. Bickers and J. Wasserstrom, "Shanghai's 'Dogs and Chinese Not Admitted' Sign: Legend, History and Contemporary Symbol," *China Quarterly* 142 (1995): 444–466.

4. John B. Powell, *My Twenty-Five Years in China* (New York: Macmillan, 1945), 3–4. See generally Arthur Henderson Smith, *Chinese Characteristics*, 3rd ed. (New York: Revell, 1894).

5. In 1923 Powell's key staff included Hollington K. Tong (Tung Hsien-kuang), who would go on to be the Republic of China's ambassador to Japan and the United States. Tong, a Kuomintang insider, worked as the assistant editor and Peking editor of the *Weekly Review* and was a journalism graduate of the University of Missouri and the Columbia University Graduate School of Journalism. Powell's younger sister Margaret (whom he called "Marg"), another University of Missouri graduate, joined the *Weekly Review* in 1917 to colead the publication.

6. In June 1923 Powell would again change the name of the magazine, this time to the *China Weekly Review*. The publication described itself as "a weekly journal published in the interest of closer financial, business and political relations between China and America and other nations."

7. "President's Reply to Critics: A Not Unfavorable Comparison with Other Republics' Beginnings," *North-China Herald*, April 28, 1923, 220.

8. R. Friedman, "An Odyssey of the Friedman Brothers" (unpublished ms., 2007), Library of Congress.

9. The passengers included Kang Tung-yi, a Chinese journalist from the well-regarded *Shun Pao* (申报, or Shanghai News), a Chinese-language newspaper based in Shanghai.

10. "The Shanghai Combine: Now Willing to Sell Stock Before Time Expires," *Peking Gazette*, January 12, 1917, 6; "The Shanghai Combine: Hope That China-German Crisis Might Overshadow the Opium Deal," *Peking Gazette*, March 8, 1917, 7; Samuel Merwin, *Drugging a Nation: The Story of China and the Opium Curse* (New York: Revell, 1908); "Men and Events," *Weekly Review*, January 20, 1923, 310; "Comm. G. D. Musso Says China Needs a Mussolini," *China Weekly Review*, March 9, 1929, 66.

11. "Traveling by Train in China: Notable Rail Developments in the Far East," in *Railway Wonders of the World*, edited by Clarence Winchester (London: Amalgamated, 1935), 2:1495-1504. Foreign media speculated that the real reason the government opposed the railroad was because of bad feng shui—the "science" of using the forces of nature to ensure that a structure is in harmony and balance with the natural world. Whatever the reason, the tracks were torn up, and the engines and carriages were unceremoniously dumped in the sea off the coast of the island of Formosa. Charles Ewart Darwent, *Shanghai: A Handbook for Travelers and Residents* (Shanghai: Kelly & Walsh, 1911), 132.

12. F. Rhea, *Far Eastern Markets for Railway Materials, Equipment, and Supplies*, Department of Commerce, Special Agents Series No. 180 (1919); E-Tu Zen Sun, "The Pattern of Railway Development in China," *Far Eastern Quarterly* 14, no. 2 (February 1955): 179–199.

13. "Traveling by Train in China," 2:1495–1504. See generally Juliet Bredon, *Peking: A Historical and Intimate Description of Its Chief Places of Interest* (Shanghai: Kelly & Walsh, 1922). With increased access to rural areas, more foreign travel authors and adventurers were writing about their experiences in China, feeding the tourism sector. See generally Henry A. Franck, *Wandering in Northern China* (New York: Century, 1923); and *Roving Through Southern China* (New York: Century, 1925).

14. "American Locomotives in China," *New York Times*, April 24, 1921, E7; "Tientsin-Pukow R.R. to Have Best Passenger Service in Asia," *Weekly Review*, Nov. 25, 1922, 448; "China Improving Railway Systems: Early Prejudices Against Modern Equipment Disappearing, and One Big Order Is Filled," *New York Times*, April 17, 1923, 36; U.S. Department of Commerce, Trade Promotion Series, No. 1, *Packing for Foreign Markets* (1924), 344–345.

15. In the foreign media, the Peking Express was also referred to as the "Blue Express" because of its steel-blue train cars. For southbound traffic, the trains were informally referred to as the "Shanghai Express." The Chinese also referred to the Shanghai-Peking line as the Jinghu railway (京滬鐵路).

CHAPTER 2: THE BANDIT CHIEF

1. English translation of proclamation issued by Sun Mei-yao, commander in chief of the Self-Governed Army for the Establishment of the Country, to the Foreign Consular Representatives, May 17, 1923, British Public Records Office, Foreign Office, 228/3252/235.

2. Sun's gang was also terrorizing both the wealthy landowners, with holdings as small as eight acres, and the foreigner missionaries of the region, including the American Presbyterian Mission. See Memorandum of the Division of Far Eastern Affairs to the Secretary of State, May 7, 1923, National Archives and Records Administration, RG 59, 393.1123 Lincheng/17, Box 4644. See generally *A Record of American Presbyterian Mission Work in Shantung Province, China*, 2nd ed.

3. "Sun Mei-yao: A Very Sordid Villain," *North-China Herald*, June 2, 1923, 593; "Bandit Chief a Reformer: Interviewed by N.C. Daily News Correspondent," *North-China Herald*, May 26, 1923, 523.

4. Chen Wu-wo, *True Facts About the Lincheng Incident* (Peking: Peking Express Press, 1923). *True Facts* is said to be a one-sided account prepared in defense of Shantung military governor Tien Chung-yu. See also Billingsley, *Bandits in Republican China*, 181–182.

5. The tuchun system—which developed rapidly after the creation of the Republic of China in 1912—benefited a handful of warlords and a horde of accomplices, all supported by an uncompensated mob of soldiers. The tuchuns were notorious for lining their pockets with tax collections, withholding pay due to troops, and openly flouting central authority. Hsi-Sheng Ch'i, *Warlord Politics in China 1916–1928* (Stanford, CA: Stanford University Press, 1976). See also Diana Lary, *Warlord Soldiers: Chinese Common Soldiers 1911–1937* (Cambridge: Cambridge University Press, 1985), 65–70; Powell, "Bandits' 'Golden Eggs,'" 914, 958; F. Hedges, "Bandits a Growing Menace in China," *Current History Magazine*, July 1923, 606; H. Bunn, "Political Causes of Chinese Banditry," *Current History Magazine*, July 1923, 603. Part of the difficulty in defining a bandit is in determining who is and who is not a bandit. The warlords tended to accuse anyone who took up arms against them of being a bandit, which included any legitimate political opposition. Rather than seeking to understand the underlying reasons for banditry, the brutal tuchuns often simply saw bandits as an antisocial, destabilizing force that took advantage of chaos, deprivation, and wars.

6. See generally Mark O'Neill, *The Chinese Labor Corps: The Forgotten Chinese Laborers of the Great War* (London: Penguin, 2014). Although many of the returnees joined the brigands, the fear that the China Labor Corps would return to China and form a strong, lawless band or army was proven to be unfounded. See N. Griffin, "Britain's Chinese Labor Corps in World War I," *Military Affairs* 40, no. 3 (October 1976): 102–108; J. Blick, "The Chinese Labor Corps in World War I," *East Asia Regional Studies Seminar, Harvard Papers on China* 9 (1955): 111–145. China remained neutral in the Great War until August 1917, when Peking declared war on Germany at the request of the United States. This led to a political crisis in Peking: there was much disagreement between warlords about whether China would actually enter the war militarily, but the war ended shortly thereafter.

7. Chen Wu-wo, *True Facts About the Lincheng Incident*; "Sun Mei-yao," 593; "Bandit Chief a Reformer: Interviewed by N.C. Daily News Correspondent," *North-China*

Herald, May 26, 1923, 523. Some considered themselves "spirit soldiers" of the I-Ho Ch'uan, the Society of Righteous Harmonious Fist ("Boxers"): deeply superstitious young men who wore scarlet-colored ribbons and aprons that they claimed had magic powers that made the wearer invulnerable to harm.

8. Powell, "Bandits' 'Golden Eggs,'" 914.

CHAPTER 3: A PICTURESQUE VIEW

1. Diary of Roland W. Pinger, "The Lincheng Incident of 1923," 87.

2. The six-hour journey from Shanghai to Nanking passes the ancient city of Soochow, which Europeans called "The Venice of the Far East" because of its countless gardens, picturesque narrow canals, and arched stone bridges; the Great Lake (Ta Hu), the third-largest freshwater lake in China, celebrated by artists and poets for the beauty of its surroundings; and the walled city of Wusih, the epicenter of China's silk industry, supplying the couturiers and garment factories of Shanghai. See Crow, *Travelers' Handbook for China*, 142–150.

3. "Pukow City Center of Rail, River Transport in Kiangsu," *China Press*, March 30, 1937, 7. A train ferry was added in the mid-1930s, but a bridge across the river would not be built until thirty years later.

4. See generally "Various Telegrams Regarding Increase of Lawlessness on the Upper Yangtze River and Recommendations by American Officers in China to Reenforce the American Gunboat Patrol, March 30, 1923-February 5, 1924," in *Papers Relating to the Foreign Relations of the United States*, 1923, 1:741–751. By treaty, the YangPat vessels had the right to patrol deep into the heartland. See generally Kemp Tolley, *Yangtze Patrol: The U.S. Navy in China* (Annapolis: Naval Institute Press, 1971).

5. Letter of Minnie MacFadden to her sister Edith MacFadden, May 1923, 1, Lucy T. Aldrich Papers, Collections of the Rhode Island Historical Society.

6. See generally Yan Xu, "The State Salt Monopoly in China: Ancient Origins and Modern Implications," in *Studies in the History of Tax Law*, ed. Peter Harris and Dominic de Cogan (London: Bloomsbury, 2017), 8:513–537.

7. George Hayim, *Thou Shalt Not Uncover Thy Mother's Nakedness: An Autobiography* (London: Quartet, 1988), 6; Edward Leopold (Eddie) Elias, "My Experience in the Hands of Shantung Bandits," British Public Records Office, Foreign Office, June 11, 1923, 228/3253/309. The Elias brothers descended from Sephardic Jews originating from Baghdad, with the maternal side being Russian Ashkenazi Jews, originally from Kiev, who later moved to Vladivostok. The Elias family prospered in Shanghai as maritime provisioners, supplying the British Navy and merchant fleets that cruised China's waters. For a history of the Sephardic Jews of Shanghai, see generally Maisie J. Meyer, *Shanghai's Baghdadi Jews: A Collection of Biographical Reflections* (Hong Kong: Blacksmith Books, 2015); *From the Rivers of Babylon to the Whangpoo: A Century of Sephardi Jewish Life in Shanghai* (Lanham, MD: University Press of America, 2003); and Hayim, *Thou Shalt Not Uncover*. Although they were British-protected persons, one consular representative would mockingly refer to them as "persons of Mesopotamian origin, somewhere around the Garden of Eden, known in the Consular trade as 'Bagdad Scotchmen.'" Memorandum of Berthold George Tours, Esq., British Consul, Tsinan (on assignment to Tsaochuang), to Sir James William Ronald Macleay, British Ambassador to China, May 21, 1923, British Public Records Office, Foreign Office 228/3253/29/5337/23/16.

8. "President's Reply to Critics," 220.

9. See "Provinces' Illegal Taxation," *North-China Herald*, May 5, 1923, 291. See generally C. Denby, "The National Debt of China—Its Origin and Its Security,"

Annals of the American Academy of Political and Social Science 68 (November 1916): 55–70; W. Straight, "China's Loan Negotiations," *Journal of Race Development* 3, no. 4 (April 1913): 369–411. Peking was even eleven months behind in paying its foreign ministry staff in various countries around the world, forcing diplomats to seek income from other sources. "Peking in Quest of a Loan," *North-China Herald*, May 5, 1923, 286; "The Bankruptcy of Peking," *North-China Herald*, May 5, 1923, 290.

10. The ongoing disbandment of troops in Shantung and the nearby provinces was not conducted in an organized fashion, and often without proper safeguards such as requiring the disarming of the troops and providing the disbanded personnel with sustainable jobs, provisions, and transport back to their hometowns. See Dispatch of Samuel Sokobin, American Consul, Kalgan Consulate, to the Secretary of State, May 9, 1923; and "Various Materials Regarding Possible Connection of Disbanded Anhwei Troops with Tientsin-Pukow Railway Hold Up," in Records of the Department of State Relating to Internal Affairs of China 1910–1929, Record Group 59, Microfilm Reel M329–33, 107–119.

CHAPTER 4: THE OUTRAGE

1. "Captured by Bandits: A Manchester Man's Adventure in China," *North-China Daily News*, March 6, 1924, 8.

2. J. B. Powell, "Personal Story of Experiences in Hands of Bandits," *Weekly Review*, May 19, 1923, 408; "Shantung Bandits All Carried Japanese Rifles," *China Weekly Review*, May 6, 1939, 296.

3. "Traveling by Train in China," 2:1495–1504. For centuries, the canal served as the primary means of transporting tribute rice and shipments of grains, silks, and other products from the rich provinces in Southeast China to Peking. The canal was a metaphor for how the power and wealth of China could concentrate in the city but flowed always from the countryside, from the people, the peasant farmers and craftsmen.

4. Powell, *My Twenty-Five Years in China*, 92–124, 93; Powell, "Personal Story," 408; "Bandits Fire on Passengers," *New York Times*, May 7, 1923, 1; J. B. Powell, "'Esteemed Guests' of the Chinese Bandits: A Personal Story of One of the Most Famous Bandit Raids in Modern History," *Asia*, November 1923, 845, 857.

5. Diary of Robert A. Allen, "Twenty-Five Days Among the Bandits," 11. The hostages heard the words "tsou" (*zǒu*, in Pinyin meaning to go, run, move, walk, or leave) and "sha" (*shā*, in Pinyin meaning to kill, shoot, or murder).

6. Pinger diary, "Lincheng Incident of 1923," 99.

7. L. Aldrich, "A Week-End with Chinese Bandits," *Atlantic Monthly*, November 1923, 672 (drafted as a letter to her sister Abby G. [Aldrich] Rockefeller from Peking, China, May 20, 1923). See also "Traveled in Care of Standard Oil Co.: Miss Aldrich's Brothers Set in Motion Corporation's Machinery in China," *New York Times*, May 7, 1923, 1.

8. "Supplementary Report by the Consular Representatives, Joint Commission of Inquiry of the Lincheng Hold-Up," June 15, 1923, British Public Records Office, Foreign Office, 228/3253/295–299. In an inquest following the incident, consular representatives found that there was no effective means of communication between the engine driver—the first person who became aware that something was wrong—and the train guard in the rear of the train. The consular representatives found that the nineteen armed guards "made a hurried exit from the rear of the train and fled without attempting to put up a fight against the brigands." The chief of the train guard, Chao Te-ch'ao, was sleeping in another car in "mufti"—civilian attire—and when the bandits seized him, he claimed to be a passenger. The supplementary report found

that the train guards were underqualified, and as admitted by Chao, they had never received proper rifle training.

9. "Report of the Joint Commission of Inquiry of the Lincheng Hold-Up," June 15, 1923, British Public Records Office, Foreign Office, 228/3253/287–294; "Report of the Joint Commission of Inquiry of the Lincheng Hold-Up," June 15, 1923, attached to the Dispatch of Minister Schurman to Secretary of State, July 26, 1923, National Archives and Records Administration, RG 59, 393.1123 Lincheng/219, Box 4646.

10. Pinger diary, "Lincheng Incident of 1923," 98.

11. "China Orders Ransom Paid for Captives," *Chicago Daily News*, May 9, 1923, 1. See also Statement of Captain G. W. Spoerry, Mrs. Allen and Mrs. Pinger, Derailment of Tientsin-Pukow Train at Lin-Cheng and Capture of Foreigners by Bandits, American Consulate General, Tientsin, May 7, 1923, H.B.M. Consulate General, Tientsin, British Public Records Office, Foreign Office 228/3252/87–88.

12. Powell, *My Twenty-Five Years in China*, 92–124, 93; "The Peking Express Outrage," *North-China Herald*, May 12, 1923, 356; Powell, "Personal Story," 407.

13. Telegram from Tientsin Consul W. Russell Brown to British Legation Peking, May 8, 1923, H.B.M. Consulate General, Tientsin, British Public Records Office, Foreign Office, 228/3252/52; Peking Dispatch, No. 225, July 25, 1917, British Public Records Office, Foreign Office, 228/3253/67; Letter of Sir Sidney Barton, Shanghai Consul-General, to Sir James William Ronald Macleay, British Ambassador to China, May 8, 1923, British Public Records Office, Foreign Office, 228/3253/69; Letter of Sir Ronald Macleay, Minister, British Legation, to the Foreign Office, May 12, 1923, British Public Records Office, Foreign Office, May 12, 1923, 228/3252/171–175; "Statement of Victor Haimovitch and Alfred Zimmerman Regarding the Capture by Bandits," May 8, 1923, H.B.M. Consulate General, Tientsin, British Public Records Office, Foreign Office 228/3252/84–85; Rothman Records, British Public Records Office, Foreign Office, 1111/301/2/10, 210, 1250. See also "Tientsin-Pukow Express Wrecked by Bandits," *North-China Herald*, May 12, 1923, 385.

14. Powell, *My Twenty-Five Years in China*, 94.

15. Aldrich, "Week-End with Chinese Bandits," 672; Minnie MacFadden to her sister Edith MacFadden, 2.

16. Lehrbas, "Miss Aldrich Tells Vivid Story of Experience: Saw Prisoner Shot," *China Press*, May 11, 1923, 1.

17. Statement of Mathilde Juliette Schoneberg, May 8, 1923, Peking, 1, Lucy T. Aldrich Papers, Collections of the Rhode Island Historical Society; Minnie MacFadden to her sister Edith MacFadden, 2.

18. Aldrich, "Week-End with Chinese Bandits," 672.

19. Minnie MacFadden to her sister Edith MacFadden, 2.

20. Lehrbas, "Miss Aldrich Tells Vivid Story of Experience," 1.

21. Aldrich, "Week-End with Chinese Bandits," 672; Lehrbas, "Miss Aldrich Tells Vivid Story of Experience," 1.

CHAPTER 5: TAKING PRISONERS

1. "Statement of Victor Haimovitch and Alfred Zimmerman." See also "Statement of Thomas Hyatt Day, Interview at American Consulate, Tientsin," before J. C. Huston, Acting Consul-General, May 8, 1923, National Archives and Records Administration, RG 59, 393.1123 Lincheng/131, Box 4644; "American Is Slain as Chinese Troops Battle Brigands," *Evening Star*, May 8, 1923, 1, 4; "Girl Faces Bullets with Bandit Terms: Miss Schoneberg, an American, Makes a Daring Trip to Arrange for Others' Ransom," *New York Times*, May 9, 1923, 1; "Grave Fears for Captives: Brigands Are Reported to Be Using Them for Shields," *New York Times*, May 9, 1923, 1.

2. Allen diary, "Twenty-Five Days Among the Bandits," 5.

3. L. Lehrbas, "China Press Man Is Victim, Escapes: Tells Thrilling Tale of Hold-Up," *China Press*, May 8, 1923, 1; "Barefoot U.S. Women Beaten by China Band," *New York American*, May 9, 1923, 2; "American Officer Slain, Peking Hears; Bandits Under Attack; Woman Freed; Our Troops May March to the Rescue," *New York Times*, May 8, 1923, 1; "Washington Ready for Drastic Action," *New York Times*, May 8, 1923, 1.

4. Allen diary, "Twenty-Five Days Among the Bandits," 6.

5. "Statement of Roland W. Pinger, June 16, 1923," 2, American Consulate, Tientsin, included with the Dispatch No. 1805 of Jacob Gould Schurman, Minister, American Legation, Peking to Secretary of State, September 13, 1923, National Archives and Records Administration, RG 59, 393.1123 Lincheng/246, Box 4646.

6. "China Orders Ransom Paid for Captives," *Chicago Daily News*, May 9, 1923, 1; Lehrbas, "China Press Man Is Victim, Escapes," 1.

7. "Statements of Mr. A. L. Zimmerman and Mr. V. Haimovitch Re Derailment of Tientsin-Pukow Train at Lin-Cheng and Capture of Foreigners by Bandits," reprinted with Dispatch of Consul, American Consulate General, Tientsin (Huston), to the Secretary of State, May 8, 1923, National Archives and Records Administration, RG 59, 393.1123 Lincheng/132, Box 4644; "Statement of Victor Haimovitch and Alfred Zimmerman."

8. Lehrbas, "China Press Man Is Victim, Escapes," 1.

9. "Tientsin-Pukow Express Wrecked by Bandits," 382.

CHAPTER 6: THE BANDITS OF PAOTZUKU MOUNTAIN

1. Lehrbas, "Miss Aldrich Tells Vivid Story of Experience," 1.

2. The Peking Express mail cars carried registered mail, which meant that they also likely transported valuables and money.

3. "Tientsin-Pukow Express Wrecked by Bandits," 380.

4. Powell, *My Twenty-Five Years in China*, 92–124, 93; Powell, "Personal Story," 407; Powell, "'Esteemed Guests,'" 845; "The Bandit Outrage: How Major Pinger's Son Was Saved from Death," *Peking & Tientsin Times*, May 16, 1923, 9.

5. Powell, *My Twenty-Five Years in China*, 92–124, 93; "Peking Express Outrage," 356; "Three Hostages Slain as Brigands Plan New Foray: Murder of Chinese Seen as Warning to Authorities Demands Must Be Met," *Evening Star*, May 16, 1923, 2; "The Bandit Outrage: How Major Pinger's Son," 9.

6. Lehrbas, "Miss Aldrich Tells Vivid Story of Experience," 1.

7. "Statement of Mathilde Juliette Schoneberg," 1.

8. "Miss MacFadden's Terrible Experience," *North-China Herald*, May 12, 1923, 386.

9. Lehrbas, "Miss Aldrich Tells Vivid Story of Experience," 1.

10. "Miss Aldrich Finds Haven in Hospital," *New York American*, May 9, 1923, 2.

11. For background information regarding the combine, see Merwin, *Drugging a Nation*; and G. E. Miller, *Shanghai, the Paradise of Adventurers* (New York: Orsay, 1937), 153–162.

12. Lehrbas, "China Press Man Is Victim, Escapes," 1.

13. "Tientsin-Pukow Express Wrecked by Bandits," 382.

14. *Montpelier Examiner*, July 26, 1918, 5; "Lloyd Lehrbas Wins Medal at University Track Meet," *Montpelier Examiner*, January 28, 1916, 4; "Lloyd Lehrbas Is Making Good," *Montpelier Examiner*, November 5, 1915, 1; "Young 'Dutch' Lehrbas Is Heard from Again," *Montpelier Examiner*, March 3, 1916, 1. In college, Lehrbas was a journalism major at the University of Wisconsin. See also Lehrbas, "China Press Man Is Victim, Escapes," 1.

15. "Captured by Bandits," 8.

16. "Statement of Mathilde Juliette Schoneberg," 1.

17. Powell, "Personal Story," 407; Powell, *My Twenty-Five Years in China*, 100–101; Aldrich, "Week-End with Chinese Bandits," 674.

18. Pinger diary, "Lincheng Incident of 1923," 102.

19. Pinger, 105.

20. Elias, "My Experience," 228/3253/318.

CHAPTER 7: THE BLACK-HEARTED GENERAL HO

1. Minnie MacFadden to her sister Edith MacFadden, 5; Scripps, "Companion of Miss Aldrich Describes Forced March to Hills as Captive of Band," United Press International, May 8, 1923.

2. "Full Story of Train Outrage," *Shanghai Times*, May 8, 1923, 1.

3. "Japanese Reported Taken," *Evening Post*, May 7, 1923, 1; "Shantung Bandits All Carried Japanese Rifles," 296; Powell, *My Twenty-Five Years in China*, 93; Powell, "Personal Story," 408. See also William Howard Gardiner, "The New World: Realities in the Far East," *Atlantic Monthly*, April 1924, 544–545. See also William Howard Gardiner Papers, Houghton Library, Harvard Library, Harvard University, Call No. MS Am 2199.

4. Article 156 of the Treaty of Versailles, which granted Germany's possessions in Shantung to Japan, triggered the May 4 movement, set off protests in Peking involving thousands of students, and forced a number of pro-Japanese officials to seek refuge in the Legation Quarter. It also prompted a nationwide boycott of Japanese goods. "Japanese Boycott in Tientsin," *North-China Herald*, April 14, 1923, 87. The Shantung citizens were also unhappy that the holy mountain of Taishan was effectively under Japanese control. Taishan has been a place of worship for at least three thousand years and is probably China's oldest sacred mountain. It saw ten thousand pilgrims daily make the ascent during the months of February and March. Shantung is the birthplace of Confucius and where thousands of pilgrims climb to the temple in his honor at the top of Taishan. "China's Holy Mountain Lost by Shantung Deal," *Sun*, September 14, 1919, 5. See generally Robert C. Forsyth, *Shantung: The Sacred Province of China* (Shanghai: Christian Literature Society, 1912); and W. Fisher, "The Oldest Place of Worship in the World," *Scientific Monthly*, June 1916, 521–535. See generally "Editorial, China's Case at Paris," *Advocate of Peace* (1894–1920) 81, no. 4 (April 1919): 109–110; G. Reid, "The Neutrality of China," *Yale Law Journal* 25, no. 2 (December 1915): 122–128; G. Reid, "Japan's Occupation of Shantung: China a Question of Right," *Journal of Race Development* 7, no. 2 (October 1916): 199–207; G. Reid, "China's Loss and Japan's Gain," *Journal of Race Development* 6, no. 2 (October 1915): 145–154; G. Reid, "China's Rights at the Peace Table," *Journal of International Relations* 10, no. 1 (July 1919): 87–98; P. Treat, "The Shantung Issue," *Journal of International Development* 10, no. 3 (January 1920): 289–312; "Editorial, Is Japan Dismantling China?," *Advocate of Peace* (1894–1920) 77, no. 9 (October 1915): 210–211; C. Elliott, "The Shantung Question," *American Journal of International Law* 13, no. 4 (October 1919); and K. Kawakami, "Japan's Acts in China," *North American Review* 210, no. 768 (November 1919): 622–634.

5. President Harding called the Treaty of Versailles the "colossal blunder of all time" and characterized the award of Shantung to Japan as the "rape of the first great democracy of the Orient." "America's Position on the Shantung Question," *Weekly Review of the Far East*, Shanghai, China (1921): 5, 16–17. "America's Position on the Shantung Question," published by John Powell's company, was a supplement to the *Weekly Review of the Far East* and was intended as supporting materials for

the Washington Conference, which commenced in November 1921. See generally J. Dewey, *China, Japan and the USA: Present-Day Conditions in the Far East and Their Bearing on the Washington Conference* (1921).

6. "China's Booming Bandit Business," *Literary Digest*, June 2, 1923, 40.

7. "China's Booming Bandit Business."

8. Known as the Torchbearers' Uprising (1852–1868), the Nien army was an alliance of clan armies purportedly one hundred thousand strong that was intended to bring down the Ch'ing Dynasty while the central government was preoccupied with the Taiping Rebellion in the South. Many influential clans in Shantung joined the Nien cause, and the clan chiefs played an important role among the Nien leaders. Most of the Nien force consisted of poor peasants, although deserters from the government militias were important as military experts. The source of their strength was the support and sympathy of the local people. After the Taiping Rebellion was crushed, the Ch'ing Dynasty focused on the Nien rebels by isolating and trapping them. The rebellion failed, and the Nien were defeated by imperial troops in 1868. See generally Billingsley, *Bandits in Republican China*, 2–3; and Elizabeth J. Perry, *Rebels and Revolutionaries in North China: 1845–1945* (Stanford, CA: Stanford University Press, 1980), 128–130, 140–145.

9. Allen diary, "Twenty-Five Days Among the Bandits," 8.

10. Minnie MacFadden to her sister Edith MacFadden, 5.

11. MacFadden, 8.

12. Powell, "'Esteemed Guests,'" 846–847.

13. Powell, *My Twenty-Five Years in China*, 98.

14. Rowlatt was forty-two years old and originally from Yorkshire, England. He worked for the British trading firm Reiss & Co. in Tientsin. He was schooled as an engineer and moved to China in 1905 at the age of twenty-four and worked in Hankow, Shanghai, and Tientsin. Rowlatt left China to enlist in the British Army during the Great War, serving in France, receiving awards for gallantry, and achieving the rank of second lieutenant. Rowlatt's American-born wife, Lillian, was waiting at home in Tientsin.

15. Pinger diary, "Lincheng Incident of 1923," 106.

16. Pinger, 106; Allen diary, "Twenty-Five Days Among the Bandits," 7.

17. "Captured by Bandits," 8.

18. "Statement of Mathilde Juliette Schoneberg," 2.

19. Pinger diary, "Lincheng Incident of 1923," 122.

20. Pinger, 178.

21. Pinger, 113.

22. Powell, "'Esteemed Guests,'" 845, 847; "Statement of M. C. Jacobson," May 8, 1923, H.B.M. Consulate General, Tientsin, British Public Records Office, Foreign Office 228/3252/74.

CHAPTER 8: THE GAUNTLET

1. Letter of Jerome A. Henley to Freeman Burbank, San Francisco, May 24, 1923.

2. In August 1921 the Yellow River broke through the north bank and laid waste to five counties, destroying roughly five hundred towns and villages. Over three million people in Shantung were at risk of floods, famine, and starvation. The Yellow River is considered the cradle of Chinese civilization, with agricultural cultures having lived on its banks for more than seven thousand years. The river gets its name from the color of the water, caused by a high level of loess silt, which results in an excessive load of sediment being deposited along the riverbanks, silting up the river and causing floods as the river seeks a new course. Even the National Committee of the YMCA supported the effort by providing education and entertainment for the workforce.

Whitham was a well-known member of the Shanghai business community, serving on the boards of the American Chamber of Commerce in Shanghai and the China Central Committee of the American Red Cross. "Dr. Shurman to Visit Yellow River Repair Enterprise," *Weekly Review*, May 5, 1923, 338.

3. "Kansan Goes to Tsingtao: Ralph Naill of Herington Goes to Chinese West Point," *Topeka State Journal*, January 10, 1921, 5; "Ralph Naill Home," *Abilene Weekly Reflector*, September 4, 1919, 6; "Gets Annapolis Appointment," *Topeka State Journal*, December 17, 1914, 10; "Ralph Naill Goes to U.S. Naval Academy," *Abilene Weekly Reflector*, May 27, 1915, 6. For a detailed historical review of the American Expeditionary Force in Siberia, see William S. Graves, *America's Siberian Adventure (1918–1920)* (New York: Peter Smith, 1941).

4. Memorandum of Vice Consul, Tsinan Consulate (Milbourne), to the Secretary of State, May 12, 1923, National Archives and Records Administration, RG 59, 393.1123 Lincheng/142, 2, Box 4644.

5. Letter of Minnie MacFadden to her sister Edith MacFadden, May 1923, 8.

6. MacFadden, 9.

7. MacFadden, 8.

8. "Statement of M. C. Jacobson," 228/3252/70–75; "Statement of Mathilde Juliette Schoneberg," 2.

9. Telegram from the Minister in China (Schurman) to the Secretary of State, May 11, 1923, National Archives and Records Administration, RG 59, 393.1123 Lincheng/32: Telegram, Box 4644.

10. "Statement of M. C. Jacobson," 228/3252/72; "Tales of Captives," *North-China Herald*, May 19, 1923, 451, 452; "Girl Faces Bullets," 1.

11. "Statement of Mathilde Juliette Schoneberg."

12. "Statement of Mathilde Juliette Schoneberg," 3.

13. "Tientsin-Pukow Express Wrecked by Bandits," 384. Kang Tung-yi, a Chinese journalist from the *Shun Pao* (申报, or Shanghai News), a Chinese-language newspaper based in Shanghai, also escaped from the bandits during the initial holdup and filed reports with his newspaper. See "津浦路匪掳乘客之纪闻" ("A Report on the Bandits Abducting Passengers on the Tientsin-Pukow Railway"), 申报 (Shun Pao), May 8, 1923, 13.

14. "Payment of Ransom by Peking Not Confirmed," *North-China Herald*, May 12, 1923, 386; "Full Story of Train Outrage," *Shanghai Times*, May 8, 1923, 1; "Tientsin-Pukow Express Wrecked by Bandits," 380.

15. "Barefoot U.S. Women Beaten," 2; "Two Yanks Shot as Chinese Fight Bandits: Brigands Make U.S. Officers Act as Shield," *Chicago Daily Tribune*, May 8, 1923, 1; "Bandits Release Women; Carry Off U.S.A. Officers Among 115 Men Captured," *Evening Post*, May 7, 1923, 1. See also "Statements of Captain G. W. Spoerry, Mrs. Allen and Mrs. Pinger Re Derailment of Tientsin-Pukow Train at Lin-Cheng and Capture of Foreigners by Bandits," reprinted with Dispatch of Consul, American Consulate General, Tientsin (Huston) to the Secretary of State, May 8, 1923, National Archives and Records Administration, RG 59, 393.1123 Lincheng/132, Box 4644.

16. "Statement of M. C. Jacobson," 228/3252/72.

17. "Statement of Mathilde Juliette Schoneberg," 3.

18. "Statement of Mathilde Juliette Schoneberg," 3.

19. "Miss Lucy Aldrich's Companion Tells of Capture," 1.

20. "Miss Lucy Aldrich's Companion Tells of Capture," 11–12; "Miss Aldrich Finds Haven," 2; Minnie MacFadden to her sister Edith MacFadden, 11.

21. When the northbound train arrived, Naill and Wiesenberg carried MacFadden to the train. Robert Paine Scripps—the twenty-eight-year-old son of media mogul

Edward Scripps of the E.W. Scripps Company—just happened to be traveling to China and gave MacFadden his compartment and helped her into the bottom berth. Scripps was on a foray to Peking as part of an around-the-world yacht trip and just missed the bandit train by two days, yet he was mistakenly featured in the global media as one of the hostages. "Chinese Bandits Hold Him Captive," *Evening Star*, May 7, 1923, 1; "Seized by Chinese Bandits," *Washington Post*, May 8, 1923, 4; "Names of Eighteen Americans Kidnapped in China; Eight Have Been Released or Escaped the Bandits," *New York Times*, May 8, 1923, 1 (correcting the record by pointing out that Scripps was not taken hostage). See also telegram from Minister in China (Schurman) to Secretary of State (Hughes), May 8, 1923, National Archives and Records Administration, RG 59, 393.1123 Lincheng/13, Box 4644.

CHAPTER 9: DIAMOND IN THE ROUGH

1. Aldrich, "Week-End with Chinese Bandits," 672; Lehrbas, "Miss Aldrich Tells Vivid Story of Experience," 1.

2. Standard Oil marketed its kerosene under the *Mei Foo* trademark—translating to "beautiful confidence" or "beautiful and trustworthy," the same Chinese characters that Socony used in its China-based company name. *Mei Foo* also referred to the name of the small glass and tin lamp that the company developed in the 1890s and mass-distributed cheaply to Chinese peasants to encourage them to switch from vegetable- and animal-based oils, which they burned in earthen bowls containing floating wicks, to the relatively cleaner kerosene. Aldrich, "Week-End with Chinese Bandits," 678–679. See "Mei Foo Lamps Are Still Shining," *New York Times*, March 15, 1959, 192.

3. "Dedicate Peking College: John D. Rockefeller Jr. Is Felicitated at Opening of Medical Centre," *New York Times*, September 21, 1921, 11; "To Dedicate Peking Institution Today: John D. Rockefeller Jr. Will Aid at Opening of New Union Medical College," *New York Times*, September 19, 1921, 14; "Rockefeller Happy: John D., Jr., Expresses Gratitude at News of Relative," *Evening Star*, May 8, 1923, 4; "Mr. Rockefeller Seeks Information," *New York Times*, May 7, 1923; "John D. Rockefeller, Jr., Doubts Report of Capture," Associated Press, May 6, 1923.

4. The consulate in Shanghai was sending "cable after cable . . . about her to distraught State Department officials and her anxious family at home." Norwood F. Allman, *Shanghai Lawyer* (New York: McGraw-Hill, 1943), 71–72. Allman was the former consul at the Shanghai US consulate. See "Miss Lucy Aldrich in Peril in China; Sister-in-Law of J.D. Rockefeller Jr., on Train from Which 150 Are Kidnapped," *New York Times*, May 7, 1923, 1; "Standard Starts Inquiries: Agents in China Seek Definite News of Miss Aldrich," *New York Times*, May 8, 1923, 2.

5. Aldrich, "Week-End with Chinese Bandits," 672; Letter of Mathilde Juliette Schoneberg, May 8, 1923, Peking, Lucy T. Aldrich Papers, Collections of the Rhode Island Historical Society; Minnie MacFadden to her sister Edith MacFadden, 1; Lehrbas, "Miss Aldrich Tells Vivid Story of Experience," 1; "Miss Aldrich Tells of Hurried Flight, Driven by Bandits," *New York Tribune*, May 11, 1923, 1; "Bandits Took Miss Aldrich Off by Herself; Treated Well by Women and Suddenly Freed," *New York Times*, May 10, 1923, 1.

6. "A Senator's Daughter," *Pacific Commercial Advertiser*, February 15, 1893, 6. See also D. Del Gais, "Two Remarkable Women/Sisters," Rockefeller Archive Center (2009).

7. *Washington Times*, August 8, 1919, 8. Aldrich's extensive collection of textiles, comprising some hundreds of items, was eventually given to the Rhode Island School of Design Museum and forms a significant part of its Asian textile archives. "Lucy Aldrich, 85, of Rhode Island: Daughter of Late Senator and Sister of Ambassador

Is Dead in Providence," *New York Times*, January 13, 1955, 27; "Miss Aldrich Left $2,500,000," *New York Times*, February 9, 1955, 11.

8. Aldrich, "Week-End with Chinese Bandits," 676.

9. Aldrich, 674, 676.

10. Aldrich, 675.

11. Aldrich, 676, 677, 678.

12. Aldrich, 675.

13. Aldrich, 676. Fruit-stone carvings are one of the most appreciated Chinese folk-art forms. They can be traced back to the Song Dynasty (960–1279) and were also very popular during the Ch'ing Dynasty (1644–1911). The most commonly used material is a peach pit, but walnuts, almonds, olive pits, and hickory nuts are also used. It was considered fashionable for high-ranking officials to wear carved fruit-pit accessories. Peaches symbolize long life, and a peach-stone carving was worn to keep demons away.

14. Aldrich, 677.

15. Aldrich, 677.

16. Aldrich, 678–679.

17. Aldrich, 680.

18. Aldrich, 680.

19. Aldrich, 678–679.

20. Aldrich, 680.

21. Aldrich, 680.

22. Aldrich, 680–681.

23. Aldrich, 680–681.

24. Aldrich, 681.

25. Lehrbas, "Miss Aldrich Tells Vivid Story of Experience," 1.

26. The painful cramping process of foot binding would begin when a girl was around five years old, and it was designed to physically alter the shape of the foot by systematically breaking the arch bones of the feet until they resembled hooves. The process was excruciating. Young girls' toes, with the exception of the big toe, were broken and bound flat against the sole of the foot, which took a triangular form. Over a two-year period, the ten-foot-long and two-inch-wide silk wrappings became tighter as the heel and sole were crushed together. The arches were broken as the girls were forced to walk long distances. Once crushed and bound, the shape could not be reversed, and the girl was effectively disabled for life. The mobility of women with bound feet was significantly limited, which also meant that they were dependent on their families. For ten centuries, continuous generations of Chinese women endured a practice that intensified female subjugation. The women walked in tiny steps and tended to walk predominantly on their heels to avoid placing weight on their broken toes. The practice also produced a particular manner of walking (seen as desirable) that relied on the thigh and buttock muscles for support. Girls enduring the process died from infection, gangrene, and necrosis. The practice continued unofficially for decades, especially in poor, rural areas of China, such as in Shantung. In 1902 Empress Dowager T'zu-hsi issued an order banning foot binding; however, after much protest the order was rescinded, and the practice continued to thrive. After the Chinese revolution, the Republic of China issued an edict in 1912 that prohibited the barbaric practice, although it was not widely implemented. See generally Wang Ping, *Aching for Beauty: Footbinding in China* (Minneapolis: University of Minnesota Press, 2000); Dorothy Ko, *Every Step a Lotus: Shoes for Bound Feet* (Berkeley: University of California Press, 2001); and Dorothy Ko, *Cinderella's Sisters: A Revisionist History of Footbinding* (Berkeley: University of California Press, 2005).

27. Aldrich, "Week-End with Chinese Bandits," 681–682.

CHAPTER 10: THE SCANDAL

1. Letter of Berthold George Tours, Esq., British Consul, Tsinan, to Sir Ronald Macleay, Minister, British Legation, May 9, 1923, British Public Records Office, Foreign Office, May 9, 1923, 228/3252/129–132.

2. Letter of Tours to Macleay, May 9, 1923.

3. Memorandum of Division of Far Eastern Affairs, State Department, to the Secretary of State, May 8, 1923, National Archives and Records Administration, RG 59, 393.1123 Lincheng/58, Box 4644; Counselor of Legation at Peking (Bell) to the Secretary of State, May 9, 1923, 393.1123 Lincheng/25: Telegram, in *Papers Relating to the Foreign Relations of the United States*, 1923, 1:632; "Schurman Suggested No Plan for Release: He Demanded That Americans Be Rescued, but Left to Peking the Method to Be Adopted," *New York Times*, May 11, 1923, 2; "State Department Starts Official Inquiry into the Kidnapping of Americans in China," *New York Times*, May 7, 1923, 1.

4. "Tientsin-Pukow Express Wrecked by Bandits," 383. See also Dispatch of John K. Davis, Consul, Shanghai, to Minister in China (Schurman), National Archives and Records Administration, RG 59, 393.1123 Lincheng/157, Box 4646.

5. Memorandum of Vice Consul, Tsinan Consulate (Milbourne), Lincheng/142, 4, Box 4644.

6. Memorandum of Vice Consul, Tsinan Consulate (Milbourne), Lincheng/142, 4–5, Box 4644.

7. Memorandum of Vice Consul, Tsinan Consulate (Milbourne), Lincheng/142, 5, Box 4644.

8. Memorandum of Vice Consul, Tsinan Consulate (Milbourne), Lincheng/142, 5–6, Box 4644.

9. "The Arrival of Dr. Jacob Schurman," *North-China Herald*, May 12, 1923, 388.

10. Memorandum of Vice Consul, Tsinan Consulate (Milbourne), Lincheng/142, 7, Box 4644.

11. Memorandum of Vice Consul, Tsinan Consulate (Milbourne), Lincheng/142, 7, Box 4644.

12. Memorandum of Vice Consul, Tsinan Consulate (Milbourne), Lincheng/142, 7, Box 4644.

13. The Minister in China (Schurman) to the Secretary of State, May 7, 1923, National Archives and Records Administration, RG 59, 393.1123 Lincheng/3: Telegram, Box 4644; Memorandum of the Division of Far Eastern Affairs to the Secretary of State, May 9, 1923, National Archives and Records Administration, RG 59, 393.1123 Lincheng/19, Box 4644; the Counselor of Legation at Peking (Bell) to the Secretary of State, 1:633–634. Thirty-year-old Major Philoon, originally from Maine, was a no-nonsense military professional who graduated from West Point, where he was the center for Army's football team. With two American consular officers and two American military officers on the ground in Tsaochuang, US officials had hoped to get more definite information about the situation. Minister Schurman's instructions to Philoon were to "proceed to the scene to act as an observer and reporter, and to use his discretion and judgment in assisting to secure the release of the captives." See "Washington Expects Results Soon in China; but Lacks Definite Information as to Captives," *New York Times*, May 10, 1923, 2. Memorandum of Vice Consul, Tsinan Consulate (Milbourne), Lincheng/142, 8, Box 4644.

14. "Pekin Sends American to Dicker with Bandits," *Sun*, May 9, 1923, 1; the Minister in China (Schurman) to the Secretary of State, May 12, 1923, National Archives and Records Administration, RG 59, 393.1123 Lincheng/43: Telegram, Box 4644.

15. Letter of Sir Ronald Macleay, Minister, British Legation, to the Foreign Office, May 12, 1923, British Public Records Office, Foreign Office, May 12, 1923, 228/3252/171–175.

16. "Kidnapping of Foreigners—Summary of Dean's (M. Batalha Freitas) Interview with Premier (Chang Shao-ts'eng)," May 8, 1923, British Public Records Office, Foreign Office, May 9, 1923, 228/3252/119–120. The diplomatic community also called for a progressive indemnity for emotional and material damages sustained by the passengers for every day after May 12. "Diplomats Demand Action: Progressive Indemnity if Captives Are Not Freed by May 12," *New York Times*, May 9, 1923, 1.

17. "Diplomats Demand Action," 1; Letter of Sir Ronald Macleay, Minister, British Legation, to the Foreign Office, May 12, 1923, 228/3252/171–175.

18. The Counselor of Legation at Peking (Bell) to the Secretary of State, May 9, 1923, 393.1123 Lincheng/25: Telegram, in *Papers Relating to the Foreign Relations of the United States*, 1923, 1:633.

CHAPTER 11: THE DRUMBEAT

1. Allen diary, "Twenty-Five Days Among the Bandits," 10.

2. Powell, "Personal Story," 407.

3. "Mrs. Verea Released: Situation of Captives Reported Desperate," *North-China Herald*, May 26, 1923, 523.

4. "Captured by Bandits," 8.

5. Pinger diary, "Lincheng Incident of 1923," 114.

6. Elias, "My Experience," 228/3253/310.

7. Allen diary, "Twenty-Five Days Among the Bandits," 10.

8. Allen, 10.

9. Elias, "My Experience," 228/3253/311.

10. "Captured by Bandits," 8.

11. Pinger diary, "Lincheng Incident of 1923," 116–117.

12. Aldrich, "Week-End with Chinese Bandits," 684.

13. See letter of Nong Yuen-lung, Station Master, Chee-tsun Station, Tientsin-Pukow Line, May 27, 1923, Lucy T. Aldrich Papers, Collections of the Rhode Island Historical Society. See also "Miss Aldrich Freed; Found in Chee-tsun," *New York Times*, May 8, 1923, 1.

14. Aldrich, "Week-End with Chinese Bandits," 685.

15. Aldrich, 685.

16. "John D. Jr. Is Relieved: Gets News of Release of Sister-in-Law While Working on Home," *New York Times*, May 8, 1923, 2; "Miss Aldrich in Hospital: Mrs. Rockefeller Is Informed Her Sister Is at Tsinan," *New York Times*, May 8, 1923, 2.

17. Cable copy of J. P. Babcock to Socony Shanghai, May 8, 1923, 3, Lucy T. Aldrich Papers, Collections of the Rhode Island Historical Society.

18. "Miss Aldrich Recovers Jewels Lost in China," *New York Times*, June 2, 1923, 14; "How Miss Aldrich Got Back Her Jewels: Search the Countryside, Boy's Lucky Discovery," *North-China Herald*, June 9, 1923, 670.

19. Aldrich, "Week-End with Chinese Bandits," 672. See also "Miss Lucy Aldrich in Honolulu," *New York Times*, August 4, 1923, 13; "Miss Aldrich Arrives," *New York Times*, August 10, 1923, 11. See also letter of Bayway Joint Conference Auxiliary to Aldrich, December 6, 1923, Lucy T. Aldrich Papers, Collections of the Rhode Island Historical Society. Aldrich received some unsolicited attention over the Lincheng affair, including being the subject of an unpublished dramatic photoplay titled "The Sacred Twin Butterflies." It oddly characterizes Aldrich's

experience as being "mysteriously carried to the Temple of Kwan Yuan, the goddess of Mercy." Unpublished manuscript of "The Sacred Twin Butterflies," Sunswan Won-Kingsing, in the Lucy T. Aldrich Papers, Collections of the Rhode Island Historical Society.

20. Powell, *My Twenty-Five Years in China*, 100–101; Allen diary, "Twenty-Five Days Among the Bandits," 15; affidavit of Leon Friedman, September 8, 1923, American Consulate, Shanghai, included with the Dispatch of Edward Bell, Acting Minister, American Legation, Peking, 393.1123 Lincheng/274.

21. In 1909 Koon Chi Cheng's father, a wealthy Cantonese merchant, sent his son to the Mill Hill School, a boarding school in northwest London. Cheng was a strong cricket player and was one of the opening batsmen on Mill Hill's second eleven in the 1912 season. Cheng returned to China after graduating from Cambridge in 1919. He converted to Christianity while in Britain.

22. Letter of John B. Powell to Major Philoon, Sunday, May 13, 1923, in the Philoon Family Papers; "Bandits Threatened to Eat Captives: Powell Tells of Anxiety and Suffering of the Foreigners Held in Shantung," *New York Times*, May 16, 1923, 7.

23. Pinger diary, "Lincheng Incident of 1923," 118–119; Allen diary, "Twenty-Five Days Among the Bandits," 15.

24. Elias, "My Experience," 228/3253/314; Pinger diary, "Lincheng Incident of 1923," 121–122.

25. Powell, "'Esteemed Guests,'" 845, 857.

26. "Bandits Threatened to Eat Captives," 7; Powell, "'Esteemed Guests,'" 845, 857. See also Pinger diary, "Lincheng Incident of 1923," 107–108.

27. Elias, "My Experience," 228/3253/313.

28. Pinger diary, "Lincheng Incident of 1923," 128–129.

29. Pinger, 102.

30. Pinger, 130.

CHAPTER 12: THE MONGREL FEAST

1. Powell, *My Twenty-Five Years in China*, 101.

2. The Counselor of Legation at Peking (Bell) to the Secretary of State, 1:632–633.

3. Pinger diary, "Lincheng Incident of 1923," 120–121.

4. Letter of Berthold George Tours, Esq., British Consul, Tsinan, to Sir Ronald Macleay, Minister, British Legation, May 11, 1923, British Public Records Office, Foreign Office, May 11, 1923, 228/3252/112, 121. Letter of Sir Ronald Macleay, Minister, to Berthold George Tours, Esq., Consul General, British Consulate, Tsinan, May 11, 1923, British Public Records Office, Foreign Office, May 11, 1923, 228/3252/141; Letter of Sir Ronald Macleay, Minister, to Berthold George Tours, Esq., Consul General, British Consulate, Tsinan, May 12, 1923, British Public Records Office, Foreign Office, May 11, 1923, 228/3252/157.

5. Letter of Berthold George Tours, Esq., British Consul, Tsinan, to Sir Ronald Macleay, Minister, British Legation, May 12, 1923, British Public Records Office, Foreign Office, 228/3252/168.

6. Powell, *My Twenty-Five Years in China*, 101.

7. Pinger diary, "Lincheng Incident of 1923," 141–142.

8. Pinger, 144.

9. Pinger, 144. See also "Bandits Claim Control of Own Regions," *North-China Herald*, May 19, 1923, 453; and "Pinger Implores That Bandits' Terms Be Complied With," *New York Times*, May 12, 1923, 1.

10. Allen diary, "Twenty-Five Days Among the Bandits," 18.

11. Pinger diary, "Lincheng Incident of 1923," 146.

12. Pinger, 149.

13. One of the Chinese captives released with Bobby and Roland was Yang Yü-hsun, the grandson of former president Yuan Shih-kai. Yang was a powerful personality and Sun Mei-yao ordered him released to avoid antagonizing the Yang family. See the Minister in China (Schurman) to the Secretary of State, May 11, 1923, National Archives and Records Administration, RG 59, 393.1123 Lincheng/38: Telegram, Box 4644; and Memorandum of Edward Bell, Consular, American Legation to Sir Ronald Macleay, Minister, British Legation, May 16, 1923, British Public Records Office, Foreign Office, 228/3252/207.

CHAPTER 13: DIPLOMACY IN ACTION

1. Report of Carl Crow to Major Arthur Bassett, Chairman, China Central Committee, the American Red Cross, July 16, 1923, in the John Powell Papers (C3662), the State Historical Society of Missouri Manuscript Collection, SHSMO Research Center, Columbia, Missouri.

2. T. Wright, "Entrepreneurs, Politicians and the Chinese Coal Industry, 1895–1937," *Modern Asian Studies* 14, no. 4 (1980): 579–602; Crow report; Memorandum on the Lincheng Incident, 4–5; Dispatch of Consul John K. Davis to Minister Schurman dated June 12, 1923, attached to the Letter from the Minister in China (Schurman) to the Secretary of State (Hughes), June 20, 1923, National Archives and Records Administration, RG 59, 393.1123 Lincheng/207, Box 4646.

3. Pinger diary, "Lincheng Incident of 1923," 84–85; Crow report.

4. Letter of Berthold George Tours, Esq., British Consul, Tsinan, to Sir Ronald Macleay, Minister, British Legation, May 14, 1923, British Public Records Office, Foreign Office, 228/3252/203. Tours's railcar accommodations the first night—apparently in a section normally used as storage for food—were not to his liking. Tours protested loudly. "No attempt had been made to furnish a resting-place for me when I arrived last night, and it was thanks to the American party, who have by priority of arrival secured a whole car to themselves and have labeled it 'The American Rescue Mission,' that I was given a room for the night in a compartment used as a storeroom," Tours said, complaining to anyone who would listen to him. "The presence of the stores had attracted enough flies to make sleep difficult, so I protested loudly this morning, and am now installed in a coupé a stage or two better than the storeroom," he went on. "A few more warm days, and the whole compound will be purgatory."

5. "One American correspondent, has even been reproached in all seriousness for being pro-American!" said Minister Schurman. The Minister of China (Schurman) to the Secretary of State, May 15, 1923, National Archives and Records Administration, RG 59, 393.1123 Lincheng/49, Box 4644. See also "The Bandit Outrage: Press Difficulties at Tsaochuang: A Haphazard and Tiresome Censorship," *Peking & Tientsin Times*, May 28, 1930, 9. Yet British consul Tours found that much of the reporting from the American press was "extra-sensational" and generated by certain journalists who were more interested in "gilding the lily for stage effect and increased circulation." Letter of Berthold George Tours, Esq., British Consul, Tsinan, to Sir Ronald Macleay, Minister, British Legation, May 19, 1923, British Public Records Office, Foreign Office, 228/3253/29.

6. "China Is Helpless to Rescue Captives: Time Limit of Diplomats' Ultimatum Expires, with Nothing Accomplished," *New York Times*, May 19, 1923, 1. See also the Counselor of Legation at Peking (Bell) to the Secretary of State, May 10, 1923, 393.1123 Lincheng/28: Telegram, in *Papers Relating to the Foreign Relations of the United States*, 1923, 1:635.

7. Memorandum of Vice Consul, Tsinan Consulate (Milbourne), Lincheng/142, 10, Box 4644.

8. E. Booker, "Tom Sawyer—Huh! He Only Lived in Missouri; We Were Kidnapped in China!," *China Press*, May 18, 1923; B. Kline, "Being Captured by Bandits Holds No Terror for Boys: Sons of Two American Army Officers Find 'Robber Men' Like Youngsters," *Japan Advertiser*, May 16, 1923.

9. Following the Boxer Rebellion, the United States Army maintained a presence in Tientsin. See generally Alfred E. Cornebise, *The United States 15th Infantry Regiment in China, 1912–1938* (Jefferson, NC: McFarland, 2004); and *The United States Army in China 1900–1938: A History of the 9th, 14th, 15th and 31st Regiments in the East* (Jefferson, NC: McFarland, 2015).

10. See 雷立柏 Leopold Leeb, Professor, 山东天主教史人物列传 (Historical List of Catholic Priests in Shandong Province [unpublished]), 人民大学 (Renmin University), December 2015. Despite the political underpinnings of its growth in China, the SVD order flourished in southern Shantung, building cathedrals, parish churches, schools, orphanages, hospitals, dispensaries, convents, seminaries, industrial workshops, and farming communities throughout. See generally Fritz Bornemann, *As Wine Poured Out: Blessed Joseph Freinademetz SVD Missionary in China 1879–1908* (Rome: Divine Word Missionaries, 1984).

11. "Bandits Threaten to Kill Prisoner," *New York Times*, May 16, 1923, 3; "Chinese Bandits Prepare to Slay Prisoners Today if Demands Fail: Grim Leader of Outlaws Demands Brigand Force Be Taken Back into Army Before Captives Are Released," *Evening Star*, May 15, 1923, 1.

12. Elias, "My Experience," 228/3253/314.

13. Allen diary, "Twenty-Five Days Among the Bandits," 21.

14. "Priest Brings Brigands' Threat to Kill Rest of Their Captives," *New York Tribune*, May 16, 1923, 4.

15. Allen diary, "Twenty-Five Days Among the Bandits," 21.

16. "Bandits Threaten to Kill Prisoner," 3; "Chinese Bandits Prepare to Slay Prisoners Today if Demands Fail," 1.

17. Allen diary, "Twenty-Five Days Among the Bandits," 22.

18. "Tientsin-Pukow Express Wrecked by Bandits," 385; "Bandits Threaten to Kill Prisoner," 3; "Chinese Bandits Prepare to Slay Prisoners Today if Demands Fail," 1.

19. Memorandum of the Division of Far Eastern Affairs to the Secretary of State, May 7, 1923, National Archives and Records Administration, RG 59, 393.1123 Lincheng/17, Box 4644. The basket of food actually came from the Yihsien Presbyterian Mission, operated by the Reverend Carroll Harvey Yerkes. The Presbyterian Mission was twenty miles east of Lincheng and the Tientsin-Pukow Railway, and it was directly connected by an elbow-shaped spur line that passed through the Tsaochuang compound to Yihsien and then south to the Grand Canal. See "Various Family Letters and Materials," Carroll and Helen Yerkes Papers (Record Group No. 153), Special Collections, Yale Divinity School Library. See also Allman, *Shanghai Lawyer*, 74–75.

20. "Bandits Threaten to Kill Prisoner," 3; "Chinese Bandits Prepare to Slay Prisoners Today if Demands Fail," 1; the Minister in China (Schurman) to the Secretary of State, May 12, 1923.

21. "Shantung Governor Wants to Quit," *New York Times*, May 12, 1923; Notice of Resignation of T'ien Chung-yu, Military Governor, Shantung Province, May 11, 1923, British Public Records Office, Foreign Office, 228/3252/189.

22. "Bandits Threaten to Kill Prisoner," 3; "Chinese Bandits Prepare to Slay Prisoners Today if Demands Fail," 1.

23. Crow was also active in the business community, including several clubs and business organizations such as the American Chamber of Commerce. See generally Paul French, *Carl Crow—A Tough Old China Hand: The Life, Times and Adventures of an American in Shanghai* (Hong Kong: Hong Kong University Press, 2006); and *Through the Looking Glass: Foreign Journalists in China, from the Opium Wars to Mao* (Hong Kong: Hong Kong University Press, 2009).

CHAPTER 14: THE AMERICAN FIXER

1. Carl Crow, "The Most Interesting Character I Ever Knew" (unpublished biography, ca. 1930, located in Carl Crow's Papers [C0041], archives of the State Historical Society of Missouri Manuscript Collection, SHSMO Research Center, Columbia, Missouri).

2. "Pekin Sends American to Dicker with Bandits," *Sun*, May 9, 1923, 1. Anderson was assisted and accompanied by Wen Shih-tsung, commissioner of foreign affairs, Nanking, Kiangsu Province, who disguised himself during negotiations to avoid being singled out and taken hostage by the bandits.

3. "China Promises to Quell Bandits: Peking Officials Will Consider General Policy to Exterminate Outlaws," *Evening Star*, May 11, 1923, 2.

4. Observers of the day believed that Japan played a key role in instigating the incident. See Gardiner, "The New World," 540, 544–545. See also William Howard Gardiner Papers, Houghton Library, Harvard Library, Harvard University, Call No. MS Am 2199. Japanese media stated that "the Peking Express in Shantung Province may prove the final straw leading to international intervention in China." See "Tokio Fears Intervention: Foreign Action Would Block Policy of Being the Intermediary for China," *New York Times*, May 9, 1923, 2; "Tokio Ready to Co-operate: Orders Charge d'Affaires at Peking to Act with Other Ministers," *New York Times*, May 11, 1923, 2.

5. "First Negotiations Abortive: A Second Attempt to Arrange with Bandits," *North-China Herald*, May 19, 1923, 453.

6. "Three Hostages Slain as Brigands Plan New Foray: Murder of Chinese Seen as Warning to Authorities Demands Must Be Met," *Evening Star*, May 16, 1923, 1; "Troops Clash with Bandits: Bandit Ultimatum Threatens Killing," *New York Times*, May 20, 1923, 1.

7. "Brigands Leaders Educated," *New York Times*, May 16, 1923, 3; "Three Hostages Slain as Brigands Plan New Foray," 2.

CHAPTER 15: THE MOUNTAIN STRONGHOLD

1. Allen diary, "Twenty-Five Days Among the Bandits," 29–30.

2. The Minister in China (Schurman) to the Secretary of State, May 16, 1923, National Archives and Records Administration, RG 59, 393.1123 Lincheng/50: Telegram, Box 4644; "Negotiations Held Up: Indefinite Delay of Dealing with Bandits Likely, Report to U.S.," *Evening Star*, May 16, 1923, 2; "Developments in Bandit Situation," *Weekly Review*, May 26, 1923, 466; "Guard over Captives Increased," *New York Times*, May 16, 1923, 3. See also the Counselor of Legation at Peking (Bell) to the Secretary of State, May 16, 1923, 393.1123 Lincheng/51: Telegram, in *Papers Relating to the Foreign Relations of the United States*, 1923, 1:639–640.

3. "Chinese Troops Engage Bandits; Captives in Peril," *Evening Star*, May 17, 1923, 1.

4. "Developments in Bandit Situation," *Weekly Review*, May 26, 1923, 466.

5. Powell, "Personal Story," 407; Allen diary, "Twenty-Five Days Among the Bandits," 28.

6. "The Bandit Outrage: Two Chinese Escape," *Peking & Tientsin Times*, May 21, 1923, 11.

7. Powell, "Personal Story," 407.

8. Elias, "My Experience," 228/3253/315-316; Allen diary, "Twenty-Five Days Among the Bandits," 28.

9. "The Bandit Outrage: Mr. Powell's Letter," *Peking & Tientsin Times*, May 22, 1923, 9.

10. "The Bandit Outrage: A Letter from Mr. Rowlatt," *Peking & Tientsin Times*, May 19, 1923, 9; Allen diary, "Twenty-Five Days Among the Bandits," 29–30.

11. Elias, "My Experience," 228/3253/316; Pinger diary, "Lincheng Incident of 1923," 155.

12. "Pawns in the Political Game," *North-China Herald*, June 2, 1923, 593; Pinger diary, "Lincheng Incident of 1923," 176.

13. Crow report, 4.

14. Crow, 5.

15. The Minister in China (Schurman) to the Secretary of State, May 23, 1923, 393.1123 Lincheng/90: Telegram, in *Papers Relating to the Foreign Relations of the United States*, 1923, 1:647; "Letter from Mr. Rowlatt: Bandits' Inaccessible Peaks," *North-China Herald*, May 26, 1923, 522.

16. "Prisoners Get Supply of Clothing and Utensils: Carl Crow, Red Cross Representative Sends Message," *China Press*, May 18, 1923.

17. Crow, "The Most Interesting Character I Ever Knew," 4–5. This was about $114,000 in today's US dollars, a hefty sum to help fund the rescue effort.

18. "Bandits Threaten Death to Captives," *New York Times*, May 19, 1923, 2.

19. Allen diary, "Twenty-Five Days Among the Bandits," 33.

20. "The Bandit Outrage: 'A Long Nightmare,'" *Peking & Tientsin Times*, May 16, 1923, 9.

21. The hostages were tortured by bugs—endless swarms of gnats, fleas, and lice. For relief, some of the prisoners rubbed their bodies in kerosene. "The Bandit Outrage: A Letter from Mr. Cheng: Neglect of Chinese Prisoners," *Peking & Tientsin Times*, May 31, 1923, 9. The captives also found that scorpions had colonized the temple compound, including their bedding, clothing, and other belongings. "The Bandit Outrage: Scorpion in Captive's Bed," *Peking & Tientsin Times*, May 28, 1923, 9.

22. Carl Crow, "The Chinese Bandit Post," *Collectors Club Philatelist*, October 1926, 223; Carl Crow, "The Facts About the Paotzuku Bandit Post," *You Cheng* (Philatelic Bulletin Shanghai) 2, no. 3 (1926): 11. See generally Wolfgang Baldus, *The Postage Stamps of the Pao Tzu Ku Bandit Post* (Munich: 2007).

23. Lehrbas, "'Bandit Stamps' Was Only a Little Carl Crow Joke," *China Press*, May 29, 1923. Crow designed a ten-cent stamp and a five-cent stamp. The printer then took the rough sketches and transferred them to lithographic stone. Approximately three hundred of each kind of stamp were made, but when they were delivered, it was found that the lithographer could not include the words "American Relief Mission." The five-cent stamp was also misprinted with "50" in error instead of simply "5." The five-cent stamp included an outline of the Paotzuku Mountain pinnacle on bright-red paper, with the word "Paotzuku" on the side. The ten-cent stamp was of black ink on beige paper and included the words "Pao Tzu Ku Bandit Post." See also Crow, "The Chinese Bandit Post," 223.

24. "The Bandit Outrage: A Letter from Mr. Rowlatt," 9; letter of Leon Friedman to Ellis Ezra and Mark Hanna, American Club, Shanghai, May 30, 1923, reprinted in Baldus, *Postage Stamps*, 36-37.

25. Letter of John B. Powell to his wife, Martha Hinton Powell, June 3, 1923 (29th Day of Captivity), in the John Powell Papers (C3662), the State Historical Society of Missouri Manuscript Collection, SHSMO Research Center, Columbia, Missouri.

26. "'Chef' Leon Friedman Is Winning Fame as Cook at Paotzuku, Says 'Larry,'" *China Press*, May 28, 1923.

27. "'Chef' Leon Friedman Is Winning Fame," 113–114.

28. "Men and Events," *Weekly Review*, January 20, 1923, 310; "Comm. G. D. Musso Says China Needs a Mussolini," *China Weekly Review*, March 9, 1929, 66.

29. Powell, *My Twenty-Five Years in China*, 109.

CHAPTER 16: THE CHILDREN

1. Crow report, 7.

2. "100 Chinese Children in the Bandits' Lair: They Crowd About Powell and Mertens, Who Scaled Paotzuku, Hoping They Were Rescuers," *New York Times*, May 22, 1923, 2; Powell, "'Esteemed Guests,'" 845, 859–860; Powell, *My Twenty-Five Years in China*, 109–111.

3. Powell, *My Twenty-Five Years in China*, 109–111.

4. Powell, 110.

5. "100 Chinese Children in the Bandits' Lair," 2.

6. Crow report, 7.

7. Crow, 7.

CHAPTER 17: THE DEADLINE

1. Letter of Berthold George Tours, Esq., British Consul, Tsinan, to Sir Ronald Macleay, Minister, British Legation, May 15, 1923, British Public Records Office, Foreign Office, 228/3252/201.

2. To help steer America's policy in Asia, President Harding relied upon Hughes, as well as his secretary of commerce, Herbert Hoover, who had extensive experience in China, having lived and worked in Tientsin for several years. Two decades earlier, Hoover had held posts as the chief engineer for the Chinese Bureau of Mines and as general manager for the Chinese Engineering and Mining Corporation. Secretary Hughes was a gifted diplomat and the architect of the Washington Conference, which had resulted in the return of Shantung to China from the Japanese. Hoover claimed that he and Secretary Hughes were not part of Harding's weekly poker party crowd and wrote in his memoirs about his objection to the game being played in the White House. Herbert Hoover, *The Memoirs of Herbert Hoover: 1920–1933, the Cabinet and the Presidency* (New York: Macmillan, 1952), 48. ("I had lived too long on the frontiers of the world to have strong emotions against people playing poker for money if they liked it, but it irked me to see it in the White House.")

3. Memorandum from the Secretary of State (Hughes) to President Warren G. Harding, May 23, 1923, National Archives and Records Administration, RG 59, 393.1123 Lincheng/114a, Box 4644.

4. Tensions between Peking and Tokyo continued to rise in 1923. Just over a month before the holdup, Peking delivered a diplomatic note to Japan seeking the abrogation of the 1915 Sino/Japan Treaty, which granted Japan significant territorial rights to the northeast region of China, including the rights to the Southern Manchuria Railroad. See "China's Ministry Challenges Japan," *New York Times*, March 25, 1923, 3; and "Various Telegrams Regarding Rejection by Japan of the Proposal by China to Abrogate the Agreements of May 25, 1915, March 27, 1923-April 5, 1922," in *Papers Relating to the Foreign Relations of the United States*, 1923, 1:826–830. In response to China's demands for a return of its territory and railroad properties, the National League of Japan—which was a group representing the leadership of Japan's political parties, business organizations, and academics—issued a resolution rejecting the demand and calling on China to "desist from all actions calculated to cause unnecessary complications."

See "Determined Attitude of Influential Japanese: Formation of National League," *North-China Herald*, April 7, 1923, 9; J. Ferguson, "Japan's Use of Her Hegemony," *North American Review* 210, no. 767 (October 1919): 456–469. The Japanese media also chimed in, stating that "China's recent note to Japan, expressing her desire to abrogate the Manchurian treaty of 1915, will, of course, serve no practical purpose. Japan, considering herself one of the great powers of the world, will not meekly submit to such a peremptory demand from a nation rent by internal discord and having no Government worthy of the name." The problem, in Japan's view, was that China was "wallowing in the mire of political intrigue and factional feuds of the worst description" and that China's woes are "of her own creation, and that her real menace lies within rather than without." K. K. Kawakami, "Japan's Civilizing Mission in Manchuria," *Current History Magazine*, May 1923, 327–329. Japanese commentators of the day were critical of the US government's approach to the Shantung question. See N. Tamura, "Facts About the Shantung Question" (unpublished ms., 1919), stating that American people are "dreadfully intoxicated by the Shantung wine" and are "confused and perplexed over the Chinese question." The *Osaka Mainichi Shimbun*, literally the Osaka Daily News, ran an editorial criticizing American naïveté over conditions in China and opined that the Lincheng Incident was a wake-up call for Washington's "imperfect knowledge and understanding of China" and representing China to the world as "a country much better than she actually is." The editorial went on to say that "the effects of such misrepresentation were particularly marked in America during the three years following the Paris conference. At one time it appeared to Americans that whatever China did was right and whatever Japan did was wrong. This curious mentality was the cause of many unfounded suspicions and misgivings in the American mind regarding Japan, and now, we are glad to say, Americans are getting a more correct knowledge of the actual conditions in China. After what has happened, Americans should realize that the Chinese themselves are to blame for the disorder in China and that Japan's policy toward China has nothing to do with it, that Japan's opinion on the Far Eastern situation is generally correct and therefore deserves greater respect, that too much sympathy for China's attempt to obstruct the legitimate activity of Japan in China is calculated to disturb the stability of the Far Eastern situation, and that it is advisable for Americans to co-operate with Japan in regard to Far Eastern questions." The *Osaka Mainichi Shimbun* essentially argued that Lincheng was a vindication of Tokyo's judgment about the inability of the Chinese government to maintain order within its territory, and it recalls the US insistence at the Washington Conference on the withdrawal of Japan from Shantung. The editorial concludes with the hope that in the future greater consideration will be given to Tokyo's opinion on conditions in China, and that the development of Japan's aspirations in China will not be obstructed. Translation of "US Learns Truth About China," *Osaka Mainichi Shimbun*, May 17, 1923, reprinted in Records of the Department of State Relating to Internal Affairs of China 1910–1929, Record Group 59, Microfilm Reel M329–33, 122–126.

    5. Memorandum from the Secretary of State (Hughes) to President Warren G. Harding, May 24, 1923, National Archives and Records Administration, RG 59, 393.1123 Lincheng/99a, Box 4644; the Minister of China (Schurman) to the Secretary of State, May 18, 1923, 393.1123 Lincheng/60: Telegram, in *Papers Relating to the Foreign Relations of the United States*, 1923, 1:641.

    6. Letter of Tours to Macleay, May 14, 1923, 228/3252/204–205.

    7. "The Gentry Fired At," *North-China Herald*, June 2, 1923, 594.

    8. "Officials to Give Selves to Brigands to Free Captives," *Evening Sun*, May 16, 1923, 1; "Hostages Are Sent to Chinese Bandits: Peking Gives Cabinet Minister and General as Pledge to Free the Foreigners," *New York Times*, May 17, 1923, 7.

9. Memorandum of the Division of the Secretary of State to the Secretary of the Navy, May 18, 1923, National Archives and Records Administration, RG 59, 393.1123 Lincheng/51, Box 4644.

10. The Eight-Nation Alliance comprised the German Empire, Japan, Russia, Great Britain, France, Italy, Austria-Hungary, and the United States. The US Navy refused to participate in the Battle of the Taku Forts, given that its commander, Admiral Louis Kempff, lacked authority from Washington to engage in combat and could act only to defend the foreign legations under siege and to rescue foreign nationals caught in the cross fire. See "Operations in China and Manchuria: The Capture of Taku Forts," in *Reports on Military Operations in South Africa and China*, Adjutant General's Office, War Department, GPO No. 33, 533–537, July 1, 1901. The Boxer Protocol called for an indemnity of 450 million taels of silver, which was equal to US$335 million at the time (or US$6.6 billion in today's dollars). See generally Diana Preston, *The Boxer Rebellion: The Dramatic Story of China's War on Foreigners That Shook the World in the Summer of 1900* (New York: Walker, 1999); and Peter Fleming, *The Siege at Peking* (New York: Harper, 1959).

11. The US Navy had three divisions of destroyers and attending fuel and repair vessels that were ordered to be concentrated off Tsingtao, Shantung Province, although the orders were officially declared to have no connection with the Lincheng Incident. Indeed, it was common for American warships stationed in the Philippines to transfer to China waters in the warmer months of the year. The Counselor of Legation at Peking (Bell) to the Secretary of State, May 16, 1923, 393.1123 Lincheng/51: Telegram, in *Papers Relating to the Foreign Relations of the United States*, 1923, 1:639–640.

12. The Minister of China (Schurman) to the Secretary of State, May 18, 1923, 393.1123 Lincheng/61: Telegram, in *Papers Relating to the Foreign Relations of the United States*, 1923, 1:642–643; the Secretary of the Navy to the Secretary of State, May 18, 1923, National Archives and Records Administration, RG 59, 393.1123 Lincheng/122, Box 4644. "It is the idea that the ships should go to Taku for the moral effect on the Chinese people and Government and to demonstrate that our just demands cannot be ignored and that our nationals must be protected," wrote the State Department to the Secretary of the Navy. Memorandum of the Division of the Secretary of State to the Secretary of the Navy, May 18, 1923, National Archives and Records Administration, RG 59, 393.1123 Lincheng/51, Box 4644. The British minister would agree with the Americans and advise the British military officials to back down on the naval maneuvers. Telegram of Sir James William Ronald Macleay, British Ambassador to China, to Admiral Sir Arthur Leveson, May 21, 1923, British Public Records Office, Foreign Office 228/3253/9–10; Telegram of Sir James William Ronald Macleay, British Ambassador to China, to Admiral Sir Arthur Leveson, May 16, 1923, British Public Records Office, Foreign Office 228/3252/199–200.

13. Telegram from Sir Sidney Barton, Shanghai Consul-General, to Sir Ronald Macleay, Minister, British Legation, British Public Records Office, Foreign Office, May 10, 1923, 228/3252/113, 122. Macleay noted that "letters from captives emphasize that use of force would be extremely dangerous to their lives." Letter of Sir Ronald Macleay, Minister, British Legation, to Foreign Office, May 31, 1923, British Public Records Office, Foreign Office, 228/3253/131. Indeed, Rowlatt wrote a letter to the British legation warning against the use of armed intervention to rescue the hostages: "Employment of armed forces seems to be out of the question if our lives are to be preserved and the matter seems to be one of bargaining and face saving while we are held as pawns in the political game." Letter of Sir Ronald Macleay, Minister, British Legation, to Foreign Office, May 31, 1923, British Public Records Office, Foreign Office, 228/3253/131.

14. Stewart had contacted Rowlatt's wife in Tientsin and asked her to send a telegram to Tsaochuang to sense out from her husband whether the brigands would accept a ransom payment for his release. Rowlatt in turn asked Consul Tours for his advice on the scheme but made it clear that he was not in favor of the idea: "I do not think it would be wise to suggest this . . . [, and it] seems to me there is a very slim chance of individual ransom being considered in the case of foreigners." Letter of Reginald H. Rowlatt to Berthold George Tours, Esq., British Consul, Tsinan (on assignment to Tsaochuang), May 26, 1923, British Public Records Office, Foreign Office, 228/3253/119. To calm his distraught wife, Rowlatt tried to explain why the ransom plan was not workable: "To make the question of ransom a little clearer, I understand the bandits have always stated that it is not ransom they are after. They want protection and non-interference. They have been harassed by the soldiers for years. Say they demanded a million dollars' ransom and got it paid and released their prisoners, the troops would then walk in and kill most of them and seize the money. They want adequate guarantees of future peacefulness and hold us until such guarantees are given— presumably endorsed by the foreign powers." Telegram text of Reginald H. Rowlatt to his wife, Lillian Rowlatt, included in Dispatch of W. Russell Brown, British Consul, Tientsin, to Sir Ronald Macleay, Minister, British Legation, May 29, 1923, British Public Records Office, Foreign Office, 228/3253/122.

15. Telegram from Sir Ronald Macleay, Minister, British Legation, to W. Russell Brown, Tientsin Consulate, May 26, 1923, British Public Records Office, Foreign Office, May 10, 1923, 228/3253/86; handwritten note of Sir Ronald Macleay, Minister, British Legation, to the Telegram from W. Russell Brown, Tientsin Consulate, May 28, 1923, British Public Records Office, Foreign Office, 228/3253/90–91; telegram from W. Russell Brown, Tientsin Consulate, to Sir Ronald Macleay, Minister, British Legation, May 26, 1923, British Public Records Office, Foreign Office, 228/3253/90–91.

16. Telegram of Sir Herbert Goffe, Consul, British Consulate, Hankow, to Sir Ronald Macleay, Minister, British Legation, June 1, 1923, British Public Records Office, Foreign Office, 228/3253/144; telegram of Sir Ronald Macleay to Sir Herbert Goffe, Consul, British Consulate, Hankow, June 1, 1923, British Public Records Office, Foreign Office, 228/3253/145.

17. Telegram of James Dolan to the Secretary of State, May 26, 1923, National Archives and Records Administration, RG 59, 393.1123 Lincheng/109: Telegram, Box 4644.

18. The Counselor of Legation at Peking (Bell) to the Secretary of State, May 15, 1923, 393.1123 Lincheng/48: Telegram, in *Papers Relating to the Foreign Relations of the United States*, 1923, 1:638; the Minister in China (Schurman) to the Secretary of State, May 11, 1923, National Archives and Records Administration, RG 59, 393.1123 Lincheng/32: Telegram, Box 4644 (the US government agreed to provide support to the Vereas on behalf of the Mexican government); Consul General in Guadalajara, Mexico (McConnico), to the Secretary of State, May 9, 1923, National Archives and Records Administration, RG 59, 393.1123 Lincheng/22: Telegram, Box 4644; "Note Verbale," May 14, 1923, British Public Records Office, Foreign Office, May 10, 1923, 228/3252/191; Circular 114, Memorandum from Wai-Chiao Pu re Mexican Captives, May 18, 1923, British Public Records Office, Foreign Office, May 10, 1923, 228/3253/59–61.

19. Letter of Reginald H. Rowlatt to Berthold George Tours, Esq., British Consul, Tsinan (on assignment to Tsaochuang), June 2, 1923, British Public Records Office, Foreign Office 228/3253/29/5337/23/34; handwritten comments of Sir Ronald Macleay to Telegram of Berthold George Tours, Esq., British Consul, Tsinan (on

assignment to Tsaochuang), to Sir Ronald Macleay, Minister, British Legation, June 1, 1923, British Public Records Office, Foreign Office, 228/3253/173.

20. Allen diary, "Twenty-Five Days Among the Bandits," 32.

21. Brian G. Martin, *The Shanghai Green Gang: Politics and Organized Crime 1919– 1937* (Berkeley: University of California Press, 1996), 67–68. Pockmarked Chin was accompanied to Lincheng by Wu K'un-shan, a key gangland deputy.

22. Letter of Berthold George Tours, Esq., British Consul, Tsinan, to Sir Ronald Macleay, Minister, British Legation, May 20, 1923, British Public Records Office, Foreign Office, 228/3253/13, 20, 22.

23. "Bandits Threatening to Shoot Captives," *North-China Herald*, May 26, 1923, 522. At the time he was released, Berubé brought down with him to Tsaochuang a thirteen-year-old Chinese girl who had been taken from the train and dragged about the countryside—forced against her will to be the concubine of one of the bandit chiefs. At the behest of Teresa Verea, the captives appealed to the bandit chiefs' sense of humanity and decency, and thus persuaded them to release the child, given her young age and fragility. After her release, she was sent home to Shanghai to be returned to her parents. "Bandits Threaten Death to Captives," 2; "Berubé Goes to Peking," *New York Times*, May 19, 1923, 2.

24. Letter of Berthold George Tours, Esq., British Consul, Tsinan, to Sir Ronald Macleay, Minister, British Legation, May 21, 1923, British Public Records Office, Foreign Office, 228/3253/62–63; the Minister in China (Schurman) to the Secretary of State, May 19, 1923, National Archives and Records Administration, RG 59, 393.1123 Lincheng/63: Telegram, Box 4644.

25. The Minister in China (Schurman) to the Secretary of State, May 20, 1923, National Archives and Records Administration, RG 59, 393.1123 Lincheng/67: Telegram, Box 4644. See also "Prisoners Removed to Heights: Paotzuku Encircled by Troops," *North-China Herald*, May 26, 1923, 524; and "The Bandit Outrage: Mexican Lady's Terrible Night Journey," *Peking & Tientsin Times*, May 22, 1923, 9.

26. Letter of Tours to Macleay, May 21, 1923, 228/3253/62–63.

27. Letter of Tours to Macleay, May 19, 1923, 228/3253/14–16; letter of Tours to Macleay, May 21, 1923, 228/3253/62–63.

28. Letter of Tours to Macleay, May 15, 1923, 228/3252/201; letter of Tours to Macleay, May 21, 1923, 228/3253/7.

29. Circular 119, Memorandum of the Diplomatic Corps to the Wai-Chiao Pu, May 21, 1923, British Public Records Office, Foreign Office, 228/3253/27, 74.

30. "Release Is Delayed by Chinese Rivalry," *New York Times*, May 19, 1923, 2.

31. Dispatch of Major Wallace C. Philoon, Assistant Military Attaché, American Legation, 4–5, to Minister Schurman dated June 12, 1923, attached to the letter from the Minister in China (Schurman) to the Secretary of State (Hughes), June 20, 1923, National Archives and Records Administration, RG 59, 393.1123 Lincheng/207, Box 4646. Consul Davis stated that "the attitude of the majority of the Shantung and national officials has furnished a striking example of the hopeless selfishness and ineptitude which characterizes the average Chinese official of today." Memorandum on the Lincheng Incident, 2–3.

32. Letter of Berthold George Tours, Esq., British Consul, Tsinan, to Sir Ronald Macleay, Minister, British Legation, May 22, 1923, British Public Records Office, Foreign Office, 228/3253/64. See also "The Bandit Outrage: The International Military Commission: Tuchun Tien Objects," *Peking & Tientsin Times*, June 4, 1923, 9. The injured Chinese soldiers were treated at Tsaochuang by LeRoy F. Heimburger, a young American physician from Missouri working for the Shantung Christian University

Hospital in Tsinan. Heimburger was onsite at Tsaochuang to be on standby to provide medical assistance to the captives, once released.

33. "Chinese Soldiers Open Attack upon Bandit Retreat: Planes and Machine Guns Used in Effort to Rescue Captives," *Evening Star*, May 27, 1923, 1; "Troops Begin Drive on Chinese Bandits: Shantung Governor Attempts to Force the Release of the 14 Foreigners," *New York Times*, May 27, 1923, 3; the Minister in China (Schurman) to the Secretary of State, May 19, 1923, National Archives and Records Administration, RG 59, 393.1123 Lincheng/62: Telegram, Box 4644; "Unpaid Troops Selling Ammunition," *North-China Herald*, May 26, 1923, 523; "The Bandit Outrage: Rifle of Tuchun's Bodyguard Stolen," *Peking & Tientsin Times*, May 21, 1923, 9, 12; "Bandits Threaten Death to Captives," 2; "Berubé Goes to Peking," 2. See also the Minister of China (Schurman) to the Secretary of State, May 20, 1923, 393.1123 Lincheng/66: Telegram, in *Papers Relating to the Foreign Relations of the United States*, 1923, 1:643–644.

34. Powell, *My Twenty-Five Years in China*, 113.

35. "Bandits' Prisoner Asks Intervention: Maj. Pinger Declares Armed Action by Powers Only Solution in China," *Evening Star*, May 30, 1923, 2.

36. Pinger diary, "Lincheng Incident of 1923," 113.

CHAPTER 18: THE SAP CLUB

1. "Held on Mountain: Three Americans Taken to Summit Prison," *Evening Star*, May 23, 1923, 1; "China Is Helpless to Rescue Captives: Time Limit of Diplomats' Ultimatum Expires, with Nothing Accomplished," *New York Times*, May 19, 1923, 1.

2. "The Bandit Outrage: Bandits Move Three Prisoners 1,800 Ft. Up," *Peking & Tientsin Times*, May 23, 1923, 9.

3. In 1923 the Woolworth building in New York City was the tallest building in the world. Letter of Lee C. Solomon to Carl Crow, American Rescue Mission, May 20, 1923, British Public Records Office, Foreign Office, 228/3253/30. See also "What It Means to Be Marooned on the Summit of Paotzuku," *North-China Herald*, May 26, 1923, 526; "The Bandit Outrage: Bandits Move Three Prisoners," 9.

4. Pinger diary, "Lincheng Incident of 1923," 112; letter of Major Roland W. Pinger from the Temple of the Clouds to Miriam Pinger, June 4, 1923, in Tientsin, in the Pinger Family Records.

5. "Held on Mountain," 1; "China Is Helpless to Rescue Captives," 1.

6. Pinger diary, "Lincheng Incident of 1923," 158.

7. Allen diary, "Twenty-Five Days Among the Bandits," 34.

8. Pinger diary, "Lincheng Incident of 1923," 160; "The Bandit Outrage: Major Pinger Describes Paotzuku Top," *Peking & Tientsin Times*, May 26, 1923, 9.

9. "Release of Allen Arouses U.S. Hope: Chinese Bandits Expected to Free All Americans Soon, Advices Say," *Evening Star*, May 31, 1923, 2.

10. Pinger diary, "Lincheng Incident of 1923," 161.

11. Pinger, 172–173.

12. Allen diary, "Twenty-Five Days Among the Bandits," 39; the Minister in China (Schurman) to the Secretary of State, May 30, 1923, National Archives and Records Administration, RG 59, 393.1123 Lincheng/118: Telegram, Box 4644.

13. Dispatch No. 541 of H. L. Milbourne, American Vice Consul, Tsinan Consulate, to the Secretary of State, May 24, 1923, and various materials Regarding Request of Shantung Provincial Assembly for Removal of the Military Governor, in Records of the Department of State Relating to Internal Affairs of China 1910–1929, Record Group 59, Microfilm Reel M329–33, 236–238. See also "The Bandit Outrage: M.P.'s Ask for Removal of Tien Chung-yu," *Peking & Tientsin Times*, May 21, 1923, 11.

14. The Minister in China (Schurman) to the Secretary of State, May 20, 1923, National Archives and Records Administration, RG 59, 393.1123 Lincheng/67: Telegram, Box 4644. See also "Utter Breakdown in Negotiations: The Bandits Increasing Demands: Charges of Intrigue and Jealousy Ruining All," *North-China Herald*, May 26, 1923, 525.

CHAPTER 19: POWELL'S CHARGE

1. "The Bandit Outrage: Bandits Drink Heavily," *Peking & Tientsin Times*, May 23, 1923, 9.

2. Elias, "My Experience," 228/3253/316; "The Bandit Outrage: Bandits Drink Heavily," 9.

3. "The Four Newly Freed," *North-China Herald*, June 9, 1923, 671; Elias, "My Experience," 228/3253/318; "The Kind of Life We Live," *North-China Herald*, June 2, 1923, 596; letter of John B. Powell to Minister Jacob G. Schurman, American Legation, Peking, May 21, 1923; "The Bandit Outrage: Interview with M. Berubé," *Peking & Tientsin Times*, May 19, 1923, 9.

4. Letter of William Smith to Berthold George Tours, Esq., British Consul, Tsinan (on assignment to Tsaochuang), May 18, 1923, British Public Records Office, Foreign Office, 228/3253/30; letter of William Smith to Carl Crow, American Rescue Mission, May 26, 1923, reprinted in "Mr. Smith's Hard Case: Urgent Plea That He at Least May Be Released," *North-China Herald*, June 2, 1923, 595; letter of Reginald H. Rowlatt to Berthold George Tours, Esq., British Consul, Tsinan (on assignment to Tsaochuang), May 17, 1923, British Public Records Office, Foreign Office, 228/3253/30.

5. "Special to New York Times," *New York Times*, June 7, 1923, 21; "Interview with Mr. Smith," *North-China Herald*, June 2, 1923, 598.

6. "Interview with Mr. Smith," 598.

7. "Bandits' Captives Take Lead in Negotiations for Release," *Weekly Review*, June 2, 1923, 22.

8. Powell, *My Twenty-Five Years in China*, 114; Allen diary, "Twenty-Five Days Among the Bandits," 40; Letter of R. H. Rowlatt of May 23, 1923, attached to the Dispatch of Berthold George Tours, Esq., British Consul, Tsinan (on assignment to Tsaochuang), to Sir Ronald Macleay, Minister, British Legation, May 25, 1923, British Public Records Office, Foreign Office, 228/3253/109–111.

9. "The Bandit Outrage: Chinese Authorities Accused of Lying," *Peking & Tientsin Times*, May 23, 1923, 9.

10. Powell, "Bandits' 'Golden Eggs,'" 914, 916.

11. "The Outlaws Intelligentsia," *North-China Herald*, June 2, 1923, 598.

12. Powell, *My Twenty-Five Years in China*, 115; the Minister of China (Schurman) to the Secretary of State, May 28, 1923, 393.1123 Lincheng/108: Telegram, in *Papers Relating to the Foreign Relations of the United States*, 1923, 1:649.

13. Powell, *My Twenty-Five Years in China*, 116–117.

14. Powell, "Bandits' 'Golden Eggs,'" 916, 956; "Bandits' Captives Take Lead," 22, 24.

15. "Washington Is Hopeful: Reports to Hughes Indicate Negotiations Are Proceeding Favorably," *New York Times*, June 1, 1923, 9. See also the Minister in China (Schurman) to the Secretary of State, May 28, 1923, 393.1123 Lincheng/108: Telegram, in *Papers Relating to the Foreign Relations of the United States*, 1923, 1:649.

16. Powell's preference to lounge with his American colleagues was instantly viewed by British Consul Tours as a diplomatic slight. Tours grumbled: "Powell's arrival has offered another opportunity of a manifestation of the American desire to 'run the whole show' and to avoid cooperation. Davis, the American Consul, simply

treated Powell as an American monopoly." Letter of Berthold George Tours, Esq., British Consul, Tsinan, to Sir Ronald Macleay, Minister, British Legation, May 28, 1923, British Public Records Office, Foreign Office, 228/3253/135. When Tours confronted Davis on why he, as the senior consul, had not received the written demands of the bandits, Davis advised him that Powell was instructed to give the document to the Chinese authorities, not the foreign consular representatives.

17. "The Bandit Outrage: The Bandit Delegates: Two Men of Good Family," *Peking & Tientsin Times*, May 30, 1923, 9; letter of Tours to Macleay, May 28, 1923, 228/3253/135.

18. Powell, *My Twenty-Five Years in China*, 118.

19. Powell, 118.

20. "Bandits Emissaries at Tsaochuang," *North-China Herald*, June 2, 1923, 597.

21. Powell, "Bandits' 'Golden Eggs,'" 956; "The Bandit Outrage: Soldiers' Vigilance: Bandit Delegates Held Up," *Peking & Tientsin Times*, May 30, 1923, 9.

22. Pinger diary, "Lincheng Incident of 1923," 182. See also "The Bandit Outrage: Morse Messages by Searchlight: How Captives on Paotzuku Top Were Kept Informed," *Peking & Tientsin Times*, June 4, 1923, 9.

CHAPTER 20: THE BREAKTHROUGH

1. Berthold George Tours, Esq., British Consul, Tsinan (on assignment to Tsaochuang), to Sir James William Ronald Macleay, British Ambassador to China, June 3, 1923, British Public Records Office, Foreign Office 228/3253/194–195.

2. Telegram of Berthold George Tours, Esq., British Consul, Tsinan (on assignment to Tsaochuang), to Sir Ronald Macleay, Minister, British Legation, May 30, 1923, British Public Records Office, Foreign Office, 228/3253/123. Some media sources refer to the village where negotiations took place as *Hsiaohsichuang* or *Wuchiaoho*. See "Bandits' Suggestion of Another Conference," *North-China Herald*, June 2, 1923, 597.

3. "Negotiations Proceeding Favorably," *North-China Herald*, June 9, 1923, 669; the Minister in China (Schurman) to the Secretary of State, May 31, 1923, National Archives and Records Administration, RG 59, 393.1123 Lincheng/119: Telegram, Box 4644; the Minister in China (Schurman) to the Secretary of State, June 1, 1923, National Archives and Records Administration, RG 59, 393.1123 Lincheng/120: Telegram, Box 4644.

4. "Men and Events," *China Weekly Review*, March 28, 1925, 110; Crow, "The Most Interesting Character I Ever Knew."

5. "Release of Allen Arouses U.S. Hope," 1; the Consul General at Shanghai (Cunningham) to the Secretary of State, May 31, 1923, 393.1123 Lincheng/117: Telegram, in *Papers Relating to the Foreign Relations of the United States*, 1923, 1:650; "Washington Is Hopeful," 9; Berthold George Tours, Esq., British Consul, Tsinan (on assignment to Tsaochuang), to Sir James William Ronald Macleay, British Ambassador to China, May 30, 1923, British Public Records Office, Foreign Office 228/3253/130.

6. The Minister in China (Schurman) to the Secretary of State, June 2, 1923, National Archives and Records Administration, RG 59, 393.1123 Lincheng/125: Telegram, Box 4644; "The Latest from Tsaochuang: Mr. Anderson Reports 'Great Progress,'" *Peking & Tientsin Times*, June 1, 1923; "Twelve Still Captives: Pinger and Solomon, Americans, Moved to Lower Level," *Evening Star*, May 31, 1923, 1; the Consul General at Shanghai (Cunningham) to the Secretary of State, May 31, 1923, 393.1123 Lincheng/117: Telegram, in *Papers Relating to the Foreign Relations of the United States*, 1923, 1:650; "Washington Is Hopeful," 9.

7. Letter of Rowlatt to Tours, June 2, 1923, 228/3253/29/5337/23/34.

8. Telegram of Berthold George Tours, Esq., British Consul, Tsinan (on assignment to Tsaochuang), to Sir Ronald Macleay, Minister, British Legation, June 1, 1923, British Public Records Office, Foreign Office, 228/3253/173; translation of Letter of Captain Raffaele Ferrajolo, M.C., Vice-Consul, Italian Consulate, Shanghai (on assignment to Tsaochuang), to General Cheng Shih-chi, June 1, 1923, British Public Records Office, Foreign Office, 228/3253/174.

9. Letter of Rowlatt to Tours, June 2, 1923, 228/3253/29/5337/23/34.

10. Berthold George Tours, Esq., British Consul, Tsinan (on assignment to Tsaochuang), to Sir James William Ronald Macleay, British Ambassador to China, May 25, 1923, British Public Records Office, Foreign Office 228/3253/103; Berthold George Tours, Esq., British Consul, Tsinan (on assignment to Tsaochuang), to Sir James William Ronald Macleay, British Ambassador to China, June 1, 1923, British Public Records Office, Foreign Office 228/3253/172; letter of Sir James William Ronald Macleay, British Ambassador to China, to Sir Sidney Barton, Shanghai Consul-General, May 29, 1923, British Public Records Office, Foreign Office 228/3253/198.

11. Letter of Berthold George Tours, Esq., British Consul, Tsinan (on assignment to Tsaochuang), to Sir Ronald Macleay, Minister, British Legation, May 28, 1923, British Public Records Office, Foreign Office, 228/3253/232. Consul Davis had strong words about the actions, or lack of action, by the other foreign consuls at Tsaochuang: "The officials of other nationalities who have been here have either accomplished nothing, or by their endeavors to obtain the release of their own nationals and by their unwarranted criticisms of and interference with the Chinese negotiators, have actually at times retarded the work of release." Memorandum on the Lincheng Incident, 2.

12. Pinger diary, "Lincheng Incident of 1923," 163.

13. Pinger, 163.

14. "Two Parties Among Bandits," *North-China Herald*, June 2, 1923, 598; Memorandum on the Lincheng Incident, 5; "Old Bandits Who Prefer a Life of Outlawry," *North-China Herald*, June 9, 1923, 671.

15. In reviewing his group of captives, Sun's impression was that Jerome Henley was the least valuable and least useful of the captives. To the irritation of many of the hostages and bandits alike, Jerome Henley was always pacing around in his pajamas and "offering a lot of advice as to what ought to be done," recalled Major Allen. Allen viewed Henley as a loudmouth who had nothing constructive to offer in terms of a realistic solution to their predicament. Rowlatt felt the same and characterized Henley as an "unmitigated nuisance" and said that "the fellow must be crazy." "Thank goodness he is not one of our nationals," pondered the British Rowlatt. Allen diary, "Twenty-Five Days Among the Bandits," 8–9; Letter of Rowlatt to Tours, June 2, 1923, 228/3253/29/5337/23/34.

16. "Four More Foreign Captives Released," *North-China Herald*, June 9, 1923, 669; "The Four Newly Freed," *North-China Herald*, June 9, 1923, 671; "Shantung Brigands Free Four Captives: Henley, American; Elias and Saphiere, British, and Verea, Mexican, Are Released," *New York Times*, June 3, 1923, 5. See also the Consul General at Shanghai (Cunningham) to the Secretary of State, June 2, 1923, 393.1123 Lincheng/123: Telegram, in *Papers Relating to the Foreign Relations of the United States*, 1923, 1:652; the Minister in China (Schurman) to the Secretary of State, June 2, 1923, National Archives and Records Administration, RG 59, 393.1123 Lincheng/125: Telegram, Box 4644.

17. "Eight Foreigners Still Held by Bandits in Shantung," *Weekly Review*, June 9, 1923, 50.

18. Pinger diary, "Lincheng Incident of 1923," 187.

19. Pinger, 187.

CHAPTER 21: FREEDOM

1. Guarantee of Sung Kwei-chi to Roy Scott Anderson, June 12, 1923, in the Roy Scott Anderson Family Papers. See "Translation of Guarantee of Sung Kwei-chi to Roy Scott Anderson," June 8, 1923, in *China Weekly Review*, April 22, 1939, 230.

2. "The Bandit Outrage: Aeroplanes Drop Pamphlets," *Peking & Tientsin Times*, May 29, 1923, 9.

3. Letter of Major Roland W. Pinger from the Temple of the Clouds to Miriam Pinger, June 11, 1923, in Tientsin, in the Pinger Family Records.

4. The diplomatic corps in Peking appointed a commission of foreign military officers to be sent to Tsaochuang to study and report on the military situation in southern Shantung arising out of the Lincheng Incident. Initially, the Chinese government was very resistant to the idea of foreign military attachés poking around Lincheng looking for evidence of fault. The central government eventually consented, and the commission arrived at Tsaochuang on June 2. The commission included officials from the key countries with citizens held hostage. In a scathing report it found evidence that "many of these Chinese government troops sympathize and fraternize with the bandits and these facts would decrease the efficiency even of these small numbers" and that given the low morale of the troops and lack of pay for months, it is "an indisputable fact that arms and ammunition are being sold by at least two of the brigades of the troops forming the cordon." The appearance of the military commission was timed to coincide with the ongoing negotiations between Roy Anderson and the brigands. The bandits construed the tour of the foreign military officers, as well as the aircraft sorties, as warlike preparations by the foreign powers. Whether intentionally or not, the commission's arrival and presence raised the stakes. See Memorandum of Instructions for the Guidance of the International Military Commission, June 1, 1923, British Public Records Office, Foreign Office, 228/3253/142; and Report of the International Military Commission, June 6, 1923, reprinted in Records of the Department of State Relating to Internal Affairs of China 1910–1929, Record Group 59, Microfilm Reel M329–33, 805–814, 808. See also "The Bandit Outrage: Foreign Military Commission," *Peking & Tientsin Times*, June 4, 1923, 9.

5. The Minister in China (Schurman) to the Secretary of State, June 6, 1923, 393.1123 Lincheng/136: Telegram, in *Papers Relating to the Foreign Relations of the United States*, 1923, 1:652; telegram of Marshal Tsao Kun (Paoting) to Roy Scott Anderson (Tsaochuang), June 8, 1923, in the Roy Scott Anderson Family Papers. See also "Translation of Telegram of Marshal Tsao Kun (Paoting) to Roy Scott Anderson (Tsaochuang), June 8, 1923," in *China Weekly Review*, April 22, 1939, 230; the Minister in China (Schurman) to the Secretary of State, June 11, 1923, National Archives and Records Administration, RG 59, 393.1123 Lincheng/141: Telegram, Box 4644; the Minister in China (Schurman) to the Secretary of State, June 6, 1923, National Archives and Records Administration, RG 59, 393.1123 Lincheng/135: Telegram, Box 4644; and Memorandum on the Lincheng Incident, 2. (The translation of Tsao's telegram reads as follows: "Mr. Anderson: You have acted as a negotiator in the Lincheng bandit case and, in spite of the hot weather and the hardships, have exercised your full energy as a mediator. I greatly appreciate this. As the case has now been discussed and a solution has been found, please do not hesitate to give the several guarantees demanded by the bandits, in order that both Chinese and foreign captives may be relieved from danger at an early date. I greatly hope that the case will now be settled in this manner. I, therefore, send you this telegram trusting that you will note the same. Tsao Kun.")

6. Pinger diary, "Lincheng Incident of 1923," 187–188.

7. Letter of Bandit Chieftains to General Cheng Shih-chi, June 10, 1923, British Public Records Office, Foreign Office, 228/3253/260.

8. Guarantee of Roy Scott Anderson, June 12, 1923, in the Roy Scott Anderson Family Papers. See "Translation of Guarantee of Roy Scott Anderson, June 8, 1923," in *China Weekly Review*, April 22, 1939, 230. Anderson's guarantee states, "To the Most Honorable Chief Sung Kwei-chi and all other Chiefs, I, Roy S. Anderson, am an American citizen and a friend of China, in life and death. As the brethren in the mountains are having hard times, as all Tan Chai [chiefs] have shown genuine sincerity in their actions and words in all the conferences, and as they are willing to submit, I am willing to guarantee that my brethren will be organized into an army and made officers and privates. There shall be no more than three thousand people and the number of unarmed men shall not exceed five hundred. The Government will undertake to support two thousand and seven hundred people while all Tan Chai shall make arrangements to pay the remaining three hundred men, themselves. I am also willing to guarantee that after the brethren are 'called and pacified,' all their former crimes will be pardoned by the Government. After they are organized, their pay as agreed upon will be given to them according to their ranks, every month, by the Government. This guarantee shall be effective three years from the day of signing. After you, my brethren, have submitted, you shall, for the sake of your country and fellow citizens, be loyal to your country and keep the order of the army, so that the whole nation, seeing that you are serving the country, will praise your spirit of sacrifice. Roy S. Anderson."

9. One of the key guarantors for the bandits was Sun Mei-yao's uncle, Sung Kwei-chi, perceived as a community leader and "elder brother." Guarantee of Chief Sung Kwei-chi to Roy Scott Anderson, June 12, 1923; "Guarantee of Roy Scott Anderson to Bandit Chief Sun Kwei-chi, June 12, 1923," in the Roy Scott Anderson Family Papers. See also "Translation of Guarantee of Roy Scott Anderson to Sung Kwei-chi (Sun Mei-yao), June 8, 1923," 230.

10. Powell, "Bandits' 'Golden Eggs,'" 914, 956.

11. "Bandits Set Free 8 Foreign Captives, Ragged and Worn: Prisoners, Who Include 4 Americans, Get Baths and Food, Then Start for Shanghai," *New York Times*, June 13, 1923, 1.

12. Pinger diary, "Lincheng Incident of 1923," 193.

13. Pinger, 193–194. As negotiations lingered on, Anderson began to realize that the Chinese captives—Professor Hung and Chi Cheng included—were not part of the deal. But Anderson knew that once a deal was cut with the bandits and they were mustered into the army, there would be less of a reason to continue to hold the Chinese captives or the children held at the top of Paotzuku Mountain. Getting the foreign captives released was a first step. But Po-Po Liu took the position that the more sophisticated Chinese captives could be ransomed.

14. Pinger, 193–194. The Shantung authorities criticized Professor Hung and Chi Cheng for their escape from the bandits, claiming that doing so had put the other Chinese captives left behind at risk. Because Hung and Cheng were deeply embedded with the foreign captives, the foreigners reassured the two that they had done the right thing and should have no regrets.

15. Telegram of Berthold George Tours, Esq., British Consul, Tsinan (on assignment to Tsaochuang), to Sir Ronald Macleay, Minister, British Legation, June 12, 1923, British Public Records Office, Foreign Office, 228/3253/250.

16. Davis defended the efforts of General Cheng Shih-chi, who he thought demonstrated "commendable coolness, fearlessness, and firmness" under such trying circumstances. Dispatch of Consul John K. Davis to Minister Schurman dated June 12, 1923, 3–4.

17. "The Bandit Outrage: A Letter from Mr. Cheng," 9. While in captivity, Chi Cheng wrote to his business associates asking for them to send provisions to the Chinese captives. "The foreigners are getting their food supplies every other day from the station and I am one of the lucky Chinese who is allowed to share with them," wrote Chi Cheng to his colleagues at China Merchants. "The rest of the Chinese captives are struggling along without proper provisions and clothing," and "nobody seems to be doing anything for them outside, but the little food they send in every now and then was stolen by the bandits, so these poor Chinese prisoners get nothing at all." The Cambridge graduate went on to encourage his coworkers to raise awareness of the plight of the Chinese prisoners: "I wonder if you would be so kind as to put some *kicks* both in the Foreign and Chinese newspapers to the above question. Nobody appears to be looking after the interests of the Chinese prisoners at all."

CHAPTER 22: A PALACE COUP

1. Memorandum on the Lincheng Incident, 7.

2. The local press described the festive scene at the station as follows: "Then pandemonium broke loose, there was a grand rush of wives and daughters and the bearded men were almost thrown to the ground under the impetus of the greetings and kisses they received. A moment's pause until each man was identified, then followed individual cheers for him. Hats were thrown into the air and men cheered themselves hoarse, while tears streamed down the cheeks of those near and dear." "Captives' Arrival at Shanghai," *North-China Herald*, June 16, 1923, 746–747.

3. "Captives' Arrival at Shanghai," 746–747.

4. "Chinese Cabinet Resigns; Bandit Episode Weakened It," *New York Times*, June 7, 1923, 1; "The Peking Cabinet's Resignation," *North-China Herald*, June 9, 1923, 649; the Minister in China (Schurman) to the Secretary of State, March 9, 1923, 893.00/4907: Telegram, in *Papers Relating to the Foreign Relations of the United States*, 1923, 1:504–505. Prior to his resignation, Premier Chang Shao-tseng told the press that the diplomatic corps was to blame for the Lincheng Incident: "The Government authorities have done their utmost to have both foreign and Chinese captives released but as yet that has not been effected. One reason for this is the fact that at the outset the diplomatic corps brought too much pressure to bear on the Government which fettered it in its action. The officials realizing from past experience with bandits knew that force must be applied. This was proved in the case of the capture of missionaries by the Honan bandits. A peaceful course having been taken to date, the more the Government treats with these bandits the more difficult it becomes to settle up. This delay in settlement cannot be branded as inability on the part of the Chinese Government." See "An Interview with the Premier," *Peking Daily News*, June 1, 1923, reprinted in and attached to Circular 144 Regarding Lincheng Incident: Statements of Premier and Diplomatic Body Protest, June 8, 1923, British Public Records Office, Foreign Office, 228/3253/257–258.

5. The Li Yuan-hung government "was faced with many other difficulties, including *Lincheng outrage*," wrote Minister Schurman. See the Minister in China (Schurman) to the Secretary of State, June 7, 1923, 893.002/128: Telegram, in *Papers Relating to the Foreign Relations of the United States*, 1923, 1:507–508.

6. There was clearly a plan in place by the Chihli Party's generals—Marshal Tsao Kun, Wu Pei-fu, and Feng Yu-hsiang—to force President Li Yuan-hung out of Peking and to put Tsao Kun in his place. Tsao was the head of the predominant military and political clique in North China, to whom the presidential chair kowtowed. Tsao was upset at Li for his refusal to allow Chang Ying-hua, the finance minister, to arrange a loan for Tsao's presidential campaign. Tsao had been warned by his allies to postpone

his own presidential aspirations until such time as the country would have a permanent constitution, which was then about 90 percent completed, but he ignored such advice. "Peking Service: Cabinet and President at Loggerheads: The Quarrel over the Octroi Post," *Peking & Tientsin Times,* June 5, 1923, 9; "Interview with the Premier"; telegram of American Minister (Schurman), American Legation, Peking, to the Secretary of State, June 13, 1923, in Records of the Department of State Relating to Internal Affairs of China 1910–1929, Record Group 59, Microfilm Reel M329–33, 216; the Minister in China (Schurman) to the Secretary of State, June 14, 1923, 893.00/5047: Telegram, in *Papers Relating to the Foreign Relations of the United States,* 1923, 1:510–511, ¶ 221.

7. "'The Highest Question': Tsao Kun's Omnipresence and His Thirst for the Presidency: Will It Profit Him?," *North-China Herald,* June 16, 1923, 763; "President Li and His Enemies: Illuminating Account of the Methods Used to Drive Him from Office," *North-China Herald,* June 16, 1923, 763; "President Li Still Showing Fight: An Absolute Burlesque of Government," *North-China Herald,* June 23, 1923, 794; "President Li Yuan-hung Interviewed," *China Advertiser,* June 16, 1923, reprinted in Records of the Department of State Relating to Internal Affairs of China 1910–1929, Record Group 59, Microfilm Reel M329–33, 710; the Minister in China (Schurman) to the Secretary of State, June 14, 1923, 1:510–511, ¶ 221.

8. Telegram of American Minister (Schurman), American Legation, Peking, to the Secretary of State, June 14, 1923, in Records of the Department of State Relating to Internal Affairs of China 1910–1929, Record Group 59, Microfilm Reel M329–33, 224–225. Li fled to Japan in July 1923 and returned to his home in Tientsin in 1924. He never held another public office. He is buried on the grounds of the Central China Normal University in Wuhan.

9. "Constitution Making in Peking," *North China Star,* June 23, 1923, reprinted in Records of the Department of State Relating to Internal Affairs of China 1910–1929, Record Group 59, Microfilm Reel M329–33, 705–706.

10. "Chinese Derelicts of Paotzuku," *North-China Herald,* July 7, 1923, 3; "Chinese at Paotzuku," *North-China Herald,* June 23, 1923, 793; "Lincheng Outrage: Chinese Captives Now Released," *North-China Herald,* June 30, 1923, 871; Powell, *My Twenty-Five Years in China,* 111.

CHAPTER 23: BETRAYAL

1. Proclamation of Chang P'ei-jung, Assistant Commander-in-Chief for Bandit Suppression in Four Provinces and Defense Commissioner of Yenchow and Colonel Wu K'o-chang of the 17th Regiment of the 5th Division, December 20, 1923, attached to the Dispatch Regarding Execution of Sun Mei-yao and Disbandment of His Forces, American Consul (Tenney), Tsinan Consulate, to the Secretary of State, January 5, 1924, 393.1123 Lincheng/277, National Archives and Records Administration, RG 59, 393.1123 Lincheng/207, Box 4646. The translation of the proclamation reads, "Sun Mei-yao was a notorious bandit leader. He was responsible for the Lincheng outrage, in connection with which Chinese and foreigners were kidnapped to bring pressure to bear upon the Government. No robbers in history have done so much harm to the country as Sun Mei-yao. The dishonor and loss of dignity suffered by the country fills one with indignation. His lawless acts in permitting his men to commit crimes, interfere with civil affairs and disturb the peace and good order of the district, are too many to enumerate. Sun Mei-yao was arrested and executed on December 19th. To do this is to deal with the ringleader and to satisfy Chinese and foreigners as well."

2. Tien Chung-yu resigned from his post as the military governor of Shantung in July 1923 because of the Lincheng Incident. Tien moved his family to Tientsin, and he never returned to Shantung. He was later given a new and flowery title of *Shan Chiang*

Chun, meaning a member of the College of Marshals, which was intended to emulate the Japanese Council of Elder Statesmen, a group that acts in an advisory capacity to the government. Tien went into retirement and, bankrolled by his accumulated wealth, purchased a large home in the French Concession in Tientsin. Dispatch No. 541 of H. L. Milbourne, May 24, 1923, 236-238. See also "The Bandit Outrage: M.P.'s Ask for Removal of Tien Chung-yu," *Peking & Tientsin Times*, May 21, 1923, 11.

3. Dispatch Regarding Execution of Sun Mei-yao, American Consul (Tenney), Tsinan Consulate, to the Secretary of State, December 22, 1923, 393.1123 Lincheng/278, National Archives and Records Administration, Box 4646; Dispatch Regarding Execution of Sun Mei-yao and Disbandment of His Forces, American Consul (Tenney), Tsinan Consulate, to the Secretary of State, December 28, 1923, 393.1123 Lincheng/276, National Archives and Records Administration, Box 4646; Dispatch Regarding Execution of Sun Mei-yao and Disbandment of His Forces, January 5, 1924.

4. "Banditry, Bunco and Boobery," *China Weekly Review*, August 11, 1923, 358.

5. "The Execution of Sun Mei-Yao," *North-China Herald*, December 29, 1923, 878; "Sun Mei-yao Bandit Chief, Is Executed for 'Mutiny,'" *China Press*, December 21, 1923, 1; "Notes," *China Weekly Review*, February 23, 1924, 466 (confirming decapitation of Sun Mei-yao and capture of bandit chief Wang Feng-wu); "Sun Mei-yao's Execution: Cheng Shi-chih's Report to Peking," *Peking & Tientsin Times*, December 22, 1923, 1; "Brigadier General Sun Mei-yao," *Peking & Tientsin Times*, December 29, 1923, 1.

6. Proclamation of Chang P'ei-jung, December 20, 1923.

7. Powell, *My Twenty-Five Years in China*, 123; "Various Letters from Carroll Yerkes," Carroll and Helen Yerkes Papers (Record Group No. 153), Special Collections, Yale Divinity School Library.

8. Dispatch Regarding Execution of Sun Mei-yao, December 22, 1923; Dispatch Regarding Execution of Sun Mei-yao, December 28, 1923; Proclamation Posted at Lincheng Train Station Re Execution of Sun Mei-yao (Chinese version), December 19, 1923, Carroll and Helen Yerkes Papers (Record Group No. 153), Special Collections, Yale Divinity School Library.

9. Powell, *My Twenty-Five Years in China*, 123. ("Anderson telephoned me and stated in great indignation that he had just received word that the Governor of Shantung had violated the agreement and through some subterfuge had enticed the bandits away from their guns and had massacred some six hundred of them with machine guns," recalled Powell.)

10. Although it was a mere coincidence, Anderson died on the same day as Sun Yat-sen. "Roy S. Anderson Dies in Peking," *New York Times*, March 13, 1925, 19; "An American in China," *New York Times*, March 14, 1925, 12. The former Lincheng captives raised funds for the construction of a memorial monument at Anderson's grave in Peking. Anderson was buried in the British Cemetery, gravesite number 85A, outside the Western Wall (Hsi-pien Men) of Peking (and currently under Beijing's second ring road). See "Men and Events," *China Weekly Review*, March 28, 1925, 110; Crow, "The Most Interesting Character I Ever Knew."

11. Allman, *Shanghai Lawyer*, 71–72.

12. Dispatch Regarding Disbandment of Sun Mei-yao's Forces, Execution of Po-Po Liu, American Consul (Tenney), Tsinan Consulate, February 4, 1924, 393.1123 Lincheng/292, National Archives and Records Administration, RG 59, 393.1123 Lincheng/207, Box 4646.

13. Dispatch Regarding Disbandment of Sun Mei-yao's Forces, February 4, 1924; Proclamation Posted at Lincheng Train Station.

EPILOGUE: THE MYTH AND MEMORY OF LINCHENG

1. "China's War Lords Keep 2,000,000 Men Under Arms: Great Standing Armies Are Stationed in the Various Provinces and Their Shifting Allegiance Makes for Uncertainty in All Affairs of the Nation," *New York Times*, April 27, 1930, 8; Ch'en, "Defining Chinese Warlords and Their Factions," 563–600.

2. "Chinese Villages Massacred: Missionaries Report Slaughter by Bandits in the Interior," *New York Times*, January 13, 1927, 4 (in 1927 in the Shantung village Wangchihpao, bandits killed more than a thousand villagers); "American Plant Looted: Chinese Bandits Seize the Texas Company Premises at Yunho," *New York Times*, April 19, 1934, 10. Some foreigners held hostage by bandits in the early twentieth century would subsequently write about their experiences. See generally Harvey J. Howard, *Ten Weeks with Chinese Bandits* (New York: Dodd, Mead, 1926); Clifford Johnson, *Pirate Junk: Five Months Captivity with Manchurian Bandits* (London: Jonathan Cape, 1934); Barbara Jurgensen, *All the Bandits of China: Adventures of a Missionary in a Land Ravaged by Bandits and Warlords* (Minneapolis: Augsburg, 1965); Anton Lundeen, *In the Grip of Bandits* (Rock Island, IL: Augustana, 1925); Tinko Pawley, *My Bandit Hosts* (London: Stanley Paul, 1935); and Geraldine Taylor, *With P'u and His Brigands* (Philadelphia: Sunday School Times, 1922).

3. "Declaration of the First Hunan Peasant Congress, December 1926," in Mao Tse-tung, *Selected Works of Mao Tse-tung (1917–1949)* (Peking: People's Publishing House/Foreign Language Press), 1:109–110. The communists did not initially seek to crush the bandit phenomenon but rather to recruit, transform, and use the brigands to their own advantage. Mao successfully tapped the disorganized power base of banditry and at the same time sought to eliminate it. By 1949, communist troops, including former brigands, controlled all of mainland China and founded the People's Republic of China. After 1949, bandit suppression continued as the communists demilitarized the countryside and specifically targeted those engaged in anticommunist guerrilla warfare or who were resistant to Mao's leadership. In 1951 the communists reported to have liquidated 1.15 million native bandits in the central-south region of China (one of six administrative regions in existence at the time), with a reported 28 percent (or 322,000) of the bandits gunned down through mass executions. The remainder were detained under a forced nationwide reformation-through-labor program, with 2 percent of the detainees under suspended death sentences. These numbers are assumed to be much higher in the southern and western parts of the country, where insurgencies continued into the mid-1950s. See Denis A. Warner, *Hurricane from China* (New York: Macmillan, 1961). Mao's reference to the Lincheng Incident as a peasant revolt and his overall interpretation of both the events and the Communist Party's views thereof may have different meanings depending upon one's views on party history. For the Chinese perspective on Mao's reference to the Lincheng Incident, see 陈友良 (Youliang Chen), 毛泽东盛赞的土匪孙美瑶传奇 (The Legend of Bandit Sun Mei-yao, Praised by Mao Zedong), 枣庄学院学报 (Zaozhuang College Journal) 25, no. 4 (August 2008); 赵杰 (Jie Zhao), 惟一受到毛泽东称赞的土匪孙美瑶为什么要制造临城大劫案 (Why Did Sun Mei-yao, the Only Bandit Praised by Mao, Create the Lincheng Incident?), in 毛泽东盛赞的土匪孙美瑶传奇 (The Legend of Bandit Sun Mei-yao, Praised by Mao Zedong), 名家讲坛 (Journal of Legality Vision), 2011, 6; 孙钱云 (Qianyun Sun), 孙美瑶和世界唯一"土匪邮票"传奇 (The Legend of Sun Mei-yao and the Only Bandit Postage Stamp in the World), in 毛泽东盛赞的土匪孙美瑶传奇 (The Legend of Bandit Sun Mei-yao, Praised by Mao Zedong), 名家讲坛 (Journal of Legality Vision), 2011, 14; 许志强 (Zhiqiang Xue), 中共为什么要肯定抱犊豪杰孙美瑶 (Why Should the Communist Party Affirm Sun Mei-yao?), in 毛泽

东盛赞的土匪孙美瑶传奇 (The Legend of Bandit Sun Mei-yao, Praised by Mao Ze-dong), 名家讲坛 (Journal of Legality Vision), 2011, 15. But other Chinese researchers did not take the view that Sun Mei-yao was a hero. See 李维民 (General Weimin Li, Academy of Military Sciences), "民国第一恐怖案"不能美化—再议临城劫车案 (The "First Terrorist Case of the Republic of China" Cannot Be Glorified—The Case in Lincheng Is Discussed Again), 军事历史 (Journal of Military History) 5 (2008): 69. (General Li, a professor at the PRC Academy of Military Sciences, stated that the bandits should not be regarded as heroes, given their cruelty to the local villagers.)

4. The Lincheng Incident has been the topic of research by Chinese academics trying to make sense of the events from a geopolitical perspective, with some observers faulting the Republican government for its weakness in dealing with foreign governments during the Lincheng Incident. See 徐基中 (Jizhong Xu), 临城劫车案中的民国政象及国民党的政治诉求—基于《民国日报》对临案报道的考察 (The Political Situation and the Kuomintang's Political Appeals in the Case of Lincheng Car Hijacking: A Case Study on the Republic of China's Daily Reports), 史研究, November 2011; 新闻陈无我 (Wuwo Chen), 临案纪实 (Lincheng True Facts) 1923, Peking Express Press; 临城劫车案文电一组 (Published Telegrams of the Lincheng Incident), 中国第二历史档案馆 (Second Historical Archives of China, Nanjing); 别琳 (Lin Bie), 临城劫车案引发的中外交涉 (Sino-Foreign Negotiations in the Lincheng Hijack Case), 四川师范大学学报 (社会科学版) (Sichuan Normal University [Social Science Edition]), 32, no. 4 (July 2005): 84; 范明明 (Mingming Fan), 临城劫车案及其善后 (Lincheng Incident and Its Consequences), 兰州大学 (Lanzhou University), April 2011; 临城劫车案 Lincheng Hijack Case (or Lincheng Incident), 枣庄政协文史委员会 Culture and Historical Records Committee, CPPCC Zaozhuang, 1996; 陈友良 (Youliang Chen), 情与理之间：《太平洋》杂志对临城劫车案的评论 (Between Emotion and Reason: A Discussion [Pacific Magazine] of the Lincheng Incident), Zaozhuang College Journal 枣庄学院学报 (Zaozhuang College Journal) 25, no. 4 (August 2008).

5. The Chinese Chargé d'Affaires (Yung Kwai) to the Secretary of State, May 4, 1923, 793.003 C73/41, in *Papers Relating to the Foreign Relations of the United States*, 1923, 1:620–621; the Secretary of State (Hughes) to the Chinese Minister (Sze), May 11, 1923, 793.003 C73/41, in *Papers Relating to the Foreign Relations of the United States*, 1923, 1:621; and "An Interview with the Premier," *Peking Daily News*, June 1, 1923, reprinted in the Minister in China (Schurman) to the Secretary of State, June 1, 1923, 793.003 C73/46: Telegram, in *Papers Relating to the Foreign Relations of the United States*, 1923, 1:622–623, ¶ 192. See also "Extraterritoriality: Question of Abolition Said to Be Postponed Indefinitely," *North-China Herald*, June 9, 1923, 650.

6. "An Interview with the Premier," *Peking Daily News*, June 1, 1923, reprinted in the Minister in China (Schurman) to the Secretary of State, June 1, 1923, 793.003 C73/46: Telegram, in *Papers Relating to the Foreign Relations of the United States*, 1923, 1:622–623, 192.

7. Separate from the diplomatic corps, the foreign business community was enraged by the Lincheng Incident and called for military intervention to protect the lives and property of foreigners in China. Before the last hostages were released, the American Chamber of Commerce in Peking unanimously adopted a resolution condemning the Lincheng Incident and called upon the foreign powers to take immediate action to protect the lives of both foreigners and Chinese nationals. Letter of the American Chamber of Commerce in Peking to Secretary of State Charles Evans Hughes, June 9, 1923, and Resolution of the American Chamber of Commerce in Peking dated June 8, 1923, reprinted in Records of the Department of

State Relating to Internal Affairs of China 1910–1929, Record Group 59, Microfilm Reel M329-33, 405–406, 526–528. See also "Suggestions by U.S. Chamber of Commerce in Peking as to Foreign Intervention," *North-China Herald*, June 23, 1923, 798. The American community in Shanghai, led by the American Association of China and the American Chamber of Commerce in Shanghai, took a much stronger approach and cabled Secretary of State Charles Hughes in Washington, sternly criticizing the United States government for its handling of the Lincheng Incident and calling for foreign military intervention in China. The Shanghai American organizations argued that "American prestige and business are being destroyed by the lack of strong action" by the US government and demanded, among other things, the disarmament of the Chinese troops and their return to their homes; the placing of Chinese finances under foreign supervision; the placement of foreign military troops on the lines of communication, both land and water; and the placement of foreign military garrisons at strategic points throughout China. See "American Chamber and Association Demand Action by the Powers: Organizations Draw Scathing Indictment of Chaotic Condition in China," *China Press*, June 15, 1923, 1; and telegram of the American Chamber of Commerce Shanghai to the Secretary of State, June 13, 1923, reprinted in Records of the Department of State Relating to Internal Affairs of China 1910–1929, Record Group 59, Microfilm Reel M329-33, 221–223. The position of the American business community was met with significant pushback by the Chinese media, business organizations, and influential Chinese community leaders. See letter of Quo Tai-chi to Major Arthur Bassett, President, American Chamber of Commerce in China, June 19, 1923, reprinted in Records of the Department of State Relating to Internal Affairs of China 1910-1929, Record Group 59, Microfilm Reel M329-33, 655, 662-664. Prominent Chinese newspapers such as *Shih Pao*, *Shun Pao*, and *Sin Wan Pao* objected to the American organizations' demands, which they believe amounted to foreign control of China. "The six recommendations of the American Chamber of Commerce may be summed up in a single phrase, i.e., international control of China." Translation of Newspaper Clippings, Shih Pao, June 21, 1923, reprinted in Records of the Department of State Relating to Internal Affairs of China 1910-1929, Record Group 59, Microfilm Reel M329-33, 650, 651-652; translation of Newspaper Clippings citing Chinese General Chamber of Commerce, Shanghai, Shun Pao, June 22, 1923, reprinted in Records of the Department of State Relating to Internal Affairs of China 1910-1929, Record Group 59, Microfilm Reel M329-33, 856, 859-860. ("It appears now in the China Press that the American Chamber of Commerce at Shanghai is loudly uttering sentiments which imply international control of China while the Chinese people are struggling for a popular government.") Translation of Newspaper Clippings citing Provincial Guilds in Shanghai, Shun Pao, June 23, 1923, reprinted in Records of the Department of State Relating to Internal Affairs of China 1910-1929, Record Group 59, Microfilm Reel M329-33, 856, 861-862.

8. At the request of the diplomatic corps, the Wai-Chiao Pu (Foreign Ministry) organized a Joint Commission of Inquiry of the Lincheng Hold-Up. As expected, each of the Chinese members of the Joint Commission who worked for the Tientsin-Pukow Railroad placed all blame for the incident on the brigands and found "no evidence before the Commission which justified the assumption that the Train Employees and the railway guards and gangers were in league with the bandits." In the supplementary report, the foreign consuls gave a blistering review of the joint commission's findings as "incomplete and inconclusive" because the members of the commission were interested parties—namely the railroad officials—and thus could not be objective. The consular representatives further found the Shantung civil

authorities at fault for not being aware of the movements of bandits in their districts and stated that they should have been in constant and immediate contact with the railway authorities and the military. The consular representatives saved their most scathing comments for the military authorities: "Seeing that the condition of the country near the Shantung-Kiangsu-Anhwei border has been notorious for years owing to the presence of bandits, and seeing that military operations against the bandits were in actual progress at the time of the Lincheng outrage, we consider that great blame attaches to the military, from the Military Governor downwards, for permitting a bandit coup of such an extensive nature, involving passage with about one hundred captives through the military lines, to take place within a few miles of the military operation." The report also criticized the military governor—Tuchun Tien—for not paying his troops for eighteen months, although he had the money in hand, and, as a result, the military operations against the brigands became a "farce." The supplementary report further questioned how the military allowed the bandits to carry off the captives over a distance of thirty miles into the hills during the first thirty-six hours when the troops had established contact with the bandits within several hours of the derailment. See Report of the Joint Commission of Inquiry of the Lincheng Hold-Up, June 15, 1923, British Public Records Office, Foreign Office, 228/3253/287-294; Report of the Joint Commission of Inquiry of the Lincheng Hold-Up, June 15, 1923, attached to the Dispatch of Minister Schurman to Secretary of State, July 26, 1923, National Archives and Records Administration, RG 59, 393.1123 Lincheng/219, Box 4646; and Supplementary Report by the Consular Representatives, Joint Commission of Inquiry of the Lincheng Hold-Up, June 15, 1923, British Public Records Office, Foreign Office, 228/3253/295-299.

9. The indemnity amount paid to the former hostages was roughly $5.7 million in today's US dollars. See telegram of Minister in China to the Secretary of State, February 23, 1925, in *Papers Relating to the Foreign Relations of the United States*, 1923, 1:709; dispatch of Minister in China to the Secretary of State, March 31, 1925, National Archives and Records Administration, RG 59, 393.1123 Lincheng/303, Box 4646; "China Pays $300,000 in Lincheng Claims to Indemnify Train Bandits' 24 Captives," *New York Times*, February 22, 1925, 1; "China Pays Our Claims: Indemnifies Victims of Bandit Raid on Train in 1923," *New York Times*, March 7, 1925, 4; telegram of Minister in China (Schurman) to the Secretary of State, February 26, 1925, National Archives and Records Administration, RG 59, 393.1123 Lincheng/295, Box 4646. The Chinese media strongly objected to the foreign governments' demands for indemnity, given the view that the Lincheng Incident was viewed as a criminal matter and not the fault of the Peking government. See 临城土匪大掠津浦车 (Bandits from Lincheng Take Hostages from Train), 东方杂志 (Oriental Magazine) 20, no. 8 (1923); 临城劫车后的官匪交涉 (Negotiations Between Government and Bandits After Lincheng), 东方杂志 (Oriental Magazine) 20, no. 9 (1923); 临城劫车案中的十六国赔偿通牒提出了 (Compensation Proposal from Sixteen Countries) 东方杂志 (Oriental Magazine) 20, no. 14 (1923); 十六国临案通牒的答复 (Reply to Compensation Proposal from Sixteen Countries), 东方杂志 (Oriental Magazine) 20, no. 18 (1923).

10. Memorandum of the Division of Far Eastern Affairs, State Department, July 6, 1923, attached to Telegram No. 261, from American Embassy London to the Secretary of State, July 2, 1923, National Archives and Records Administration, RG 59, 393.1123 Lincheng/193, Box 4646.

11. Russky "shared the popular belief that a soldier was only a bandit in uniform, who ate seed as well as crop, leaving the peasants to beggary or starvation," as Major Pinger recalled. Pinger diary, "Lincheng Incident of 1923," 124, 190.

12. Some of the former hostages prepared statements, diaries, and letters that were unpublished. See generally "Statement of Thomas Hyatt Day, Interview at American Consulate, Tientsin, before J. C. Huston, Acting Consul-General," May 8, 1923, National Archives and Records Administration, RG 59, 393.1123 Lincheng/131, Box 4644; R. Friedman, "An Odyssey of the Friedman Brothers" (2007), Library of Congress; Minnie MacFadden to her sister Edith MacFadden; "Statement of Mathilde Juliette Schoneberg"; statements of Mr. A. L. Zimmerman and Mr. V. Haimovitch Re Derailment of Tientsin-Pukow Train; Pinger diary, "Lincheng Incident of 1923"; Allen diary, "Twenty-Five Days Among the Bandits"; affidavit of Leon Friedman; Elias, "My Experience," 228/3253/308; statement of Spoerry, Allen, and Pinger, Derailment of Tientsin-Pukow Train at Lin-Cheng, 228/3252/87–88; statement of Roland W. Pinger, June 16, 1923, 2, American Consulate, Tientsin, included with the Dispatch No. 1805 of Jacob Gould Schurman, Minister, American Legation, Peking to Secretary of State, September 13, 1923, National Archives and Records Administration, RG 59, 393.1123 Lincheng/246, Box 4646; and statement of Jerome Henley, June 21, 1923, American Consulate, Tientsin, included with the Dispatch of Edward Bell, Acting Minister, American Legation, Peking, National Archives and Records Administration, RG 59, 393.1123 Lincheng/303, Box 4646. Sixteen years after the Lincheng Incident, the US government would publicly release its communications concerning the affair. See "State Department Publishes 'Lincheng Bandit' Correspondence," *China Weekly Review*, April 15, 1939, 198–202; "US Minister Schurman Took Lead in Pressing for Release of Lincheng Captives," *China Weekly Review*, April 22, 1939, 230–234; "Shantung Bandits, Generals and Control of Government Railways," *China Weekly Review*, April 29, 1939, 263–268; and "Lessons from Lincheng: Tuchuns of 1923— Japanese Warlords of 1939," *China Weekly Review*, May 13, 1939, 335–339.

13. Powell, *My Twenty-Five Years in China*, 123–124; C. Alcott, *My War with Japan* (1943), 284–285. Prison guards stole Powell's shoes, and his feet froze in the unheated, vermin-infested cell. Gangrene developed, which eventually resulted in the amputation of both of his feet. He never fully recovered from his wounds and died at Walter Reed General Hospital in February 1947 at the age of fifty-seven.

14. Aldrich, "Week-End with Chinese Bandits," 672; "Lucy Aldrich, 85, of Rhode Island," 27; "Miss Aldrich Left $2,500,000," 11.

15. "Echo of Lincheng Outrage: Captive's Appreciation of Efforts of Messrs. S. T. Wen and Carl Crow," *North-China Herald*, August 25, 1923, 543; Earl A. Selle, *Donald of China* (New York: Harper, 1948), 236–237; "Men and Events," *China Weekly Review*, March 28, 1925, 110; Crow, "The Most Interesting Character I Ever Knew."

16. Letter of Major Robert A. Allen to the Secretary of State, May 29, 1925, National Archives and Records Administration, RG 59, 393.1123 Lincheng/308, Box 4644.

17. "Echo of Lincheng Outrage," 543; letter of John B. Powell to Carl Crow, June 19, 1923, in the John Powell Papers (C3662), the State Historical Society of Missouri Manuscript Collection, SHSMO Research Center, Columbia, Missouri; letter of Major Roland Pinger to Carl Crow, August 2, 1923, in the John Powell Papers (C3662), the State Historical Society of Missouri Manuscript Collection, SHSMO Research Center, Columbia, Missouri; letter of Edward Elias to Carl Crow, June 8, 1923, in the John Powell Papers (C3662), the State Historical Society of Missouri Manuscript Collection, SHSMO Research Center, Columbia, Missouri; letter of American Minister Jacob Gould Schurman to Carl Crow, July 11, 1923, in the John Powell Papers (C3662), the State Historical Society of Missouri Manuscript Collection, SHSMO Research Center, Columbia, Missouri. Crow authored dozens of books on various

subjects such as China travel and culture, including *The Chinese Are Like That* (1938); *My Friends the Chinese* (1938); *Four Hundred Million Customers* (1937); *Foreign Devils in the Flowery Kingdom* (1940); *Master Kung* (1940); *I Speak for the Chinese* (1937); *The Travelers' Handbook for China* (1913); and *Handbook for China* (1921, 1925, 1933). The American Rescue Mission was supported by Robert McCann, who worked for Whitham's Asia Development Company. Crow recognized that "a great part of the success" of the mission was a result of McCann's efforts. Later, McCann was imprisoned by the Japanese in World War II for almost four years, one of the longest civilian captivities recorded. Following the war, he returned to Tientsin in 1946 to reopen his business to support American companies. He refused to leave China after the Communist takeover in 1949 and was arrested and convicted by the Communist government on charges of espionage. McCann was released in April 1961 after ten years in captivity. See Robert Ezra McCann Papers, Collection No. 76040, Hoover Institution Archives, Stanford University.

18. The British consul Tours stated that the system worked with the "regularity and precision of a postal service, and reflects the highest credit on its organizers, the head of who is Mr. Carl Crow, a Shanghai merchant, who has, I understand, voluntarily given up his time to this work." Berthold George Tours, Esq., British Consul, Tsinan (on assignment to Tsaochuang), to Sir James William Ronald Macleay, British Ambassador to China, May 20, 1923, British Public Records Office, Foreign Office 228/3253/29/5337/23/34.

19. "At the time we thought they were a rather silly joke," recalled Major Pinger. "The newspaperman took them for the real thing and hence the demand," he said. Letter of Major Roland W. Pinger from the Temple of the Clouds to Miriam Pinger, June 11, 1923, in Tientsin, in the Pinger Family Records. The stamps created a sensation in the world of philately, with stamp collectors purportedly paying tens of thousands of dollars for covers that included the stamps. Telegram of Berthold George Tours, Esq., British Consul, Tsinan (on assignment to Tsaochuang), to Sir James William Ronald Macleay, British Ambassador to China, June 3, 1923, British Public Records Office, Foreign Office 228/3253/196. See generally Baldus, *Postage Stamps*.

20. See generally French, *Carl Crow*; and *Through the Looking Glass*.

21. Leon's philanthropy was lifelong, and when he died in 1961 at the age of seventy-seven, he left $2 million (approximately $17.5 million today) to charity, including donations to the Rambam Cancer Research Institute in Haifa, Israel, which built a monument in his honor, with this inscription: "In Memory of Leon Friedman with Hope for a Better World." "Haifa's Cancer Research Institute Dedicated," *Jerusalem Post*, April 1969.

22. "Men and Events: Honored," *China Weekly Review*, May 11, 1940, 396; "Aide to MacArthur Named," *New York Times*, June 8, 1942, 4; "Col. Lehrbas Gets Post," *New York Times*, January 4, 1946, 29; "Lehrbas Gets Army Assignment," *New York Times*, February 26, 1942, 8.

23. See 雷立柏 (Leopold Leeb, professor), 山东天主教史人物列传 (Historical List of Catholic Priests in Shandong Province [unpublished]), 人民大学 (Renmin University), December 2015.

24. Although there was no evidence that the foreigners were targeted for their religious beliefs, more than half of the final eight captives were Jewish—including Sephardic and Ashkenazic Jews—and the only foreigner killed in the affair, Joseph Rothman, was Jewish. This was more of a reflection of the diversity of nationalities and identities of the foreigners who lived and worked in China in the early twentieth century. See generally Meyer, *From the Rivers of Babylon to the Whangpoo*, 145–155; and *Shanghai's Baghdadi Jews*, 372–375.

25. "Lincheng Captives: Entertained at Dinner by French Consul-General," *North-China Herald*, July 7, 1923, 37.

26. John B. Powell, "Ma Chang Invented in China Spreads All over the World," *China Weekly Review*, June 30, 1923, 1 (article written by Powell featuring Lee Solomon's factory in Shanghai).

AFTERWORD

1. Quoting the Platform Sutra of the Sixth Patriarch, which is notable in Chinese Buddhism.

INDEX

Li Jianjun

James M. Zimmerman is a Beijing-based lawyer who has lived and worked in China for more than twenty-five years. He is among China's leading foreign lawyers and represents companies and individuals confronted with the political and legal complexities of doing business in Mainland China. He is the author of the *China Law Deskbook*, published by the American Bar Association, and is frequently featured as a political commentator on US-China relations in various print and broadcast media around the globe. He is the former four-term chairman of the American Chamber of Commerce in China. In addition to Beijing, he maintains a home in San Diego, California.

PublicAffairs is a publishing house founded in 1997. It is a tribute to the standards, values, and flair of three persons who have served as mentors to countless reporters, writers, editors, and book people of all kinds, including me.

I. F. STONE, proprietor of *I. F. Stone's Weekly*, combined a commitment to the First Amendment with entrepreneurial zeal and reporting skill and became one of the great independent journalists in American history. At the age of eighty, Izzy published *The Trial of Socrates*, which was a national bestseller. He wrote the book after he taught himself ancient Greek.

BENJAMIN C. BRADLEE was for nearly thirty years the charismatic editorial leader of *The Washington Post*. It was Ben who gave the *Post* the range and courage to pursue such historic issues as Watergate. He supported his reporters with a tenacity that made them fearless and it is no accident that so many became authors of influential, best-selling books.

ROBERT L. BERNSTEIN, the chief executive of Random House for more than a quarter century, guided one of the nation's premier publishing houses. Bob was personally responsible for many books of political dissent and argument that challenged tyranny around the globe. He is also the founder and longtime chair of Human Rights Watch, one of the most respected human rights organizations in the world.

. . .

For fifty years, the banner of Public Affairs Press was carried by its owner Morris B. Schnapper, who published Gandhi, Nasser, Toynbee, Truman, and about 1,500 other authors. In 1983, Schnapper was described by *The Washington Post* as "a redoubtable gadfly." His legacy will endure in the books to come.

Peter Osnos, *Founder*